Advanced Word Processing

Microsoft® Word 2010

Susie H. VanHuss, Ph.D.
Distinguished Professor Emeritus
University of South Carolina

Connie M. Forde, Ph.D.
Mississippi State University

Donna L. Woo
Cypress College, California

COLLEGE KEYBOARDING

LESSONS 56–110

18th Edition

SOUTH-WESTERN
CENGAGE Learning™

Australia • Brazil • Japan • Korea • Mexico • Singapore • Spain • United Kingdom • United States

Visit our company website at **www.cengage.com**

For your course and learning solutions, visit **www.cengage.com/highered**

Cengage Learning products are represented in Canada by
Nelson Education, Ltd.

USA
Mason, OH 45040
5191 Natorp Boulevard
South-Western Cengage Learning

ISBN-10: 0-538-49540-5

ISBN-13: 978-0-538-49540-0

connection with, sponsorship, or endorsement by such owners.
respective owners. South-Western disclaims any affiliation, association,
purposes only and may be trademarks or registered trademarks of their
The names of all products mentioned herein are used for identification

countries.
a registered trademark of Microsoft Corporation in the U.S. and/or other
Microsoft Office screen captures: © Microsoft Corporation. Microsoft is

Keyboarding Pro DELUXE 2 illustrations: © Cengage Learning

© 2011, 2008 South-Western, Cengage Learning

Sr. Rights Specialist, Text: Mardell Glinski Schultz

Photo Researcher: Bill Smith Group

Sr. Rights Specialist, Photos: Deanna Ettinger

Design, Ltd.
© penfold, iStock; illustration, Grannan
Cover Image: © Markus Dziable, iStock;

Cover Designer: Grannan Design, Ltd.

Internal Designer: Grannan Design, Ltd.

Sr. Art Director: Tippy McIntosh

Copyeditor: Gary Morris

Production Service: PreMediaGlobal

Sr. Print Buyer: Charlene Taylor

Sr. Media Editor: Mike Jackson

Sr. Content Project Manager: Martha Conway

Associate Marketing Manager: Shanna Shelton

Editorial Assistant: Conor Allen

Mary Todd, Todd Publishing Services
Consulting Editors: Catherine Skintik;

Sr. Developmental Editor: Dave Lafferty

Sr. Acquisitions Editor: Jane Phelan

Vice President/Marketing: Bill Hendee

Schmohe
Vice President/Editor-in-Chief: Karen

Jack W. Calhoun
Vice President of Editorial, Business:

Donna L. Woo

Susie H. VanHuss, Connie M. Forde,

Eighteenth Edition

Advanced Word Processing, Lessons 56–110,

SOUTH-WESTERN
CENGAGE Learning

Contents

It Keeps Getting Better

One Series: the Right Number of Lessons

Make your life easier with proven textbooks and software that have the appropriate number of lessons for today's course. Plenty of documents and a strong instructional model combine to build confidence and proficiency in keyboarding, formatting, and word processing skills. The new **18th edition** merges the strengths of the *Essentials* series and the efficiencies of the *Certified Approach.*

Web Reporter for In-Class or Online Courses

Online courses just got easier with Web Reporter. Students use their browser to send instructors assignments. Instructors can manage their classes, view documents, and utilize the gradebook with ease.

Keyboarding Pro DELUXE 2: Your KEY to Success

NEW! Keyboarding Pro DELUXE 2™ now checks formats as well as keystrokes, helping you build the skills needed to create professional documents and meet the challenges of the digital workplace. It's engaging, interactive, easy to navigate, and provides motivating, instant feedback.

College Keyboarding solutions have a track record of ensuring success, and they just keep getting better. You can rely on the new 18th edition to provide print and digital solutions for *Microsoft Word 2010* that work for you. *College Keyboarding 18e* builds on its time-tested tradition to teach, improve, and assess proficiency in Keyboarding and Word Processing skills, ensuring classroom and workplace success.

Reliable, Dependable, Easy to Use

Correct techniques, an abundance of crafted drills, and a variety of meaningful routines keep lessons fun and build skill. Both the textbook lessons and software teach new *Word 2010* commands, introduce new documents, and apply what is learned.

Formats Now Checked

Keyboarding Pro DELUXE 2 now checks formats and keystrokes, including commands such as fonts, alignment, spacing, merge, tables, and more.

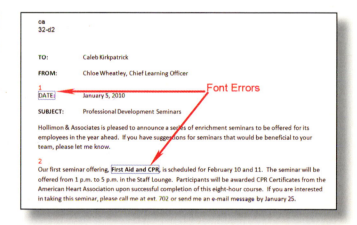

Greater Document Support

Keyboarding Pro DELUXE 2 works hand-in-hand with each Lesson. New textbook features help you, too.

Troubleshooting helps you along the way by providing tips on difficult portions of the lesson.

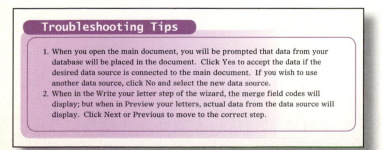

Quick Check solutions let you know you're on the right track.

Always Fresh, Always New

The lessons are completely updated with an abundance of new documents and additional practice. New topics include meeting, travel, and news documents, legal and medical documents, and improved coverage of employment documents.

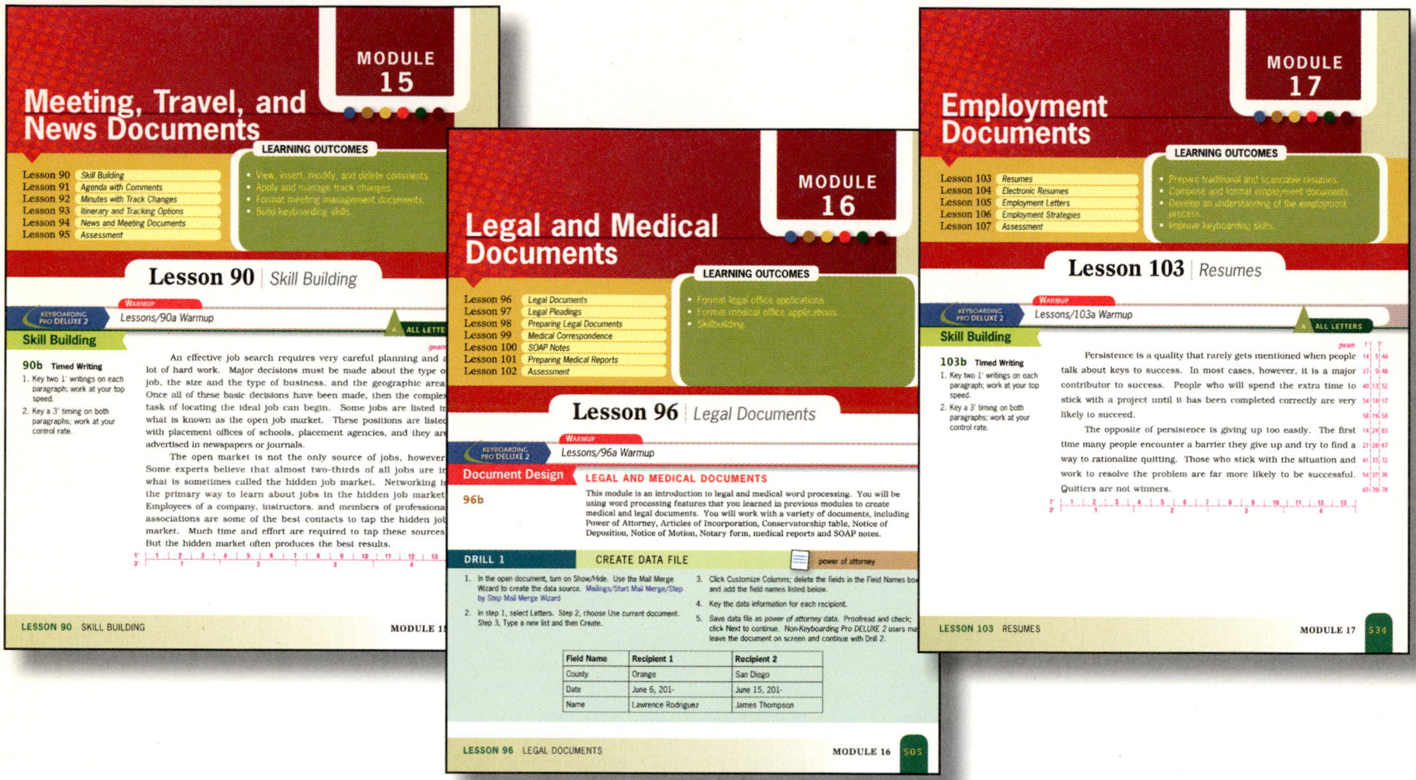

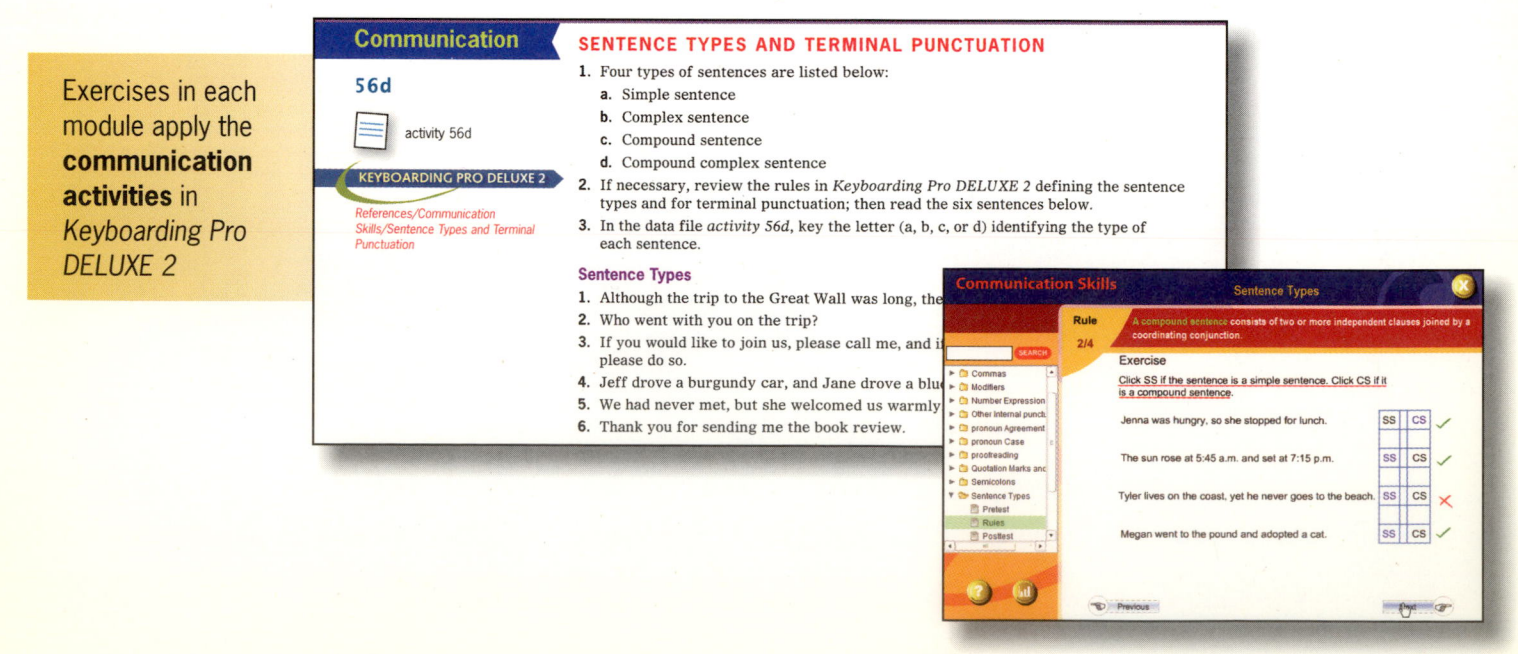

Communication Skills Integrated

Exercises in each module apply the **communication activities** in *Keyboarding Pro DELUXE 2*

The Path to Learning Microsoft® Word 2010

Follow the highlighted **Path of the Ribbon** (Tab/Group/Command) to learn the relevant steps of new commands. Drills apply each new command; once again, apply the path.

Path introduced here

Path reinforced here

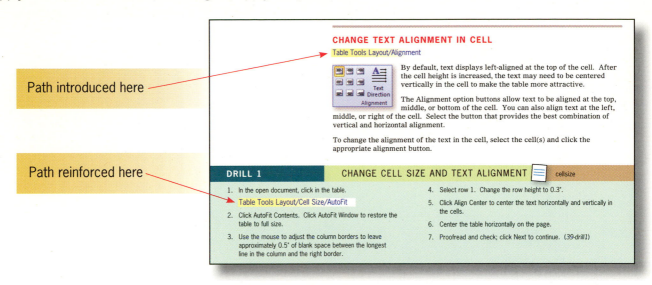

NEW: **Updated Videos** for the Reference section in *KEYBOARDING PRO DELUXE 2*! Includes updated videos for *WORD 2010* to guide and apply various *WORD* skills.

Extra Practice Builds Confidence and Success

Technique Drills and **Quick Review** provide extra practice to strengthen accuracy and techniques.

Skill Builders 4 and 5 provide extra reinforcement.

Timed Writings are always within easy reach. **Error diagnostics** tracks errors by row, finger, and reach and then provides drills to help reduce errors

Corrective drills provide instant practice for immediate improvement

College Keyboarding 18e: It Keeps Getting Better

This comprehensive series now merges the strength of the *Essentials* series and the efficiencies of the *Certified Approach* in one series. *College Keyboarding 18e* has a new lesson structure: **Lessons 1–55** focus on keyboarding, word processing, and formatting; **Lessons 56–110** move into more advanced word processing commands and provide loads of document formatting reinforcement; the **Complete Course (Lessons 1–120)** adds 10 additional lessons with topics for certification.

Keyboarding and Word Processing Essentials, Lessons 1–55, 18e
978-0-538-49538-7
Master the keyboarding and formatting skills most important for career success, including formatting business documents with Microsoft® Word 2010.

Keyboarding and Word Processing, Complete Course, Lessons 1–120, 18e
978-0-538-49647-6
The Complete Course adds 10 additional lessons with topics for certification.

Keyboarding Pro DELUXE 2 Student License Package
978-0-840-05335-0
Keyboarding Pro DELUXE 2 now checks document formats and fully supports Lessons 1–110.

Reviewers

SHARON BREEDING
Bluegrass Community and Technical College, Regency Campus
Lexington, KY

KAREN CARPENTER
West Georgia Technical College–LaGrange West Campus
LaGrange, GA

MARILYNE CLEEVES
Cuesta College
San Luis Obispo, CA

WENDY CONLEY
Learey Technical Center
Tampa, FL

SHARON COOPER
Sullivan University
Louisville, KY

ALDENE FRICKS
St. Louis Community College at Meramec
St. Louis, MO

CHRISTINE GREENE
Genesee Community College & Jamestown Community College
Jamestown, NY

CORA NEWMAN
Technical College of the Lowcountry
Beaufort, SC

To Our Teachers and Students

Thank you for choosing our keyboarding materials. We have designed them to make it easy to teach and learn keyboarding, formatting, and *Word 2010* skills. We hope they meet your needs and wish you much success in developing these valuable career skills.

Your College Keyboarding authors
Susie VanHuss
Connie Forde
Donna Woo

www.collegekeyboarding.com

You are about to tap into the best print and digital tools available for keyboarding and word processing instruction. Quite simply, South-Western provides **Tools that Work**, tools that have prepared thousands of students for success in school and beyond. Following is a brief discussion of the technology tools that accompany *College Keyboarding 18e, Lessons 56–110*:

- *Keyboarding Pro DELUXE 2*
- *Web Reporter*
- Website Resources

KEYBOARDING PRO DELUXE 2

Keyboarding Pro DELUXE 2 is the perfect companion for either online or in-class keyboarding instruction. This all-in-one keyboarding and document processing software will launch either *Microsoft Word 2010* or *Word 2007*; it is compatible with *Windows 7, Windows Vista,* or *Windows XP. Keyboarding Pro DELUXE 2* includes 110 lessons. Lessons 56–110 focus on the following:

- Keypad lessons and timings
- Timed Writings with error diagnostics
- Drills customized to correct the pattern of errors each student experiences
- Format and keystroke error checking

- Videos of proper keyboarding techniques, *Word 2010* commands, and tutorials for using *Keyboarding Pro DELUXE 2*
- Multimedia review of communication skills and document formats with activities

MAIN MENU

The Main menu includes the primary tabs to use the software and navigation buttons to execute common commands.

Lessons Keyboarding drills are keyed both from the screen and from the textbook. The number of lessons available on the Lesson menu depends on the length of your course. A red checkmark appears after the lesson name when it is completed.

Skill Building Use **Technique Builder** to practice the drills found in Skill Builders 4–5 in the textbook. **Drill Practice** recommends drills to correct the errors you make most frequently on Timed Writings. Review the Error Diagnostic Report for full details.

Skill Building
Quick Review
Technique Builder
Drill Practice

Timed Writings Easy access to all timings is available from the Timed Writings tab as well as from the lessons. Error Diagnostics tracks specific accuracy problems and then provides drills by row, by finger, or type to improve accuracy. Your 3–5 best and last 40 timings are reported on the Timed Writing Report.

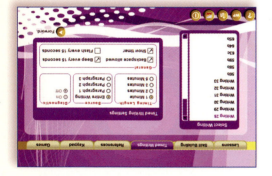

References Videos reinforce the *Word 2010* commands that are presented within lessons. **Communication Skills** reviews 16 common language arts topics; each includes a pretest, posttest, rules, examples, and exercises to check understanding. **Document Formats** illustrate and review common document formats. **Tutorials** teach you to transfer your student record and troubleshoot issues.

References
Word 2007 Presentations
Communication Skills
Document Formats
Tutorials
Presentation Link
Movies

Keypad You will learn the numeric keypad by touch and build your skill. Keypad timed writings build skill.

CREATING YOUR STUDENT RECORD

Launch *Keyboarding Pro DELUXE 2*: From the Start menu, select Programs, then South-Western Keyboarding, and click *Keyboarding Pro DELUXE 2*.

Create your student record (one time only). The student record reflects your work.

1. Select **New User** from the Login screen.
2. Complete the required fields. Record your security question and answer; keep this information in a safe location.

Non-distance learning class: Select your class from the Class drop-down menu. Ignore Class Code. If you are creating the student record on a **flash drive**, see the *Keyboarding Pro DELUXE 2 User's Guide* for instruction. Subsequently when logging in, select your name from the Log In screen and key your password. If you do not see your name, click the Folder icon; browse to locate your student record.

Distance learning class:

Important: If you created a student record for Lessons 1–55, you must choose a unique Username for this second course.

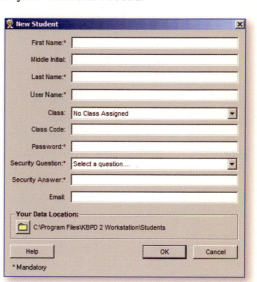

Leave the Class field empty. Copy and paste your **Class Code** to the Class Code field.

- Locate the document provided by your instructor with the Class Code.

- Double-click the Class Code to select it. Right-click the Class Code and choose *Copy*.

- Toggle (Alt + Tab) to the New Student dialog box and paste the Class Code in the Class Code field. To paste, right-click in the Class Code field, and choose *Paste*.

- Click OK. The software will issue a **Student ID**.

If you create your student record at school, you will need to download it to your home computer. Do **not** create a second student record. To download your student record to your home computer, click **Locate Online Student** from the Login screen and copy/paste in your Class Code and Student ID. This is a one-time process. (See *User's Manual*.)

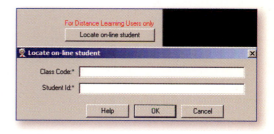

3. Transfer your student record if appropriate. See the videos under References.

- To transfer your student record to a flash drive, use the Export command.

- If you are using Web Reporter, select Yes when logging out to upload your work.

COMPLETING DOCUMENTS IN WORD 2010

Follow the Standard Procedures when completing documents. *Keyboarding Pro DELUXE 2* will also launch *Word 2007*; however, when new *Word 2010* commands such as Text Effects are integrated within the documents, the software will not check the command.

Standard Procedures for *Word* Documents

1. Key and format the document following the textbook directions.

2. Proofread and verify formats. Preview for placement.

3. Check the document when you are completely satisfied. Mistakes will be counted and shown above each paragraph and errors will be highlighted. Formatting error are displayed in blue.

4. Select Display Error List for an explanation of each error.

5. Scroll to the bottom of the screen to view the report of errors, gwam, number of errors, etc. Print if directed by instructor.

6. Click NEXT to move to the next application.

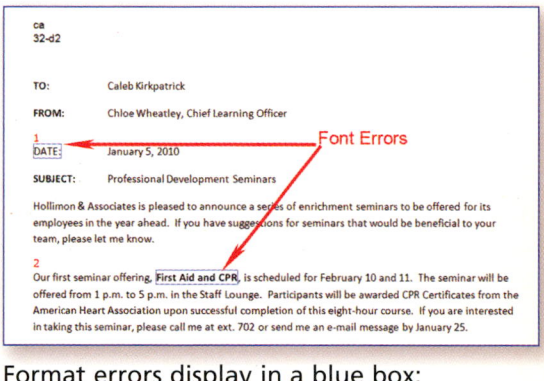

Format errors display in a blue box; errors are numbered.

When you choose a word processing activity, the Document Options dialog box displays:

Begin new document begins a new pass.

Open an existing document opens an activity so that you can can continue to work. Edits are numbered in sequential order (Edit 1, Edit 2, etc.).

Print document prints the document in *Word* format; errors are not marked.

Check existing document checks and displays results.

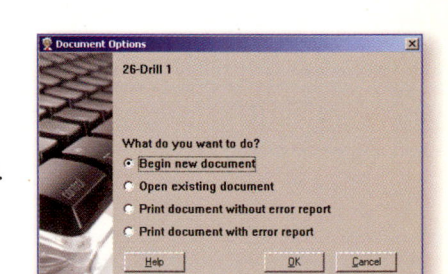

When selecting a word processing application from the Lessons menu, *Word* launches and the Document Toolbar displays in the upper right corner. **Back** saves the document without checking it. **Check** compares your document to the solution, reports your results, and grades the document if appropriate. NOTE: A document must be 90 percent complete or it will not be checked. When the checked document displays, the Document Toolbar changes: **Error List** identifies the type of mistakes. **Next** takes the user to the next exercise without closing *Word*.

Back Check

Error Next
List

Reports Numerous reports are available from the menu bar. Each report hyperlinks to a specific lesson or document. Instructors can view these same reports in Web Reporter or the Instructor Utility.

Reports | Option | Help
Summary Lessons 1-25
Summary Lessons 26-110
Skill Building Report...
Timed Writings...
Cumulative Error Diagnostic..
Document and Production Tests
Performance Graphs ▶
Grade Book

Web Reporter

Web Reporter is an easy solution for online users to send assignments to the instructor. The relationship with the Web Reporter is established when you create your student record and paste in the Class Code. For best results when using Web Reporter, use a direct connection to the Web rather than a wireless connection. To use Web Reporter, you'll need to re-enter various information you added when you created your student record. Log into Web Reporter to view comments from your instructor or grades posted to the various assignments or production tests.

To access Web Reporter, enter your user name, password, security question and answer, and e-mail.

Web Resources www.collegekeyboarding.com

The website has several resources to enrich your experience, give you immediate feedback, and help you master the word processing concepts. From the website, choose *College Keyboarding 18e*, and then *Lessons 56–110*. **Data files**, organized by module, are available for download; simply click on the link, download, and unzip the file. If you are using *Keyboarding Pro DELUXE 2*, these files will open automatically; occasionally you will be directed to insert a file, in which case you will need to access the data files. Flash cards, chapter quizzes, practice quizzes, web links, and more are also provided to increase your engagement and help you master the course. These chapter resources are also available as a **WebTutor Toolbox** for use with Blackboard, Angel, and other learning management systems.

ELECTRONIC MAIL

Electronic mail (or **e-mail**) is a message sent by one computer user to another. E-mail was originally designed as an informal, personal way of communicating. However, it is now used extensively in business. For business use, e-mail should not be casual or informal.

Business writers compose e-mail messages in two ways. First, the writer may compose the entire communication (or message) in the body of the e-mail. Second, the writer may compose a brief e-mail message and then attach electronic documents to it. Distribution of electronic documents via e-mail is a common business practice; these documents include many types of document formats, e.g., memos, letters, reports, contracts, worksheets, and presentations. It is important for the business writer to recognize the importance of attractive and acceptable formats of all documents, including e-mail messages.

Using e-mail requires an e-mail program, an e-mail address, and access to the Internet.

Address e-mail. Key and check the address of the recipient, and always supply a subject line. Also, key the e-mail address of anyone who should receive a copy of the e-mail.

Format the body of an e-mail single-spaced; double-space between paragraphs. Do not indent paragraphs. Limit the use of bold, italics, and uppercase. For business use, avoid abbreviations and emoticons (e.g., BTW for *by the way* or :- for wink).

Attach electronic documents to an e-mail message using the attachment feature of the e-mail program. The attached file can then be opened and edited by the recipient.

CREATE AN E-MAIL ACCOUNT

If you do not have an e-mail account, several companies provide free e-mail service. The following directions can be used to create a Hotmail account:

1. Use an Internet browser to go to www.*hotmail.com*.

2. If you do not have a Hotmail account, click the Sign up button and key the information to set up your e-mail account.

USE E-MAIL TO SEND A DOCUMENT

The process of sending a document via e-mail is simple. You can create, format, and edit the document in *Word*; when you are ready to send the document, use the Send Using E-mail command and choose to send the document as an attachment. Your e-mail screen opens with the *Word* file as an attachment. *Microsoft Word* must be on the receiver's computer to open your document. If the receiver does not have *Word*, or if you do not want the reader to be able to edit your document, you can choose to send the attachment in PDF or XPS format. *Word* will save the document in the PDF or XPS format and then attach a copy to your e-mail.

If you save the document on a web server, such as Windows Live Space or SkyDrive, you can use the option to Send a Link. This creates an e-mail and places a link to the saved file on the web server; the recipient clicks the link to open the file.

Word provides five options for sending documents you create as an e-mail:

Send as Attachment	An e-mail message is created with a copy of the document as an attachment.
Send a Link	The document must be saved to a web server before this option becomes available. This creates an e-mail message with a link to the document.
Send as PDF	*Word* saves a PDF version of the document and then creates an e-mail with the PDF attachment.
Send as XPS	Saves an XPS version of the document and then creates an e-mail with the XPS attachment. (XPS format is similar to PDF but not as widely used.)
Send as Internet Fax	You must subscribe to an Internet fax service before using this option. *Word* sends the document to that service for faxing.

To use e-mail to send a document:

File/Save & Send/Send Using E-mail

1. Key the document and save it.
2. Follow the path to display options for sending the e-mail, such as Send as Attachment. Select one of the options.
3. Your e-mail program opens a new message, with the document name listed as an attachment and also in the Subject line. If you selected the Send a Link option, the link is displayed in the e-mail message box.
4. Key the address of the person to whom you are sending the e-mail; key your message.
5. Send the e-mail.

Know Your Computer

The numbered parts are found on most computers. The location of some parts will vary.

1. **CPU (Central Processing Unit):** Internal operating unit or "brain" of computer.

2. **CD-ROM drive:** Reads data from and writes data to a CD or DVD.

3. **Monitor:** Displays text and graphics on a screen.

4. **Mouse:** Used to input commands.

5. **Keyboard:** An arrangement of letter, figure, symbol, control, function, and editing keys and a numeric keypad.

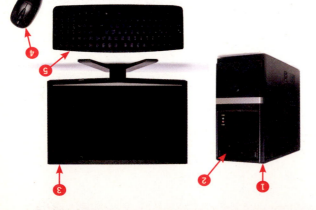

KEYBOARD ARRANGEMENT

1. **Alphanumeric keys:** Letters, numbers, and symbols.

2. **Numeric keypad:** Keys at the right side of the keyboard used to enter numeric copy and perform calculations.

3. **Function (F) keys:** Used to execute commands, sometimes with other keys. Commands vary with software.

4. **Arrow keys:** Move insertion point up, down, left, or right.

5. **ESC (Escape):** Closes a software menu or dialog box.

6. **TAB:** Moves the insertion point to a preset position.

7. **CAPS LOCK:** Used to make all capital letters.

8. **SHIFT:** Makes capital letters and symbols shown at tops of number keys.

9. **CTRL (Control):** With other key(s), executes commands.

10. **ALT (Alternate):** With other key(s), executes commands. Commands may vary with software.

11. **Space Bar:** Inserts a space in text.

12. **ENTER (return):** Moves insertion point to margin and down to next line. Also used to execute commands.

13. **DELETE:** Removes text to the right of insertion point.

14. **NUM LOCK:** Activates/deactivates numeric keypad.

15. **INSERT:** Activates insert or typeover.

16. **BACKSPACE:** Deletes text to the left of insertion point.

Level +3

DOCUMENT DESIGN MASTERY

JOB APPLICATION FORM

Learning Outcomes

Document Design Skills

+ To design and prepare attractive documents.

+ To organize content effectively with tables and graphics.

+ To enhance report formats with design elements that add structure, provide a consistent image, and increase readability.

+ To create merged documents with envelopes and labels.

Word Processing Skills

+ To review and apply basic *Word 2010* commands.

+ To learn and apply *Word 2010* commands to create and format effective documents.

Communication Skills

+ To review and improve basic communication skills.

+ To produce error-free documents and apply language arts skills.

Keyboarding

+ To improve keyboarding speed and accuracy.

d. *Henry and choo*: Size 2.1" high; apply a Bevel Perspective Left, White picture style.

    e. *Molly 2*: Size 2.6" high; apply a Metal Rounded Rectangle picture style.

    f. *Kosh 2*: Size 2.4" high; apply a Metal Rounded Rectangle picture style.

9. Insert a Tiles footer; show the footer on both pages. Key the address in the left placeholder; select the text and change the font size to 9 points so that the entire address will fit. Select the text in the right placeholder (*Page* + number) and change the font to 9 points to match the left side.

10. Preview the document. Check to see that it is a two-page document and that the pictures are placed and sized appropriately.

11. Check and close. (*proj3-d11*)

IT STOCK/JUPITER

! WORKPLACE SUCCESS

Influencing Others

Effective leaders can influence others to do things even though they have no authority over them. The ability to influence others is a valuable career skill for upward job mobility.

There is no one right or wrong way to go about influencing others. However, effective leaders tend to use techniques that have common characteristics. Some examples are:

- They approach the situation from the perspective of the other person rather than from their own. They have learned how to use empathy effectively.

- They make the effort to show the benefits to the other person.

- They try to get agreement on the big concepts before getting into the details that bog people down.

- They use good human relations skills and make it easy for the other person to grant requests.

Participating in meetings with individuals from different departments provides an excellent opportunity to learn how to influence other people. A good way to get started is to observe leaders who are able to bring a group to a consensus even though the discussion might have begun with very diverse positions. Meetings provide an opportunity to demonstrate good communication skills, leadership skills, and good time management and organization skills as well as good negotiation skills.

Skill Builder 4

DINODIA PHOTOS/JUPITER IMAG...

DRILL 15

Keystroking Patterns

Key each line once for fluency; DS between groups.

3rd row

1 it we or us opo pop you rut rip wit pea lea wet pit were quiet
2 pew tie toe per rep hope pour quip rope your pout tore rip quirk

Home row

3 ha has kid lad led last wash lash gaff jade fads half sash haggle
4 as dad had add leg jug lads hall lass fast deal fall leafs dashes

1st row

5 ax ban man zinc clan bank calm lamb vain amaze bronze back buzzer
6 ax sax can bam zag cab mad fax vans buzz caves knack waxen banana

---

A ALL LETTERS

1. Take a 1' writing on each paragraph.
2. Take one 3' or one 5' writing on both paragraphs.

Optional: Practice as a guided writing.

1/4'	1/2'	3/4'	gwam 1'
8	16	24	32
9	18	27	36
10	20	30	40
11	22	33	44
12	24	36	48
13	26	39	52
14	28	41	56
15	30	45	60
16	32	48	64
17	34	51	68
18	36	54	72

Standard Plan for Guided Writing Procedures

1. Take a 1' writing on paragraph 1. Note your *gwam*.
2. Add four words to your 1' *gwam* to determine your goal rate.
3. Set the timer for 1' and the Timer option to beep every 15".
4. From the table at the left, select from Column 4 the speed nearest your goal rate. Note the ¼' point at the left of that speed. Place a check mark at each ¼' goal.
5. Take two 1' guided writings on paragraphs 1 and 2 striving to meet your ¼' goal.

Writing 28

gwam 3' | 5'

Who is a professional? The word can be defined in many ways. Some may think of a professional as someone who is in an exempt job category in an organization. To others the word can denote something quite different; being a professional denotes an attitude that requires thinking of your position as a career, not just a job. A professional exerts influence over her or his job and takes pride in the work accomplished.

Many individuals who remain in the same positions for a long time characterize themselves as being in dead-end positions. Others who remain in positions for a long time consider them- selves to be in a profession. A profession is a career to which you are willing to devote a lifetime. How you view your pro- fession is up to you.

	3'	5'
	4	2	32
	8	5	35
	12	7	37
	17	10	40
	21	13	43
	25	15	45
	28	17	47
	32	19	49
	36	22	52
	40	24	54
	45	27	57
	49	29	59
	50	30	60

3' | 1 | 2 | 3 | 4
5' | 1 | 2 | 3

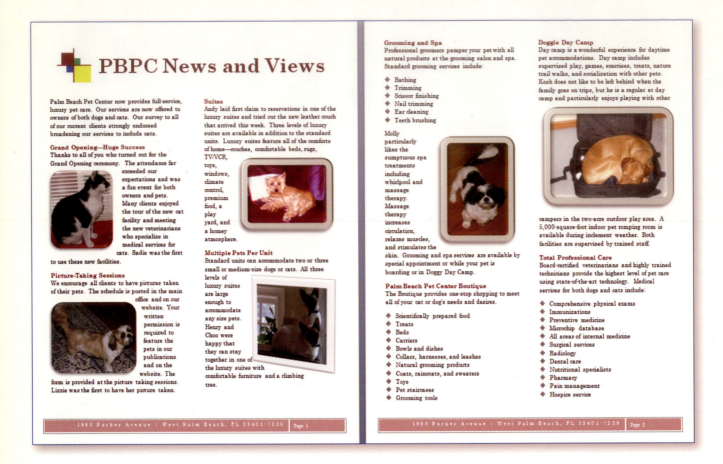

1. In a new document, apply Narrow margins.

2. Tap ENTER once and insert the *pbpc logo* data file; apply Tight text wrapping.

3. Key **PBPC News and Views** (do not spell out PBPC); apply 36-point, Dark Red, Text 2 Heading font and bold.

4. Change font to 11-point, Automatic color Body font. Tap ENTER twice and insert a Continuous section break.

5. On the line below the section break, insert the *pbpc newsletter* data file. Select the text and format using two equal-width columns.

6. Format all headings using Heading 5 and apply bold.

7. Change the bullets by using the bullet (◈) from the Wingdings 2 font. Use Decrease Indent to position the bullets at the left edge of the column.

8. Insert the pet pictures from the data files in the order shown below and apply the formats specified for each picture. Crop each picture close to the image of the pet as shown in the illustration above. Compress all pictures and apply Tight text wrapping to all pictures except *kosh 2*.

   a. *Sadie*: Size 2" high; flip the image horizontally; apply a Bevel Rectangle picture style.

   b. *Lizzie 2*: Size 1.8" high; apply a Bevel Rectangle picture style.

   c. *Andy couch*: Size 1.7" high; adjust color: Saturation: 200%; apply a Metal Rounded Rectangle picture style.

 TIP

1. To get Heading 5 to display, click the last heading that displays in Styles.

2. Repeat step 1 until Heading 5 displays.

DRILL 16

Keyboarding Technique

Key each line once for fluency; DS between groups.

1st
1 Zam and six lazy men visited Cecil and Bunn at a bank convention.
2 Zane, much to the concern of Bev and six men, visited their zone.

2nd
3 Jill said she wished that she had fed Dale's dog a lot less food.
4 Jake Hall sold the glass flask at a Dallas "half-off" glass sale.

3rd
5 Did either Peter or Trey quip that reporters were out to get you?
6 Either Trey or Peter tried to work with a top-quality pewter toy.

4th
7 18465 97354 12093 87541 09378 34579 74629 45834 28174 11221 27211
8 02574 29765 39822 07623 17659 20495 39481 10374 32765 77545 22213

KEYBOARDING PRO DELUXE 2 | **Timed Writings**

A | **ALL LETTERS**

1. Take three 1' writings on each paragraph.
2. Take one 5' writing or two 3' writings. Proofread; circle errors; determine *gwam*.

Option: Practice as a guided writing.

			gwam
1/4'	**1/2'**	**3/4'**	**1'**
8	16	24	32
9	18	27	36
10	20	30	40
11	22	33	44
12	24	36	48
13	26	39	52
14	28	41	56
15	30	45	60
16	32	48	64
17	34	51	68
18	36	54	72

Writing 29

gwam 3' 5'

Students, for decades, have secured part-time jobs to help   4 2 52
pay for college expenses. Today, more students are gainfully   8 5 54
employed while they are in college than ever before. Many of 12 7 57
them are employed because their financial situation requires that 17 10 59
they earn money. Earnings from jobs go to pay for tuition, 21 12 62
books, living costs, and other necessities. Some work so that 25 15 64
they can own cars or buy luxury items; others seek jobs to gain 29 17 67
skills or to build their vitas. These students are aware that 33 20 69
many organizations prefer to hire a person who has had some type 38 23 72
of work experience than one who has had none. 41 24 74

Students often ask if the work experience has to be in 44 27 76
exactly the same field. Obviously, the more closely related the 49 29 78
experience, the better it is. However, the old adage, anything 53 32 81
beats nothing, applies. Regardless of the types of jobs students 57 34 84
have, they can demonstrate that they get to work regularly and on 62 37 86
time, they have good human relations skills, they are organized 66 40 89
and can manage time effectively, and they produce good results. 70 42 91
All of these factors are very critical to employers. The bottom 75 45 94
line is that employers like to use what you have done in the past 79 47 97
as a predictor of what you will do in the future. 82 49 99

3' | 1 | 2 | 3 | 4 |
5' | 1 | 2 | 3 |

Document 10
Itinerary

dcs itinerary

Use the *dcs itinerary* data file and the information below to prepare an itinerary for Mr. Schmidt. Preview, proofread, and check; click Next to continue. (*proj3-d10*)

Trip: Chicago, Illinois Tuesday, March 14 – Thursday, March 16, 201-

Trip destination: Meet in Chicago with potential suppliers of upscale merchandise for the Pet Boutique

Departure: March 14; Midtown Airlines; depart on Flight 2846 at 5:45 p.m.

Flight connections: One stop in Atlanta; same aircraft; arrive 7:45 p.m.

Ground transportation: Picked up by Executive Cars; Confirmation #OH493802; 312-555-0121

Hotel: Chicago Levernoir, 725 N. Michigan Avenue; Confirmation #87B0376519

Return: March 16; Midtown Airlines; Flight 8937 at 7:45 a.m.

Flight connections: Direct, nonstop flight; arrives 9:43 a.m.

March 15 Breakfast: 7:15 | Hotel

8:30 | Roger Demus, Elegant Puppy Mart, 312-555-0136 | 34 E. Division Street

10:30 | Mark Lane, Chicago Pet Spa Supplies, 312-555-0196 | 17 E. Scott Street

Lunch: 12:15 | Lynn Marcus, Marcus Pet Boutique Supplies, 312-555-0137 | Hotel Levernoir Bistro

2:00 | Martin Walker, Anna Metz, and Leslie Walker, Walker Furniture, 312-555-0186 | 2408 S. State Street

4:00 | Leon Ranson and Jan Anders, Pet Boutique Specialties, 312-555-0147 | Meet in hotel lobby; drive to Pet Boutique Specialties

Dinner: 8:30 | Elaine Beswick, President, and Rae LaFevre, Design Director, Pet Boutique Specialties | Charlie Truluck Restaurant

Comments: Reservations for lunch and dinner in your name.

Document 11
Newsletter

pbpc newsletter
sadie, lizzie 2, andy couch
henry and choo
molly 2, kosh 2

Palm Beach Pet Center will use the newsletter you design as the standard style that will be used for all newsletters in the future to create a consistent image. The body of the newsletter has already been keyed; you will insert the text and format it. Before you begin, review the illustration on the next page. Pay particular attention to the following items:

- Placement of logo and text for the banner heading.
- Placement of the pictures of pets that are featured throughout the newsletter.
- Type and position of the bullets used.
- Format of the headings.

DRILL 17

Number reaches

Key each line once at a comfortable rate; practice difficult lines.

1 My staff of 11 worked 11 hours a day from May 11 to June 11.
2 Her flight, PW 222, lands at 2:22 p.m. on Thursday, June 22.
3 We 3, part of the 333rd Corps, marched 33 miles on August 3.
4 Car 444 took Route 4 east to Route 44, then 4 miles to Aden.
5 The 55 wagons traveled 555 miles in '55; only 5 had trouble.
6 Put 6 beside 6; result 66.   Then, add one more 6 to get 666.
7 She sold 7,777 copies of Record 77, Schubert's 7th Symphony.
8 In '88, it took 8 men and 8 women 8 days to travel 88 miles.
9 The 9 teams, 9 girls and 9 boys, depart on Bus 999 at 9 a.m.
10 Million has six zeros; as, 000,000.   Ten has but one; as, 0.

| 1 | 2 | 3 | 4 | 5 | 6 | 7 | 8 | 9 | 10 | 11 | 12 | 13 |

A ALL LETTERS

Writing 30

	gwam	3'	5'

Planning, organizing, and controlling are three of the — 4 | 2 | 65
functions that are familiar to all sorts of firms. Because these — 8 | 5 | 68
functions are basic to the managerial practices of a business, — 12 | 7 | 71
they form the very core of its daily operations. Good managerial — 17 | 10 | 73
procedures, of course, do not just occur by accident. They must — 21 | 13 | 76
be set into motion by people. Thus, a person who plans to enter — 25 | 15 | 78
the job market, especially in an office position, should study — 30 | 18 | 81
all of the elements of good management in order to apply those — 34 | 20 | 83
principles to her or his work. — 36 | 22 | 85

Leadership is another very important skill for a person — 40 | 24 | 87
to develop. Leaders are needed at all levels in a business to — 44 | 26 | 89
plan, organize, and control the operations of a firm. A person — 48 | 29 | 92
who is in a key position of leadership usually is expected to ini- — 52 | 31 | 95
tiate ideas as well as to carry out the goals of a business. — 57 | 34 | 97
Office workers who have developed the qualities of leadership are — 61 | 37 | 100
more apt to be promoted than those without such skills. While — 65 | 39 | 102
leadership may come naturally for some people, it can be learned — 70 | 42 | 105
as well as be improved with practice. — 72 | 43 | 106

Attitude is an extremely important personality trait that — 76 | 46 | 109
is a big contributor to success in one's day-to-day activities. — 80 | 48 | 111
Usually a person with a good attitude is open-minded to the ideas — 85 | 51 | 114
of others and is able to relate with others because he or she has — 89 | 53 | 117
an interest in people. Thus, one's attitude on the job often — 93 | 56 | 119
makes a great difference in whether work gets done and done — 97 | 58 | 122
right. Because teamwork is a part of many jobs, developing a — 101 | 61 | 124
good attitude toward work, people, and life seems logical. — 105 | 63 | 126

3' | 1 | 2 | 3 | 4 |
5' | 1 | 2 | 3 |

Document 9
Form for Itinerary

Mr. Schmidt travels frequently to visit with suppliers and potential suppliers for Palm Beach Pet Center. Create an itinerary form using a table for his approval.

1. Use Narrow margins. Tap ENTER once and insert a 2-column, 18-row, Light List – Accent 6 table. Place brackets around the variable information that would be selected and replaced. Key the text shown below. Adjust column widths as indicated.

2. Format the first row 1.2" high. Apply 20-point Heading font to the first line and 16-point Heading font to the next three lines. Apply Align Center to text.

3. Format the remaining rows 0.4" high and apply Align Center Left to all text.

4. After you complete the travel information section, merge the cells in row 9 and leave it blank. Then split each of the columns in the remaining rows and format them as shown below. Apply Bold to the headings in row 10.

5. Proofread and check; click Next to continue. *(proj3-d9)*

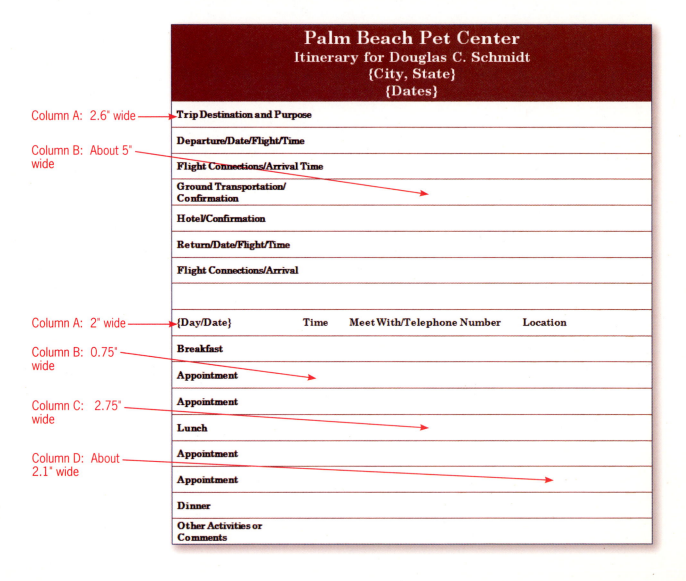

DRILL 18

Improve response patterns

Key each line once; DS between 4-line groups; work at a controlled rate; repeat drill.

direct reaches: reaches with the same finger; keep hands quiet

1 brand much cent numb cease bright music brief jump special carved
2 create mumps zany mystic curve mummy any checks brag brunch after
3 Bradley broke his left thumb after lunch on a great hunting trip.
4 After having mumps, Cecil once saw June excel in a funny musical.

adjacent reaches: keep fingers curved and upright

5 were junior sad yuletide trees polo very join safe property tweed
6 tree trio trickle tripod quit excess was free easy million option
7 Gwen and Sumio are going to be quite popular at the Western Club.
8 Fred said we were going to join the guys for polo this afternoon.

double letters: strike keys rapidly

9 dill seem pool attic miss carry dragged kidded layoff lapped buzz
10 commend accuse inner rubber cheer commission football jazz popper
11 Tammy called to see if she can borrow my accounting book at noon.
12 Lynnette will meet with the bookseller soon to discuss the issue.

KEYBOARDING PRO DELUXE 2   **Timed Writing**

A **ALL LETTERS**

Writing 31

	gwam	3'	5'
Working at home is not exactly a new phenomenon, but the con-	12	2	47
cept is growing quite rapidly. For many years, people have worked	26	5	50
at home. In most instances, they were self-employed and operated	39	8	52
a business from their homes. Today, the people who work at home	52	10	55
fit into a variety of categories. Some own their own businesses;	65	13	58
others bring extra work home after the workday ends. A key change	79	16	60
is the large group of people who are employed by huge organizations	92	18	63
but who work out of home offices. These employees are in jobs that	106	21	66
include sales, creative, technical, and a host of other categories.	120	24	69
The real change that has occurred is not so much the numbers	12	26	71
of people who are working at home and the variety of jobs, but the	26	29	74
complex tools that are now available for doing the job. Technology	39	32	76
has truly made the difference. In many cases, clients and customers	53	35	79
are not even aware that they are dealing with individuals working	66	37	82
at home. Computers, printers, fax machines, telephone systems,	79	40	84
and other office equipment enable the worker in the home to function	93	42	87
in the same way as workers in a typical business office.	104	45	89

1' | 1 | 2 | 3 | 4 | 5 | 6 | 7 | 8 | 9 | 10 | 11 | 12 | 13 |
5' | 1 | 2 | 3 |

Interestingly, the list provided was developed by a leading authority on preventive health care for pets (Citation 1). While many differences exist in the health-care needs of pets compared to the needs of their owners, many similarities also exist. Dr. Bradford says that common sense is the key to wellness for pets.

Palm Beach Pet Center Wellness Plan (Heading 1)

In response to the many requests from clients, Dr. Erin Faulk interviewed a young veterinarian (Citation 2), who is a former student of Dr. Bradford's, and whose research focuses on the components of effective pet wellness programs. As a result of that interview, Dr. Guidice was hired to develop the Palm Beach Pet Center Wellness Program. Dr. Guidice currently serves as the director of the program. In addition to the standard components listed above, the program utilizes highly trained technicians to monitor pet health and wellness (Citation 3).

(Insert *wellness report* data file here)

Source Information for Citations

Citation 1

Type: Book | **Author:** Bradford, Monica C. | **Title:** Wellness for Pets, A Scientific Analysis | **Year:** 2010 | **City:** Phoenix | **Publisher:** Arizona Veterinary Society Publishers

Note: Edit the citation to add page number: 86

Citation 2

Type: Interview | **Interviewee:** Guidice, David | **Title:** leave blank | **Interviewer:** Faulk, Erin | **Year:** 2010 | **Month:** October | **Day:** 26

Citation 3

Type: Journal | **Author:** Graham, A. Christopher | **Title:** Highly Trained Technicians Monitor Pet Wellness | **Journal Name:** New Mexico Pet Wellness Journal | **Year:** 2010 | **Pages:** 18-23

Writing 32

gwam ♂'

Many small businesses fail. Surprisingly, though, many | 4

people are still willing to take a chance on starting one of | 8

their own. A person who is willing to take the risks necessary | 12

to manage a business in order to receive the potential rewards is | 17

called an entrepreneur. In a sense, such individuals are pio- | 21

neers who enjoy each step on the way to achieving objectives that | 25

they have determined to be important. This type of person has | 29

had a profound impact on shaping our economy and our quality of | 34

life. | 34

What does it take to start a business venture, and what | 38

kinds of people make it work? Obviously, the desire to make | 42

money and to be one's own boss are two basic incentives, but | 40

these alone are not enough to guarantee success. Two qualifica- | 50

tions common to most successful entrepreneurs, whatever field | 54

they are in, are an attentiveness to detail and a knack for | 58

solving day-to-day problems without losing sight of long-range | 62

goals. | 63

While there is a high risk in organizing any new business, | 67

the entrepreneur who is successful is seldom someone who could be | 71

considered a gambler. Most gamblers expect to have the odds | 75

against them. On the other hand, a clever businessperson sees to | 80

it that the odds are as good as possible by getting all of the | 84

facts and planning carefully before going ahead. Luck helps, to | 88

be sure, but a new business enterprise depends far more on good | 92

ideas and detailed plans. | 94

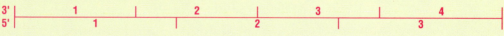

3' | 1 | 2 | 3 | 4
5' | 1 | 2 | 3

Document 8
Report with Citations

wellness report
pbpc cover page

TIP

Remember to break the link between the sections for both the header and the footer. Set the number on the first page of the report to 1.

The Veterinary staff has drafted the information for a report to distribute to clients. They have asked you to prepare the report.

1. Key the report shown below. Insert citations where noted. Use MLA style. Source information for the citations is presented at the end of the document.

2. Apply custom dog bullets for the items that are bulleted.

3. Insert the *wellness report* data file where noted. Apply the formats noted in the comments; then delete all comments.

4. Generate a bibliography on a new page at the end of the document.

5. Insert a Next page break at the beginning of the document and insert the *pbpc cover page* data file. Complete the placeholders and add a Dark Red, Text 2 Box border to the cover page.

6. Number the pages using Rounded Rectangle 3 at the top of the page. Format using Dark Red, Text 2 Shape Fill and center the text. Do not show the page number on the cover page or first page of the report.

7. Preview to ensure that the format is correct and that pages are numbered correctly.

8. Proofread and check; click Next to continue. (*proj3-d8*)

The Palm Beach Pet Center Wellness Plan **(Title style; shrink to fit on one line)**

For Healthy and Happy Pets **(Subtitle style)**

Many families that own pets think of those pets as part of their family. Today, families express more concern about wellness for their families than was the case some years ago. And, not surprisingly, that concern also applies to the wellness of their pets. Many clients have asked Palm Beach Pet Center to provide them with sound information in a non-technical manner about wellness for pets. This report is designed to address issues of wellness for pets and to announce the new Palm Beach Pet Center Wellness Plan.

Wellness for Pets **(Heading 1)**

When you ask people what they think should be included in a successful wellness program for their families, most people will provide a list of items such as the one that follows.

- Good nutrition
- Exercise to improve fitness
- Drink a substantial amount of water
- Weight control
- Preventive health care
- Preventive dental care
- Effective medical care when needed
- Avoidance of bad habits
- Effective social interaction
- Safety awareness—avoiding hazardous things

DRILL 19

Opposite hand reaches

Key at a controlled rate; concentrate on the reaches.

	1 yj my say may yes rye yarn eye lye yap any relay young berry
y/t	2 tf at it let the vat tap item town toast right little attire
	3 Yesterday a young youth typed a cat story on the typewriter.
	4 bf but job fibs orb bow able bear habit boast rabbit brother
b/n	5 nj not and one now fun next pony month notice runner quicken
	6 A number of neighbors banked on bunking in the brown cabins.
	7 gag go gee god rig gun log gong cog gig agog gage going gang
g/h	8 huh oh hen the hex ash her hash ah hush shah hutch hand ache
	9 Hush; Greg hears rough sounds. Has Hugh laughed or coughed?
	10 row or rid air rap par rye rear ark jar rip nor are right or
r/u	11 cut us auk out tutu sun husk but fun cub gun nut mud tug hug
	12 Ryan is sure you should pour your food from an urn or cruet.

| 1 | 2 | 3 | 4 | 5 | 6 | 7 | 8 | 9 | 10 | 11 | 12 |

A ▶ **ALL LETTERS**

Writing 33

	gwam	3'	5'

Most people think traveling is fun because they associate | 4 | 2
travel with exciting vacations. People who have to travel as | 8 | 5
part of their jobs have a very different view of travel. They | 12 | 7
are more prone to view business travel as a hassle than a plea- | 16 | 10
sure. Business travelers often have to work under less than | 21 | 12
ideal circumstances. While they are away from the office, regu- | 25 | 15
lar work tends to pile up; and they often return to find stacks | 29 | 17
of work waiting for them. Many business travelers learn to uti- | 33 | 20
lize wisely the waiting time that is a part of most travel. | 37 | 22

A successful business trip requires careful planning. The | 41 | 25
typical business traveler tends to think of a trip as a success | 45 | 27
if two conditions are met. The business goals must be achieved, | 50 | 30
and the trip must be totally free of headaches. The person mak- | 54 | 32
ing the trip has to worry about achieving the business goals, but | 58 | 35
a good travel agent can relieve the traveler of many of the wor- | 63 | 38
ries of making travel arrangements. A good checklist can help to | 67 | 40
ensure that all the personal items as well as business items | 71 | 43
needed for the trip will be handy when they are needed. | 75 | 45

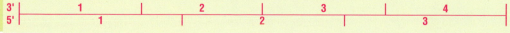

| 3' | 1 | 2 | 3 | 4 |
| 5' | 1 | 2 | 3 | |

Document 7

Invitation

maggie
kosh
molly
andy
lizzie

1. In the open document, apply a Dark Red, Text 2 Box border to the page. Use the Page Color Fill Effects to apply Parchment texture.

2. Insert the five pictures from the data files in the order listed. Crop the pictures close to each dog as shown in the illustration below. Size each picture 2" high. Position the pictures against the top border and within the side borders. Make the following picture corrections:

   a. *Maggie*: Sharpen: 25%; Brightness: 0% Contrast: +20%.
   b. *Kosh*: Sharpen: 25%; Brightness: 0% Contrast: +40%. Flip the picture horizontally.
   c. *Molly*: Sharpen: 25%; Brightness: +20% Contrast: +20%.
   d. *Andy*: Sharpen: 50%; Brightness: +20% Contrast: +20%.
   e. *Lizzie*: Sharpen: 25%; Brightness: +20% Contrast: +20%.

3. Draw a text box directly below the pictures; size it 0.3" high and extend it from side border to side border. Apply Dark Red, Text 2 Shape Outline. Key the names of the dogs in the order shown above; apply Dark Red, Text 2 font color and bold italic. Use the Space Bar to position the names under the pictures as shown in the illustration below.

4. Click in the text box and apply Shape Fill, No Fill.

5. Key the text shown below. Begin at 4.2" and center the text. Apply Lucida Calligraphy, 18-point, Dark Red, Text 2 font.

6. Proofread and check; click Next to continue. (*proj3-d7*)

Join your friends and their families

for the

Grand Opening of the new facilities

Refreshments, tours, and seminars

Sunday, April 18, 3:30 p.m.

at the

Palm Beach Pet Center

1985 Parker Avenue

West Palm Beach

Word 2010 Review

LEARNING OUTCOMES

- Review and apply *Word 2010* commands.
- Build keyboarding skills.

Lesson 56 | *Home Tab Commands*

Review Commands

- Font Group
- File Menu
- Mini and Quick Access Toolbars
- Paragraph Group
- Clipboard Group
- Styles Group
- Editing Group

KEYBOARDING PRO DELUXE 2

WARMUP

Lessons/56a Warmup

A   ALL LETTERS

Skill Building

56b   Timed Writing

1. Key a 1' writing on each paragraph; work to increase speed. Use wordwrap.
2. Key a 3' timing on both paragraphs.

	gwam	1'	3'
Good plans typically are required to execute most tasks		11	4
successfully. If a task is worth doing, it is worth investing		24	8
the time that is necessary to plan it effectively. Many people		37	12
are anxious to get started on a task and just begin before they		50	17
have thought about the best way to organize it. In the long run,		63	21
they frequently end up wasting time that could be spent more		75	25
profitably on important projects that they might prefer to tackle.		89	30
A task plan may or may not include organizational steps. The		13	34
better a plan is organized, the more likely the execution of the plan will		28	39
be successful. The way you plan and organize a task generally will		42	44
depend on how frequently it has to be done. For tasks that are done		56	48
occasionally, determine the quickest and the easiest way to complete		70	53
the job. For repetitive tasks, try to automate them to save future time.		85	58
The importance of the job is another factor that should be considered.		99	63

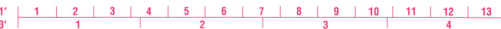

1' | 1 | 2 | 3 | 4 | 5 | 6 | 7 | 8 | 9 | 10 | 11 | 12 | 13 |
3' | 1 | 2 | 3 | 4 |

7. Insert a 2-column, 20-row table and format as follows:

   a. Apply Medium Shading 1 – Accent 6 table style. Size all rows 0.3" high; apply Align Center Left text alignment.

   b. Merge the cells in both the *Veterinary Operations* and the *Retail and Service Operations* rows; apply Heading font in White and Dark Red, Text 2 shading.

   c. Key the table shown below.

   d. Preview to ensure that the document fits on one page.

8. Use Select All and save as a Quick Part with the name and description **PBPC Contact**. Select the Insert content in its own page option.

9. Proofread and check; click Next to continue. *(proj3-d6)*

TIP

Remember to replace *Student's Name* with your name in both the *Veterinary Operations* and the *Retail and Service Operations* sections.

Veterinary Operations	
Erin A. Faulk, DVM	Managing Partner
Student's Name	Business Manager
Jan Cotter	Intern
Kathryn Moreau, DVM	Director, Surgical Services
Charles Lee	Technician, Surgical Services
Timothy T. Juk, DVM	Director, Internal Medicine
Ann Taylor	Technician, Internal Medicine
David P. Guidice, DVM	Director, Wellness Program
Lynn West	Technician, Wellness Program
Retail and Service Operations	
Douglas C. Schmidt	Managing Partner
Student's Name	Business Manager
Jan Cotter	Intern
Lynn Babcock	Manager, Grooming and Spa
Mark Jones	Assistant Manager, Grooming and Spa
Aaron Barr	Manager, Boutique
JoAnn Jameson	Assistant Manager, Boutique
Lisa Owens	Manager, Boarding and Pet Care
Jan Marcus	Assistant Manager, Boarding and Pet Care

HOME TAB COMMANDS

This module reviews *Word 2010* commands. *Keyboarding Pro DELUXE 2* has video presentations for instruction on the commonly used *Word* commands as well. The references for these commands are shown in each lesson. You can search for a specific command in the References. If you used *Keyboarding and Word Processing Essentials, Lessons 1–55*, you are already familiar with these procedures.

Keyboarding Pro DELUXE 2 will launch or open *Microsoft Word* automatically when you choose the first activity to be done in *Word*. The software manages files automatically; it opens data files and checks, saves, and closes documents for you. Non-*Keyboarding Pro DELUXE 2* users: Download the data files from www.collegekeyboarding.com and save them to your hard drive or flash drive following the instructions on the website. See the Reference Guide for instructions on how to unzip these files.

★ TIP

Standard operating procedures (SOPs) are tasks you do without being told. It is your responsibility to follow the SOPs on each document you prepare.

If you are not using *Keyboarding Pro DELUXE 2*, you will need to save your documents in a folder for each module (*Module 9* for this module) and use the filename shown in the last step of each drill or application.

STANDARD OPERATING PROCEDURES

1. Use the current date on documents requiring a date unless a specific date is provided. Replace 201- with the current year when you see it in a date.

2. Replace xx with your initials at the bottom of letters or memos.

3. Tap ENTER three times to place the date at 2" on letters or for the title of a report.

4. Use attachment or enclosure notations when the content of a document indicates something is attached or enclosed.

5. When you have completed a document, preview it, use Spelling & Grammar and other proofing tools to check the document, and proofread it carefully.

6. Print the document unless your instructor directs you otherwise.

7. Check and close the document.

PATH

Home/Font/Command

The Ribbon contains three basic components:

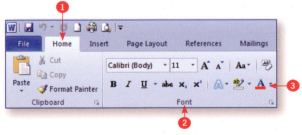

1 **Tabs**—located at the top of the Ribbon. Home, the first tab, is shown above. When you click a different tab, the Ribbon displays commands that relate to that tab.

2 **Groups**—contain a number of related items. The names are positioned at the bottom of the Ribbon below each group. The group indicated above is the Font group, which you will use to format text in this lesson.

3 **Commands**—the buttons, the boxes for entering information, and the menus that provide a choice of options. The command indicated above is the Text Color command. Clicking the drop-list arrow next to a command will display additional options.

Type of Function (Heading 1)

Mark reported that the management team wanted the function to appeal to families and to be pet friendly. JoAnn and Jan agreed to work with Mark on appropriate food and beverages to serve. Pet treats will be provided as well. The team agreed that small group tours should be hosted by a staff member in each area to showcase the state-of-the-art facilities and equipment. The veterinary staff should conduct a brief seminar on the latest trends in the medical care of pets.

Document 6
Company Contact Sheet

pbpc logo

TIP

Tap ENTER before applying shading or font color.

Mr. Schmidt asked you to prepare a company contact sheet that could be handed out or e-mailed to clients and potential clients.

1. Set a 0.7" custom top margin.

2. Insert the *pbpc logo* and apply Square text wrapping; position as shown in the illustration below.

3. Key **Palm Beach Pet Center** on the first line; apply Dark Red, Text 2, 20-point bold Heading font. Tap ENTER and apply Normal style to remove formats.

4. Tap ENTER and key **Contact Information**; apply 16-point Heading font; select the heading and apply Dark Red, Text 2 shading, and White font color.

5. Key the contact information shown below. Remove the space after each paragraph except the last one. Apply Dark Red, Text 2 to the vertical bar in the telephone line.

6. Key **Key Contacts**; apply formats from step 4 above.

Follow the directions on the next page for keying and inserting the table.

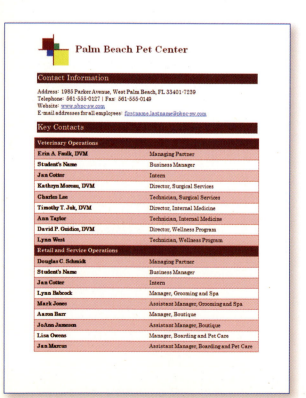

Address: 1985 Parker Avenue, West Palm Beach, FL 33401-7239

Telephone: 561-555-0127 | Fax: 561-555-0149

Website: www.pbpc-sw.com

E-mail addresses for all employees: firstname.lastname@pbpc-sw.com

PATH, CONTINUED

Home/Font/Command

Note that the path shown above (Home/Font/Command) guides you in the location of commands. To follow the path: Click the tab (Home); then look for the group label (Font) at the bottom of the Ribbon, and finally select the desired command (such as Font Size or Bold). The path will be provided for most commands throughout this textbook to assist you in locating commands quickly and easily.

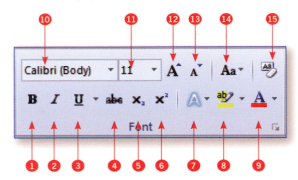

1 Bold **2** Italic **3** Underline **4** Strikethrough **5** Subscript **6** Superscript

7 Text Effects **8** Text Highlight Color **9** Font Color **10** Font **11** Font Size

12 Grow Font **13** Shrink Font **14** Change Case **15** Clear Formatting

---

DRILL 1   **FORMAT TEXT**   text formats

1. Open the data file *text formats*.
2. Read each sentence carefully and apply the command as directed.
3. Review all commands applied.
4. Proofread and check; click Next to continue. (*56-drill1*)

! WORKPLACE SUCCESS

Self-Management

Self-management is telling yourself what to do rather than waiting to be told what to do by someone else. Self-managed people make many of the daily decisions that affect their lives. To be effective in the workplace, employees must develop self-management skills.

Self-management is a concept that has worked well in the medical world with patients who have chronic diseases. Patients learn how to deal with pain; use medication appropriately; and manage factors such as exercise, nutrition, and new treatment evaluation. They learn to rely on themselves rather than on medical professionals to manage the disease.

Today, self-management is being applied to business and education. It is especially important in career management. Self-managed employees are typically low-maintenance and high performers.

Grand Opening Planning Session

Vet Conference Room	10:30 a.m.	March 8, 201-
10:30	Overview	Your Name
10:35	Date and Time of Opening	Team
10:40	Type of Function	Mark Jones
10:50	Invitation List	Lynn Babcock
11:00	Promotion Options	Aaron Barr
11:15	Budget	Your Name
11:30	Wrap Up	Your Name

Document 5
Minutes

 minutes

Prepare minutes from the Team Meeting for Planning the Grand Opening.

1. Key the minutes shown below. Insert the data file *minutes* at the end of the minutes you keyed. Use Show/Hide to remove extra spaces that are not needed.
2. Format as suggested in the comments. Remove the highlight reminding you to add your name. Make sure your name is added each time it is indicated.
3. Use Plain Number 3 for page numbers. Do not show the page number on the first page.
4. Proofread and check; click Next to continue. (*proj3-d5*)

Grand Opening Planning Session **(Title style)**

Minutes—March 8, 201- **(Subtitle style)**

The Grand Opening Planning Team met on March 8, 201- at 10:30 a.m. in the Vet Conference Room. Team members present were Lynn Babcock, Aaron Barr, Mark Jones, JoAnn Jameson, Jan Marcus, Mary Todd, and (Your Name).

Overview **(Heading 1)**

(Your Name) reported that Mr. Schmidt and Dr. Faulk requested that the team plan an event to mark the completion of new pbpc facilities. pbpc has been open during the renovation of the old facilities and the construction of the new facilities. All work has been completed, and the furnishings will be in place in approximately two to three weeks.

Date and Time **(Heading 1)**

The team discussed the advantages and disadvantages of a weekday event versus a weekend event and an afternoon versus an evening event. The group agreed that a Sunday afternoon would probably attract the largest group and selected April 18 at 3:30 p.m. as the date and time.

FILE MENU

File/Command

 The File tab located in the upper-left corner of the Ribbon provides you with all of the commands that you need to work with files. When you click the File tab with only a blank document open, a menu drops down with the commands shown on the left and the most recently opened documents on the right. **Note:** The path for the File tab (File/Command) is used for working with files on the File menu because the File menu is available for all tabs on the Ribbon. Note the pin is engaged on the first file shown below. Pinned files remain on the Recent Documents list; other files rotate off as new files are added. You can pin a document by clicking the pin.

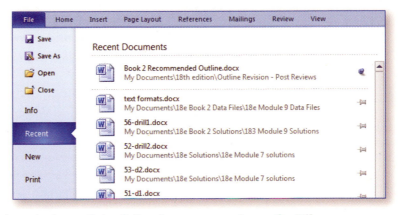

Review the descriptions of the following commands on the File menu.

Save—saves the document with the same name.

Save As—saves the document with a new name or to a new location.

Open—opens an existing document.

Close—closes a document and leaves *Word* open.

Recent—lists up to 20 documents you recently worked with that can be opened by clicking the desired document.

New—provides a list of document types that you can choose to create.

Print—displays the printing options on the left side of the screen and a preview of the document on the right side.

TIP

Remember that *Keyboarding Pro DELUXE 2* does most of these file management tasks for you. However, if you are using *Word* to prepare personal business documents or papers for other classes, you will need to manage your own files.

TIP

Remember when you are managing your own files to click the File tab any time you want to use a command to work with files—New, Open, Close, Save, Save As, or Print.

DRILL 2   FILE COMMANDS

1. Open *56-drill1* and preview the document, noting the formats applied in each sentence.

2. Key your name on the line below the last sentence; clear the formatting on this line.

3. Print a copy of the document.

4. Proofread and check; click Next to continue. (*56-drill2*)

CREATE A NEW FOLDER

The first time you save a document, clicking either Save or Save As will display the Save As dialog box. The Save As dialog box also gives you an opportunity to create a new folder in which to save the document.

shared drive. Please note that the attached procedure is labeled PBPC #1 Document Processing Standards. The PBPC #1 label indicates that the procedures outlined in this document apply to all Palm Beach Pet Center documents that are prepared for internal and external use. Procedures that apply only to the Veterinary Operations are labeled PBPC-VO, and those that apply only to the Retail and Service Operations are labeled PBPC-RSO.

Document 3
Letter

 pbpc letterhead

Do not include your initials since this letter has your signature. To enhance your productivity, save your closing lines as a Quick Part.

1. In the open document, prepare the following letter for your own signature. Be sure to include your full name and new title.

2. Send Mr. Schmidt a copy of the letter; use his name and title: **Douglas C. Schmidt, Managing Partner | Retail and Service Operations**

3. Proofread and check; click Next to continue. (*proj3-d3*)

Mr. Mark Anderson | Placement Director | Florida Tides College | 2044 Palm Beach Lakes Boulevard | West Palm Beach, FL 33409-6502

Last year you assisted me in obtaining an internship at pbpc. The internship was a very valuable experience for me. My internship not only gave me an opportunity to apply the knowledge and skills I acquired in the business program at Florida Tides; it also was a great learning experience that led to a permanent position.

I have recently been named the business manager of pbpc. As you might remember, pbpc is a thriving new business that resulted from a joint venture between Dr. Erin A. Faulk, a veterinarian, and Mr. Douglas C. Schmidt, an entrepreneur.

We would like to hire an intern who is academically successful, has leadership skills, and can work without close supervision. A job description listing the specific skills required is enclosed. Could you please recommend some of your outstanding junior or senior students for this position?

Document 4
Agenda

Your next task is to prepare an agenda for a meeting of the Grand Opening Planning Team.

1. Key the agenda shown on the next page. Apply Title style to the meeting title and Subtitle style to the subtitle. After keying the subtitle, set a center tab at 3.25" and a right tab at the right margin.

2. Before you key the body of the agenda, modify the tabs as follows: Set a left tab at 1"; remove the center tab, and change the tab at the right margin to a leader tab.

3. Add this note at the bottom of the agenda: **Note: Bring Facilities Master Plan to the meeting.**

4. Add a Draft 1 watermark to the document. Participants will be given an opportunity to make additions to the agenda.

5. Proofread and check; click Next to continue. (*proj3-d4*)

To save a document in a new folder:

File/Save or Save As

1. With the document open, click Save or Save As to display the Save As dialog box.
2. Click the New folder button to create a new folder in which to store the document. The new folder displays in blue.
3. Click in the name box and key the name of the folder, such as *Module 9*.
4. Click Open or double-click the new folder (Module 9) to open it.
5. Key the filename in the File name box and click Save.

New folder

Name box

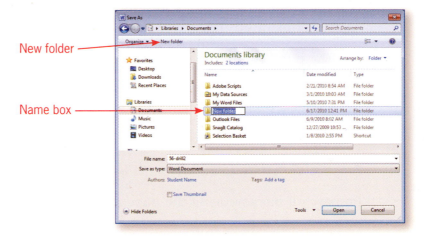

SAVE TO USB MEMORY DEVICE (FLASH DRIVE)

To save a document in a new folder on another drive:

File/Save As/Computer/Removable Disk

1. With the document open, click Save As to display the Save As dialog box.
2. Insert your USB memory device (flash drive) into a USB port.
3. Click Computer, find the Removable Disk (flash drive) on your computer, and double-click it to open it. It displays in the location box. Note that you can create a new folder on the flash drive by clicking New folder.
4. Select or key the filename.
5. Click Save.

Computer

Removable Disk

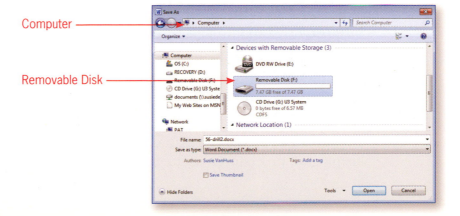

pbpc has developed standard operating procedures for all phases of its operation. Document processing standards apply to all employees in both the veterinary and the retail operations. Documents are a key part of our image and branding. Therefore, the logo, colors, fonts, and document styles must be used consistently throughout pbpc. A style guide is provided on the shared drive. Accurate documents are critical; errors not only create a bad impression, but they could also create medical problems and liability issues.

Proofread, preview, and print each document you prepare.

Use the standardized guide for naming and saving all files. Save a copy of each document on the shared drive if it will be accessed by others.

Use the pbpc standard document theme for each document you prepare.

Create a building block based on the pbpc letterhead so that you can insert it in documents when needed.

Write out pbpc in all documents; do not abbreviate the name.

Prepare all letters using the pbpc letterhead.

Prepare all memos using the pbpc memo form.

Use complete names in the closing lines of letters you prepare for the managing partners; they will sign first names on letters to individuals they know well.

Use the document style guide for preparing all documents.

Apply a draft watermark on documents that are still in draft form.

Use software features to automate as many processes as possible.

Share tips with other employees to enhance productivity.

Document 2
Memo

 pbpc memo

1. Open *pbpc memo* and key the memo shown below from Doug Schmidt to All Employees.
2. List the attachment as: **Attachment: PBPC #1 Document Processing Standards**.
3. Proofread and check; click Next to continue. (*proj3-d2*)

SUBJECT: Standard Operating Procedures

Our management team has worked with most of you to develop standard operating procedures for all phases of our operations. Procedures will be reviewed and revised on a continual basis. All employees are encouraged to review procedures and suggest ways to improve pbpc operations.

The business manager has been designated as the person responsible for keeping all procedures up to date. The procedures will be stored on the

MINI TOOLBAR

The Mini toolbar provides a shortcut to apply frequently used formatting commands. When you select text, the Mini toolbar appears in a very light or faded view. You may have noticed the toolbar when you selected text to format in Drill 1. To darken the Mini toolbar, move the mouse pointer toward it. You can click a button from this toolbar to apply a format. This toolbar simplifies editing text by positioning frequently used commands at the point at which they are needed.

To use the Mini toolbar:

1. Select text to which you want to apply a commonly used format.

2. Move the mouse pointer toward the Mini toolbar when it appears in a faded view.

3. Click the command(s) that you want to apply when the Mini toolbar darkens.

QUICK ACCESS TOOLBAR

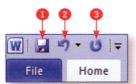

The Quick Access Toolbar is located in the upper-left corner of the screen above the File and Home tabs. The Quick Access Toolbar provides a shortcut or one-click option for the following frequently used commands. Additional commands can be added to the Quick Access Toolbar.

TIP

The Quick Access Toolbar is available from all tabs on the Ribbon.

❶ **Save**—preserves the current version of a document or displays the Save As dialog box to save a new document.

❷ **Undo**—reverses the most recent action you have taken (such as inserting or deleting text or removing formats). The drop-list arrow displays a list of the commands that you can undo. Selecting an item on the list will undo all items above it on the list.

❸ **Redo**—reverses the last undo; it can be used several times to redo the past several actions. This command can also be used to repeat actions.

To customize the Quick Access Toolbar:

1. On the Quick Access Toolbar, click the Customize Quick Access Toolbar button to display the commands.

2. Click the desired command that you wish to add to the Quick Access Toolbar. Note that the default commands Save, Undo, and Redo are already on the toolbar.

DRILL 3   QUICK ACCESS TOOLBAR

1. Add the following commands to the Quick Access Toolbar: Quick Print and Print Preview.

2. Key the two sentences below and apply italic format to *Undo* and bold to *Redo* in Sentence 1.

3. Undo the bold to *Redo* and apply italic to it in sentence 1.

4. Apply underline and italic to *Quick Access Toolbar* in sentence 2.

5. Undo the italic in sentence 2.

6. Redo the italic in sentence 2.

7. Use the Quick Access Toolbar to preview and print this document.

8. Proofread and check; click Next to continue. (*56-drill3*)

1. Undo and Redo are useful editing tools.

2. Customize the Quick Access Toolbar to add frequently used commands.

PBPC Fonts

Heading font: Century Schoolbook 11 point

Body font: Century 11 point

Effects

Effects: Office

Productivity Tools

Create AutoCorrect options as shown below.

File/Options/Proofing/AutoCorrect Options

pbpc   Replace with: **Palm Beach Pet Center**

eaf   Replace with: **Erin A. Faulk, DVM**

dcs   Replace with: **Douglas C. Schmidt**

Remember to add other AutoCorrect Options for names or phrases that you key repeatedly to be more productive.

★ TIP

It is acceptable to use the initials *pbpc* in themes, filenames, and similar applications.

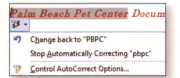

To reverse an AutoCorrect action such as retaining *PBPC* as initials, press CTRL + Z or select the text, click the AutoCorrect down arrow, and select the desired option.

STANDARD OPERATING PROCEDURES (SOPs)

1. Proofread, preview, and print each document you prepare.
2. Use the Palm Beach Pet Center letterhead and memo data files for letters and memos.
3. Use the PBPC custom theme for all documents.
4. Spell out *pbpc* as *Palm Beach Pet Center* each time it appears in documents.
5. Use block letter style with open punctuation for all letters.
6. Use *Dear* + the title and last name as the salutation on all letters unless directed to use the individual's first name.
7. Add enclosure or attachment notations and copy notations when they are referenced in a letter or memo.
8. Use the current date on all memos, letters, and reports unless directed otherwise. Use standard format for reports and meeting documents. (Apply Title style and position title at 2".)
9. Use the standard cover page with the logo for multiple-page reports.

Document 1
Procedures

Mr. Schmidt reviewed with you the standard operating procedures that are shown above. He and Dr. Faulk asked you to work with them to standardize a format for the procedures that have been developed for all areas of Palm Beach Pet Center. The procedures will be stored electronically on a shared drive. Each procedure will begin with an explanatory paragraph followed by bulleted or numbered procedural steps.

1. Key the procedures shown on the next page.
2. Apply Title style to the title **Standard Operating Procedures** and Subtitle style to the subtitle **PBPC #1: Document Processing Standards**. Do not spell out *PBPC*.
3. Apply square bullets to the list of procedures after the introductory paragraph.
4. Add a Blank footer and key: **Last revised on (Current date).**
5. Proofread and check; click Next to continue. (*proj3-d1*)

PARAGRAPH GROUP

Home/Paragraph/Command

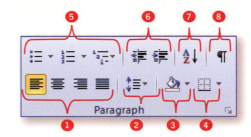

Some paragraph commands are positioned together in subgroups separated from one another by divider bars. The following overview presents the commands by the subgroups. Some paragraph commands will be applied in this lesson; others will be taught in later lessons.

1 **Alignment commands**—Align Text Left, Center, Align Text Right, and Justify—specify how text lines up.

2 **Line and Paragraph Spacing**—determines the amount of space between lines of text and before and after paragraphs.

3 **Shading**—applies color as a background for text and paragraphs.

4 **Border**—applies and removes inside and outside borders and horizontal lines.

5 **Bullets, Numbering, and Multilevel List**—apply formats to lists of information. Bullets and Numbering present information on one level whereas Multilevel List presents information in a hierarchy.

6 **Decrease and Increase Indent**—move all lines of a paragraph to the right or left.

7 **Sort**—alphabetizes selected text or arranges numerical data in ascending or descending order.

8 **Show/Hide**—displays paragraph markings and other nonprinting characters.

To apply paragraph formats:

Home/Paragraph/Command

1. Click in a single paragraph or select multiple paragraphs to which a format is to be applied.
2. Click the command to be applied.

DRILL 4   PARAGRAPH FORMATS   paragraph formats

1. Open the data file *paragraph formats*.
2. Read the directions shown in blue carefully, and apply each command as directed.
3. Preview the document to ensure that all commands were applied.
4. Proofread and check; click Next to continue. (*56-drill4*)

Palm Beach Pet Center II

LEARNING OUTCOMES

- Apply keying, formatting, and word processing skills.
- Create a variety of documents.
- Follow standard operating procedures.
- Work independently and with few specific instructions.

PALM BEACH PET CENTER II

Palm Beach Pet Center
1985 Parker Avenue | West Palm Beach, FL 33401-7239
Telephone: 561-555-0127 | Fax: 561-555-0159 | www.pbpc-sw.com

In Palm Beach Pet Center I, you worked as an intern with Dr. Erin A. Faulk, a veterinarian, and Mr. Douglas C. Schmidt, an entrepreneur, in a new joint venture named Palm Beach Pet Center. The new business integrated a veterinary clinic with a full-service luxury pet boarding, grooming, and boutique center. Palm Beach Pet Center is located near a very high income residential and resort area. Palm Beach Pet Center has become a very successful venture much earlier than expected. Because of your excellent work as an intern, you have been hired as the business manager.

Palm Beach Pet Center has recently made changes to enhance its corporate image and to develop a strong brand. The new logo and letterhead information is shown above. Your focus in Palm Beach Pet Center II is to ensure that all documents enhance the corporate image and that productivity tools are used effectively to improve your productivity.

Prior to beginning the jobs, you must create the custom document theme on your computer so that you can use it for all documents you create. Letterhead and memo forms are provided in the data files, but you will need the theme for reports, newsletters, and other documents that you prepare. Information for creating the custom theme is shown below. Save colors as **PBPC**; save fonts as **PBPC**; and save the theme as **PBPC**.

PBPC Colors

Text/Background – Dark 2: Red, Accent 2, Darker 50%

Text/Background – Light 2: Tan, Text 2

Accent 1: Dark Red (Standard Color)

Accent 2: Blue (Standard Color)

Accent 3: Green (Standard Color)

Accent 4: Yellow (Standard Color)

Accent 5: Dark Blue (Standard Color)

Accent 6: Red, Accent 2, Darker 25%

Hyperlink: Blue (Standard Color)

Followed Hyperlink: Purple (Standard Color)

CLIPBOARD GROUP

An overview of the four editing commands the Clipboard group contains is provided below. The Clipboard is used to store up to 24 items of text or graphics that have been cut or copied so they can be used in other locations. The Office Clipboard task pane is illustrated below on the right. It is accessed by clicking the small arrow (called the Dialog Box Launcher) located at the lower-right corner of the Clipboard group. Items can be pasted by using the Paste button or from the Clipboard. Note that you can paste items individually or all at one time.

Cut—removes the selected text from its current location.

Paste—positions the text that was cut in another location.

Copy—makes an additional copy of the selected text.

Format Painter—enables you to copy the format of one paragraph to another.

The Paste Option buttons shown below provide a live preview of what text will look like when it is pasted.

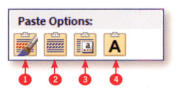

❶ Keep Source Formatting ❷ Merge Formatting

❸ Use Destination Theme ❹ Keep Text Only

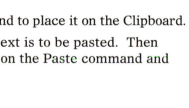

To cut, copy, or paste text:

Home/Clipboard/Cut, Copy, or Paste

1. To cut or copy text, select the text and click the command to place it on the Clipboard.
2. To paste the text, place the insertion point where the text is to be pasted. Then click either the Paste command or the drop-list arrow on the Paste command and select the desired Paste option.

To copy a paragraph format to a single paragraph:

Home/Clipboard/Format Painter

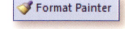

1. Click in the paragraph that has the desired format and then click the Format Painter.
2. Drag the Format Painter across a paragraph to copy the desired format to it.

To copy a paragraph format to multiple paragraphs:

1. Click in the paragraph that has the desired format and then double-click the Format Painter to keep it turned on.
2. Drag the Format Painter across each paragraph to copy the desired format to it.
3. Click Format Painter to turn it off or tap ESC.

markets. However, time per trip is significantly lower in the smaller cities due to greater traffic in the larger markets during the evening hours as well as during the typical business hours.

Services

The mix of services is composed of business executive services, major event services, and general limo services. The primary services are those provided for business executives. Business executive services include an array of services depending on the needs of the customer. Business services are provided to executives of the company and to guests who visit the company.

Strategy

Pommery Limo Service strives to become the dominant limo service in the cities it serves. Pommery also plans to expand its geographic area over the next three years. Pommery's core competencies involve providing safe, high-quality, luxury services that are cost effective. All other services provided are designed to facilitate and enhance the continual development of the core competencies.(5) To implement this strategy, Pommery Limo Service must expand its service in the cities it currently serves as well as expand into other areas.

Footnotes

1. The number of passengers accommodated far exceeds the number of trips made per month.

2. The next regional office will serve the Atlantic Coast region. The location has not yet been determined.

3. Airport trips also tend to increase the time per trip in larger cities with major airports.

4. Major events and general limo services average two to four passengers per trip. Executive travel averages one or two passengers per trip.

5. Currently, 72 percent of our customers provide repeat business. More than 30 percent of our business customers use our services more than 25 times per month.

BOOKMARK

www.collegekeyboarding.com
Module 18 Practice Quiz

DRILL 5 — EDITING COMMANDS

1. In the open document, turn on Show/Hide.

2. Read the directions shown in blue carefully, and apply the command as directed.

3. Delete the directions in blue below the title and any extra paragraph markers.

4. Proofread and check; click Next to continue. (*56-drill5*)

STYLES GROUP

Preformatted styles such as title and heading styles can easily be applied to text. The size and resolution of your screen determines how many styles display in the Styles gallery.

More button

To apply styles:

Home/Styles/Styles

1. Click in the text to which you want to apply the style, and then click the desired style in the Styles gallery.

2. To view additional styles, click the More button to expand the gallery.

DRILL 6 — STYLES

styles

1. In the open document, click in the first line and apply Title style.

2. Apply Subtitle style to *Use the Quick Styles Gallery.*

3. Apply Heading 1 style to *Heading 1* and Heading 2 style to *Heading 2*.

4. Proofread and check; click Next to continue. (*56-drill6*)

EDITING GROUP

The Find command is used to locate text or objects. It includes the Go To command—an excellent navigation tool. Replace is used to substitute new text or formatting for that which was found.

To find and replace text:

Home/Editing/Find or Replace

1. Click Find to display the Navigation pane -or- Replace to display the Find and Replace dialog box.

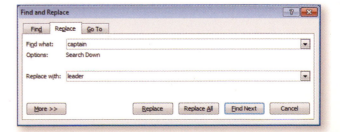

Pommery Facts

Company Overview

Pommery Limo Service (Pommery) is a company specializing in providing limousine services. Pommery is headquartered in Chicago, Illinois, with its main office located at 1340 N. Astor Street.

Mission

Pommery's mission is to:

Provide its customers with safe, reliable transportation, quality service, and outstanding value.

Offer its employees an environment that fosters teamwork and customer service and that also rewards integrity and productivity.

Deliver superior value to its shareholders.

Company

Pommery Limo Service, a Delaware corporation founded in January 2008, currently has a fleet of 192 stretch limos and 450 executive cars. Pommery provides limo service for more than 65,500 trips per month.(1)

An experienced, highly competent management team leads Pommery Limo Service. Senior management emphasizes teamwork, empowerment, productivity, and employee development. Employee stock options provide incentives to employees to focus on quality, productivity, and profitability. The organization chart on the next page shows our Senior Executive team.

The executive team is in the process of developing a team of regional presidents. Our first regional president, Miyo Mitsui, was named in the Southwest region. The new regional office in Houston serves other cities in Texas, Louisiana, Oklahoma, Colorado, and Arizona.(2)

[Insert SmartArt graphic here]

Pommery Limo Service became profitable in its tenth month of existence and continues to be profitable. The company operates as a lean, efficient organization. Average costs per mile (ACM) have dropped approximately 10 percent. Yield per vehicle has increased more than 25 percent.(3)

Market

Pommery Limo Service provides service to destinations in 18 cities in 12 states located in the Midwest, Southwest, and Atlantic Coast regions. The more than 65,500 trips per month provide transportation services to a much larger group of passengers.(4) The primary market is defined by city size. In large cities, trips per vehicle per day are more than double those in smaller

2. Key the text to locate in the search box of the Navigation pane -or- in the Find what box in the Find and Replace dialog box. The text that contains the search text will display in the Navigation pane, and the words will be highlighted in the document.

3. Key replacement text in the Replace with box on the Find and Replace dialog box.

4. Click Find Next and then click Replace -or- Replace All.

To navigate using Go To:

Home/Editing/Find/Go To

1. Follow the path to display the Go To tab on the Find and Replace dialog box.

2. Select the desired option such as Page or Footnote.

3. In the Enter box, key the desired item, such as the page number or footnote number.

DRILL 7 — FIND AND REPLACE

 find and replace

1. In the open document, find *captain* one time and replace it with *leader*.

2. Find *objectives* and replace with *goals* each time the word occurs in the document.

3. Find *synergy* and read the next sentence, which explains what synergy means.

4. Use the Go To command to go to footnote 1. Add **Effective** to the title of the seminar so that it reads *Effective Team Leadership*. Check the formatting of the title to make sure it is consistent.

5. Proofread and check; click Next to continue. (*56-drill7*)

Communication

56d

 activity 56d

KEYBOARDING PRO DELUXE 2

References/Communication Skills/Sentence Types and Terminal Punctuation

SENTENCE TYPES AND TERMINAL PUNCTUATION

1. Four types of sentences are listed below:
   a. Simple sentence
   b. Complex sentence
   c. Compound sentence
   d. Compound complex sentence

2. If necessary, review the rules in *Keyboarding Pro DELUXE 2* defining the sentence types and for terminal punctuation; then read the six sentences below.

3. In the data file *activity 56d*, key the letter (a, b, c, or d) identifying the type of each sentence.

Sentence Types

1. Although the trip to the Great Wall was long, the view was worth the time and cost.

2. Who went with you on the trip?

3. If you would like to join us, please call me, and if you would like to bring a guest, please do so.

4. Jeff drove a burgundy car, and Jane drove a blue one.

5. We had never met, but she welcomed us warmly.

6. Thank you for sending me the book review.

Terminal Punctuation

1. In the Terminal Punctuation section, add the appropriate punctuation at the end of each sentence.

2. Proofread and check; click Next to continue. (*56d*)

When you complete a document, proofread it, check the spelling, and preview for placement. Click the Check button when you are ready to error-check the test. Review and/or print the document analysis results.

110c

Assessment

 Continue

 Check

110-d1

Report

 pommery logo

1. Key the report shown on the next page with footnotes and a cover page. Apply Hardcover theme.

2. Apply Title style and Subtitle style to the title and subtitle on the first two lines.

3. Apply Heading 1 style to all headings in the report.

4. Apply square bullets to the three mission paragraphs in the *Mission* statement.

5. Insert footnotes where noted in parentheses () in the text. Key the footnotes that are shown at the end of the report.

6. Insert a SmartArt Name and Title Organization Chart at the top of page 2. Key and format as follows:
   a. Top shape: **Patrick Ray**; Title: **President & CEO**
   b. Assistant shape: **Lynn West**; Title: **Executive Assistant**
   c. Left shape, bottom row: **Da-Shawn Archie**; Title: **Senior VP & CFO**
   d. Center shape: **Anna Garcia**; Title: **Senior VP & COO**
   e. Right shape: **Mason Lee**; Title: **Executive VP**
   f. Make sure the titles for the four executives have the same size font—9 points; the Assistant title will be 8 points to fit in the placeholder.
   g. Format the graphic 2.6" by 6" and position in Top Center with Square Text Wrapping. Tap ENTER below the graphic and key the next paragraph.

7. Insert a Continuous section break at the top of the first page and insert a Pinstripes cover page. Format as follows:
   a. Key the title and subtitle in the appropriate placeholders; pick the current date; key the company name and your name in the appropriate placeholders.
   b. Insert the *pommery logo* data file. Position the logo in Middle Center with Square Text Wrapping.

8. Insert a Motion (Odd Page) header. Remember to break the link for both the header and footer before inserting the header to number the pages.

9. Change the page number to 1 on the first page of the report; do not show the number on the first page.

10. Preview and proofread the report carefully.

11. Check and close. (*110-d1*)

56-d1

Format Text and Paragraphs

1. In a new document, tap ENTER three times and key your name; right-align it; and then key the document left-aligned using Calibri 11-point font. Apply commands from the Mini toolbar when possible.

2. Apply Cambria 14-point bold font to the title and center it. Convert the title to uppercase.

3. Justify the first paragraph below the title.

4. Use the Format Painter to justify the paragraph below the heading *Topic Sentences*.

5. Convert the title to capitalize each word; apply Title style and shrink the font so that it fits on one line.

6. Apply Heading 1 style to the three side headings.

7. Find *oneness* and replace it with *unity* each time it occurs; find *insure* and replace it with *ensure* one time.

8. Use the Go To command to move to the second heading, *Topic Sentences*; select the heading and then highlight it in Turquoise.

9. In the second bulleted item, move *logically* after *linked*.

10. Check and close. (*56-d1*)

Paragraphs—Building Blocks For Effective Writing

Good writers pay attention to one of the key building blocks for effective writing—paragraphs. The length of paragraphs affects readability. Good paragraph length averages 4 to 8 lines.

Paragraph Structure

Three concepts are used in structuring paragraphs effectively:

- Oneness—all sentences in the paragraph relate to one topic.
- Coherence—ideas within the paragraph are linked to each other logically. Using carefully selected transitional words to link ideas also builds coherence.
- Emphasis—important ideas are stressed and less important ideas are de-emphasized.

Topic Sentences

Topic sentences are not required; however, most good paragraphs do have topic sentences. Typically, a topic sentence is used to begin or end a paragraph because it is given more emphasis in these positions.

Writing Strategy

1. Outline the ideas before writing—check to see that all ideas are related.
2. Draft the paragraph.
3. Edit the paragraph carefully to insure that it has oneness, coherence, and that important ideas are emphasized.
4. Proofread and finalize the paragraph.

Lesson 110 | Assessment

WARMUP

Lessons/110a Warmup

A   ALL LETTERS

Skill Building

110b   Timed Writing

1. Key one 3' timed writing on each paragraph; key at your control rate.

2. Key one 5' timed writing; key at your control rate.

	gwam	3'	5'

Today, a huge number of white-collar workers use computers in their daily work. Most of these workers also have access to the Internet. Using the Internet for work purposes is becoming more and more common and, most of the time, is quite effective. Some organizations are finding, though, that a number of their workers do abuse the Internet. The abuse tends to occur in two forms.

The first type of abuse they find is that a large number of employees visit sites that are not related in any way to their work. Some of the sites that workers visit contain material that is very offensive to others. The problem is more serious when offensive e-mails or material from websites are sent to other employees. In some cases, the courts have found that these materials create a hostile work environment. The second type of abuse is the waste of work time. Employees who spend excessive amounts of time surfing the Internet simply are not doing the work they are paid to do.

A number of large companies are trying to deal with this problem by buying software that they use to track the sites that workers access from their computers. These companies warn all of their employees that visiting offensive sites at work can have major consequences and might even result in job loss. They tend to be a little more lenient on the time abuse issue and often treat the Internet the same way that they deal with the telephone. Limited personal use of the Internet or e-mail is not a major problem. If the use becomes excessive, then action is taken.

gwam 3' / 5':
4 | 2
8 | 5
13 | 8
17 | 10
21 | 13
26 | 15
30 | 18
34 | 21
39 | 23
43 | 26
48 | 29
52 | 31
56 | 34
61 | 36
65 | 39
69 | 41
73 | 44
78 | 47
82 | 49
87 | 52
91 | 54
95 | 57
100 | 60
103 | 62

3' | 1 | 2 | 3 | 4
5' | 1 | 2 | 3

Lesson 57 | Insert Tab Commands

Review Commands

- Tables Group
- Illustrations Group
- Text Group
- Pages Group

WARMUP

Lessons/57a Warmup

Skill Building

57b   Textbook Keying

1. Key each line, concentrating on using good keying techniques. Tap ENTER twice after each 4-line group.
2. Repeat the drill if time permits.

1 Sand castles are fun to build but are poor shelter in a downpour.

adjacent reaches

2 The Hoosiers scored three points in the fourth to avoid an upset.

3 Her articles are going to be reported in an edition of the paper.

4 Fewer people attend West Point to play polo than to join a choir.

5 A dazed beggar scattered after a red car swerved on a wet street.

one hand

6 Mimi feasts on milky eggs at noon after I feed Kipp plum dessert.

7 Mo started ragweed tests in a vacated garage after greeting Dave.

8 You debate Phil after I defeat John; rest up, you brave braggart!

9 Handiwork is busy work, but it's also a memento of a rich entity.

balanced hand

10 The hairy ape bit the fish, but the apricot and corn lay dormant.

11 Henry may dismantle an authentic antique auto for Zoe's sorority.

12 An Irish auditor quit work at the city and ambled to the fields.

Review Commands

57c

INSERT TAB

The Insert tab contains seven groups of commands—Pages, Tables, Illustrations, Links, Header & Footer, Text, and Symbols. Some of the groups and commands within those groups were not taught in Lessons 1–55 or will be reviewed in depth in future lessons and will not be included in this lesson. This lesson is designed to provide a quick review of some of the key commands.

KEYBOARDING PRO DELUXE 2

References/Word 2010 Commands/Lessons 38–40

TABLES GROUP

The Tables group is used to insert tables. Tables can be created by using the grid or the Insert Table command on the Insert Table menu. Tables can be designed and formatted using the Table Tools tabs. Tabs like Table Tools Design and Layout are sometimes called *contextual tabs* because they display in the context of working with a particular item such as a table, picture, shape, SmartArt, or clip art. Contextual tabs are accessed by clicking in the table or on the graphic.

Table Tools | Design | Layout

1. Prepare an announcement that will be sent to all Pommery Limo Service employees.

2. Apply Hardcover theme, Landscape orientation, and Narrow margins.

3. Tap ENTER 11 times to position the insertion point at 4.4". Increase the font size to 18 points and key the information shown below. Center the text. Apply italic to *RSVP*.

4. Insert a Horizontal Scroll Banner from Shapes. Size it 1.5" high by 10" wide and align the top of the shape with the first blank paragraph on the page.

5. Key the text **Pommery Limo Service—Company Picnic**; grow the font to 36 points to fill the banner; apply Fill – White, Drop Shadow text effect.

6. Use the keyword *picnic* and search clip art for a suitable clip to depict a picnic. Size it 2.0" high and center it below the banner. (See illustration below.)

7. Proofread and preview the document.

8. Check and close. (*109-d3*)

Pommery Limo Service—Company Picnic

Saturday, May 15 from 10:30 a.m. to 7:30 p.m.

Lakeshore Shelter 10

Bring the family

Celebrate Pommery's best quarter ever!

Food, beverages, and recreational activities provided

RSVP by May 10 to Jenna.Newell@pommerylimo.com

Saturday, May 15 from 10:30 a.m. to 7:30 p.m.

Lakeshore Shelter 10

Bring the family

Celebrate Pommery's best quarter ever!

Food, beverages, and recreational activities provided

RSVP by May 10 to Jenna.Newell@pommerylimo.com

! WORKPLACE SUCCESS

Employee Empowerment

Employee empowerment refers to allowing employees to participate actively in decision making relative to their jobs. Employees cannot truly be empowered unless they have the knowledge, skills, and ability to make good decisions that affect their jobs. Empowerment requires training and experience as well as a desire on the part of the individual employee to make contributions and decisions relative to the job being performed.

To create a table using the Table grid:

Insert/Tables/Table

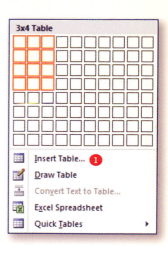

3x4 Table

1. Position the insertion point where the table is to be inserted and follow the path to display the Insert Table menu.

2. Drag on the grid to select the number of columns and rows needed for the table. Note that Insert Table changes to indicate the number of columns and rows, such as 3 × 4 Table.

3. Click the left mouse button to display the table in the document.

4. Click the first cell to key text. Use the TAB key to move to the next cell.

- Insert Table... ❶
- Draw Table
- Convert Text to Table...
- Excel Spreadsheet
- Quick Tables

To create a table using the Insert Table command:

Insert/Tables/Table/Insert Table

Insert Table

Table size
Number of columns: 5
Number of rows: 2

AutoFit behavior
- Fixed column width: Auto
- AutoFit to contents
- AutoFit to window

Remember dimensions for new tables

OK   Cancel

1. Repeat step 1 above.

2. Click Insert Table ❶ to display the Insert Table dialog box.

3. Use the spin arrows to select the number of columns and rows or key the number in the box.

4. Click the first cell to key text. Use the TAB key to move to the next cell.

DRILL 1   CREATE TABLE

1. In a new document, tap ENTER three times and create a 2-column, 3-row table.

2. Key the data shown in the table on the right.

3. Proofread and check; click Next to continue. (57-drill1)

Anderson East	5,000
Anderson West	2,500
River View	9,000

TABLE LAYOUT

The tools on the Table Tools Layout tab are used to format and change the structure of tables. The Table Tools Layout tab contains six groups of commands—Table, Rows & Columns, Merge, Cell Size, Alignment, and Data. In this lesson, you will work with the following commands in these groups:

- Commands in the Rows & Columns group to insert and delete rows and columns.
- Commands in the Merge group to merge or split cells.

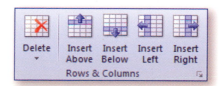

Delete | Insert Above | Insert Below | Insert Left | Insert Right
Rows & Columns

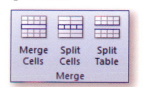

Merge Cells | Split Cells | Split Table
Merge

    d. Use the appropriate formula to multiply the data in column B times 225 to complete column C. Apply the number format #,##0.

    e. Add a row at the bottom of the table; key **Totals** in column A and use the appropriate formula to sum columns B and C; use the same number format as used for the data in the columns.

3. Verify that the numbers are correct.

4. Add a copy notation for **Patrick V. Ray** and your initials.

5. Proofread and continue to next document. (*109-d2*)

Miyo Mitsui | Da-Shawn Archie | Current date | Investment Results

Thank you for giving me the opportunity to participate on the Grand Opening program. You put together an excellent group of potential investors. You and Pat both did a superb job in presenting Pommery Limo Service as a very successful, client-oriented company and as having tremendous momentum and growth potential.

Having a very receptive audience makes it much easier to showcase the investment opportunities that Pommery Limo Service offers. Several individuals in the audience have followed up and have already committed to making an investment in the company. Their commitments are shown in the following table.

Houston Investors		
Names	Shares	Dollar Value
Robert and Courtney Blakewood	500	
Carlos and Gabriela Ramirez	575	
Andrew and Laura Blankenship	610	
Jacob and Naomi Goldberg	850	
Christopher and Rebecca Alvarez	998	

Several other participants have expressed an interest in the company and requested additional information. We will follow up with them and try to convert them to investors.

TABLE LAYOUT, CONTINUED

- Commands in the Cell Size group to change the height of rows, change the width of columns, and AutoFit the contents of the table.

- Commands in the Alignment group to position text in cells.

- Commands in the Table group to select or center the table.

To change a table layout:

Table Tools Layout/Rows & Columns, Merge, Cell Size, Alignment, or Table

- To insert rows or columns, click where the new column or row is to be inserted; click Insert Above, Insert Below, Insert Left, or Insert Right in the Rows & Columns group.

- To delete a column or row, position the insertion point in that row or column; click Delete in the Rows & Columns group and select the desired Delete option.

- To merge cells, select the cells; click Merge Cells in the Merge group.

- To split a cell, click in it; click Split Cells in the Merge group and choose the number of rows and columns.

- To change the height of a row or width of a column, click in it; use the Width and Height spin arrows in the Cell Size group to change the size as desired.

- To apply AutoFit, click in the table; click AutoFit in the Cell Size group and select AutoFit Contents or AutoFit Window.

- To align text in a cell, click in the cell; click the desired position in the Alignment group.

- To center a table horizontally, click in it; click Properties in the Table group; in the Alignment group, select Center.

DRILL 2   TABLE LAYOUT

1. Open *57-drill1* and insert a column to the right of column B. Key the following data in the column:

   $200,000 – 325,000
   $300,000 – 395,000
   $125,000 – 175,000

2. Insert a row above row 1; key the following headings in the three cells:

   Development | **Number of Units** | **Price Range**

3. Add another row above the top row and merge the cells; increase the height of the row to 0.3".

4. Key the title **New Developments**; increase the font size to 16 point; and apply Align Center.

5. Apply AutoFit to Contents.

6. Center the table horizontally.

7. Proofread and check; click Next to continue. (*57-drill2*)

When you complete a document, proofread it, check the spelling, and preview for placement. When you are completely satisfied, click the Continue button to move to the next document. Click the Check button when you are ready to error-check the test. Review and/or print the document analysis results.

109-d1

Letter

 pommery lth

1. Key the following letter in the open document.
2. Use the current date, the standard greeting line, and your initials.
3. Proofread and continue to the next document. (*109-d1*)

Dr. Daniel B. McAngus | President and CEO | St. Simon Medical Group | 8 E. Pearson Street | Chicago, IL 60611-2068

This letter confirms our dinner at the Chicago WestMark Club next Friday at 8:15 p.m. for a party of twenty. We are pleased that you and your five senior officers and their spouses can join our senior executive team for dinner. Our trip coordinator will arrange for each of you to be picked up at home and brought to the Club.

Dr. McAngus, we appreciate serving your company for the past year, and it is always a pleasure for us to serve you. We especially appreciate the introduction you gave us to the Rexford Medical Group, and the excellent recommendation that your senior officers gave them about our services. We finalized our contract with the Rexford Medical Group and will begin providing transportation services to them next week. Your support was instrumental in our successful negotiations with this new group.

We look forward to having the opportunity to get to know your executive team better and to a very delightful dinner and evening.

Sincerely | Patrick V. Ray | President and CEO

109-d2

Memo

pommery memo

1. Key the memo on the next page in the open document.
2. Create a 2-column, 7-row table; split column B into two columns and distribute the columns equally; format the table as follows:
   a. Apply Medium Shading 1 – Accent 1 Table Style.
   b. Merge the cells in row 1; increase the height to 0.4"; center the title vertically and horizontally; apply 14-point Heading font and White Font color.
   c. Bold and center the column headings in columns B and C and center the data in those columns.

TABLE DESIGN

The tools on the Table Tools Design tab can be used to make a table more attractive and enhance its readability. In this lesson, you will work with Table Styles.

Table Styles

To apply table styles:

Table Tools Design/Table Styles

1. Click in the table to display the Table Tools tabs and follow the path to Table Styles. Click the More button to display the Table Styles gallery.

2. Move the mouse pointer over each table style until you find the desired one. Use the scroll bar, if needed, to view all available styles.

3. Click a style to apply it to the table.

DRILL 3   TABLE DESIGN

1. Open *57-drill2* and apply Medium Grid 3 – Accent 1 Style.

2. In columns B and C, select the column headings and the data in the three cells below each column head and apply Align Center.

3. Center the table horizontally.

4. Proofread and check; click Next to continue. (*57-drill3*)

ILLUSTRATIONS GROUP

Graphics can be used to enhance documents and to clarify or simplify concepts. In this lesson, you will review the Picture, Clip Art, Shapes, and SmartArt commands.

KEYBOARDING PRO DELUXE 2

References/Word 2010 Commands/Lessons 49–50

PICTURE AND CLIP ART

Pictures are photographs or other images created in software other than *Word*; they are accessed by browsing your files. Clip art is a media file that can be accessed by using keywords to search for the appropriate clip provided in *Office* software or online.

To insert a picture or clip art:

Insert/Illustrations/Picture or Clip Art

- Click at the position you wish to insert a picture, follow the path, and click Picture to browse your files and select the picture to be inserted.

- Follow the path and click Clip Art to display the Clip Art task pane. Key a word or phrase in the Search for box to locate the desired type of clip art. Accept the defaults and click Go. Scroll to locate the desired clip and click it to insert it.

Lesson 109 | Assessment

Skill Building

gwam | 3' | 5'

109b Timed Writing

1. Key one 3' timed writing on each paragraph; key at your control rate.
2. Key one 5' timed writing; key at your control rate.

Most people find it amazing that mobile telephones can create a | 4 | 3
number of etiquette and safety problems. The use of hand-held, | 9 | 5
mobile telephones has increased dramatically in the past few years. | 13 | 8
Just because a mobile telephone can be taken almost anywhere does | 18 | 11
not mean that it is appropriate to use it in any place it can be | 22 | 13
carried. Common sense and good manners seem to have been forgotten | 26 | 16
when it comes to using a mobile telephone. | 29 | 18

The major safety hazard of using a hand-held telephone results | 33 | 20
from its use in moving automobiles. A significant percentage of | 38 | 23
all accidents is the result of drivers being distracted. Of all the | 42 | 25
distractions reported, the most frequent are those that occur while | 47 | 28
a driver is holding a telephone in one hand and trying to drive | 51 | 31
at the same time. A hands-free telephone is not as dangerous, but | 56 | 33
it can still cause a driver to be distracted. | 59 | 35

The etiquette problem is the result of a person speaking on | 63 | 38
a telephone in a place that disturbs another person. Either the | 67 | 40
individual doing this just does not care or does not realize how | 71 | 43
rude he or she is being to another person. It is not unusual to | 76 | 45
see signs that prohibit the use of a mobile telephone in meeting | 80 | 48
rooms, restaurants, movie theaters, concert halls, and a number | 84 | 51
of other places. What is most shocking is that these signs are | 88 | 53
necessary. Except in rare cases, a telephone should not be used | 93 | 56
in these places. What has happened to basic courtesy? | 96 | 58

```
3' |    1         2         3         4
5' |    1         2         3
```

Click the picture or clip art and use the tools on the Picture Tools Format tab to apply a Picture Style, arrange the picture, adjust it, or size it.

To format pictures or clip art:

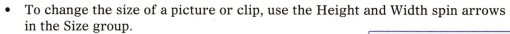 Picture Tools Format/Arrange, Size, Adjust, or Picture Styles

- To move a picture or clip, click Wrap Text in the Arrange group; select a style such as Square and drag the clip or picture to the desired position.

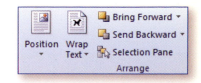

- To position a picture or clip, click Position in the Arrange group; select the desired position with text wrapping.

- To change the size of a picture or clip, use the Height and Width spin arrows in the Size group.

- To cut off unwanted portions of a picture on one side, click Crop in the Size group; drag the cropping handle inward. To crop the same amount on two sides, press CTRL while you drag the handle. The cropping line will illustrate what is being cut off. To finish, click off the picture.

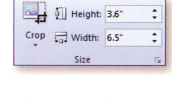

- To reduce the file size of a picture or clip, click Compress Pictures in the Adjust group; click OK to accept the defaults and compress the picture.

- To apply a style to a picture or clip, use the Picture Styles More button to display all styles in the Picture Styles gallery; click the desired style to apply it.

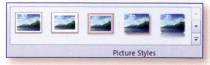

DRILL 4   PICTURE   castle

1. In a new document, insert *castle* from the data files and position in Top Center with Square Text Wrapping.

2. Crop approximately 0.75" from the top and bottom of the picture.

3. Compress the picture; accept the defaults.

4. Size the picture 2.5" high.

5. Apply Bevel Rectangle picture style.

6. Preview the picture.

7. Proofread and check; click Next to continue. (*57-drill4*)

Footnotes

1. The vehicle utilization rate in large cities is 32% higher than in mid-size cities.

2. The fleet currently consists of 192 stretch limos and 450 executive cars.

Information for Basic Pie SmartArt

1. Founder 28.68%

2. Business Community 24.25%

3. Senior Officers 16.75%

4. Outside Directors 15.67%

5. Employees 14.65%

QUICK ✔

- ✓ Is the logo positioned in the Middle Center of the cover page?
- ✓ Is Title style applied to the table of contents, and is it positioned at 2"?
- ✓ Is the table of contents numbered *ii* in the center of the footer?
- ✓ Does the first page of the Business Plan begin at 2" and have no number displayed?
- ✓ Does the header contain *Business Plan* and correct Arabic page numbers?

Communication

108c Compose Letter

pommery lth

TIP

You will complete this job in *Keyboarding Pro DELUXE 2*, but the composition will not be checked by *Keyboarding Pro DELUXE 2*.

1. Use Pommery letterhead and compose a letter from Mr. Patrick Ray to:

   Mr. Michael G. White | White and Burge Associates | 437 N. Rush Street | Chicago, IL 60611-3501

2. Supply the appropriate greeting line and use the Quick Part for the closing lines.

3. Provide the following information for Mr. White.

   a. Thank him for giving Pommery Limo Service an opportunity to supply a quote for providing service for 80 guests for a VIP Gala his company is sponsoring at the Chicago Medallion Center one month from today (specify the date).

   b. Mr. White indicated he would like to discuss the quote with a Pommery Limo Service representative next Friday if possible. Invite Mr. White to have lunch with Mr. Ray on Friday of next week at 12:30 p.m. at the Chicago WestMark Club.

   c. Mr. Ray will bring the Pommery quote with him to lunch. Ask for the information in the bulleted list below to be e-mailed by next Wednesday.

      • What is the desired average number of guests per limousine?

      • Please provide a list of the pick-up locations that are more than five miles from the Chicago Medallion Center.

      • What are the expected arrival and departure times for guests?

4. Close the letter with a forward-looking statement about providing service for White and Burge Associates.

5. Edit the letter carefully, preview, and proofread.

6. Check and close. (*108c*)

1. Search Clip Art using the keyword *castle*.

2. Select and insert a landscape-oriented clip of a castle.

3. Crop the picture as desired and size it 3" high.

4. Apply Square text wrapping and use the mouse to drag to the approximate horizontal center.

5. Apply Bevel Rectangle picture style and preview.

6. Proofread and check; click Next to continue. (*57-drill5*)

SHAPES

Individual shapes can be added to a document, or a number of shapes can be combined to create a more complex drawing. Tools on the Drawing Tools Format tab can be used to apply a shape style; to change the shape fill, outline, or effects; to size the shape to specific dimensions; to position it; and to group multiple shapes.

To add a shape to a document:

Insert/Illustrations/Shapes

1. Follow the path to display the gallery of shapes; click the desired shape; then click in the document where you want to position the shape and drag to draw the shape the desired size.

2. To add text to the shape, click on it and key the text.

To format a shape using the Drawing Tools commands:

Drawing Tools Format/Shape Styles/Shape Fill, Shape Outline, Shape Effects, Shape Styles

- Select the shape and then click the Shape Styles More button to display the Shape Styles gallery; click the desired style to apply it.

- Click the drop-list arrow on Shape Fill, Shape Outline, or Shape Effects and choose a fill color, outline color and weight, or a shape effect.

> ⭐ **TIP**
>
> To create a perfect circle or square (or to constrain the dimensions of other shapes), press and hold SHIFT while you drag.

> ⭐ **TIP**
>
> Shapes can be sized or moved with the mouse. Dragging the sizing handles at the corners will retain the proportion of the shape.

1. Draw a Sun shape from the Basic Shapes category; size the shape 5" high and 5" wide.

2. Apply Light 1 Outline, Colored Fill – Blue, Accent 1 shape style; change the fill to Yellow from the Standard Colors.

3. Insert the text **Sunshine makes me smile!** in the shape.

4. Center the text, apply bold, and increase the font size to 24 point.

5. Position the shape in Middle Center with Square Text Wrapping.

6. Proofread and check; click Next to continue. (*57-drill6*)

SMARTART

SmartArt consists of predesigned diagrams that help to simplify complex concepts. SmartArt layouts are grouped into nine categories: List, Process, Cycle, Hierarchy, Relationship, Matrix, Pyramid, Picture, and layouts from Office.com. You can elect to view all of the layouts or the layouts in one of the categories.

Program Information

Welcome	11:30
Ms. Miyo Mitsui | Southwest Regional President	
Company Overview	11:40
Mr. Patrick V. Ray | President and Chief Executive Officer	
Investment Opportunities	11:50
Mr. Da-Shawn Archie | Chief Financial Officer	
Luncheon	12:15
Tour of Regional Office	1:15

108-d4

Report

business plan
pommery logo

TIP

Remember to break the links between the first and second sections of the header and the footer. Go to page 363 of Lesson 73 in Module 12 for a complete review of the procedures for numbering the pages of a report with preliminary pages. If you have trouble, review the Troubleshooting Tips on page 364.

1. In the open document, format the Business Plan using standard report format. Note that the data file includes formatting instructions in a blue color for the title, subtitle, headings, and where to insert footnotes and the SmartArt graphic. After you have followed these instructions, delete them, including any extra spaces after headings.

2. Apply square bullets to the three segments under the *Industry* heading.

3. Insert the footnote references where indicated and key the footnotes shown on the next page.

4. Insert a Basic Pie SmartArt Layout where indicated in the data file and format as follows:

   a. Change the colors to Colorful – Accent Colors.

   b. Select the gray shape and add a shape after. Then add another shape after the one just added.

   c. Key the information shown on the next page beginning with the exploded piece of the pie (piece that appears outside of the pie). The percentages should be from high to low as you move clockwise.

5. Click at the top of the first page; insert the Pinstripes cover page and then a blank page for the table of contents. Click again at the top of the first page of the report and insert a Continuous section break. Format the cover page as follows:

   a. Key the title and the company name as the subtitle in the appropriate placeholders; pick the current date; delete the company name placeholder; and key **Patrick V. Ray** as the author in the appropriate placeholder.

   b. Insert the *pommery logo* data file. Position the logo in Middle Center with Square Text Wrapping.

6. Number the preliminary pages with lowercase Roman numerals in the center of the footer; add a Motion (Odd Page) header. Key the report title in the header.

7. Generate the table of contents and apply Title style to the heading.

8. Preview, proofread, and check; click Next to continue. (*108-d4*)

To insert and add text to SmartArt:

Insert/Illustrations/SmartArt

1. Position the insertion point where you want to add the graphic, and follow the path to open the Choose a SmartArt Graphic dialog box.

2. Click the SmartArt layout you wish to insert.

3. Click in each shape and key the desired text. -or- Click Text Pane on the SmartArt Tools Design tab that displays with the diagram and key the text in the Text Pane.

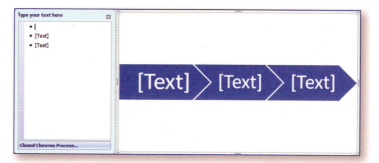

To add shapes to SmartArt:

SmartArt Tools Design/Create Graphic/Add Shape

1. Click the shape before or after which you want to add another shape, and follow the path to add a shape.

2. Repeat the process until you have as many shapes as you need in the layout.

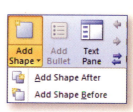

DRILL 7　　　　SMARTART

1. Insert the Basic Chevron Process SmartArt layout; click in the shape at the right side and then click Add Shape.

2. Key the text shown at the right in the Text Pane.

3. Position in the Top Center with Square Text Wrapping.

4. Proofread and check; click Next to continue. (57-drill7)

- Plan
- Prepare
- Practice
- Deliver

TEXT FROM FILE

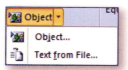

Text from File is an option on the Object command in the Text group that is used to insert entire document files. In earlier drills, you created graphics and inserted them in *Word* documents. These documents can be inserted in other documents using the Text from File command.

To insert a document file:

Insert/Text/Object/Text from File

1. Position the insertion point where you wish to insert a file; click the drop-list arrow on Object and select Text from File.

2. Select the file you wish to insert and click Insert.

5. Create the second column of page 1:

    a. Tap ENTER as many times in column 2 as you did in column 1 to reach 6.4".

    b. Key the Southwest Regional Office address and web address shown below, pressing SHIFT + ENTER after each line except the last one. Apply the same font formatting as for the address in column 1.

    c. Insert Gradient Fill – Dark Red, Accent 1 WordArt at the top of the column and key the title **Pommery Limo Service**; shrink the font to 24 points; tap ENTER and key the second line **Grand Opening**; center the text.

    d. Click in the paragraph at 2.8". Use the keywords *car with chauffeur* and search for clip art. Enter the clip shown in the illustration below or a similar one. If necessary, size it 2.5" high. Change text wrapping to In Front of Text.

6. Insert a Column break after the web address in column 2 to move to page 2. Apply Normal style and center alignment. Insert a Column break to go to the second column.

7. Tap ENTER twice and apply Dark Red, Accent 1 font color. Key the title **Program**; apply 24-point font; tap ENTER, change to 12-point font, and key **October 16, 201-**; press SHIFT + ENTER and key **Board Room**.

8. Tap ENTER, change to left alignment, and set the following tabs: 0.5" left tab and 3.75" right leader tab. Key the text on the next page as shown in the illustration below. Remove space between subitems.

9. Preview, proofread, and check; click Next to continue. (*108-d3*)

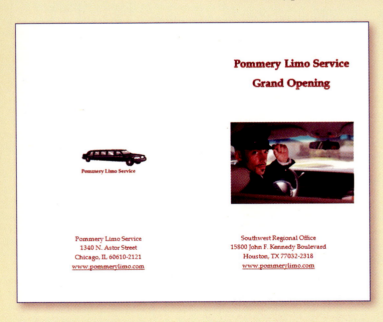

Pommery Limo Service Address and Web Address

Pommery Limo Service | 1340 N. Astor Street | Chicago, IL 60610-2121 | www.pommerylimo.com

Southwest Regional Office Address and Web Address

Southwest Regional Office | 15800 John F. Kennedy Boulevard | Houston, TX 77032-2318 | www.pommerylimo.com

PAGES GROUP

The Pages group contains commands to insert a cover page from built-in styles, a blank page, or a page break.

To insert a cover page:

<mark>Insert/Pages/Cover Page</mark>

1. Position the insertion point where you wish to insert a cover page and display the gallery of Built-In cover page styles; click the desired style to insert it.

2. Click in each placeholder and key the appropriate text or insert the date.

To insert a blank page or page break:

<mark>Insert/Pages/Blank Page</mark> or Page Break

- Position the insertion point where you wish to insert a blank page and click Blank Page.

- Position the insertion point where you wish to insert a page break and click Page Break.

★ TIP

Page break shortcut:

Press CTRL + ENTER.

DRILL 8　　　　**PAGES AND TEXT GROUPS** developments, cape, smartart

1. In a new document, insert the Pinstripes cover page. Key or insert the information below in the placeholders to complete the cover page. Note that a blank page is inserted after the cover page.

2. Insert the data file *developments* on the blank page; click in the second blank paragraph below the table if necessary and then click Blank Page to insert a blank page.

3. Use the keywords *Atlantic ocean* to search clip art and insert a clip showing ocean and shore. Size the clip art 4" high. Center the paragraph in which the clip is inserted. Apply Beveled Matte, White picture style.

4. Click in the paragraph in which the clip is inserted and tap ENTER; then click Page Break to move to the next page. Insert the data file *cape*. Size the picture 4" high. Apply Beveled Matte, White picture style. Compress the picture.

5. Click in the paragraph in which the picture is inserted and tap ENTER. Use the shortcut (CTRL + ENTER) to insert a blank page. Insert the data file *smartart* on the blank page.

6. Proofread and check; click Next to continue. (*57-drill8*)

Title: Sample Graphics

Subtitle: For Demonstration Purposes

Date: Insert today's date.

Company name: Key your school's name.

Author's name: Key your name.

Board of Directors

Ms. Natalie Bass | Transportation Consultant | RTA and Associates | 3829 Quincy Avenue | Denver, CO 80237-2756

Mr. Herman Davis | Chief Sustainability Officer | Davis and Jeansonne Associates | 1300 Lamar Street | Houston, TX 77010-3013

Ms. Betsy Burge | President and CEO | Associated Travel Services | 28 W. New York Street | Aurora, IL 60506-4121

Mr. Joseph Perkins | Senior Vice President | River Industries | 340 W. Belmont Avenue | Chicago, IL 60657-4892

Current date

«Appropriate fields for inside address»

«GreetingLine»

Thank you for a thorough review of the initial draft of our Business Plan. We reviewed the questions raised and suggestions that you made at the last meeting. We believe we have addressed all of the questions and incorporated the suggestions in the enclosed version of the Business Plan.

You will note that the financial sections have been expanded significantly as you requested. We also included a table showing the current stock ownership. The diversity of ownership provides a major strategic advantage for the company.

Please review this version very carefully. If you have questions, please call me prior to our meeting on Friday of next week. If the Board is comfortable with this version of the Business Plan, we will ask you to vote on the final approval at the meeting.

We look forward to seeing you next week.

108-d3

Program

  pommery logo

★ **TIP**

Remove the hyperlink from the web address in both columns.

1. Format a two-page program that will be printed front and back. Review the illustration on the next page prior to keying the document. Remember to use the Hardcover theme.

2. Set Moderate margins; apply Landscape orientation.

3. Format the document in two equal-size columns 3.75" wide with 1.5" spacing.

4. Create the first column of page 1:

   a. Tap ENTER 16 times and key the Pommery Limo Service Headquarters address and web address shown on the next page at 6.4"; apply 14-point, Dark Red, Accent 1 font color; press SHIFT + ENTER after each line except the web address line; center the text.

   b. Insert the *pommery logo* from the data files; use the default size (0.83" by 2.17"). Position it at the vertical and horizontal center of the column.

   c. Insert a Column break after the web address to move to the second column. Apply Normal style to the paragraph at the top of the column.

57-d1

Report with Table and Graphics

 career perspectives

1. Insert an Austere cover page in a new document. Use the information below to complete the cover page.

2. Key the title, subtitle, and first paragraph of the report shown below. Tap ENTER three times to position the title at 2". Apply Title style to the title and Subtitle style to the subtitle.

3. Insert the data file *career perspectives* after the first paragraph. Note the data file contains three errors. Proofread and correct these errors. Apply Heading 1 style to the three headings.

4. Insert the table shown below following the third paragraph below the subtitle. Apply the following formats:

   a. Add a column to the right of the first column shown below; key **Age** in the first cell and move the numbers from the first column to the new column.

   b. Add a row above row 1; merge the cells and increase the height to 0.4". Key the title **Chief Executive Officers Under Forty**, and apply 14-point Cambria font.

   c. Select the other rows and increase the height to 0.3".

   d. Apply Colorful List – Accent 1 table style to the table.

   e. Apply Align Center to the table title and to column B; apply Align Center Left to columns A and C.

5. Apply bullets to the four skills and experience requirements.

Cover Page Information:

Date: Today | Company: Meetze University | Author: Lynn C. King

Title: Career Perspectives | Abstract: This document provides information to assist organizations in evaluating students as potential employees. It also provides students with useful information in preparing for their careers.

Title: Career Perspectives

Subtitle: A Dual Perspective

Organizations and students tend to view careers from very different perspectives. Organizations tend to focus on finding employees who match their qualification requirements and culture very closely and who are mature and can begin contributing immediately. Most of the positions available for new employees are entry or mid-level positions. Successful, relevant experience often provides the basis for evaluating potential employees.

REVIEW

Insert Space Before Paragraph

Home/Paragraph/Line and Paragraph Spacing/Add Space Before Paragraph

To add space after the table, turn Show/Hide on, click the paragraph, and add space before the paragraph.

Table:

Chief Executive Officer		Type of Company
Cameron R. McMillan	38	Financial services
Zachary L. Hartman	34	Electronic publishing
Olivia J. Rosenbloom	37	Real estate development
Jonathan C. McKenzie	32	Technology
Jeremiah B. Newton	35	Medical devices

   c. Insert a row between *Senior Officers* and *Business Community* and key the following data: **Outside Directors 117,525** shares **15.67** percent.

   d. Bold and center the column headings for columns B and C; center the data in column B; set a decimal tab at 5.5" to position the data in column C.

   e. Use the appropriate formula to sum the columns; use the same number format as used for the data in the columns.

4. Proofread and check; click Next to continue. (*108-d1*)

Thank you, Roberto, for an excellent review of the Pommery Limo Service Business Plan. We will revise the plan and incorporate the suggestions you made. We especially appreciate the financial analysis that you provided for the industry and the comparison of Pommery to the industry data.

We will also include the following table that you suggested we prepare:

Pommery Limo Service Stock Ownership		
Group	Shares	Percent of Stock Issue
Employees	109,875	14.65
Senior Officers	125,625	16.75
Business Community	181,875	24.25
Founder	215,100	28.68
Total		

We expect to complete the revision of the plan today and send it to the Board of Directors. I think they will be pleased when they see this version. We have addressed all of the issues raised at the last meeting.

Again, thank you for an excellent job in a very short timeframe.

108-d2

Mail Merge Letters

  108-d2 main

⭐ **TIP**

Save the closing lines from *Sincerely* through your initials as a Quick Part for future use. Use **Ray Closing Lines** for the name and description.

1. Use mail merge to create a block-style letter with open punctuation. The body of the letter and the names and addresses of the Board members are shown on the next page. Set up the data source with title, first name, and last name as separate fields. Use the field *position* for the job title. Save as *108-d2 data source*.

2. Use the greeting line with Dear Title Last name format. Use the closing lines: **Patrick V. Ray | President and Chief Executive Officer**.

3. Add the **Business Plan** enclosure notation and a copy notation for **Executive Officers**.

4. Preview and proofread the document and then merge the data source and the main document.

5. Check; click Next to continue. (*108-d2*)

DISCOVER

Change the SmartArt Color Scheme

SmartArt Tools Design/ SmartArt Styles/Change Colors

★ 6. Insert a Segmented Pyramid SmartArt before the heading *Packaging Skills Effectively* and insert the text shown below. On the SmartArt Tools Design tab, change colors to Colorful – Accent Colors style. Apply White Outline SmartArt style; size the SmartArt 4" high and 6.5" wide.

7. Insert clip art depicting a business meal after the last paragraph of the report. Use the keywords *business lunch* and search for an appropriate clip. Apply the following formats:

   a. Size the clip art 4" high and 6" wide.

   b. Apply Metal Rounded Rectangle picture style and center the clip art.

8. Note that the pages of this report have not been numbered. You will review numbering pages in a document with sections in Module 12.

9. Preview, proofread, check, and close. (*57-d1*)

Segmented Pyramid Text:

- Technical Skills
- Soft Skills
- Experience
- Conceptual Skills

QUICK ✔

Check your document against the illustration below.

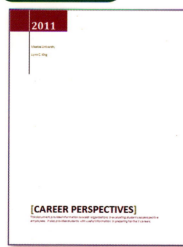

Review and Assessment

Lesson 108   *Document Review*
Lesson 109   *Assessment*
Lesson 110   *Assessment*

LEARNING OUTCOMES

- Review and format basic documents.
- Demonstrate ability to format a variety of documents.
- Demonstrate keyboarding skills.

Lesson 108 | Document Review

WARMUP

KEYBOARDING PRO DELUXE 2   *Lessons/108a Warmup*

A ALL LETTERS

Skill Building

108b Timed Writing

1. Key one 1' timed writing on each paragraph; work for speed.
2. Key one 3' timed writing; work at your control rate.

	gwam	3'	5'
Reports are one of the best means by which busy executives	4	2	26
at any level of a business can keep well informed. The pertinent	8	5	29
data in reports can be used to solve a wide variety of problems	13	8	31
that arise, make any changes that may be required, analyze	16	10	34
results, and make precise, timely decisions.	19	12	36
The quality of the plans and decisions made on the basis of	23	14	39
the information found in reports depends in large measure on how	28	17	41
well the reports are produced. A good report is a thorough and	32	19	43
objective summary of all pertinent facts and figures. If reports	36	22	46
are not well produced, the firm will surely suffer.	40	24	48

3' |———1———|———2———|———3———|———4———|
5' |————1————|————2————|————3————|

Applications

108-d1

Memo

pommery memo

1. Use Hardcover theme for all documents in this module.
2. Complete the memo heading in the open template using the following information:
   Roberto Hernandez | Anna Westin | Current date | Business Plan Review
3. Key the memo shown on the next page. Format the 3-column, 7-row table as follows:
   a. Apply Medium Shading 1 – Accent 1 table style.
   b. Merge the cells in row 1; increase the height to 0.4"; center the title vertically and horizontally; apply 14-point Heading font and White font color.

Lesson 58 | Page Layout Tab Commands

Review Commands

- Themes Group
- Page Setup Group
- Page Background Group
- Paragraph Group
- Indent and Tabs on Ruler

A   ALL LETTERS

Skill Building

58b Timed Writing

1. Key a 3' timed writing, working for speed.
2. Key a 3' timed writing, working for control.

	gwam	3'	5'

You may be familiar with the expression that we live in an
information age now. People interpret this expression in a host of
diverse ways, but most people agree on two key things. The first
thing is that a huge amount of information exists today; some even
think we suffer from information overload. The second thing is that
technology has changed the way we access that huge pool of data.

Some people are quick to point out that a big difference exists
between the quantity and the quality of information. It is very
critical to recognize that anyone who has access can simply post
information on the Internet. No test exists to screen for junk
before something is posted. Some of the data may be helpful and
valid. However, much of it must be analyzed quite carefully to
judge if it is valid.

Just how do you judge if the data you have accessed is valid?
Some of the same techniques that can be used with print media can be
applied with electronic media. A good way to assess material is to
examine its source carefully. What do you know about the people who
provided this information? Is the provider ethical and qualified
to post that information? If you cannot unearth the answer to this
question, you should be wary of trusting it.

gwam	3'	5'
	4	2
	8	5
	13	8
	17	10
	22	13
	26	16
	30	18
	35	21
	39	23
	43	26
	48	29
	52	31
	53	32
	58	35
	62	37
	67	40
	71	42
	75	45
	80	48
	83	50

3' | 1 | 2 | 3 | 4
5' | 1 | 2 | 3

Review Commands

58c

KEYBOARDING PRO DELUXE 2

References/Word 2010
Commands/Lessons 26–30 and 44

PAGE LAYOUT TAB

The Page Layout tab contains five groups: Themes, Page Setup, Page Background, Paragraph, and Arrange. Many of the commands in these groups will be reviewed or taught in later modules. This lesson provides a review of some of the key commands.

Guides for Selecting References

Deciding who to select as references is a very important strategic decision. Give careful thought to the individuals you select as references.

Criteria for Selection

The key is to select individuals who know you well, will provide a strong, positive recommendation, and who can support your ability to do the job for which you are applying. Employers and former employers can attest to your job performance as well as colleagues and team members. Instructors can also provide valuable insight into academic ability and share workplace attributes, such as attendance, punctuality, and ability to work with others. Friends, relatives, neighbors, or others who the prospective employer might view as biased in your favor should not be selected as references unless they are employees of the company considering you for a position.

The references selected for one position may not be as strong for a different position. Banking professors may be a better choice for a position in a bank, whereas marketing professors may be a better choice for a similar position in a public relations firm. Use references who can legitimately give you a good recommendation and who also would have credibility with the company.

Permission to Use References

Not only is it good manners to request permission to list a person as a reference; it is strategically important to do so. If a person hesitates, do not select that person as a reference. Hesitation is a sign that the person may not give you as strong a recommendation as you would like to have. Requesting permission gives you an opportunity to refresh the person's memory about you and to update him or her on recent accomplishments. You should also confirm position titles and contact information to ensure that you provide the employer with accurate information. Thank your references and update them after the job search process has been completed.

Sharing the List of References with Employers

Several different practices exist for sharing the reference list.

- If your resume is less than a page long, you may want to add several references to fill the page.
- Refer the employer to career services at your college or university or other agency that maintains and distributes records for applicants.
- Include a statement on the resume indicating that a separate list of references will be provided on request. Take the list to all interviews.

Be extremely careful about posting reference information to your website. Many references object to having their information posted on the Internet and will not serve as a reference if you post it. Posting information to an applicant tracking system on a secure company website usually is acceptable.

BOOKMARK

www.collegekeyboarding.com
Module 17 Practice Quiz

THEMES GROUP

A theme consists of a set of colors, heading and body fonts, and effects that are applied to all parts of a document. A theme can be applied from a gallery of built-in themes or from a custom theme that the user develops.

To apply a document theme:

Page Layout/Themes/Themes

1. Follow the path and click the drop-list arrow to display the gallery of Built-In themes.
2. Click the document theme you wish to use.

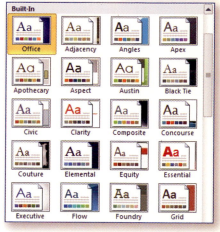

DRILL 1   **THEMES**

1. Open *57-d1* and display the gallery of Built-In themes. Hold the mouse over six of the themes to preview them. Note the color and font differences.

2. Click Clarity to apply the theme.

3. Click the drop-list arrows for Colors, Fonts, and Effects and note the options for the Clarity theme.

4. Preview the document; note the changes in the cover page, title, headings, table, and SmartArt.

5. Proofread and check; click Next to continue. (*58-drill1*)

PAGE SETUP GROUP

The Page Setup group commands are used to change the way text is displayed on the page.

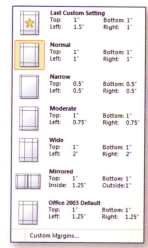
MARGINS

Margins are the distance between the edge of the paper and the text of a document. The default margins for *Word 2010* are 1" at the top, bottom, right, and left. On the gallery of preset margins options, the default margins are called Normal. The space between the left and right margins is called the line of writing. ✳ Custom margins can also be set.

To change margin settings:

Page Layout/Page Setup/Margins

1. Follow the path to display the gallery of margins options.
2. Click the desired margins option.

107-d1

Follow-up Letter

huang letterhead

1. In the open document, key the following letter that Po-Ling Huang used to follow up on the first resume she sent out. Use block style. Follow-up letters can be very effective in bringing attention to your resume.

2. Proofread, preview, and click Next to continue to the next document. (*107-d1*)

Mr. Coleman Stanberry | Managing Editor | Forde Financial News | 840 Montclair Road | Birmingham, AL 35213-1943

Recently I applied for a position as a junior graphic designer at *Forde Financial News*. Since writing to you, I have additional qualifications that I wish to report to you.

My enclosed resume has been updated to include my recent first-place award in the College Graphic Design Category of the National Collegiate Graphic Design Association. This award, the most prestigious award presented by NCGDA, was established to recognize the excellent work of the most aspiring graphic design student. I am most honored to have received this distinction by academia.

Mr. Stanberry, I would like the opportunity to discuss with you the valuable contributions I can make to your newspaper. Please write or call me at the address or phone number listed in the letterhead.

107-d2

Interview Checklist

1. Key the Interview Checklist shown below. Use customized bullets for the checklist. Tap ENTER three times and key the title: **Prepare for Success.** Apply Title style.

2. Key the subtitle: **Develop an Interview Checklist**. Apply Subtitle style.

3. Proofread, preview, and click Next to continue to the next document. (*107-d2*)

Preparation is an important key to success in job interviewing. Use this simple checklist as you prepare for a job interview. Seek the advice of experts and continue to add items to this checklist.

- ☑ Am I comfortable with my knowledge about the company?
- ☑ Am I prepared to dress professionally for the interview?
- ☑ How long will it take me to get to the interview at least 15 minutes early?
- ☑ What materials should I take to the interview?
- ☑ Am I prepared for questions that might be asked of me, and what are the best answers to these questions?
- ☑ Do I know the interviewer's name, and can I pronounce it correctly?
- ☑ How do I handle the handshake?
- ☑ When should I be seated?
- ☑ How important is eye contact?
- ☑ What does my body language tell the interviewer?
- ☑ What questions can I ask the interviewer?
- ☑ Am I comfortable with the answers to the previous questions?
- ☑ If not, I need to do more preparation for the interview.

107-d3

Report

1. Key the report on the next page. Use Title style, default theme, Heading 1 style for headings, and Plain Number 3 page numbers.

2. Check and close. (*107-d3*)

PAGE ORIENTATION

The size of standard paper is 8.5" × 11". Orientation provides another way of positioning information on a page. The default option, Portrait, positions text so that the top edge of the paper is 8.5" wide. Landscape positions text so that the top edge of the paper is 11" wide.

To change page orientation:

Page Layout/Page Setup/Orientation

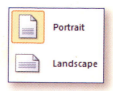

1. Follow the path and click the drop-list arrow on the Orientation command.

2. Select desired orientation (either Portrait or Landscape).

DRILL 2   MARGINS AND PAGE ORIENTATION   building blocks

1. In the open document, apply Narrow margins to the document.

2. Change the page orientation to Landscape.

3. Change the document theme to Verve.

4. Proofread and check; click Next to continue. (*58-drill2*)

PAGE BACKGROUND GROUP

The Page Borders command is used to place a border around a whole document, a section, or the first page.

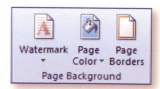

To apply a page border:

Page Layout/Page Background/Page Borders

★ **TIP**

The color palette displayed to select page border colors is determined by the theme applied.

1. Follow the path to display the Borders and Shading dialog box.

2. Select the Setting, Style, Color, Width, and the portion of the document to which the border is to be applied.

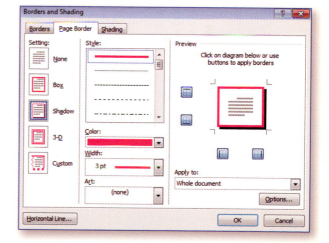

DRILL 3   PAGE BORDER

1. Open *58-drill2*, change the page orientation to Portrait, and the margins to Moderate.

2. Apply a Pink, Accent 1, 3-point Shadow, solid-line border to the whole document.

3. Proofread and check; click Next to continue. (*58-drill3*)

Lesson 107 | Assessment

A ALL LETTERS

Skill Building

107b Timed Writing
Key two 3' timed writings.
Work at your control rate.

	gwam	3'	5'

How are letters and other documents produced in the modern office? They are prepared in a number of ways. Just a few years ago, with rare exceptions, a document was composed by a manager who either wrote it in longhand or dictated it. Then, one of the office staff typed it in final form. Today, the situation is quite different. Office staff may compose and produce various documents, or they may finalize documents that were keyed by managers. In some cases, managers like to produce some or all of their documents in final form.

	3'	5'
	4	2	52
	8	5	54
	13	8	57
	17	10	60
	21	13	62
	25	15	65
	29	18	67
	34	20	70
	36	22	71

Many people question how this dramatic change in the way documents are prepared came about. Two factors can be cited as the major reasons for the change. The primary factor is the extensive use of computers in offices today. A manager who uses a computer for a variety of tasks may find it just as simple to key documents at the computer as it would be to prepare them for office personnel to produce. The other factor is the increase in the ratio of office personnel to managers. Today, one secretary is very likely to support as many as six or eight managers. Managers who share office staff find that they get much quicker results by finalizing their own documents when they compose them.

	3'	5'
	40	24	73
	44	26	76
	48	29	78
	52	31	81
	57	34	83
	61	37	86
	65	39	89
	70	42	91
	74	44	94
	78	47	96
	82	49	99

3' | 1 | 2 | 3 | 4 |
5' | 1 | 2 | 3 |

Applications

107c

Assessment

 Continue

 Check

When you complete a document, proofread it, check the spelling, and preview for placement. When you are completely satisfied, click the Continue button to move to the next document. Click the Check button when you are ready to error-check the test. Review and/or print the document analysis results.

PARAGRAPH GROUP

The Indent command in the Paragraph group specifies the amount of space the lines of a paragraph are indented on the left and right sides.

To indent text:

Page Layout/Paragraph/Indent

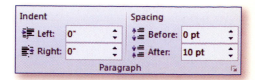

- Use the spin arrows to increase or decrease the indent on the left or right.

DRILL 4   INDENT

1. Key the text shown below.

2. Indent the quote below 0.5" on both the left and right sides.

3. Proofread and check; click Next to continue. (*58-drill4*)

> President and Chief Executive Officer Daniel J. Suggs welcomed the members of the Compensation Committee and said to them:
>
> > The Compensation Committee has a critical role in ensuring the future of the company. The key issue is to develop a compensation plan that is fair to shareholders and that can be used to attract and retain the top-level talent needed to lead the company over the next five years.

INDENT AND TABS ON RULER

Display the Ruler if it is not already displayed. To display the Ruler, click the View Ruler button above the scroll bar on the right side of the screen.

The Left Indent marker **1** and the Right Indent marker **2** are located on the ends of the Ruler. The tab selector on the left side indicates the type of tab.

Indent Markers

Note the three markers at the left end of the Ruler **1**. The downward-pointing triangle is the First Line Indent marker. The upward-pointing triangle is the Hanging Indent marker. The square marker below the triangles is the Left Indent marker. At the right end of the ruler, the Right Indent marker is an upward-pointing triangle.

To set indents using the ruler:

- To set a left indent, click the square Left Indent marker and drag it to the desired position.

- To set a right indent, click the Right Indent marker and drag it to the desired position.

these individuals know you are in the job market and telling them that you value their advice may be all you need for someone to suggest that you contact a particular company.

Searching the hidden job market takes time and effort, but it produces excellent results. Those who take the easy route and search only the generally advertised sources often miss out on the best opportunities.

Heading 1 style →

Interviews

Networking also helps to gain interviews. For example, if an individual who is on the Board of Directors of a company suggests that you contact the company for possible employment, mentioning that in the application letter is likely to ensure that you will be interviewed. Application documents and networking are both designed to find potential sources of jobs and to gain an interview—not to get a job. It would be extremely rare to be hired without having been interviewed by that company.

Heading 2 style →

Interview Preparation

Companies spend a significant amount of time preparing for interviews. They ensure that applicants invited to interview have the requisite skills and education; they ensure that the right people are available to participate in the interview; and they design opportunities to obtain additional information about the candidate. For example, a meal is frequently included in the interview visit. The main objective might be to observe the candidate in a social setting to determine if he or she would be able to interact effectively with customers and clients in a social setting.

They expect applicants to do even more preparation. Applicants need to learn as much as possible about the company, its philosophy, products, customers and clients, and many other types of information. The website and the annual report are excellent sources of that information. Networking contacts may even be better sources. Applicants also need to learn how to make a good impression—particularly a good first impression. Often decisions are made in the first five minutes of an interview. The remainder of the time is spent trying to confirm if the initial impression was correct.

Numerous factors are critical—appearance, eye contact, handshake, punctual arrival, and way in which you treat staff at all levels who meet and greet you.

Heading 2 style →

Interview Follow-Up

Following up with a thank-you letter and additional information gives you an advantage over people who do not follow up. Keeping in contact and providing more information confirms your serious interest in the position and demonstrates that you put major effort into the things you do.

Tabs

3 The tab selector located on the left side of the Ruler indicates the type of tabs that are set on the ruler. Depending on the size of your screen, the tab selector may not be adjoining the Ruler.

4 Bar tab   Inserts a vertical bar at the tab position.

5 Left tab   Aligns text at the left.

6 Center tab   Centers text at this position as it is keyed.

7 Decimal tab   Aligns numbers at the decimal point.

8 Right tab   Aligns text at the right.

To set a tab: Click the tab selector, select desired type, and click the Ruler where you want to set the tab.

To clear a tab: Click the tab marker on the Ruler and drag it down off the Ruler.

To move a tab: Click the tab marker on the Ruler and drag it to the new location.

DRILL 5   INDENT AND TABS ON RULER

1. Set the following tabs: 0.5" bar tab, 1" left tab, 3.25" center tab, 5" decimal tab, and 6.25" right tab.

2. Key the four lines of tabulated data in the drill below, tap ENTER, and then clear the bar tab from the Ruler.

3. Key the introductory sentence; then tap ENTER, drag the indent markers in 0.5" on the left and the right, and key the quote.

4. Select the four lines of tabulated data; drag the center tab to 3" and the decimal tab to 4.5".

5. Proofread and check; click Next to continue. (*58-drill5*)

1	Jan Maxwell	Business	3.98	Freshman
2	Lynn Jackson	Psychology	3.45	Sophomore
3	Jordan Lindsey	Music	3.82	Junior
4	Leslie Coker	Engineering	3.76	Senior

Mr. Monahan introduced the four students who were being honored at the Founders Day celebration and said:

These four students are not only outstanding scholars; they are outstanding leaders and citizens in every respect. The students are leaders in key student and professional organizations on campus. They also devote many hours each week providing service to the needy in our community.

responses from employers. Even if you submit 100 applications and you receive 99 rejection letters, you are 100 percent successful if one of the applications produces a job that truly meets your career objective.

Heading 2 style ⟶ ## Targeted Search

A targeted search focuses on a few carefully selected and well-researched job opportunities. A job market analysis is conducted to determine which companies may be the prospects for your job search, and your efforts are focused on these opportunities.

Heading 1 style ⟶ # Job Market Analysis and Search

Many decisions are involved in a job market analysis. Some of these decisions include:

- Geographical area you wish to consider
- Preference of a small or large company
- Specific industry or if the career option is available in multiple industries

Each of these decisions is important because different markets have to be tapped depending on the decision.

Heading 1 style ⟶ # Sources of Jobs

Once the decisions on the geographic area, company size, and industry are made, then sources of jobs must be analyzed. Sources can be put in two categories: the advertised market and the hidden job market.

Heading 2 style ⟶ ## Advertised Job Market

Many jobs are advertised in the public market—newspaper ads, school placement offices, employment agencies, and governmental agency listings. Many jobs are also listed on the Internet. Employment specialists estimate that about a third of all jobs are listed in these public sources.

Heading 2 style ⟶ ## Hidden Job Market

Many jobs—particularly those at the higher levels and with higher compensation—are not advertised in the open market. Two of the best ways to tap the hidden job market are to talk to knowledgeable individuals and to read specialized publications. Well-informed people in a field are more likely to know about jobs in that field. Often jobs that are not advertised in the general market are listed in publications read by people in a certain field, such as banking, insurance, or public relations.

Networking is a good way to tap the hidden job market. You can start by listing people you know who may be able to provide you with information about jobs in the field, location, and industry of interest. Friends, relatives, and business associates (bankers, lawyers, doctors, association members, etc.) are all sources of job information. A friendly letter or telephone call letting

(continued)

1. In a new document, apply Moderate margins and Equity theme. Tap ENTER three times and key the title **Tailgating**, and then key the subtitle **An Entrepreneurial Perspective**. Apply Title style to the title and Subtitle style to the subtitle. Then key the document shown below; make the corrections in the two paragraphs with the proofreaders' marks.

2. Insert the data file *tailgating* after the last paragraph.

3. Indent the five-sentence quote in the first paragraph 0.5" from both the right and left sides.

4. Apply Heading 1 style to the first three headings and Heading 2 style to the last three headings.

5. Use square bullets and Sentence case (capitalize the first word) for the two sets of bulleted items.

6. Preview, proofread, check, and close. (58-d1)

Most people view tailgating as a social event that occurs in parking lots prior to and after sporting events. Thomas Blackmon, a well-known sports historian, said: Tailgating began at college football games when people had to arrive early in order to get a parking space. They brought food and beverages to consume while waiting for the football game to begin. The popularity of tailgating skyrocketed and expanded to numerous other sporting events at the college, professional, and high school levels. In addition, the amount of time spent tailgating extended significantly. Tailgating also became popular at concerts and other outdoor events.

Early Entrepreneurial Ventures

College students were some of the early entrepreneurs who saw an opportunity to make ~~a significant amount of~~ money assisting fans with the preparation and set up of extensive tailgates. They realized that fans ~~who flew in for~~ *out-of-town* ~~games~~ wanted these experiences, but it was difficult for them to make ~~the~~ *all of* arrangements. These entrepreneurial students arranged for rental items and *for a tailgate* provided services including [tents, tables, chairs, food, beverages, setup services ~~and~~ cleanup services.] *place on separate lines; delete commas; apply bullets.* In the process, they made a substantial profit. Affluent local fans soon found these services to be attractive, and the businesses grew.

Supply and Services Ventures

As tailgating became more sophisticated, the demand for supplies increased significantly and numerous businesses cropped up. Typical supplies available include [flags, pennants, tents, chairs with logos, paper products, food service *Apply bullets* items, tubs, coolers, umbrellas, portable grills, ~~and~~ novelty items.] The best selling items are those with officially licensed logos of the team. *The second best selling items are those in team colors.*

Lesson 106 | *Employment Strategies*

106b

USING EFFECTIVE EMPLOYMENT STRATEGIES

The first three lessons of this module focused on preparing effective employment documents. You also had an opportunity to learn about the impact of technology on employment, particularly applicant tracking systems as well as electronic and scannable resumes. While employment documents and systems are very important, they represent only a portion of the total employment process. This process consists of seven steps:

1. Self-analysis
2. Job analysis
3. Job market analysis
4. Job search
5. Preparation and submission of application materials
6. Interviews
7. Follow-up activities

The report that follows focuses on job market analysis, job search, and the interview process.

Applications

106-d1

Report

1. Apply Aspect document theme and key the report shown below.
2. Apply Rounded Rectangle 3 page numbers formatted with Light 1 Outline, Colored Fill – Orange, Accent 1 Shape Style; do not show page numbers on first page.
3. Preview, check, and close. *(106-d1)*

Title style ⟶ Effective Employment Strategies

Successful employment strategies focus on both the prospective employer and the prospective employee. The ultimate goal for both parties is to match the right person with the right position—a win-win situation for both the company and the new employee.

Heading 1 style ⟶ Job Search Perspectives

Job seekers typically approach the employment process from one of two philosophically different perspectives.

Heading 2 style ⟶ Comprehensive Search

The comprehensive approach involves mass producing employment documents and transmitting them to as many companies as you can locate. The hope is that a few of these mass solicitations may generate positive

(continued)

Memos and Letters

LEARNING OUTCOMES

- Format memorandum.
- Format block and modified block business letters with special features.
- Format two-page memos and letters.
- Create envelopes with special notations.
- Improve keying speed and accuracy.

Lesson 59 | Memos

New Commands
- Save as template
- Header

KEYBOARDING PRO DELUXE 2

WARMUP

Lessons/59a Warmup

A ALL LETTERS

Skill Building

59b Timed Writing

1. Key a 1' timed writing on each paragraph. Work to increase speed.
2. Key a 3' timed writing on both paragraphs.

	gwam	3'	5'

If you wish to advance in your career, you must learn how to   4 | 2 | 37
make good decisions. You can develop decision-making skills by   8 | 5 | 39
learning to follow six basic steps. The first three steps help   13 | 8 | 42
you to see the problem. They are identifying the problem, ana-   17 | 10 | 44
lyzing the problem to find causes and consequences, and making   21 | 13 | 47
sure you define the goals that your solution must meet.   25 | 15 | 49

Now you are ready to solve the problem using the last three   29 | 17 | 52
steps. They include finding alternative solutions to the prob-   33 | 20 | 54
lem, analyzing each of the alternatives carefully to locate the   37 | 22 | 57
best solution, and putting the best solution into action. Once   41 | 25 | 59
you have implemented a plan of action, check to make sure that   46 | 27 | 62
it meets all of your objectives. If it does not, then determine   50 | 30 | 64
if the problem is with the solution or with the way it is being   54 | 33 | 67
implemented. Always keep all options open.   57 | 34 | 69

```
3' |----1----|----2----|----3----|----4----|
5' |-----1-----|-----2-----|-----3-----|
```

105-d4

Job Refusal Letter

1. In a new document, insert the letterhead Quick Part you created for Po-Ling Huang in *105-d1*.

2. Key the letter shown below to Mr. Miguel Mendoza as a block letter.

3. Proofread and check; click Next to continue. (*105-d4*)

Mr. Miguel Mendoza
Director, Human Resources
Blackmon Development Corporation
548 Poplar Street
Macon, GA 31201-2752

Dear Mr. Mendoza

Yesterday, I received your offer for a position as a management trainee in the Human Resources Department of Blackmon Development Corporation. Your offer is very interesting and very competitive. I also received an offer yesterday for a position as a junior graphics designer for a financial newspaper.

Although the position you offered is a very desirable one and I have considered it very carefully, it does not give me the opportunity to apply my graphic design and information technology skills immediately. Therefore, I have decided to accept the other position because it is more directly related to my long-term career goals.

I do appreciate Blackmon Development Corporation offering me a position and the many courtesies that were extended to me during my interview and visit to Macon. Blackmon Development Corporation is an excellent company, and I wish you much success in finding the right person for the position you have available.

Sincerely

Po-Ling Huang

105-d5

Compose Job Acceptance Letter

1. Use your personal letterhead and write an acceptance letter for the position you applied for at VanHuss Enterprises (*105-d2*).

2. Confirm a starting salary that you think appropriate for the position and a starting date of one month from today.

3. Proofread and check; click Next to continue. (*105-d5*)

105-d6

Compose Job Acceptance Letter

1. Compose a thank-you letter to your instructor for providing you with a reference for the position at VanHuss Enterprises.

2. Tell your instructor that you received the job offer and that you have accepted it.

3. Express your appreciation for the job offer and indicate how helpful you thought the reference was.

4. Edit and proofread the letter carefully.

5. Check and close. (*105-d6*)

SAVE AS TEMPLATE

A template is a set of predefined styles for a particular type of document. The purpose of a template is to reuse it when needed. Templates are available for formatting numerous types of documents, and others can be downloaded on the Microsoft website. However, when existing documents are unique, it is useful to save them as a template.

By default, templates are saved to the Templates folder within the program. In a classroom environment, you will want to save templates you create to a USB memory device (flash drive) or another location.

To save a document as a template:

File/Save As

1. Click the File tab and then Save As. The Save As dialog box displays.

2. *Save to a USB memory device (flash drive):* Select My Computer and browse to the flash drive.

   -or-

   Save to a hard drive: By default the software will save to the Templates folder.

3. In the File name box, key an appropriate template name such as **memo**.

4. In the Save as type box, click the down arrow and select Word Template. Click Save. The extension *.dotx* is assigned automatically.

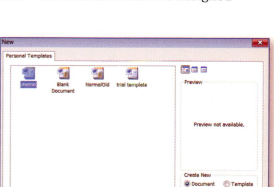

To use the template:

File/New

Saved to a flash drive: Click the File tab and select New. From the Available Templates pane, browse to locate the desired template. Click OK.

-or-

Saved to a hard drive: Click the File tab and select New. From the Available Templates pane, choose My templates; browse to locate the desired template. Click OK.

DRILL 1   SAVE AS TEMPLATE

1. Position the insertion point at 2". Key the memo heading **TO:**, **FROM:**, **DATE:**, and **SUBJECT:**. Turn off bold after each heading, and tab to the 1" tab mark.

2. In the DATE line of the heading, insert the Date command and check to update automatically.

3. Tap ENTER after you key all headings and then save as a template. Your instructor will tell you where to save it. *Keyboarding Pro DELUXE 2:* Your document will be saved as a *Word* file and not as a template.

4. Proofread and check; click Next to continue. (*59-drill1 memo template*)

105-d1

Application Letter

1. In a new document, create a letterhead for Po-Ling Huang using the following directions:

   a. Key the name at the top position in the header (.5").

   b. Apply Title style and tap ENTER.

   c. Key the address; add a square symbol between elements of the address as shown on the previous page. Space twice before and after the symbol. Apply Dark Blue, Text 2 font color to the symbols. Tap ENTER and click outside of the header.

   d. With the Insertion point at the first line below the header, click Line Spacing and Add Space Before Paragraph. Insert the current date.

2. Save the letterhead as a Quick Part with the name and description, **Huang Letterhead**.

3. Review the letter carefully before keying it; pay particular attention to the callouts that explain the strategy for writing the letter.

4. Key the letter shown using block style.

5. Proofread and check; click Next to continue. (*105-d1*)

105-d2

Compose Application Letter

1. In a new document, create a letterhead using your name and address information.

2. Compose an application letter for the position you are seeking. Your instructor told you that VanHuss Enterprises has that position available.

3. Your instructor provided you with the following address:

   Mr. Ray VanHuss

   Director of Human Resources

   VanHuss Enterprises

   3200 Trenholm Road

   Columbia, SC 29204-3335

4. Format the letter using block style.

5. Enclose your resume.

6. Edit the letter carefully; check to see that you followed the strategy illustrated in the letter you keyed in *105-d1*.

7. Proofread and check; click Next to continue. (*105-d2*)

105-d3

Thank-You Letter After Interview

1. In a new document, insert the Quick Part letterhead you created for Po-Ling Huang in *105-d1*. Remember to add space before the paragraph when you insert the current date. The date should be positioned at 2".

2. Key the letter shown below to Mr. Coleman Stanberry as a block letter.

3. Proofread and check; click Next to continue. (*105-d3*)

Thank you for taking time to talk with me about the position as a junior graphic designer at *Forde Financial News*.

I appreciated the comprehensive tour and the information you provided about the Graphic Design Department. This group of professionals is very fortunate to be equipped with the most up-to-date hardware and software and an outstanding staff development program. Consequently, your subscribers are the real winners.

Mr. Stanberry, I would like the opportunity to work at *Forde Financial News* and to contribute to the popularity and success of this outstanding newspaper. I am eager to receive a call from you.

Sincerely | Po-Ling Huang

1. Open *59-drill1 memo template*, the memo template created in Drill 1.

2. Key the memo to **Corey Zinn** from **Mallorie McBride**. The subject is **Travel Reimbursement Forms**.

3. Non-*Keyboarding Pro DELUXE 2* users: Click the File tab and Save As. In the Save as type box, select *Word* Document. In the File name box, key **59-drill2**. You do not want to save over the template.

4. Proofread and check; click Next to continue. (*59-drill2*).

The itinerary for my business trip to Chicago next week is attached. I am driving to Chicago and need detailed maps to each of the locations listed on the itinerary.

I will return to the office Monday morning and would like to review the information at that time. Thank you very much.

HEADER

A header contains text or copy that is keyed in the top margin of the page. Generally, the header is suppressed on the first page. In this module you will prepare a header for a two-page memo and letter.

To insert a header for a memo:

Insert/Header & Footer/Header

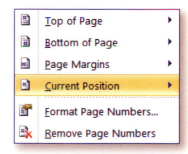

1. Follow the path to display the Built-In gallery of Header styles. Click the Blank style.

2. Key the name of the recipient and tap ENTER.

3. Key **Page** followed by a space.

4. From the Header & Footer group, click the Page Number drop-list arrow and choose Current Position. Choose the Plain Number style. Tap ENTER.

5. In the Insert group, click Date & Time. Select the month, day, and year format (October 10, 201-). Tap ENTER to leave a blank space between the header and the first line of the text.

6. In the Options group, select Different First Page  to suppress the header on the first page of the memo.

Scott Collins
Page 2
Current date — Tap ENTER once after date to leave blank line.

The enclosed packet of material provides you with detailed information about the testing software and costs for a site license. Our sales representative, Susan Wyman, will call you next week to answer questions you might have about the software.

Po-Ling Huang

1001 Hogan Street, Apartment 2A ▪ Mobile, AL 36617-1001 ▪ 334-555-0103 ▪ plhuang@cotheru.edu

Current date

Mr. Coleman Stanberry
Managing Editor
Forde Financial News
840 Montclair Road
Birmingham, AL 35213-1943

Dear Mr. Stanberry

Establish a point of contact and state the job you are applying for → My bachelor's degree with double majors in graphic design and information technology and my graphic design work qualify me for the position of a junior graphic designer for *Forde Financial News* that you advertised.

Convey key qualifications → As a result of my comprehensive four-year program, I am skilled in the latest Office suite as well as the current versions of desktop publishing and graphics programs. In addition, my excellent research and writing skills played a very important role in the Cother University Design Award I received last month. Being able to locate the right resources and synthesize those data into useful information for your readers is a priority I understand well and have practiced in my positions at the Cother University Alumni Office and the Cother University Library.

State how the employer will benefit from your qualifications → My technical and communication skills were applied as well as I worked as the assistant director and producer of the *Cother University Alumni News*. I understand well the importance of meeting deadlines and also producing a quality product within budget that will increase newspaper sales.

Request an interview → After you have reviewed the enclosed resume as well as my graphic design samples located on my Web page at www.cotheru.edu/plhuang, I look forward to discussing my qualifications and career opportunities with you at *Forde Financial News*.

Sincerely

Po-Ling Huang

Enclosure

EDIT HEADER

Insert/Header & Footer/Header

To edit a header, follow the path and click Edit Header. An alternate method is to double-click in the header section of the document. To move to the text of the memo, double-click in the memo—not the header.

To remove a header, follow the path and click Remove Header.

DRILL 3	CREATE HEADER	collinsmemo

1. In the open document, create a header for the second page of the memo. Include the recipient's name, page number, and date. Tap ENTER once after keying the date. Do not print the header on the first page.

2. Add an enclosure notation and a copy notation to **Susan Wyman**.

3. Proofread and check; click Next to continue. (59-drill3)

Communication

59d Commas

1. Key your name on the first line and at the left margin.

2. For each group of sentences, select the sentence that has applied the use of commas correctly. Key the sentence number and then key the letter that corresponds to the correct sentence, e.g., (1a).

3. Proofread and check; click Next to continue. (59d)

KEYBOARDING PRO DELUXE 2

References/Communication Skills/Commas

1a. The legislators voted on Policy #2083 on May 23, 2010, at 5 p.m.
1b. The legislators voted on Policy #2,083 on May 23, 2010 at 5 p.m.

2a. To view Michelle's entire social networking site I need her permission.
2b. To view Michelle's entire social networking site, I need her permission.

3a. The parents volunteered to bring coffee, juice, milk, and pastries.
3b. The parents volunteered to bring coffee juice milk and pastries.

4a. Several club members designed an attractive logo, and the fundraising committee created an online store for selling merchandise displaying the logo.
4b. Several club members designed an attractive logo and the fundraising committee created an online store for selling merchandise displaying the logo.

5a. Mr. Rankin explained "Upload your essay to the class blog by Monday at 9 a.m."
5b. Mr. Rankin explained, "Upload your essay to the class blog by Monday at 9 a.m."

6a. The independent film festival will be held in Baton Rouge, Louisiana, on May 11–15.
6b. The independent film festival will be held in Baton Rouge, Louisiana on May 11–15.

7a. Chef Nate I appreciate your answering my questions about organic gardening on your blog.
7b. Chef Nate, I appreciate your answering my questions about organic gardening on your blog.

If your resume is mailed or faxed, the letter serves as a cover. If your resume is transmitted electronically, the letter may have to be incorporated within an e-mail or as an attachment to an e-mail. Always follow the instructions provided by the organization.

Review Po-Ling Huang's application letter on the next page.

THANK-YOU LETTER AFTER INTERVIEW

Good manners dictate that you should write a thank-you letter very soon after an interview—preferably the day of or the day after the interview. Many people do not write a thank-you letter; therefore, writing one helps you to create a good impression. The thank-you letter can be a powerful tool because you know more about the job than you did when you applied. You can use it to reinforce your strengths and show specifically how they match the job requirements.

1. Begin with a warm, sincere thank you.
2. Reaffirm your interest in the position.
3. Point out several specific things that were of interest or that matched your strengths.

REQUEST FOR REFERENCE

Good strategy and good manners dictate that you ask for permission by telephone, e-mail, or letter to use a person's name as a reference before you use it. Telephone and e-mail are better for individuals with whom you have a current relationship. Letters are preferable for those with whom you have not had recent contact. If your name has changed, be sure to indicate your name at the time you were enrolled in classes with or employed by the person. Above all, select references who will give you a good recommendation. Thank-you notes after the reference are a nice touch.

1. Introduce yourself and make the request.
2. Tactfully present information about the classes or work you did for the person, if appropriate.
3. Suggest that you will call to confirm the person's willingness to be a reference.

JOB ACCEPTANCE OR REFUSAL LETTERS

Most companies require a written acceptance of a job offer. It is much easier to write the acceptance letter than the refusal letter. Always decline a position graciously. In the future, that company may have a position you would like to accept or may even become a customer or client.

Acceptance Letters

1. Express your delight in accepting the position.
2. Confirm specific details, such as salary and starting date.
3. End on a friendly, optimistic note about your future with the company.

Refusal Letters

1. Begin with a buffer or neutral statement to cushion the bad news.
2. Present the reasons tactfully and let them lead to the decline.
3. End on a friendly note thanking the employer for considering you.

MEMORANDUMS

59e

KEYBOARDING PRO DELUXE 2

References/Document Formats/Memo

Memos, which are less formal than letters, are used for correspondence within an organization. E-mail has reduced the number of memos significantly; however, many companies require that e-mail messages only contain information that will not be needed in the future. Memos are keyed, saved as a document, and stored and maintained as a part of the company's records management system.

Memos may be printed on plain paper and sent in plain or interoffice envelopes, but they are more often transmitted as an attachment to an e-mail. Study the formatting guidelines below and refer to the full model on the next page.

TO: Maxine Cagiano, Heather Lewis, Benjamin Morgan

FROM: Aaron Redding

DATE: March 15, 201-

SUBJECT: Executive Vice President Screening

The Human Resources Department has forwarded to our screening committee five complete applications for the executive vice president position. Letters of acknowledgment have already been mailed to all applicants.

The work of this screening committee is outlined in the enclosed schedule. Please read the schedule carefully noting your specific responsibilities regarding telephone interviews with references. Refer to pages 130-140 of the *Employment Guide* for legal responsibilities in conducting interviews and use the interview template when conducting your interviews.

Our committee will meet on Thursday, April 1, at 9 a.m. in the third floor conference room to hear your reports and to narrow the list of candidates to three. These three individuals will be invited for an interview.

Thank you for your commitment to this important assignment.

xx

Enclosure

Heading:

- Begin the memo about 2" from the top of the page.
- Format the memo heading in bold and uppercase.
- Tap TAB once or twice after each heading to align the text that follows each item. You may also set a left tab at 1" and tap TAB once.
- Tap the ENTER key once after each line of the heading.

Body:

- Use the 1.15 default line spacing. Tap ENTER once after each paragraph.

Notations:

- Tap ENTER once after the body and key reference initials.
- Key the enclosure or attachment notation one line below the reference initials.
- Key the copy notation one line below the enclosure notation or one line below the reference initials if no enclosure notation is needed.

Distribution Lists:

When memos are sent to more than one person, key the names after the word *TO:* and separate them with commas, or key them in a list. Generally, names should be in alphabetical order by last name or listed in order of rank.

TO: Maxine Cagiano, Heather Lewis, Benjamin Morgan or TO: Maxine Cagiano
                                                                                     Heather Lewis
                                                                                    Benjamin Morgan

Lesson 105 | Employment Letters

Skill Building

105b Timed Writing

1. Key a 1' timed writing on each paragraph, working at your top rate.
2. Key a 3' timed writing, working to improve keying techniques.

	gwam	1'	3'

Have you ever given serious thought to owning your own business? The idea of being an entrepreneur appeals to many people and frightens many others. To some people, being your own boss is what draws them to the concept. To others, being boss means being responsible for everything and that is quite scary.

Maximizing results in a new enterprise requires far more than just knowledge in the area. Many people who have super ideas and who know a business well cannot make it succeed because they do not have the critical management or financial skills needed. Others do not realize the time required, nor are they willing to devote extra time to the venture.

Individuals who have the skills, knowledge, passion, and the willingness to devote the time needed find owning their own businesses the most rewarding thing they can do. They also need to surround themselves with people who can bring the talents that they do not possess to the business. Building a very good team can also make a big difference between making a new venture a success or a failure.

gwam 1' | 3'
12 | 4
26 | 9
39 | 13
53 | 18
63 | 21
13 | 25
27 | 30
41 | 35
55 | 39
68 | 44
72 | 45
13 | 49
27 | 54
41 | 58
54 | 63
67 | 67
81 | 72

3' | 1 | 2 | 3 | 4 |

Document Design

105c

APPLICATION LETTERS

The purpose of an application letter is to obtain an interview—not to get a job. Most organizations will not hire anyone on the basis of just a letter, resume, or application form. Application letters vary depending on how you learned of the position. It is important that the letter shows how your skills match the requirements of the job that is available. Design an attractive personal letterhead for your application letter— never use a company's letterhead. A personal letterhead looks more professional than plain paper with a return address. Block style is generally preferred.

A good strategy for writing an application letter is to:

1. Establish a point of contact if possible.
2. Specify the job that you are seeking.
3. Convey your key qualifications.
4. Interpret your major qualifications in terms of employer benefit.
5. Request an interview.

Tap ENTER 3 times; at 2"

TO: Maxine Cagiano, Heather Lewis, Benjamin Morgan ↓ 1

FROM: Aaron Redding ↓ 1

DATE: March 15, 201- ↓ 1

SUBJECT: Executive Vice President Screening ↓ 1

The Human Resources Department has forwarded to our screening committee five complete applications for the executive vice president position. Letters of acknowledgment have already been mailed to all applicants.

The work of this screening committee is outlined in the enclosed schedule. Please read the schedule carefully noting your specific responsibilities regarding telephone interviews with references. Refer to pages 130-140 of the *Employment Guide* for legal responsibilities in conducting interviews and use the interview template when conducting your interviews.

Our committee will meet on Thursday, April 1, at 9 a.m. in the third floor conference room to hear your reports and to narrow the list of candidates to three. These three individuals will be invited for an interview.

Thank you for your commitment to this important assignment. ↓ 1

Typist's first and last initials xx ↓ 1

Enclosure

Memo

Po-Ling Huang

PERMANENT ADDRESS
583 Post Oak Road
Savannah, GA 31418-0583
912-555-0171

TEMPORARY ADDRESS (May 30, 201-)
1001 Hogan Street, Apt. 2A
Mobile, AL 36617-1001
334-555-0103
plhuang@cotheru.edu

CAREER OBJECTIVE
To obtain a graphic design position with an opportunity to advance to a management position.

SUMMARY OF ACHIEVEMENTS
Bachelor's degree with double major in graphic design and information technology; certified in major software applications and programming language. Relevant work experience in two organizations; earned design award.

EDUCATION
B.S. Graphic Design and Information Technology (double major), Cother University, Mobile, Alabama. May 2010. GPA: 3.8 on 4.0 scale (Magna Cum Laude).

SPECIAL SKILLS
Microsoft Certified Application Professional. C++ Certification. Know Java and Visual Basic Script programming languages. Keyboarding skills: 70 wpm.

EXPERIENCE
Cother University Alumni Office. Mobile, Alabama. Assistant editor and producer of the Cother University Alumni News, 2008 to present.
* Designed layout and production of six editions; met every publishing deadline; received the Cother University Design Award.
* Assisted editor in design of Alumni Office webpage (www.cotheru.edu/alumni).

Cother University Library, 2006-2008.
* Created Multimedia Catalog using computerized database.
* Prepared monthly and annual reports using database.
* Designed brochure to promote library services (www.cotheru.edu/lib/plhuang/samples/brochure).

Po-Ling Huang   Page 2

HONORS AND ACTIVITIES
Dean's Scholar (3.5 GPA or higher), President, Cother University Graphic Design Association, Recipient of Cother University Design Award.

REFERENCES
Letters from references and a transcript are available from Cother University Placement Office, Cother University, P.O. Drawer 3418, Mobile, AL 36617-3418, 334-555-0134.

Communication

104d

word usage

KEYBOARDING PRO DELUXE 2

References/ Communication Skills/Word Usage

The following list contains sets of words that are often confused and misused.

1. Check the list carefully to make sure that you know how the words on the list should be used.

2. If you are not sure how all of the words should be used, take one of the following actions:

   a. Go to the References in *Keyboarding Pro DELUXE 2*; in the Communication Skills section, click Word Usage and review the rules for each set of words.

   b. Look up the words in a traditional or online dictionary.

3. In the open document, key the correct option in the first column for each sentence.

4. Check and close. (*104d*)

1. accept/except
2. affect/effect
3. bad/badly
4. complement/compliment
5. ensure/insure
6. farther/further
7. good/well
8. it's/its
9. principal/principle
10. their/there/they're
11. to/too/two
12. who's/whose

TWO-PAGE MEMORANDUMS

1. Begin the text on the second and succeeding pages at 1".
2. Create a header ❶ that includes the recipient's name, page number, and date on separate lines, and suppress the header on the first page.
3. In a two-page memo, at least two lines of the last paragraph are on the page with the header.

TO:	Scott Collins
FROM:	Vikram Yadama
DATE:	Current date
SUBJECT:	Automated Test Development and Generation System

Scott Collins
Page 2
Current date

The enclosed packet of material provides you with detailed information about the testing software and costs for a site license. Our sales representative, Susan Wyman, will call you next week to answer questions you might have about the software.

Applications

59-d1
Memo

1. Key the memo on page 286.
2. Proofread and check; click Next to continue. (*59-d1*)

59-d2
Two-Page Memo

▶▶ **REVIEW**

Document Theme
Page Layout/Themes/Themes

1. Open *59-drill1 memo template*, the memo template created in Drill 1.
2. Key the two-page memo below. Apply the Adjacency document theme.

    TO: Publication Staff; **FROM:** Dustin Parikh, Technology Coordinator;

    SUBJECT: External Review Accolades and Suggestions

3. Autofit the contents of the table and apply the Colorful Shading – Accent 2 table style. Drag the decimal tab in the second and third columns to center the numbers horizontally in the cells. Center the table horizontally on the page.
4. Add an appropriate second-page header.
5. Check and close. (*59-d2*)

Recently an external study of our training manuals and supplementary materials was conducted at the request of Tom Pearson, Vice President of Training. Reviewers applauded our thoroughness in instructions and our clarity in explaining complex tasks. Additionally, we received high marks on accuracy of directions and grammatical correctness. I am very pleased to report these accolades to you. Your commitment to training materials that are both accurate and thorough is commendable, and that commitment makes our training programs very popular with our public.

The professional appearance of our documents continues to set us apart from our competition. Two areas were noted by our reviewers that will further enhance our documents. Please read the following descriptions and software directions. If time permits and if practice is needed, please complete the short exercises.

(continued)

FORMATTING ELECTRONIC RESUMES

The ten tips that follow are designed so that the text can be (1) scanned easily into any applicant scanning system, (2) imported directly into a resume-building system, or (3) easily pasted in segments in the various fields of an online resume-building system.

1. Use a short line length—typically 80 or fewer characters for text-only resumes. Use normal margins for scannable resumes.

2. Use a sans serif True Type font such as Arial, Calibri, or Consolas.

3. Position your name on a line by itself at the top followed by your contact information; key a heading on the second page if a second page is needed.

4. Format section headings in uppercase.

5. Left-align all text including headings.

6. Avoid tabs, tables, bold, italic, underline, and graphics. Use the Space Bar to position text.

7. Use hyphens, asterisks, or other symbols from the keyboard to replace bullets or serve as a section divider. Space twice after asterisks or other symbols to separate the "bullet" from the text.

8. Print the scannable resume using a high-quality laser printer.

9. Use high-quality white or cream paper.

10. Proofread copy carefully; use checking tools. You can copy text to online resume builders or into an e-mail.

★ TIP

If you are in an actual job search and a text-only resume is requested by a company, prepare it in *Word* (not using *Keyboarding Pro DELUXE 2*).

1. Click Save as and key the filename.

2. In the Save as type box, select Plain Text.

All of your documents in this module will be saved by *Keyboarding Pro DELUXE 2*.

Applications

104-d1
Scannable Resume

1. Follow the tips above to format the resume you prepared for Po-Ling Huang in *103-d1* as a scannable resume. Use 11 pt. Calibri font for the entire document including headings. Do not use a table or tabs. Remove vertical bars (|). Tap ENTER twice to use a 1.7" top margin.

2. Key a heading on the first line of the second page—position name on the left and **Page 2** at the right margin. Use the Space Bar to position text at the right. See illustration on the next page.

3. Proofread and check; click Next to continue. (*104-d1*)

104-d2
Text Only Resume

1. Open *104-d1* and change the margins to wide.

2. Move the second-page heading to the first line on the page and reposition the page number at the right side.

3. Proofread and check; click Next to continue. (*104-d2*)

104-d3
Personal Scannable Resume

1. Reformat your personal resume as a scannable resume.

2. Review your *Summary of Achievements* or *Profile* as well as other sections of your resume. Make sure it contains many keywords that actually describe you and also fit the description of the job that you wish to obtain. If not, revise to include more keywords.

3. Proofread and check; click Next to continue. (*104-d3*)

59–d2

continued

Decimal Align in Tables

When preparing professional tables, use the decimal align tab to align decimals. Set the tab so that the numbers appear centered in the table. Using right alignment will align the decimals; however, the numbers will display at the right of the column. Use the following directions to align the tabs in the table below.

1. Select the cells where the decimal tab is needed.
2. From the Ruler, click the Tab alignment button until the decimal tab displays.
3. Point to the Ruler and click to set the decimal tab in the desired location.
4. Drag the tab as needed to center the numbers in the column.

After the table style is applied, set a decimal tab to center numbers in the second and third columns.

PICC RATE INCREASES		
Federal PICC Recovery	First Line	Additional Line
Primary Residence	$0.53	$1.50
Single-Line Business	$0.53	$2.75
Multi-Line Business	$2.75	$2.75
ISDN	$15.00	$13.50

Align Numbered List at the Decimal

The automatic numbering of the software does not allow a numbered list to be aligned at the decimal if digits are larger than a single digit. One simple way to align the numbers at the decimal is to deselect automatic numbering as follows:

1. Click File and then Options.
2. Click Proofing in the left pane.
3. Click AutoCorrect Options and then click the AutoFormat As You Type tab.
4. Under Apply as you type, deselect the Automatic numbered lists option. Click OK.

After you have turned off the automatic numbering option, set a decimal tab at the desired location. Tap the Tab key to move to the decimal tab and key the numbered items. Because the automatic numbering is not selected, you must key the number and the period. To align two-line items, drag the hanging indent marker on the Ruler to the beginning of the text. To practice this concept, open the file *practice1* on the shared drive, *Forde* folder. Follow the directions in this file.

If you have any additional suggestions for the publishing of our training materials, please e-mail them to me by next Friday. Again, thank you for your professionalism and commitment.

ELECTRONIC RESUMES

An electronic resume is simply a file containing a resume that is transmitted to the potential employer by e-mail, posting to a website, or pasting into the resume builder portion of an applicant tracking system (a software database that manages resumes). A scannable resume is a paper-based document that is transmitted to a potential employer usually by regular or overnight mail services so that it can be scanned using OCR technology into the company applicant tracking system. Not all resumes scan accurately, so it pays to learn as much as possible about the system that manages your resume. In fact, some companies request a "text-only" resume—meaning no formatting with tabs, tables, graphics, or text enhancements such as bold, color, or italic.

Checking the websites of many companies (of varying sizes) to see what information they provided about submitting a resume produced a wide range of alternatives. Many of them provided multiple alternatives, and size of company was not always a good indicator of the company's preference. Here are some samples of what you might find if you do an Internet search.

- Submit your resume by mail, *Word* document, or PDF file attached to an e-mail, post to a specified website, or use our resume builder to submit online.
- All resumes must be submitted by attaching a *Word* document to an e-mail; we do not accept hand delivery, mail, or other resume submission methods.
- To apply for a position, use our resume builder to submit your information.
- Submit a text-only resume following instructions on this website.
- Contact information on career page includes address, telephone, fax, and e-mail address—no indication of preferred way to receive information.

Note: The content of a resume does not change to make it an electronic or scannable resume; the format changes. A well-written resume can be reformatted to meet all of these styles.

KEYWORDS

Keywords are usually nouns. Typically, resumes are written in an action-oriented style, which means verbs are used rather than nouns. Sophisticated applicant tracking systems will pick up verbs as well as nouns; however, less sophisticated systems may not do so. Some resume-writing experts recommend putting a section of keywords at the beginning of the resume. Others think that this may do more harm than good. While the keyword section may get more initial "hits" in the software screening process, it may have a negative effect when the employer reads the resume.

A good alternative is to work keywords carefully into each section of the resume. Also, use keywords only when they truly apply to you. Padding a resume is never a good idea. Preparing various styles of resumes and then tailoring each one to the specific company increases your chances of being successful in your job search.

The resumes that you formatted in Lesson 103 were designed to be printed. These resumes could also be attached to an e-mail and meet the criteria that some companies specify—submit a *Word* file attached to an e-mail. The difference between a scannable resume and a text-only resume is that the former has limited formatting and the latter is just text. For many systems, PDF documents are not easy to search. Often when a one-page resume is formatted as a scannable or text-only resume, it will become a two-page resume. In that case, key a heading on the second page.

Lesson 60 | *Block Letters*

New Commands • Create and save Quick Parts • Modify Quick Parts

WARMUP

Lessons/60a Warmup

New Commands

60b

KEYBOARDING PRO DELUXE 2

References/Word 2010
Commands/Lesson 60

BUILDING BLOCKS OVERVIEW

Documents can be segmented into parts called building blocks that can be saved and reused in other documents. Building blocks also include built-in formats from galleries such as Cover Page and Header & Footer. Building blocks consist of formatted text, images, or other objects, such as closing lines of letters or letterhead with memo heading.

CREATE QUICK PARTS

The Quick Parts Gallery is one of the galleries of building blocks. A Quick Part is created by selecting a segment of formatted text or an image and saving it in the Quick Parts Gallery for reuse in other documents. You may save the closing lines of a letter or the memo heading. The text and format can be used in new letters or memos without rekeying them. When you create the building block, save the following information about the new building block.

Name	Key a unique name that suggests the content of the building block.
Gallery	Click the down arrow to view all the galleries.
Category	General is a broad category to use or create your own category name.
Description	Key a brief description of the building block.
Save in	Name of an open template. Typically, you will use *Building Blocks*.
Options	The options include: Insert content only, Insert content in its own paragraph, or Insert content in its own page.

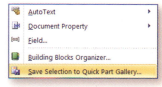

To create a content building block that can be used in other documents:

Insert/Text/Quick Parts

1. Select the text you want to save as a building block. Make sure the text is formatted in the way you plan to use it.

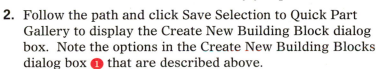

2. Follow the path and click Save Selection to Quick Part Gallery to display the Create New Building Block dialog box. Note the options in the Create New Building Blocks dialog box ❶ that are described above.

3. Key the name of the building block (if you want to change the default name that displays) and the description. For now, use the other options that are filled in—Quick Parts Gallery, General Category, Save in Building Blocks, and Insert content only. Click OK.

TIP

The paragraph mark (¶) must be selected to include formatting in the text you save as a building block. Use Show/Hide to make sure that the paragraph mark is selected.

Lesson 104 | Electronic Resumes

WARMUP

Lessons/104a Warmup

Skill Building

104b Textbook Keying

1. Key each line once, concentrating on good techniques. Tap ENTER twice after each 3-line group.
2. Repeat if time permits.

	1	polio freezer join dirt lion threw polo grew loop crew poppy sack
adjacent	2	were audio sad pool tree guy free joint western rope sorter quiet
	3	We were going to the pool or to sit under a tree for a few hours.
	4	decide gum cent jump brave hunt brunt greed cede kick draft funny
direct reach	5	fervor numb break cedar junked zany craft many brace lunch recess
	6	Cecil and Hunt decided to go after lunch to jump on a trampoline.
	7	junk was pun free hill brave hunk draw mull extra you web million
one hand	8	pumpkin exact pink creased hymn grade imply few noon career puppy
	9	Phillip was, in my opinion, a great, jolly puppy Jim gave my Mom.
	10	eight flake dish map kale jam name quake rigid oak turn social us
balanced hand	11	shrub throw spent whale visor world profit roam mentor clay blame
	12	The ornament is an authentic antique; so is the clamshell emblem.

! WORKPLACE SUCCESS

Applicant Tracking Systems

Understanding how companies track resumes is very important to a successful job search. Many, if not most, medium- and large-size companies manage their job recruitment process by using an applicant tracking system. They request electronic resumes or scan paper-based resumes into their system. Once a resume has become a part of an applicant tracking system, the software then determines from all resumes received which ones will be reviewed by the potential employer. Keywords are used to match the resume to the job description. The best way to format a resume depends on the software used by the company that receives it. To get the best results, check the company's website for information about submitting a resume.

CHRIS RYAN/OJO IMAGES/JUPITER IMAGES

SHORTCUT

Key the name or part of the name of the Quick Part and tap F3 to enter the Quick Part.

To add Quick Parts to a document:

Insert/Text/Quick Parts

1. Position the insertion point where you wish to insert the Quick Part in the document.

2. Follow the path and view the list of Quick Parts you have added.

3. Click the Quick Part you wish to insert. Repeat these steps for each Quick Part you want to add to the document.

DRILL 1   CREATE QUICK PART

1. Open *59-drill1 memo template*.

2. Select the entire document (CTRL + A).

3. Save the selection as a Quick Part.

4. Key the name and description **memo heading**; then click OK.

DRILL 2   USE QUICK PART

1. Insert the building block *memo heading*.

2. Complete the memo heading with you as the sender and your instructor as the recipient of the memo. The subject is **Memo Heading Inserted as Building Block**.

3. Proofread and check; click Next to continue. (*60-drill2*)

To modify and save building blocks with the same name:

Insert/Text/Quick Parts/Save Selection to Quick Part Gallery

TIP

Your Quick Parts may not save to your lab computer upon exit. If possible, complete the drills and applications in this lesson before you exit *Word*.

1. In a new blank document, insert the building block that you want to change.

2. Make the changes to the text; then select it and save the selection to the Quick Parts Gallery using the same name and description.

3. Respond Yes to the query *Do you want to redefine the building block entry?* to save the building block with the same name.

DRILL 3   MODIFY A BUILDING BLOCK   mfletterhead

1. In the open document, insert the building block *memo heading* below the letterhead. Position the heading to begin at 2".

2. In the FROM part of the heading, key your name.

3. Save the building block in the Quick Parts Gallery as **memo heading with letterhead** and description (**my memo heading with letterhead**).

4. Proofread and check; click Next to continue. (*60-drill3*)

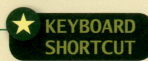

103-d1

Resume

KEYBOARD SHORTCUT

Nonbreaking Hyphen

CTRL + SHIFT + hyphen

1. Key the model resume on the previous page. Use *Word 2010* defaults.

2. Use Title style for the name. After the address, insert a horizontal line; format it using Blue, Accent 1. Use a nonbreaking hyphen in all ZIP Codes and phone numbers in the resume.

3. Format the body as a 2-column table; use Table Grid with no borders; adjust width of first column to 1.5". Tap ENTER to leave a blank line after each entry in the row. Use Cambria, uppercase, bold for the headings. Be sure to remove the bullets in the blank lines.

4. Proofread and check; click Next to continue. (*103-d1*)

103-d2

Resume Planner

resume planner

Po-Ling Huang used a planning document to map out her qualifications for a graphic design position. Use the data file *resume planner* to plan your resume. It is important that you use accurate information. Do not make up information. The goal is to learn how to present yourself in the best possible manner.

1. Use *103-d1* as a model for the headings and content of your resume, but adapt it to meet your needs and job objective.

2. Write a career objective that matches the type of position you would like to have.

3. Add headings that would assist you in showcasing your qualifications; delete headings that would not be helpful to you. You may change headings. For example, instead of using *Summary of Achievements,* some people might prefer to use *Profile*. The resume tells your story—use the style and the headings that best meet your needs.

4. Proofread and check; click Next to continue. (*103-d2*)

103-d3

Job Search

1. Use the Internet to locate job listings in a city or area where you would like to live.

2. Key a list of two or three jobs that you would like to have. Key the URL so that you can locate the information again if you need to.

3. Either copy the advertisement or job description or print it for each job.

4. Match the job requirements to your qualifications; select the best match.

5. Proofread and check; click Next to continue. (*103-d3*)

103-d4

Personal Resume

1. Open *103-d2* and use the Resume Planner to prepare a resume for the job you identified in *103-d3*. Insert a page break at the top of the open document and create your resume on the blank page.

2. Use copy and paste to add segments of information from the Resume Planner to your resume; use the style illustrated in *103-d1*. Delete the information in the Resume Planner after you complete the resume.

3. Try to keep the resume to one-page; if it goes to a second page, add a header with your name and the page number. Do not show the header on the first page.

4. Check and close. (*103-d4*)

BUSINESS LETTER REVIEW

The block letter style is a typical business letter format in which all letter parts are keyed at the left margin. The standard letter parts and the required spacing are reviewed below and illustrated on the following page. This letter also illustrates open punctuation style—no punctuation after the salutation and the complimentary closing.

LETTER PARTS

Letterhead: Preprinted stationery that includes the company name, logo, address, and other optional information, such as a telephone number, e-mail address, or Web address.

Dateline: Date the letter is prepared. Position at about 2". Begin at least 0.5" below the letterhead.

Hill University Cultural Center

3840 Cedar Mill Parkway ✗ Athens, GA 30606-4384 ✗ 607-555-0192 ✗ Fax: 607-555-0193

Letterhead

May 25, 201- Dateline

Attention Order Department
Redmon Publishers
5280 Circle Point
Long Beach, CA 90840-0792   Letter address

Ladies and Gentlemen Salutation

The Cultural Center at Hill University is hosting a summer workshop entitled "Women of the Mountains." Elizabeth is our keynote speaker, and we know our attendees will be clamoring for her exciting book, *The Legacy of Mountain Women*.   Body

A purchase order with shipping instructions for 100 copies of Ms. Gainwright's book is enclosed. These books must be delivered to the Massey Convention Center during the first week in June where they will be stored until the seminar on June 15.

If you have questions regarding this order, please call me at 10 a.m. and 2 p.m. on Thursday and Friday. We appreciate your assisting us with this order and special delivery.

Sincerely Complimentary closing

Erin Bland, Coordinator Writer's name and title

xx Reference initials

Enclosure Enclosure notation

c   John Connor
        Angela Ward Copy notation

Letter address: Complete address of letter recipient. Tap ENTER two times after the date. Generally includes receiver's name, company name, street address, city, state (one space after the state), and ZIP Code. Include personal title (Mr., Ms., Dr.). Capitalize the first letter of each word. Remove the added space between the lines of the letter address.

Salutation (or greeting): Tap ENTER one time after the letter address. Include a courtesy title with the name, e.g., Dear Mr. Nibert. Use *Ladies and Gentlemen* when addressing a company.

Body: Message of the letter. Tap ENTER one time after the salutation. Use the 1.15 default line spacing; tap ENTER once between paragraphs.

Complimentary closing: Formal good-bye. Tap ENTER one time after the body. Capitalize only the first letter of the first word of the closing.

Writer's name and title: Tap ENTER two times after the complimentary closing. Include a personal title (Mr., Ms.) only if it is not apparent to the reader if the person is male or female (Jan, Pat, Chris). Key the name and title on either one or two lines, whichever gives better balance. Use a comma to separate name and title if on one line. If two lines are used, remove the added space between the two lines.

Reference initials: Tap ENTER one time after the writer's name and title. Replace xx with your initials. Include no spaces or periods.

Enclosure notation: Tap ENTER one time after the reference initials. If multiple enclosures are listed, set a tab at 1" and remove added space between lines.

Copy notation: Tap ENTER one time after the reference initials or enclosure notation if an enclosure notation is included. If multiple copies are listed, set a tab at 0.5" to align and remove added space between lines.

Po-Ling Huang

Permanent Address: 583 Post Oak Road | Savannah, GA 31418-0583 | Telephone: 912-555-0171

Temporary Address: (May 30, 201-): 1001 Hogan Street, Apt. 2A | Mobile, AL 36617-1001 | Telephone: 334-555-0103 | plhuang@cotheru.edu

CAREER OBJECTIVE	To obtain a graphic design position with an opportunity to advance to a management position.
SUMMARY OF ACHIEVEMENTS	Bachelor's degree with double major in graphic design and information technology; certified in major software applications and programming language. Relevant work experience in two organizations; earned design award.
EDUCATION	B.S. Graphic Design and Information Technology (double major), Cother University, Mobile, Alabama. May 2010. GPA: 3.8/4.0 (Magna Cum Laude).
SPECIAL SKILLS	Microsoft Certified Application Professional. C++ Certification. Know Java and Visual Basic Script programming languages. Keyboarding skills: 70 wpm.
EXPERIENCE	Cother University Alumni Office. Mobile, Alabama. Assistant editor and producer of the Cother University Alumni News, 2008 to present.

- Designed layout/production of six editions; met every publishing deadline; received the Cother University Design Award.
- Assisted editor in design of Alumni Office webpage (www.cotheru.edu/alumni).

Cother University Library, 2006-2008.

- Created Multimedia Catalog using computerized database.
- Prepared monthly and annual reports using database.
- Designed brochure to promote library services (www.cotheru.edu/lib/plhuang/samples/brochure).

HONORS AND ACTIVITIES	Dean's Scholar (3.5 GPA or higher), President, Cother University Graphic Design Association, Recipient of Cother University Design Award.
REFERENCES	Letters from references and a transcript are available from Cother University Placement Office, Cother University, P.O. Drawer 3418, Mobile, AL 36617-3418	Telephone: 334-555-0134.

Haas Plumbing Supply Co.
1010 Greenbrier Hill
Ironton, OH 45638-1010

Tap ENTER 3 times; 2"

September 22, 201- ↓ 2

Ms. Charise Rossetti
149 West Fifth Street   } Remove Space After Paragraph
St. Albans, WV 25177-4900 ↓ 1

Dear Ms. Rossetti ↓ 1

All of the employees at Haas Plumbing Supply are pleased that you are completing an internship at our company headquarters. One of your duties will be to assist Mr. Joseph Burns in preparing the daily correspondence. We know that your training at Highview Community College has prepared you well for this task.

Remember that the correspondence our customers receive from us is one of the ways that they evaluate our effectiveness as a business. Our outgoing letters must be as perfect as we can make them in layout, content, grammar, and punctuation. This will impress upon our customers that we have a company-wide commitment to excellence. Our correspondence manual is enclosed for your review.

Your internship agreement is also enclosed. Please read carefully and submit the signed copy when you report to Mr. Burns on September 28 at 8 a.m. Again, we are pleased to have you working in our organization.

Sincerely ↓ 2

Gerald Haas } Remove Space After Paragraph
President

xx ↓ 1

Align enclosures at 1"

Enclosures: Correspondence Manual } Remove Space After Paragraph
                  Internship Agreement

c   Joseph Burns } Remove Space After Paragraph
        Ellis Wiseman

Align copy notations at 0.5"

Block Letter with Open Punctuation

RESUMES

A resume is a summary of your qualifications; it is the primary basis for the interviewer's decision to invite you for an interview. Prior to preparing a resume, complete a self-analysis, identifying your career goals and job qualifications. Most resumes contain some or all of the following information.

Po-Ling Huang

Permanent Address: 583 Post Oak Road | Savannah, GA 31418-0583 | Telephone: 912-555-0171

Temporary Address: (May 30, 201-): 1001 Hogan Street, Apt. 2A | Mobile, AL 36617-1001 | Telephone: 334-555-0103 | plhuang@cotheru.edu

CAREER OBJECTIVE	To obtain a graphic design position with an opportunity to advance to a management position.
SUMMARY OF ACHIEVEMENTS	Bachelor's degree with double major in graphic design and information technology; certified in major software applications and programming language. Relevant work experience in two organizations; earned design award.
EDUCATION	B.S. Graphic Design and Information Technology (double major), Cother University, Mobile, Alabama. May 2010. GPA: 3.8/4.0 (Magna Cum Laude).
SPECIAL SKILLS	Microsoft Certified Application Professional. C++ Certification. Know Java and Visual Basic Script programming languages. Keyboarding skills: 70 wpm.
EXPERIENCE	Cother University Alumni Office. Mobile, Alabama. Assistant editor and producer of the Cother University Alumni News, 2008 to present. • Designed layout/production of six editions; met every publishing deadline; received the Cother University Design Award. • Assisted editor in design of Alumni Office webpage (www.cotheru.edu/alumni). Cother University Library, 2006-2008. • Created Multimedia Catalog using computerized database. • Prepared monthly and annual reports using database. • Designed brochure to promote library services (www.cotheru.edu/lib/plhuang/samples/brochure).
HONORS AND ACTIVITIES	Dean's Scholar (3.5 GPA or higher), President, Cother University Graphic Design Association, Recipient of Cother University Design Award.
REFERENCES	Letters from references and a transcript are available from Cother University Placement Office, Cother University, P.O. Drawer 3418, Mobile, AL 36617-3418	Telephone: 334-555-0134.

Identification: Your name, telephone numbers, address, e-mail address, and Internet address. Students may list a temporary and permanent address.

Career Objective: Indicate the type of position to let the employer know your specific career goal.

Summary of Achievements: Summary of your most important achievements. Emphasize special or unique skills (foreign language, computer skills, etc.).

Education: Diplomas or degrees earned, schools attended, and dates. Include majors and grade-point averages when it is to your advantage to do so.

Experience: Job titles, employers, dates of employment, a brief description of the positions, and major achievements—not a listing of activities. Use active voice and concrete language; for example, "Handle an average of 200 customer orders per week." List information in the same order for each position.

Honors and Activities: Specific examples of leadership potential and commitment.

References: Information on how to obtain references. Usually a separate list of references is given to the interviewer upon request.

Items within the sections of the resume are arranged in reverse chronological order (most recent experiences listed first). Which section is presented first? From your self-analysis, you will determine which one of your qualifications is the strongest. If work experience is stronger than education, present this section first. A recent college graduate would present education first.

A major consideration in preparing an effective resume is the overall attractiveness of the resume. Use high-quality paper; print on a laser printer using effective layout design that will allow your resume to appear professionally created. However, do not overdo the design.

SPECIAL LETTER PARTS

You have reviewed the standard letter parts that are present in business letters. Other special features may be included, depending on the needs of the document. When special parts are added to a letter, they cause it to move down farther on the page. Always preview letters to determine if starting at 2" results in the most attractive appearance. If necessary, adjust the date higher on the page allowing adequate space between the letterhead and the date. Be sure the date begins 0.5" below the letterhead.

An **attention line** is used to direct a letter to a position or department within an organization. It is keyed as the first line of the letter address. Whenever an attention line is used to direct a letter to a department, division, or company, the correct salutation is *Ladies and Gentlemen*. If it is used for a specific position title, then the salutation would be Dear (position title), such as *Dear Office Manager*. See illustration of an attention line on pages 291 and 298.

> Attention Accounting Department
> Chou and Chou Furniture Company
> First Street and First Avenue
> Olympia, WA 99504-6480
>
> Ladies and Gentlemen:

A **copy notation** (c) indicates that a copy of the document has been sent to the person(s) listed. Key the copy notation one line below the reference initials or enclosure notation (if used). Tap TAB to align the names. If necessary, click the Undo Automatic Capitalization button after keying the copy notation to lowercase the letter c.

Align at 0.5"

A **blind copy notation** (bc) indicates that others are receiving a copy of the letter without the addressee's knowledge. Tap ENTER one time after the reference initials, enclosure notation, or copy notation (if any). The blind copy notation appears on copies but not on the original. Align multiple recipients at the 0.5" tab. **Note:** E-mail messages containing attached letters may be addressed with blind copy recipients.

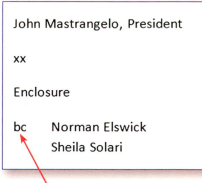

Appears on copies, but not on the original

Applications

60-d1

Block Letter

1. Key the block letter on page 292 with open punctuation. Begin the date at about 2".
2. Align the enclosure notations at a tab set at 1".
3. Send a copy to **Joseph Burns** and **Ellis Wiseman**; align the names at a 0.5" tab.
4. Remove the added space between the letter address, writer's name and title, enclosures, and individuals receiving copies of this letter.
5. Select the letter address and create an envelope; add it to the document.
6. Proofread and check; click Next to continue. (*60-d1*)

Employment Documents

LEARNING OUTCOMES

- Prepare traditional and scannable resumes.
- Compose and format employment documents.
- Develop an understanding of the employment process.
- Improve keyboarding skills.

Lesson 103 | Resumes

KEYBOARDING PRO DELUXE 2

WARMUP

Lessons/103a Warmup

A **ALL LETTERS**

Skill Building

103b Timed Writing

1. Key two 1' writings on each paragraph; work at your top speed.
2. Key a 3' timing on both paragraphs; work at your control rate.

	gwam	1'	3'

Persistence is a quality that rarely gets mentioned when people | 14 | 5 | 44

talk about keys to success. In most cases, however, it is a major | 27 | 9 | 48

contributor to success. People who will spend the extra time to | 40 | 13 | 52

stick with a project until it has been completed correctly are very | 54 | 18 | 57

likely to succeed. | 58 | 19 | 58

The opposite of persistence is giving up too easily. The first | 14 | 24 | 63

time many people encounter a barrier they give up and try to find a | 27 | 28 | 67

way to rationalize quitting. Those who stick with the situation and | 41 | 33 | 72

work to resolve the problem are far more likely to be successful. | 54 | 37 | 76

Quitters are not winners. | 60 | 39 | 78

```
1' | 1 | 2 | 3 | 4 | 5 | 6 | 7 | 8 | 9 | 10 | 11 | 12 | 13 |
3' |     1     |       2       |      3      |      4      |
```

60-d2

Create Quick Part

 bland

1. In the open document, select the closing lines of the letter (complimentary closing through reference initials) and create a Quick Part named **Bland Closing Lines**.
2. Key the description **Bland Closing Lines**.
3. Click Next to continue. You will use the Quick Part in the next document.

60-d3

Block Letter

 redmon

REVIEW

Envelopes

Mailings/Create/Envelopes

1. In the open document, format the letter in block letter style and open punctuation. Apply correct spacing and position the dateline appropriately.
2. Position the date **May 25** at 2". Send the letter to **Attention Order Department** | **Redmon Publishers** | **5280 Circle Point** | **Long Beach, CA 90840-0792**.
3. Provide an appropriate salutation when an attention line is used.
4. Insert the building block *Bland Closing Lines*, created in *60-d2* above.
5. Review the letter to determine if an enclosure notation is needed.
6. Send a blind copy to **John Connor** and **Angela Ward**.
7. Create an envelope and add to the letter.
8. Proofread and check; click Next to continue. (*60-d3*)

60-d4

Block Letter

1. Format the block letter with open punctuation. Begin at 2". Insert the Date command and check to update automatically. Remove the added space between the letter address and writer's name and title.
2. Review the letter to determine if an enclosure notation is needed.
3. Create an envelope and add to the letter.
4. Check and close. (*60-d4*)

Ms. Sarah Atkinson | 1234 Elm Lane | Bronx, NY 10466-1234

Good news! Our newest litter of smooth-coated collies is now four weeks old. The enclosed photograph shows these adorable quadruplets with their purebred mother.

Because of your interest in a collie for a family pet, we are writing to you before the public announcement of this litter is released. As you know, our smooth-coated collies are always placed weeks before they are old enough to leave our kennel.

Please call our office at 718-555-0198 Monday through Saturday to arrange a time for you and your family to visit our kennel and see these exquisite puppies for yourselves. You will not want to miss this special opportunity to take one of these puppies home with you.

Sincerely | Andrew Rogers | Kennel Manager

1. Use New from existing to create a new document using *100-d1*, the SOAP note form. Save as *102-d2*.

2. Fill in the form with the following information:

   Lucas, Steve

   Patient No. **# 22653**; Age: **42**

   Allergies: **None known**

   Meds: **Esomeprazole Magnesium**

   T: **99.0**; P: **80**; R: **15**; B/P: **118/76**

   C/O: **Pain left elbow**; Date: **4-10-201-**

3. Center the text vertically in the cells.

4. Check and close. (*102-d2*)

S	Pt injured left elbow two days ago in fall from rollerblades. Complains of pain on outside of elbow, superficial.
O	No inflammation; slight hematoma; limited ROM on left elbow FLEXION.
A	Treatment: lateral epicondyle 15 minute hot pack every day for a week and help with passive ROM. Ask pt to apply a hot pack at home twice a day. Diagnosis: Lateral epicondylitis on left.
P	Pt will return twice a week to reduce pain and increase ROM.

BOOKMARK

www.collegekeyboarding.com
Module 16 Practice Quiz

Lesson 61 | *Modified Block Letters*

New Commands
- Use Building Blocks Organizer
- Create New Building Block Category

New Commands

61b

BUILDING BLOCKS ORGANIZER

Both the built-in building blocks provided when *Word* was installed and any building blocks you created are listed in the Building Blocks Organizer. Note that the Quick Part *memo heading*, which you created in Lesson 60, is shown in the illustration below. It is saved in the Quick Parts Gallery in the General category. When you click one of the building blocks, a preview is shown at the right. Note that you can insert building blocks from the Building Blocks Organizer into a document or you can delete the building block itself. Building blocks can be sorted by Name, Gallery, Category, Template, Behavior, or Description.

To work with building blocks in the Building Blocks Organizer:

Insert/Text/Quick Parts/Building Blocks Organizer

1. Follow the path to display the Building Blocks Organizer.

2. To sort a column in the Building Blocks Organizer, click the heading of the Name column. If you know the name of the building block, click Name to sort by the name. If you want to look for it by Gallery or Category, click that heading to sort the building blocks.

3. To insert a building block in a document, click where you want the building block to be placed; then click the desired building block in the Building Blocks Organizer list, and click Insert.

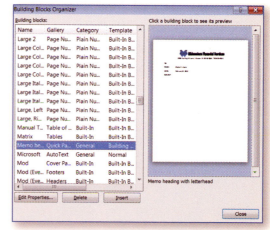

4. To delete a building block from the Building Blocks Organizer, select the building block, click Delete, and then click Yes.

DRILL 1   USE ORGANIZER

1. Key your name, select it, and save it as a building block. Key **My Name** as the name of the building block and as the description. Click OK.

2. Delete your name that you keyed (not the building block); leave the document open.

3. Display the Building Blocks Organizer. Click the Name column to sort it.

4. Locate the building block you created for your name (*My Name*) and insert it in the document.

5. Select the building block *My Name*, and delete it from the Building Blocks Organizer. Close the drill, but do not save it.

102-d1

**Pleading Form with Table
List of Trial Exhibits**

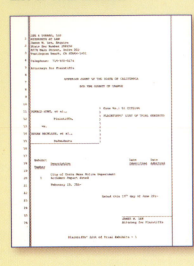

1. Use the Pleading form with 26 lines template to create the Plaintiffs' List of Trial Exhibits.

2. Insert a table for the Exhibit Number section. Turn on Show/Hide; click on the ¶ and change the line spacing to 1.0. Adjust column widths. Remove borders and underline column heads.

3. Continue to the next document. (*102-d1*)

LEE & DURAND, LLP

ATTORNEYS AT LAW

James W. Lee, Esquire

State Bar Number 202256

8578 Main Street, Suite 202

Huntington Beach, CA 92646-1801

Telephone: 714-555-0174

Attorneys for Plaintiffs

SUPERIOR COURT OF THE STATE OF CALIFORNIA
FOR THE COUNTY OF ORANGE

DONALD HURT, et al.,

Plaintiffs,

vs.

SUSAN RECKLESS, et al.,

Defendants

Case No. 01 CC05144

PLAINTIFFS' LIST OF TRIAL EXHIBITS

Exhibit Number	Description	Date Identified	Date Admitted
1	City of Costa Mesa Police Department Accident Report dated February 15, 201-		

Dated this 19th day of June 201-

JAMES W. LEE

Attorney for Plaintiffs

CREATE A NEW CATEGORY

Only one category, General, is provided for saving Quick Parts. However, you can create a new category so that you will not have an excessive number of building blocks in one category. A new category can be created when you are saving a new building block, or you can create a new category by editing the properties of a current building block.

To save a building block to a new category:

Insert/Text/Quick Parts/Save Selection to Quick Part Gallery

1. Select the text or image you wish to save.
2. Follow the path to display the Create New Building Block dialog box.
3. Click the down arrow on Category and select Create New Category ❶.
4. Key the name you wish to use and click OK.

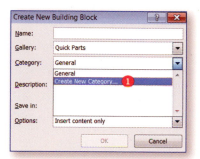

To create a new category by modifying the building block properties:

Insert/Text/Quick Parts/Building Blocks Organizer

1. Follow the path to display the Building Blocks Organizer.
2. In the Building Blocks Organizer, select the building block that you wish to modify, and click Edit Properties to display the Modify Building Block dialog box.
3. Click the drop-list arrow on Category and select Create New Category ❶.
4. Key the name you wish to use and click OK twice.
5. Click Yes to redefine the entry; then click Close.

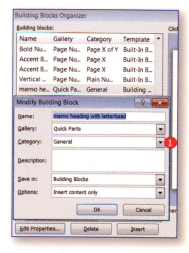

DRILL 2   CREATE NEW CATEGORY

1. Key your name and right-align it.
2. Select your name and save it as a building block as follows: Name: Your Name; Description: Your Name; Category: Create a new category named **Personal**. Click OK and click OK again.
3. Delete your name; leave the document open.
4. Sort the Building Blocks Organizer by Category and find your name.
5. Sort the Building Blocks Organizer by gallery; note that your name is saved in the Quick Parts Gallery.
6. Insert it in the document.
7. Proofread and check; click Next to continue. (*61-drill2*)

Lesson 102 | Assessment

Skill Building

gwam | 1' | 3'

102b Timed Writing

1. Key two 1' timed writings on each paragraph; work for speed.
2. Key one 3' timed writing on both paragraphs.

Forms provide both a productive and an effective way to collect data. Designing an effective form often does not happen quickly, but the time spent can be justified quite easily. The time spent creating a form is productive because once the form has been finished, it can be used multiple times.

14	5	48
28	9	52
42	14	57
56	19	62
60	20	63

Forms provide an effective way of collecting data because they add structure. Forms can be set up so that the data is organized in exactly the way the designer wants to collect it. Analyzing data can be simplified by the way in which the form is structured. Information is also much easier to tabulate from data on a well-designed form.

14	25	68
27	29	72
41	34	77
56	39	82
69	43	86

1'	1	2	3	4	5	6	7	8	9	10	11	12	13	14
3'		1			2			3			4			5
5'			1				2				3			

Applications

102c

Assessment

 Continue

 Check

When you complete a document, proofread it, check the spelling, and preview for placement. When you are completely satisfied, click the Continue button to move to the next document. Click the Check button when you are ready to error-check the test. Review and/or print the document analysis results.

1. Display the Building Blocks Organizer.

2. Sort the entries by clicking the Name column.

3. Select *memo heading with letterhead* and click Edit Properties.

4. Click the down arrow on the Category box and select Create New Category. Key the category name **CK Building Blocks**. Click OK.

5. Change the name and description of the building block to **memo heading + letterhead**.

6. Click OK and then click Yes to redefine the building block.

7. Sort by category and then insert the *memo heading + letterhead* building block into the document.

8. Proofread and check; click Next to continue. *(61-drill3)*

Document Design

MODIFIED BLOCK LETTER

61c

KEYBOARDING PRO DELUXE 2

References/Document Formats/Modified Block Letter

The only difference between the block and modified block style letters is the placement of the dateline, complimentary close, and the writer's name and title. These lines begin at the horizontal center of the page. Study the illustration of a modified block letter on the next page. Begin the letter by setting a tab at the center of the page. To determine the position of the tab, subtract the side margins from the center of the paper (4.25" − 1.0" = 3.25").

Tap TAB before keying the dateline, complimentary close, and the writer's name and title. Remember to remove the extra spacing between the letter address and other short lines. Review the model modified block letter on the next page.

Note: If the letter has already been keyed and you are changing it to modified block format, select the entire document and then set the tab at 3.25". If default tabs are being used for multiple enclosures or multiple copy notations, select the letter from the date line through the sender's name and title; then set the tab at 3.25".

MIXED PUNCTUATION

Although most letters are formatted with open punctuation, some businesses prefer mixed punctuation. To format a letter using mixed punctuation, key a colon after the salutation and a comma after the complimentary close.

Monica A. Carter
Communication Consultant
100 Main Street
Clinton, MS 39056-0503

Tab 3.25" ———→ July 11, 201-

Attention Communication Department
Professional Document Designs, Inc.
9345 Blackjack Boulevard
Kingwood, TX 77345-9345

Ladies and Gentlemen:

Modified Block Style Letters

Modified block format differs from block format in that the date, complimentary close, and the writer's name and title are keyed at the center point. Set a left tab at 3.25" and tap the Tab key to move the insertion point to the center of the page.

Paragraphs may be blocked, as this letter illustrates, or they may be indented 0.5" from the left margin. We suggest using block paragraphs so that the additional key strokes are not needed.

We recommend that you use modified block style only for those customers who request it. Otherwise, we urge you to use block format, which is more efficient. Please refer to the model documents in the enclosed *Communication Experts Format Guide*.

Sincerely,

Tab 3.25"

Monica A. Carter
Communication Consultant

xx

Enclosure

bc   Lyndon David, Account Manager

Dear Mr. Hathorn:

Sincerely,

Summary and Recommendations

Personality testing suggests the use of repression and dissociation that prevent him from having to remember or relive past painful experiences. Repressed feelings of frustration may return to be acted out behaviorally. Christopher may tend to not take responsibility for his actions or may minimize them.

It may be important for the staff to assess, in an ongoing fashion, indications of the degree of personality fragmentation that Christopher experiences. Some exploration of whether or not he remembers past events that have been reported by other family members may assist with this.

Christopher needs to learn techniques of anger management. He should be taught to become aware of when he is beginning to become angry so that he can voluntarily learn to control his behavior. Christopher may have much difficulty learning to access the signs that he is beginning to become upset. He may need to practice a variety of techniques in order to control his behavior and then later resolve the problem verbally.

An additional focus should be on his relational skills. Assisting him in becoming sensitive to reading cues and the teaching of some empathy and conscious awareness would also help improve his functioning level.

QUICK ✓

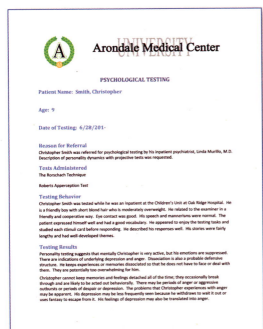
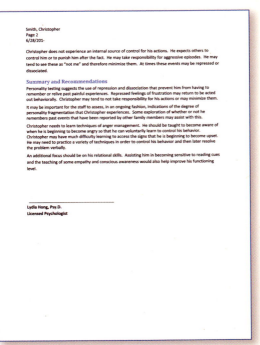

101-d3

Monica A. Carter
Communication Consultant
100 Main Street
Clinton, MS 39056-0503

Tap ENTER 3 times; 2"

Tab 3.25" → July 11, 201-

Attention Communication Department ← *Attention line*
Professional Document Designs, Inc.
9345 Blackjack Boulevard
Kingwood, TX 77345-9345

Ladies and Gentlemen: *Mixed punctuation*

Modified Block Style Letters *Subject line*

Modified block format differs from block format in that the date, complimentary close, and the writer's name and title are keyed at the center point. Set a left tab at 3.25" and tap the Tab key to move the insertion point to the center of the page.

Paragraphs may be blocked, as this letter illustrates, or they may be indented 0.5" from the left margin. We suggest using block paragraphs so that the additional key strokes are not needed.

We recommend that you use modified block style only for those customers who request it. Otherwise, we urge you to use block format, which is more efficient. Please refer to the model documents in the enclosed *Communication Experts Format Guide*.

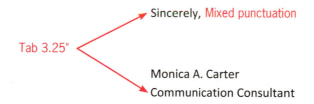

Sincerely, *Mixed punctuation*

Tab 3.25"

Monica A. Carter
Communication Consultant

xx

Enclosure

bc   Lyndon David, Account Manager *Not printed on the addressee's copy*

Tab 0.5"

Modified Block Letter With Mixed Punctuation

1. Follow the steps in *101-d2* to create a Psychological Testing report for Christopher Smith.
2. Check and close. (*101-d3*)

Patient Name: Smith, Christopher

Age: 9

Date of Testing: 6/28/201-

Reason for Referral

Christopher Smith was referred for psychological testing by his inpatient psychiatrist, Linda Murillo, M.D. Description of personality dynamics with projective tests was requested.

Tests Administered

The Rorschach Technique

Roberts Apperception Test

Testing Behavior

Christopher Smith was tested while he was an inpatient at the Children's Unit at Oak Ridge Hospital. He is a friendly boy with short blond hair who is moderately overweight. He related to the examiner in a friendly and cooperative way. Eye contact was good. His speech and mannerisms were normal. The patient expressed himself well and had a good vocabulary. He appeared to enjoy the testing tasks and studied each stimuli card before responding. He described his responses well. His stories were fairly lengthy and had well-developed themes.

Testing Results

Personality testing suggests that mentally Christopher is very active, but his emotions are suppressed. There are indications of underlying depression and anger. Dissociation is also a probable defensive structure. He keeps experiences or memories dissociated so that he does not have to face or deal with them. They are potentially too overwhelming for him.

Christopher cannot keep memories and feelings detached all of the time; they occasionally break through and are likely to be acted out behaviorally. There may be periods of anger or aggressive outbursts or periods of despair or depression. The problems that Christopher experiences with anger may be apparent. His depression may be less frequently seen because he withdraws to wait it out or uses fantasy to escape from it. His feelings of depression may also be translated into anger.

Christopher does not experience an internal source of control for his actions. He expects others to control him or to punish him after the fact. He may take responsibility for aggressive episodes. He may tend to see these as "not me" and therefore minimize them. At times these events may be repressed or dissociated.

SPECIAL LETTER PARTS

Two additional letter parts are introduced in this lesson. Adding special letter parts may cause the letter to move farther down the page, so always preview the letter for attractive placement. If necessary, move the date higher on the page, but be sure the date begins 0.5" below the letterhead.

A **reference line** is used to direct the reader to source documents or to files. Tap ENTER one time after the letter address.

A **subject line** provides the reader with a short description of the purpose of the letter. Tap ENTER one time after the salutation. Key the subject line using initial caps or UPPERCASE. It may be preceded by the word *Subject*, but often it is not. A subject line and reference line are rarely both used in one letter.

Ms. Allison Raymond
P.O. Box 3100
Natchez, MS 39120-2030

Re: Order No. R1084

Dear Ms. Raymond:

Dear Mr. Jones:

Projected Sales Figures

The sales figures for the first quarter have been released.

! WORKPLACE SUCCESS

Letters

Letters should be carefully planned. List all the points that need to be covered and make sure they relate to the main purpose of the letter. Letters need to be accurate and written in a timely manner. Business letters often have financial implications, so check to make sure that all stated facts are accurate.

Letters are a more formal means of communicating than are e-mails, text messages, or memos. Letters should be formal and factual, and at the same time be reader friendly. If the letter is part of a package, limit the cover letter to one page and relegate technical details to enclosed documents. Avoid language that is specific to gender, race, or religion in all business correspondence. For example, use words such as workforce rather than manpower and chairperson rather than chairman.

101-d2

Psychological Testing Report

1. Use New from existing to open a copy of *101-d1*, the Psychological Testing report form.

2. Key the psychological testing report for Maria Perez. Patient Name, Age, and Date of Testing should be keyed on the same line as the heading. The rest of the report is keyed under the repective side heading; click the ¶ below the heading and key the text.

3. Insert a header at the top of the second page that consists of the patient's name (Perez, Maria), the page number, and the date of the testing. For the page number, key the word **Page** and then insert the page number. Choose Plain Number in the Current Position. Choose Different First Page to suppress the header on the first page.

4. Format the report; place the Summary and Recommendations section on the second page.

5. Check and close. (*101-d2*)

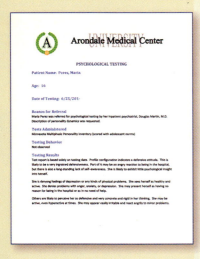

Patient Name: Perez, Maria   **Age:** 16   **Date of Testing:** 6/25/201-

Reason for Referral

Maria Perez was referred for psychological testing by her inpatient psychiatrist, Douglas Martin, M.D. Description of personality dynamics was requested.

Tests Administered

Minnesota Multiphasic Personality Inventory (scored with adolescent norms)

Testing Behavior

Not observed

Testing Results

Test report is based solely on testing data. Profile configuration indicates a defensive attitude. This is likely to be a very ingrained defensiveness. Part of it may be an angry reaction to being in the hospital, but there is also a long-standing lack of self-awareness. She is likely to exhibit little psychological insight into herself.

She is denying feelings of depression or any kinds of physical problems. She sees herself as healthy and active. She denies problems with anger, anxiety, or depression. She may present herself as having no reason for being in the hospital or as in no need of help.

Others are likely to perceive her as defensive and very concrete and rigid in her thinking. She may be active, even hyperactive at times. She may appear easily irritable and react angrily to minor problems.

Summary and Recommendations

At the time Maria Perez took the test she appeared to be defensive and minimizing problems. On an ongoing basis she may have a lack of insight into her difficulties. Further testing may help describe her problems in more detail. She may lower her defensiveness so that she is more open to acknowledging and working on areas of difficulty as she adapts to the Unit and begins to feel more comfortable in the environment.

Applications

61-d1

Modified Block Letter

1. Key the model modified block letter on page 298 with mixed punctuation. Set a left tab at 3.25" for keying the date, complimentary close, writer's name, and title. Note that it includes an attention line, subject line, and blind copy notation.

2. Before keying the blind copy notation, set a left tab at 0.5".

3. Add an envelope to the letter.

4. Proofread and check; click Next to continue. *(61-d1)*

61-d2

Building Blocks

 TIP

Allow time to complete these applications before exiting *Word*.

1. Open *61-d1*, select the closing lines of the letter (complimentary closing through reference initials, including the tab before *Sincerely*), and create a Quick Part named **Carter closing lines**. *Hint:* Begin selecting at the left margin so you will select the tab before *Sincerely*. Save it in a new category you create named **Carter Building Blocks**. Key the description **Carter closing lines modified block with mixed punctuation**.

2. Click Next to continue. You will use this building block in the next document.

61-d3

Modified Block Letter

 global

1. In the open document, format the document as a modified block letter with mixed punctuation. Position the dateline at the appropriate position.

2. Read the letter and compose an appropriate subject line. Omit the word *Subject*.

3. After the last paragraph, insert the *Carter closing lines* building block you created in *61-d2*.

4. Proofread and check; click Next to continue. *(61-d3)*

61-d4

Modified Block Letter

1. Format the modified block letter and use mixed punctuation. Supply necessary letter parts.

2. Add the reference line **Re: Order No. S3835**.

3. Send a copy to **Eric Leiu**. Set a tab at 0.5" to key the notation.

4. Add an envelope to the letter.

5. Proofread and check; click Next to continue. *(61-d4)*

Current Date | Dr. Jeneve Dostorian, Instructor | Merritt College |

319 North Jackson Street | Jacksonville, FL 32256-0319

Your TIME+ personal manager software was shipped to you this morning by next-day air service. We realize that your time is valuable, and installing incorrect software is not a good use of your time. However, we are glad to learn that your students benefited from your demonstration of the software.

Easy-to-follow instructions for installing the new software over the current software are enclosed. You will also note on your copy of the invoice that you were billed originally for the TIME software. The TIME+ software is $99 more; however, we are pleased to provide it at no extra cost to you.

An additional bonus for choosing TIME+ is the monthly newsletter, *Managing Time with TIME+*. You should receive your first copy by the first of the month.

Sincerely, | Veronica Scrivner | Customer Service Manager

Lesson 101 | *Preparing Medical Reports*

Document Design

MEDICAL REPORT FORMS

Formats may vary slightly at different medical facilities; however, all medical reports contain similar sections: the heading, body, and conclusion. The **heading** contains pertinent information necessary to identify the patient. The heading is keyed at the top of the report; some headings are quite lengthy and can take up to one-third of the first page. The **body** of the report contains the observations, testing results, and/or findings. The **conclusion** includes the diagnosis and recommendations.

Applications

101-d1

Medical Report Form

 arondale logo and name

1. Use New from existing to open a copy of *arondale logo and name*. You will be creating the form for the psychological testing report shown on the next page.

2. Center the heading **PSYCHOLOGICAL TESTING** in all caps at approximately 2"; apply Heading 1 style.

3. Key the side headings at the left margin and apply Heading 2 style to each. Tap ENTER twice after each heading.

    Patient Name:

    Age:

    Date of Testing:

    Reason for Referral

    Tests Administered

    Testing Behavior

    Testing Results

    Summary and Recommendations

4. After keying the last heading, tap ENTER four times. Set a left underline tab at 3" for the physician's signature. Key the physician's name and title below the line. Apply the Strong style to the physician's name and title. Remove space afer paragraph.

    Lydia Hong, Psy.D.

    Licensed Psychologist

5. Check and close. (*101-d1*)

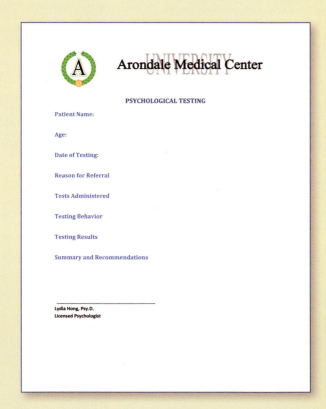

61-d5

Building Blocks

1. Key your personal title with first and last name, address, city, state, and ZIP Code on three lines. See sample shown in *61-d6* below.

2. Select the three lines and save as a Quick Part named **My Return Address**. Save it in the category Personal that you created in *61-drill2*. If the category is not on your computer, create the category now.

3. Edit your return address that is still on the screen by adding your middle initial. Select it and save the building block with the same name (*My Return Address*) and category (*Personal*).

4. Go to the Building Blocks Organizer, sort by Category, and locate the *Personal* building block you have created. Click on *My Return Address* and change the title to **My Address**.

5. Proofread and check; click Next to continue. You will use this building block in the next document.

61-d6

Single Envelope

1. Key a single envelope to the following address. Include your address as the return address using the Quick Part created in *61-d5*. *Hint:* Click in the return address box and key the name of the Quick Part or part of the name and tap F3.

2. Check and close. (*61-d6*)

Mr. David Rieder
1832 Nottingham Drive
Bloomington, IL 61704-1832

DOCUMENT 3 SOAP NOTE BODY

S	Pt complains of pain in the right knee; tripped and fell 6/17/201-.
O	Inflammation/hematoma on right anterior medial patella; decreased ROM right knee, with flexion, extension.
A	Diagnosis: Pre-patella bursitis. Treatment: R.I.C.E. on right patella anterior medial with ice pack twice a day for 4-6 weeks. Stay off right leg. ADL: rest knee; ice right anterior knee morn/night; elevate.
P	Stay off right leg. Rest; ice morn/night; elevate. Week 1: decrease pain; week 2: increase ROM.

QUICK ✔

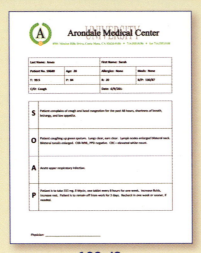

100-d2

WORKPLACE SUCCESS

DARRIN KLIMEK/DIGITAL VISION (RF)/JUPITER IMAGES

Confidentiality

Information contained in a patient's record is confidential and should not be revealed without the patient's consent unless required by law. Confidentiality must be protected in order for patients to feel comfortable about revealing personal information. Health professionals are obligated to report findings of the following nature:

- A patient has threatened another person, and there is reason to believe that the threat may be carried out.

- Knife and gunshot wounds and injuries that may indicate child abuse must be reported.

- Communicable diseases, such as AIDS, hepatitis, and sexually transmitted diseases, must be reported.

Lesson 62 | Multiple-Page Letters

Skill Building

62b Textbook Keying

Key each line once; concentrating on using good keying techniques. Tap ENTER twice after each 2-line group.

az
1 Zen and Ozzie zealously played the anthem in the Aztec Jazz band.
2 Batz went to Phoenix, Arizona, to take a math quiz he had missed.

by
3 Boyd drove by the Blue Bayou to bypass the roadblocks at the Bay.
4 By daybreak, Mary will stop by to bake a birthday cake for Jayne.

cx
5 Please carry the X-ray from exit C to exit X for Cece and Xavier.
6 Carol can meet Xian at the exit doors following the movie Exodus.

dw
7 Don walked the dog at dawn when he dwelled in his downtown condo.
8 Did Dwight drive Wendy to the new drive-in or the new drive-thru?

figures
9 The 12 teams spent $3,489.00 on groceries for the 567 boy scouts.
10 Judy's 13 puzzles had 60,789 pieces, but 524 pieces were missing.

| 1 | 2 | 3 | 4 | 5 | 6 | 7 | 8 | 9 | 10 | 11 | 12 | 13 |

Document Design

62c

KEYBOARDING PRO DELUXE 2

References/Document Formats/ Letter with Special Parts

TWO-PAGE LETTERS

Letters that are more than one page in length require special layout considerations. Use letterhead paper for the first page only. For additional pages, use plain paper that matches the letterhead in quality and color. Be sure that there are at least two lines of text from the final paragraph of the body on the last page with the closing lines. Study the full-page model on pages 304–305.

To format multi-page letters:

1. Position the date on the first page approximately 2" from the top of the page. Be sure the date begins 0.5" below the letterhead.
2. Begin the text on the second and succeeding pages at 1".
3. Create a header ❶ that includes the recipient's name, page number, and date on separate lines, and suppress the header on the first page.

December 1, 2010

Dr. Kristin Morris
529 Fifth Street
Sacramento, CA 94203-8571

Dear Dr. Morris

Dr. Kristin Morris ❶
Page 2
December 1, 2010

Please send a reply by the end of the week to give us ample time to process your request. I look forward to serving your technology needs.

1. Use New from existing to create a new document using *100-d1*.

2. Fill in the form with the information for Document 2. **Note:** *Pt* is the abbreviation for patient. Spell out the word *patient* when keying the notes.

3. Proofread and check; click Next to continue. (*100-d2*)

4. Repeat the above steps for Document 3 (*100-d3*).

5. Check and close. (*100-d3*)

Field Names	Document 2	Document 3
Last Name	Jones	Pham
First Name	Sarah	Loriana
Patient No.	10680	31048
Age	20	27
Allergies	None	Bee stings
Meds	None	None
T	99.5	98.5
P	84	62
R	20	15
B/P	130/87	112/72
C/O	Cough	Pain in right knee
Date	6/9/201-	6/21/201-

DOCUMENT 2 SOAP NOTE BODY

S	Pt complains of cough and head congestion for the past 48 hours, shortness of breath, lethargy, and low appetite.
O	Pt coughing up green sputum. Lungs clear, ears clear. Lymph nodes enlarged bilateral neck. Bilateral tonsils enlarged. CXR-WNL, PPD negative. CBC—elevated white count.
A	Acute upper respiratory infection.
P	Pt is to take 333 mg. E-Mycin, one tablet every 8 hours for one week. Increase fluids, increase rest. Pt is to remain off from work for 3 days. Recheck in one week or sooner, if needed.

SPECIAL LETTER PARTS

Two additional letter parts are introduced in this lesson. Adding special letter parts may cause the letter to move farther down the page, so always preview the letter for attractive placement. If necessary, move the date higher on the page. Be sure the date begins 0.5" below the letterhead.

A **postscript**, often used to emphasize information or to gain attention as in a sales letter, is keyed one blank line below the last notation. Do not begin with *PS*.

A **mailing notation** such as FACSIMILE, OVERNIGHT, CERTIFIED, SPECIAL DELIVERY, or REGISTERED provides a record of how the letter was sent. Other notations such as CONFIDENTIAL or PERSONAL indicate how the recipient should treat the letter.

Key special notations in UPPERCASE at the left margin one line below the date. On the envelope, notations that affect postage right-aligned below the stamp (about line 1.3"). Key envelope on-arrival notations, such as Confidential or Personal, below the return address (about line 1").

> John Mastrangelo, President
>
> xx
>
> Enclosure
>
> Use modified block for whenever

> December 14, 201-
>
> CERTIFIED
>
> Attention Division 2
> Clinard Security Services
> 207 Hollyhill Avenue
> Downers Grove, IL 60515-0935
>
> Ladies and Gentlemen

To add notations to an envelope:

1. Click the Add to Document button.

2. Position the insertion point one line space below the return address or about 1". Key the recipient's notation—e.g., CONFIDENTIAL—at the left margin.

3. Position the insertion point on about 1.3". Click the Align Text Right button. Key the mailing notation, e.g., CERTIFIED.

Dwight Reed
209 North Palm Street
Maysville, KY 41056-2332

1" CONFIDENTIAL ←———————————— Mailing notation ————————————→ CERTIFIED 1.3"

Attention Division 2
Clinard Security Services
207 Hollyhill Avenue
Downers Grove, IL 60515-0935

1. Click the Paragraph Dialog Box Launcher to display Indents and Spacing tab. Click the Tabs button at the bottom of the dialog box.
2. Key the tab position in the Tab stop position box. Select the desired alignment.
3. Under Leader, select option 4.
4. Click the Set button so that the tab setting displays in the Tab stop position box.
5. Repeat steps 1–4 for each tab that needs to be set, then OK.

DRILL 1   USING THE UNDERLINE TAB

1. Set a left, underline tab at 2.75".
2. Set a left tab, with no leaders at 3.0".
3. Set a right, underline tab at 6.5".
4. Turn on Show/Hide. Key **Name**, tap Space Bar, and then tap TAB twice.
5. Key **Address** and tap Space Bar; then tap TAB. Tap ENTER.
6. Key **Work Phone** and **Cell Phone** with an underscore following each.
7. Proofread and check; click Next to continue. (*100-drill1*)

Applications

100-d1

Create SOAP Note form

 arondale letterhead

1. Use New from existing to create a new document using *arondale letterhead*.
2. Create a table at approximately 2" for the patient's vital signs. Bold the text and change the row height to .4"; align text center left.

Last Name:		First Name:	
Patient No.	Age:	Allergies:	Meds:
T:	P:	R:	B/P:
C/O:		Date:	

3. Create a table for the SOAP notes. Make the letters *SOAP* 26 point and bold. Make each row height 1.25". Center-align the letters.
4. Select column B and change the alignment to Align Center Left; text will be centered vertically in the box when the note is keyed.
5. Modify the footer to make the tab at 3.25" a center underline tab. Place the physician's signature line in the footer. (See page 523.)
6. Preview the document and adjust vertical placement as needed.
7. Proofread and check; click Next to continue. (*100-d1*)

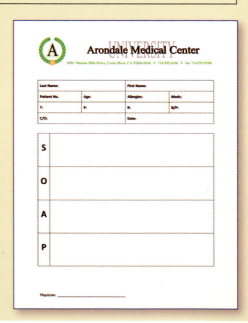

BETHANY ISNER

598 Garden Street, Apartment 25 ▪ Carlsbad, NM 88220-1001 ▪ 575-555-0109 ▪ bisner@fhsc.edu

Current date

CERTIFIED Mailing notation in UPPERCASE

Dr. Denton Dulaney, Chairperson
Curriculum Specialist Search Committee
Lynn State University
323 University Avenue
Santa Fe, NM 87507-1742

Re: Position #1839-13 Reference line

Dear Dr. Dulaney:

It is my pleasure to apply for the position of curriculum specialist as advertised in the *Bulletin of Educational Positions*. As you can see from my enclosed resume, I have extensive experience in the area of curriculum design and instruction. I am excited about the prospect of using my knowledge and experience in this area to strengthen your program.

In my current position with the Forest Hills School District, I am responsible for overseeing the curriculum development of all business education programs at the secondary level throughout the district. I meet regularly with secondary teachers, content specialists, advisory boards, industry representatives, and state legislators. These contacts provide me with a variety of viewpoints concerning the construction of curriculum. Without considering all of the available sources of input, it would be impossible to develop a curriculum that would address the needs of today's workforce.

In addition to supervising curriculum development, during the past five years I have been loaned to three other school districts to help with their curriculum development. Each assignment gave me the opportunity to use and expand my expertise in my field. These experiences in particular are significant when considering the knowledge base that I can bring to the classroom.

I also have classroom experience at the secondary level. After obtaining my bachelor's degree, I taught business education for Finton Public Schools. During the five years that I held this position, I completed both my master's and doctoral degrees. After completing the degrees, I taught for two years at Shadowland Community College. These invaluable experiences of developing curriculum for and teaching in both secondary and postsecondary schools will make it possible for me to guide curriculum development for the state of New Mexico to a point where teachers are prepared to excel at whatever teaching level they seek.

Lesson 100 | *SOAP Notes*

Document Design

100b

SOAP NOTES

All medical offices keep recorded notes of the patient's office visit, which are commonly called SOAP notes. SOAP notes contain the patient's complaints, the physician's findings, and the physician's assessment and plan for treatment. The letters *S O A P* stand for Subjective, Objective, Assessment, and Plan.

S—SUBJECTIVE (what the patient tells the physician)

O—OBJECTIVE (the physician's findings as a result of a physical exam or evaluation)

A—ASSESSMENT (the physician's diagnosis or impression of the problem)

P—PLAN (the planned treatment for the patient)

Physician signature line in footer

Arondale Medical Center

8501 Mission Hills Drive, Costa Mesa, CA 92626-0186 ◆ 714.555.0186 ◆ fax 714.555.0188

Last Name:		First Name:	
Patient No.	Age:	Allergies:	Meds:
T:	P:	R:	B/P:
C/O:		Date:	

S	
O	
A	
P	

Physician: _____

Command Review

100c

SET UNDERLINE TAB

Home/Paragraph/Indents and Spacing/Tabs

Leader tabs, which are most often used to guide the reader's eye across the page, can also be used to create the underlines for signatures. The advantage of using an underline tab to create underlines is all of your underlines can align evenly. Using the underscore key on the top row of the keyboard would be more time consuming and may not result in underlines evenly aligned at the right.

Dr. Dulaney, I look forward to hearing from you to discuss your employment needs. I can be reached at 505-555-0199 Monday through Friday. Your advertised position and my curriculum development experiences certainly appear to be a good fit.

Sincerely,

Dr. Bethany Isner

xx

Enclosure

c   Dr. Owen Strickland

Please view my teaching portfolio at www.teachingfolios.com/bisner. Postscript

Pneumonia Vaccine Recommended

A pneumonia shot is highly recommended for all adults 65 years of age and older who have not had this vaccine. Individuals between the ages of 2 and 65 with chronic medical conditions who have not had this vaccine should also get this shot. The pneumonia vaccine prevents the most common cause of bacterial pneumonia that can result in hospitalization or death.

Disease Surveillance Update

The table below contains a summary of the surveillance data obtained from county health departments in 2010. No incidences of Congenital Rubella Syndrome or Rubella were reported in the state during the 2010 year.

Disease	Age Groups		
	0-4 Years	5-17 Years	18+ Years
Hepatitis A	123	305	534
Hepatitis B	83	215	350
Measles	25	47	13
Pertussis	305	278	153
Tetanus	17	31	43

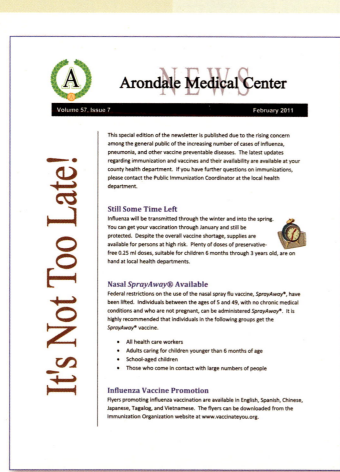

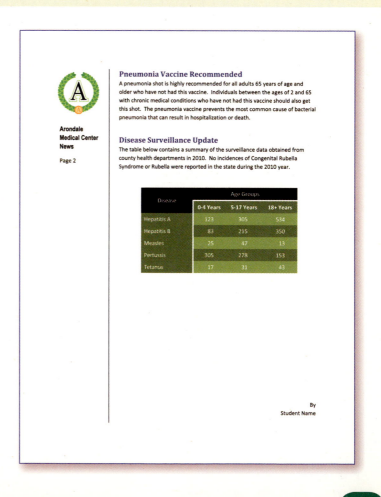

DRILL 1

ENVELOPE WITH NOTATIONS

 barrington

1. In the open document, key the mailing notation **CERTIFIED** one line below the date.

2. Create an envelope and add to the document.

3. Position the insertion point at about 1.3" on the envelope and click the Align Text Right button. Key the mailing notation **CERTIFIED**.

4. Proofread and check; click Next to continue. (*62-drill1*)

DRILL 2

ENVELOPE WITH NOTATIONS

 barrington

1. In the open document, key the mailing notation **CONFIDENTIAL** one line below the date.

2. Create an envelope and add to the document.

3. Position the insertion point at about 1" on the envelope and key the mailing notation **CONFIDENTIAL** at the left margin.

4. Proofread and check; click Next to continue. (*62-drill2*)

Applications

62–d1

Two-Page Letter

1. Key the two-page letter as shown on pages 304–305. Note the illustration of many of the special letter parts learned in this module.

2. Create a header to include the three required items of a multiple-page header. Tap ENTER once after the date to leave one blank line between the header and the letter. Suppress the header on the first page.

3. Create an envelope and add the mailing notation **CERTIFIED**.

4. Proofread and check; click Next to continue. (*62-d1*)

62–d2

Edit Letter

 franz

1. Format the letter as a modified block letter with mixed punctuation.

2. Position the dateline appropriately.

3. Add the following special letter parts:

   Subject line: **Automated Test Development and Generation System**

   Copy notation: **Susan Wyman** (*Hint:* Set left tab appropriately.)

   Blind copy notation: **Crystal Hager**

   Postscript: Move the last sentence of the letter to the appropriate location for a postscript.

4. Add an appropriate header for the second page and suppress it on the first page.

5. Create an envelope and add to the document.

6. Proofread and check; click Next to continue. (*62-d2*)

62–d3

Envelope

1. Create an envelope for Crystal Hager, the recipient of a blind copy in *62-d2*. The address is **Ms. Crystal Hager, 209 Sweet Acre Drive, Decatur, AL 35601-4892**.

2. Add the envelope to the document. Add the mailing notation **CONFIDENTIAL**.

3. Check and close. (*62-d3*)

9. Format and key the table as shown on the second page. Use a decimal tab to align numbers. Change the height of all the rows to .3". Apply Dark List – Accent 3 table style. Center the text vertically in the rows. Drag the Table Move handle to move the table so that it appears centered in the second column.

10. Tap ENTER 10 times to move the insertion point to the bottom of the page. Key a byline right-aligned at the bottom of the page. Remove the space after paragraph between the lines in the byline.

11. Place the insertion point in the left column on page 2; tap ENTER 14 times. Copy the logo from the banner and place it at the top of the left column. Key **Arondale Medical Center News** using Arial Narrow font. Place the text in bold and 12 point.

12. Click on the paragraph marker below **News** and key **Page 2**.

13. Check and close. (*99-d3*)

This special edition of the newsletter is published due to the rising concern among the general public of the increasing number of cases of influenza, pneumonia, and other vaccine preventable diseases. The latest updates regarding immunization and vaccines and their availability are available at your county health department. If you have further questions on immunizations, please contact the Public Immunization Coordinator at the local health department.

Still Some Time Left

Influenza will be transmitted through the winter and into the spring. You can get your vaccination through January and still be protected. Despite the overall vaccine shortage, supplies are available for persons at high risk. Plenty of doses of preservative-free 0.25 ml doses, suitable for children 6 months through 3 years old, are on hand at local health departments.

Nasal *SprayAway*® Available

Federal restrictions on the use of the nasal spray flu vaccine, *SprayAway*®, have been lifted. Individuals between the ages of 5 and 49, with no chronic medical conditions and who are not pregnant can be administered *SprayAway*®. It is highly recommended that individuals in the following groups get the *SprayAway*® vaccine.

- All health care workers
- Adults caring for children younger than 6 months of age
- School-aged children
- Those who come in contact with large numbers of people

Influenza Vaccine Promotion

Flyers promoting influenza vaccination are available in English, Spanish, Chinese, Japanese, Tagalog, and Vietnamese. The flyers can be downloaded from the Immunization Organization website at www.vaccinateyou.org.

TIP

Registered Trademark

To add a registered trademark, follow the path below. Insert/Symbols/Symbol/ More Symbols/Special Characters.

If the superscript returns to normal font when you apply a style, select the registered trademark and reapply the superscript effect (Home/Font/Superscript).

Lesson 63 | Correspondence Review and Editing

WARMUP

Lessons/63a Warmup

63b Textbook Keying

Key each line once; concentrating on using good keying techniques. Tap ENTER twice after each 4-line group.

left hand

1 crazed bass averages dessert cedar badger affect braggart detects
2 beware greatest feet effects gag faster bazaar assess drawers ads
3 grease estate carafe awarded exerted get careers agrees beads ear
4 In my opinion, today anyone can play pool or monopoly with Jimmy.

right hand

5 honk million kimono pumpkin yolk poplin oil lumpy homily hoop lip
6 pill nylon million puppy uphill yoyo ninny opinion lion polio mum
7 Jimmy minimum pupil holly imply kinky monopoly pool union you ohm
8 Their neighbor's mangy dog and lame duck slept by a box of rocks.

Skill Building

A   ALL LETTERS

63c Timed Writing

1. Key one 3' timing on the entire writing.
2. Key one 5' timing on the entire writing.

	gwam	3'	5'

Surrogate grandparents and pet therapy might not be the types of terms that you expect to find in a medical journal, but they are concepts that are quite popular with senior citizens. Two of the most common problems experienced by senior citizens who do not live with or near a family member are loneliness and the craving to feel needed and loved. — 4 / 2; 9 / 5; 13 / 8; 18 / 11; 22 / 13; 23 / 14

Senior citizens who are healthy and who are stable mentally often can have a high-quality relationship with deprived children who do not have grandparents of their own. They often have time to spare and the desire to give these needy children extra attention and help with their school work and other needs. At first, it may seem that children gain the most from being with seniors. However, it soon becomes evident that the surrogate grandparents tend to benefit as much or even more than the children. — 27 / 16; 32 / 19; 36 / 22; 41 / 24; 45 / 27; 49 / 30; 54 / 32; 57 / 34

Both assisted-living and total-care residential facilities are using pets to keep senior citizens from feeling alone. In those cases in which a single person lives in one of the housing units, the pet can help to reduce the feeling of being alone and lonely. Even patients in the total-care units who do not communicate very much become animated and will talk to a very gentle pet brought in on a regular basis to play with the patients. — 61 / 36; 66 / 39; 71 / 42; 76 / 45; 80 / 47; 85 / 50; 87 / 51

3' | 1 | 2 | 3 | 4
5' | 1 | 2 | 3

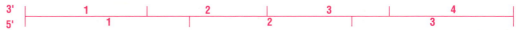

99-d2

Memorandum

 arondale memorandum

1. Use New from existing to create a new document using *arondale memorandum*.
2. Key the memo below; supply all necessary memo parts.
3. Check and close. (*99-d2*)

TO: Clinic Staff
FROM: Dr. Sabrina Rodriguez, Immunization Coordinator
SUBJECT: Procedures for Ordering Vaccines

Requests for vaccines need to be submitted on the O.C. Vaccine Order Form. The facility name that should be put on the order form is Community Clinic, Quality Care Medical Center. The authorized signature is Dr. Matthew Steward. Always review the completed form with Dr. Steward before asking him to sign the form.

Follow the instructions on the form for faxing the order to the Orange County Health Department. Refrigerator logs must be faxed with the order forms. If there are no logs, they will not send the vaccine. A vaccination record for the clinic needs to be sent to the health department each month.

Mary Wilson, at the Division of Disease Control, is in charge of disbursing the vaccine to our clinic. If you have questions regarding the order, you may call her at 714-555-0122 or e-mail her at mary.wilson@ddcontrol.gov.

99-d3

Medical Newsletter

 arondale banner heading

1. In the open document, turn on Show/Hide.
2. Place the insertion point on the ¶ below the section break. Set up the columns:
   a. Click Page Layout/Page Setup/Columns and choose More Columns.
   b. In the Columns dialog box, choose 2 columns. Deselect the box for Equal column width.
   c. Key 1" for the width of column 1. Click in the Width box for column 2; it automatically changes to 5".
   d. Place a check mark in the Line between box if necessary. Click OK.
3. Use WordArt to key **It's Not Too Late!** in the left column. Change the text wrapping to Square.
4. Rotate the title and stretch it to attractively fit in the column; see illustration on page 522. Change the Text Fill color and the Text Outline color to brown (More Fill Colors). Change the font on the WordArt to Times New Roman.
5. Click the insertion point on the ¶ in column 1. Insert a column break (Page Layout/ Breaks). The cursor moves to the top of the second column. If the title moves to the second column, move it back to the first column.
6. Key the text in the second column. Apply Heading 1 style to the side headings.
7. Insert a clip art of a clock in the second paragraph and apply Tight text wrapping. Size the picture as needed.
8. Continue keying all the text on the first page. When the cursor moves to the top of the first column on page 2, insert a column break. You may need to insert the column break twice to move the cursor to the second column. Key the text in the second column on page 2.

Applications

63-d1

Edit Memo

TIP

Refer to page REF4 to review proofreaders' marks.

1. Insert the Quick Part memo heading titled *memo heading + letterhead.* If the Quick Part is not available, key the memo heading.
2. Key the memo below to **Ann Melnick, Zackery Minga,** and **Naketa Patel** from you. Key each name on a separate line. Remove extra space between lines.
3. The subject is **Revised Schedule for Kenneth Phelps**.
4. Key the meal functions at the left margin and tap TAB before keying each name. Then center the lines.
5. Key **Attachment** for the enclosure notation.
6. Proofread and check; click Next to continue. *(63-d1)*

A copy of the final interview

~~The newly revised~~ schedule ~~for Kenneth Phelps~~ is attached. To involve more of

your in the interview process with Kenneth Phelps, we have added the *one additional person*

~~following individuals~~ to the various meal ~~events~~. *functions* Please refer to the list shown below.

Monday, 11:30 a.m. Lunch	Zackery Minga
Monday, 6:30 p.m. Dinner	Naketa Patel
Tuesday, 7:30 a.m. Breakfast	Ann Melnick

Please take time to get to know Kenneth and to evaluate his credentials.

63-d2

Block Letter

1. Format the letter in block style with open punctuation.
2. Add mailing notation **CERTIFIED** and subject line **Annual Craft Fair Booth**.
3. Create an envelope with the notation CERTIFIED positioned appropriately.
4. Proofread and check; click Next to continue. *(63-d2)*

January 10, 201- | Ms. Denise McWhorter | HandPrints, Inc. |	11
92 E. Cresswell Road | Selden, NY 11784-0293 | Dear Ms. McWhorter	24
Booth 24, your first choice, had been reserved for you	35
for the annual craft fair on May 15-17. Your booth was ex-	46
tremely popular last year, and we are very pleased to have you	59
participate in the fair again this year.	67
Our standard agreement form is enclosed. Please sign	78
the form and return it to us by April 15. Your booths will	90
have a large table and a minimum of two chairs. If you need	102
anything else for the booth, please let us know prior to the	114
opening of the fair.	119
Sincerely | Jennifer A. Reed | President | xx | Enclosure	129

99-d1

Modified Block Letter

arondale letterhead

1. Use New from existing to create a new document using *arondale letterhead.* Key the letter below in modified block style with open punctuation. Supply all necessary letter parts.

2. Center the address lines for O. C. Good Samaritan Medical Center.

3. The letter is from David Dostourian, M.D., President.

4. Proofread and check; click Next to continue. *(99-d1)*

Dr. Sabrina Rodriguez, M.D. | Immunization Coordinator | Quality Care Medical Center | 5252 Superior Road | Santa Ana, CA 92701-3088

Arondale Medical Center has an agreement with the Orange County Health Department which enables us to obtain vaccinations and supplies at no cost. These include Hepatitis A and B, influenza, and pneumococcal vaccines. The agreement requires that we keep detailed and accurate paperwork pertaining to the storage and administration of the vaccine.

The vaccine is currently being stored at:

O. C. Good Samaritan Medical Center
c/o Dr. Abrahim Jordan
1560 Broadway Avenue
Santa Ana, CA 92701-1234

The refrigerator containing the vaccine is in the infusion room. The temperature is to be measured twice a day and recorded on the form; use the thermometer in the door of the refrigerator for measuring. It is the duty of the clinic coordinator to ensure that this log is kept current. Under no circumstances should false values be added to the chart.

This agreement with Orange County Health Department provides us with an excellent opportunity to directly help the medically underserved population in the area. I am confident that you will maintain a strong relationship with the health department.

QUICK ✓

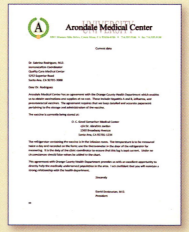

99-d1

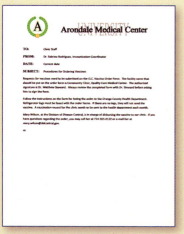

99-d2

63-d3

Modified Block Letter

1. Format the modified block letter with mixed punctuation. Position the date appropriately. Make the revisions marked on the letter. Add the correct salutation.
2. Add the reference notation **Internship #100-22**.
3. Send a blind copy to the intern mentioned in the letter.
4. Add the following postscript one line below the last notation. Remove the hyperlink.

   Please take a few minutes to review Paul's work at www.merrittcollege.edu/librarytour.htm.
5. Create an envelope with the notation **CONFIDENTIAL** positioned appropriately.
6. Proofread and check; click Next to continue. (63-d3)

Current date │CONFIDENTIAL │Ms. Louise Brown, Director │Merritt College │

750 East Wolfe Road │Vienna, WV 25105-0750

    Thank you for the opportunity to participate as an employer
    one of your technology majors,
in your internship program. Paul Zieger worked 90 hours this

summer and was an excellent *~~edition~~ addition* to our department. His

final project was a*n* interactive tutorial of the Merritt College

library. This tutorial provides an electronic tour of the

library, including the layout of the library *its holdings,* and specific

directions on locating certain materials. ¶Paul has agreed to work

(for us *part-time*) during the fall semester. Our initial plans *~~is~~ are*

for him to work with faculty in setting up and conduct*ing* private

demonstrations for classes. In addition, he will write a

second *#* tutorial for the graduate library.
¶ *Please send another excellent intern next summer.*
Sincerely │Daniel E. Romano, Director │Library Services │xx

63-d4

Edit Letter

1. Open *63-d2*. Delete Ms. Denise McWhorter as the recipient of the letter. Add the attention line **Attention Marketing Manager**.
2. Change the salutation to **Dear Marketing Manager**.
3. Create an appropriate envelope and add to the document. Click Change Document to override the current envelope. Add the mailing notation CERTIFIED on the envelope.
4. Check and close. (63-d4)

Lesson 99 | Medical Correspondence

Document Design

99b

MEDICAL CORRESPONDENCE

You will be keying medical correspondence for Arondale Medical Center. The medical center is affiliated with the Arondale University College of Medicine. The medical center is operated by private medical practitioners and university staff. You will be keying letters and reports to patients, other medical firms, government, and regulatory agencies. Arondale Medical Center sends informational newsletters and brochures to community members promoting health awareness and disease prevention.

New Command

99c

TIP

Keyboarding Pro DELUXE 2 users will need to launch *Word* manually to complete 99-drill1. For the rest of the activities that use the New from Existing Document feature, launch *Word* to use this feature or select the activities in *Keyboarding Pro DELUXE 2* to have the files open automatically.

NEW FROM EXISTING DOCUMENT

New from existing

If you wish to use the same document repeatedly, you can use the New from Existing Document feature to create new documents based on an existing document. When this feature is used, *Word* makes a copy of the existing document and places it in a new document window. This allows you to save the new document under a different name. The original document remains intact. You can use the New from existing feature repeatedly with the same document; just remember to give the copy a different name.

To create a new document from an existing document:

File/New/New from Existing

1. The New from Existing Document dialog box displays.
2. Select the file that is to be used to create a new document.
3. Click the Create New button. A copy of the document displays on the screen; save it using a different name.

DRILL 1

USE NEW FROM EXISTING TO CREATE NEW DOCUMENT

 arondale logo and name

1. Click File and then New. Click New from existing to display the New from Existing Document dialog box.

2. Select *arondale logo and name*; then click the Create New button.

3. A copy of the file displays. Notice the title bar displays an unnamed document.

4. Turn on Show/Hide; click the insertion point on the last paragraph marker. Key your name.

5. Proofread and check; click Next to continue. (*99-drill1*)

6. Use New from existing to open a copy of *arondale logo and name* again. Notice that a new unnamed document displays; your name should not be displayed on this copy.

7. Proofread and check; click Next to continue.

Lesson 64 | Assessment

Skill Building

64b Timed Writing

Key two 3' timed writings.

		gwam	3'	5'

What is a college education worth today? If you asked that | 4 | 2
question to a random sample of people, you would get a wide range of | 9 | 5
responses. Many would respond that you cannot quantify the worth of | 13 | 8
a bachelor's degree. They quickly stress that many factors other | 18 | 11
than wages enhance the quality of life. They tend to focus on the | 22 | 13
benefits of sciences and liberal arts and the appreciation they | 26 | 16
develop for things that they would never have been exposed to if | 31 | 18
they had not attended college. | 33 | 20

Data show, though, that you can place a value on a college | 37 | 22
education—at least in respect to wages earned. Less than twenty | 41 | 25
years ago, a high school graduate earned only about fifty percent | 45 | 27
of what a college graduate earned. Today, that number is quite | 50 | 30
different. The gap between the wages of a college graduate and | 54 | 32
the wages of a high school graduate has more than doubled in the | 58 | 35
last twenty years. | 59 | 36

The key factor in economic success is education. The new | 63 | 38
jobs that pay high wages require more skills and a college degree. | 68 | 41
Fortunately, many high school students do recognize the value of | 72 | 43
getting a degree. Far more high school graduates are going to | 76 | 46
college than ever before. They know that the best jobs are jobs | 81 | 48
for knowledge workers and those jobs require a high level of skill. | 85 | 51

```
3'  |    1    |    2    |    3    |    4    |
5'  |      1      |      2      |      3      |
```

Applications

64c

Assessment

When you complete a document, proofread it, check the spelling, and preview for placement. When you are completely satisfied, click the Continue button to move to the next document. Click the Check button when you are ready to error-check the test. Review and/or print the document analysis results.

 Continue

 Check

1. Open *98-d4* and insert the following information in each bookmark.
2. Set a left tab at .38" to align the address for the Recipient bookmark; remove space after paragraph.
3. Check and close. (*98-d5* and *98-d6*)

Bookmark name	Document 5	Document 6
Name	Linda Matsayama	Justin Lopez
Position	President of Matsayama Tools Inc., a California Corporation	Marketing Director of Acme Tools, a privately owned company
Address	5200 Katella Avenue, Los Alamitos, CA 90720-6314	7901 Holder Street, Cypress, CA 90631-9215
Residence	9342 Primrose Circle, Seal Beach, CA 90740-2875	3602 W. Third Street, Los Angeles, CA 90020-9215
Recipient	LINDA MATSAYAMA 9342 Primrose Circle Seal Beach, CA 90740-2875	JUSTIN LOPEZ 3602 W. Third Street Los Angeles, CA 90020-9215

QUICK ✓

Index No. 12870

NOTICE OF MOTION

      PLEASE TAKE NOTICE that upon the annexed affidavit of LOUISE TROMBLEY, sworn to the 23rd day of October, 201-, and upon all the papers and proceedings filed heretofore and had herein, the undersigned will move the Court at a Special Term to be held in and for the County of Orange, at the Courthouse in the City of Santa Ana, on the 15th day of November, 201-, at 10:30 o'clock in the forenoon, or as soon thereafter as counsel may be heard, for an order, pursuant to CPLR Section 7202(b) directing Linda Matsayama, as President of Matsayama Tools Inc., a California Corporation, of 5200 Katella Avenue, Los Alamitos, CA 90720-6314, as an individual residing at 9342 Primrose Circle, Seal Beach, CA 90740-2875, as a witness before trial, to submit to an oral examination at the offices of KRAMMER, GONZALEZ, & NGUYEN, 55 Civic Center Drive, Santa Ana, CA 92704-1288, on a day in December, 201-, to be fixed by this Court, concerning all matters necessary to the prosecution of this action, upon the ground that the witness is intimately involved with the defendant regarding the subject matter of this action and can provide testimony vital to plaintiff's case.

      PLEASE TAKE FURTHER NOTICE that pursuant to the CPLR Rule 8829(a) you are required to serve upon the undersigned at least five (5) days before the return date of this motion any answering affidavits.

                    KRAMMER, GONZALEZ, & NGUYEN
                    Attorneys for Plaintiff
                    55 Civic Center Drive
                    Santa Ana, CA 92701-0485
                    714-555-0110

TO: LINDA MATSAYAMA
      9342 Primrose Circle
      Seal Beach, CA 90740-2875

98-d5

64-d1

Memo

1. Key the memo to **Marvell Hodges**, from **Christina Hagberg, Coordinator**. Use **July 27, 201-** as the date and **August 8–9 Workshop** as the subject.

2. Continue to the next document. (64-d1)

Over seventy-five teachers have preregistered to participate in the Integrating Technology Workshop scheduled for August 8–9 at Ferguson Community College. We are very pleased with the overwhelming response to this offering.

The workshop will begin at 8 a.m. and conclude by 5 p.m. each day. Please come to Room T38 of the Continuing Education Building. You may make your housing reservation today by calling 601-555-0142. I look forward to your participating in this outstanding learning experience.

64-d2

Two-Page Block Letter

1. Key the following letter in block style with open punctuation. Position the date appropriately. Add all necessary letter parts. Mark the letter as **CONFIDENTIAL**.

2. Add the subject line **Plant Expansion to Mexico**. (Omit Subject.)

3. Send a copy to the three members of the management team listed in the letter.

4. Insert a header for the second page. Do not print the header on the first page.

5. Create an envelope and add to the letter. Add the appropriate notation.

6. Continue to the next document. (64-d2)

December 1, 201- | Ms. Candace Brennan | Brennan and Associates | 2202 Kimbrough Street | Suite A | Chesterfield, MO 63017-0420

Final approval for plant expansion out of the country has been received. The purchase of an already existing plant was decided to be cost effective. The sites being considered are Japan, Mexico, and France.

Visits will be scheduled for each of the three proposed sites. The first visit will be on January 10–12 to Voz del Cielo in Juarez, Mexico. An itinerary is enclosed for your planning purposes. Your responsibilities have been highlighted.

The small cellular phone production plant is located in Juarez, Mexico, about ten miles south of El Paso, Texas. The physical plant covers approximately 20,000 square feet and houses approximately one hundred employees.

The following management team will be meeting with us: Armando Cruz, president; Tito Gonzales, vice president of production; and Reuben Puente, vice president of marketing.

(continued)

1. Key the first two lines in bold; then tap ENTER. Change to double space. Key the remaining Notice of Motion. Indent paragraphs 1".

2. Replace the text shown in parentheses (including the parentheses) with a bookmark.

3. Tap ENTER after the last paragraph and return to 1.15 line spacing. Set a left tab at 4" and key the attorney signature block; remove space after paragraph. Key **TO:** at the left margin.

4. Proofread and check; click Next to continue. (*98-d4*)

Index No. 12870

NOTICE OF MOTION

Tap ENTER and change to double spacing

    PLEASE TAKE NOTICE that upon the annexed affidavit of LOUISE TROMBLEY, sworn to the 23rd day of October, 201-, and upon all the papers and proceedings filed heretofore and had herein, the undersigned will move the Court at a Special Term to be held in and for the County of Orange, at the Courthouse in the City of Santa Ana, on the 15th day of November, 201-, at 10:30 o'clock in the forenoon, or as soon thereafter as counsel may be heard, for an order, pursuant to CPLR Section 7202(b) directing (Name bookmark), as (Position bookmark), of (Address bookmark), as an individual residing at (Residence bookmark), as a witness before trial, to submit to an oral examination at the offices of KRAMMER, GONZALEZ, & NGUYEN, 55 Civic Center Drive, Santa Ana, CA 92704-1288, on a day in December, 201-, to be fixed by this Court, concerning all matters necessary to the prosecution of this action, upon the ground that the witness is intimately involved with the defendant regarding the subject matter of this action and can provide testimony vital to plaintiff's case.

    PLEASE TAKE FURTHER NOTICE that pursuant to the CPLR Rule 8829(a) you are required to serve upon the undersigned at least five (5) days before the return date of this motion any answering affidavits.

Tap ENTER

4" left tab

KRAMMER, GONZALEZ, & NGUYEN

Attorneys for Plaintiff

55 Civic Center Drive

Santa Ana, CA 92701-0485

714-555-0110

Tap ENTER twice

TO: (Recipient bookmark)

64–d2

continued

Three factors we must consider when preparing for this meeting are:

- Our counterparts have a different culture and customs.
- The meeting is in Mexico—not in the United States.
- We only have about three months to prepare for the meeting.

Your preparation for this visit is essential. Please begin your preparation by completing the following items:

1. Study the culture and customs of Mexico. Use the enclosed report prepared by Carlos Petrillo as a point of departure.
2. Study the book *An Easy Guide to Conversant Spanish*. Being familiar with the language will assist us in our negotiations.
3. Secure a passport. This official record will be required when we enter Mexico.

I look forward to working with you on this project.

Sincerely | Tony Wiest, President

64–d3

Modified Block Letter

1. Key the modified block letter with mixed punctuation. Use the current date. Supply necessary letter parts.
2. Check the test and close it. (*64-d3*)

Ms. Audra Meaux | 268 Marsalis Lane | Hot Springs, AR 71913-1004

Our professional staff finalized the Technology Task Force report requesting approval of four major technology enhancements for K-14. A draft copy is enclosed for your review. Please make any corrections and return the draft to us within one week so that the final report can be prepared.

The report will be sent special delivery to each school board member no later than Monday. This deadline must be followed if the item is to appear on the November 15 agenda. If we do not hear from you within one week, we will assume that you accept the draft as submitted.

Audra, thank you for your willingness to serve on the Technology Task Force.

Ryan Messamore | NTA President

 BOOKMARK

www.collegekeyboarding.com
Module 10 Practice Quiz

1. Open *98-drill1*.

2. Use the Go To command to find each bookmark, and insert the text shown in the table at the right. Note that the bookmarks shown in uppercase should have the replacement text also keyed in uppercase.

3. Proofread and check; click Next to continue. (*98-drill2*)

Go To the bookmark	Insert the following text
NAME	REBECCA PEREZ
NAME_AGAIN	REBECCA PEREZ
Address	One Main Street, Irvine, CA, 96203-4865
HUSBAND_NAME	MATEO PEREZ
HUSBAND_AGAIN	MATEO PEREZ
EXECUTOR	GREGORY LEON

Applications

98-d1

Notary Form

1. Key the notary form shown below. Replace the text that is in parentheses with bookmarks.

2. Tap ENTER two times and insert a right leader tab at 3" to create the signature line. Insert a left tab at 3.5" and key **(Seal)**.

3. Proofread and check; click Next to continue. (*98-d1*)

State of California

County of (Bookmark:County)

On (Bookmark:Date), before me, (Bookmark:Notary), personally appeared (Bookmark:Client), prove to me on the basis of satisfactory evidence to be the person whose name is subscribed to the within instrument and acknowledged to me that she executed the same in her authorized capacity and that by her signature on the instrument the person, or the entity upon behalf of which the person acted, executed the instrument.

WITNESS my hand and official seal.

Signature _____   (Seal)

98-d2 and 98-d3

Complete Notary Form

1. Open *98-d1* and insert the following information in each bookmark.

Bookmark	Document 2	Document 3
County	Orange	Los Angeles
Date	April 12, 201-	April 15, 201-
Notary	Robert Bayer, Vice President, Bank of Commerce	Andrew Park, Notary, Quicken Escrow Company
Client	Louise Ann Kruger	Mary Lou Chan

2. Proofread and check; click Next to continue. (*98-d2* and *98-d3*)

Tables

LEARNING OUTCOMES

- Create and format tables.
- Sort tables.
- Perform calculations in tables.
- Convert text and tables.
- Create documents with tables.
- Build keying speed and accuracy.

Lesson 65 | Table Layout Commands

New Commands

- Set Decimal Tabs
- Change Text Direction

KEYBOARDING PRO DELUXE 2

WARMUP

Lessons/65a Warmup

Skill Building

A   ALL LETTERS

gwam   3'

65b   Timed Writing

Key two 3' timed writings.

First-year college students are very eager about beginning the next	5
step in the journey after high school. Going away to college	9
offers many opportunities and challenges to these young students.	13
Choosing what time to attend classes, when to go to bed, when to get	18
up, what to eat each day, and how to spend their money seems fantastic	23
at an initial glance. But, wait, are these students adequately	27
prepared for the hard choices that come with these freedoms?	31
One major area in which students need help is in making good food	36
selections. Pizza, pasta, and macaroni and cheese do not make a wise	41
choice even if these foods are easy to make and affordable. Be sure	45
to have five fruits and vegetables each day and add some physical	50
activity in the schedule. Remember nutritious meals and exercise are	54
important to success in college.	56
Another problem area for students is money management. Having a	61
monthly budget will make it easier when deciding whether to go with	66
friends for an expensive meal, to go out for ice cream, to pay only	70
the minimum balance on the credit cards, or to spend student loans on	75
items that are not college expenses. Making wise decisions in these	79
important areas will be a big step toward success in college.	84

3' | 1 | 2 | 3 | 4 |

After bookmarks have been inserted in a document, you can use the Go To feature to move the insertion point to the specific bookmark. Bookmarks can be helpful when creating repetitive documents that contain variable information. **Note:** As a reminder to yourself, you may want to key a bookmark name in uppercase if the replacement text will also be keyed in uppercase.

To insert a bookmark:

Insert/Links/Bookmark

1. Click the insertion point at the position where the bookmark is to be inserted. Click Bookmark to display the Bookmark dialog box.

2. Key the name of the bookmark in the Bookmark name box.

3. Click the Add button. Repeat steps 1–3 for each bookmark to be inserted.

DRILL 1 **INSERT BOOKMARK** bookmark

1. Turn on Show/Hide.

2. Delete the text #1 bookmark. Create a bookmark named **NAME**.

3. Replace the text #2 bookmark with a bookmark named **NAME_AGAIN**. (Insert the underscore between words.)

4. Replace the text #3 bookmark with a bookmark named **Address**.

5. Replace the text #4 bookmark with a bookmark named **HUSBAND_NAME**.

6. Replace the text #5 bookmark with a bookmark named **HUSBAND_AGAIN**.

7. Replace the text #6 bookmark with a bookmark named **EXECUTOR**.

8. Proofread and check; click Next to continue. (*98-drill1*)

To use the bookmarks:

Home/Editing/Find/Go To

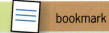

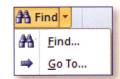

1. In the document in which you inserted bookmarks, click the Find drop-list arrow and select Go To. The Find and Replace dialog box displays with the Go To tab selected.

2. In the Go to what pane, select Bookmark.

3. Click the Enter bookmark name drop-list arrow and select the name of the bookmark. Click the Go To button.

4. Click Close. The insertion point displays at the position of the bookmark.

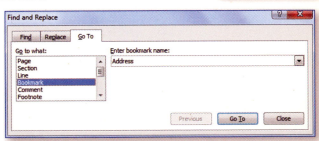

In this module, you will be using your knowledge of creating and editing tables to work with advanced table features such as inserting formulas, performing sorts, inserting graphics, and converting text to tables. In this lesson, you begin with a review of table layout options.

CHANGE TABLE LAYOUT

You will recall that once the table has been created, two additional tabs display at the top of the Ribbon; they are the Table Tools Design tab and the Table Tools Layout tab. The Table Tools Layout tab contains features that allow you to change the structure or layout of the table in the following ways.

Insert and Delete Rows and Columns

Table Tools Layout/Rows & Columns

Click the insertion point where the new row or column is to be inserted. If several rows or columns are to be inserted, select the number you want to insert. Then choose the desired Insert option.

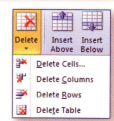

Click the insertion point in the row or column to be deleted. If more than one row or column is to be deleted, select them first. Click the Delete drop-list arrow and select the appropriate item to be deleted in the drop-down menu that displays.

Merge and Split Cells

Table Tools Layout/Merge/Merge Cells or Split Cells

The Merge Cells and Split Cells features make it possible to create complex table designs. Merge can join cells horizontally or vertically. A common use for the merge feature is to combine the cells in the first row of a table so the table heading can be positioned there.

Merge cells by selecting the cells to merge and clicking the Merge Cells command.

Cells in rows or columns can be split to create new columns or rows. A common use for this feature is to create multiple columns below a single cell. This allows for a heading that spans multiple columns as well as individual column headings below that heading.

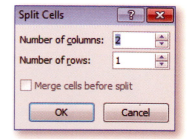

Split cells by clicking in the cell to be divided, or by selecting multiple cells to divide, and then clicking the Split Cells command. Enter the number of columns or rows into which the selected cell(s) will be divided.

Lesson 98 | Preparing Legal Documents

Communication

98b

1. Review the rules for number expression on page REF2 in the *Reference Guide*. The rules are also available under Communication Skills on the Reference tab of the *Keyboarding Pro DELUXE 2* software.

2. Key a corrected copy of the sentences at the right.

3. Proofread each sentence on the right for errors in number expression. Then key each sentence, correcting the error in it.

4. Proofread again to ensure that you did not make any other keying errors. Correct any errors you find.

5. Proofread and check; click Next to continue. *(98b)*

NUMBER EXPRESSION

1. The deposition was, by stipulation, continued today, April twenty-nine, at 2 o'clock p.m.

2. I, Mary Doe, hereby certify that on the tenth day of January, 2010, I was the official court reporter for the proceedings.

3. The occurrence took place on May twelve, 201- at approximately two a.m.

4. We inspect the office 3 or 4 times a week.

5. Mr. Brown moved that the board accept the bid of $one hundred twenty-seven thousand.

Document Design

98c

NOTICE OF MOTION

A Notice of Motion is a routinely generated document in a legal office. (See illustration in the Quick Check on page 517 and in the document to be keyed on page 516.) A Notice of Motion is an application for an Order addressed to the Court. Some states require that the Notice of Motion be keyed on a pleading form; other states will have it keyed on plain paper.

Documents that are routinely keyed in a legal office are often created as boilerplate documents. The data is inserted into the Notice of Motion by using the Bookmark and Go To Features. A Notice of Motion uses default margins.

New Command

98d

USING BOOKMARKS

A bookmark marks a location in a document so that you can quickly move the insertion point to the location. If more than one bookmark is inserted into a document, you will need to give each one a unique name. A bookmark name can include letters, numbers, and the underscore character. Do not include spaces in a bookmark name.

When you click in a single cell and increase column width or row height, all cells in that column increase in width or height.

Adjust Column Widths and Row Height

Table Tools Layout/Cell Size/Width or Height

Column widths can be adjusted by dragging column borders. Leave approximately 0.5" to 0.75" between the longest line and the border. Another way to adjust a column width to a precise value is to position the insertion point over a column border, press ALT, and click on the border. The column width displays in the Ruler; drag to adjust width.

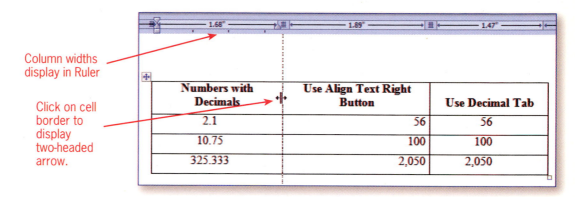

Column widths display in Ruler

Click on cell border to display two-headed arrow.

Numbers with Decimals	Use Align Text Right Button	Use Decimal Tab
2.1	56	56
10.75	100	100
325.333	2,050	2,050

Row height can also be adjusted by dragging the row border until the row is the desired height. Adjusting row height can make table text easier to read.

For more precision, use the commands in the Cell Size group to specify column width or row height. Click in a cell, or select multiple cells, and then use the spin arrows in the Cell Size group to increase or decrease column width or row height.

Change Text Alignment

Table Tools Layout/Alignment

The options in the Alignment group offer combinations of vertical and horizontal alignment that allow you to position text at the top, middle, or bottom of a table cell, as well as at the left, center, or right side of the cell.

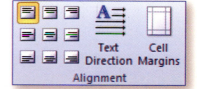

Change Table Alignment

Table Tools Layout/Table/Properties

If a table does not run the full width of the page, it is usually centered. Use the Center Alignment feature in the Table Properties dialog box to center the table horizontally on the page.

The Table Properties dialog box can also be used to set a width for the table. Place a check mark in the Preferred width checkbox and then key the desired table width in the Preferred width box, or use the spin arrows to set the width.

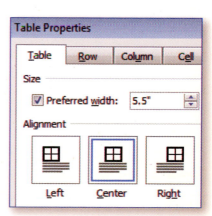

```
 1        PLEASE TAKE FURTHER NOTICE that plaintiff Henry Hurt is required to

 2   bring with him to the deposition the following records, documents, and

 3   things:

 4

 5        1. Any and all documents which substantiate the claim for property

 6           damage.

 7        2. Any and all documents which substantiate the claim for loss of

 8           earnings.

 9        3. All photographs which in any way relate to the subject matter of

10           this action.

11                                            Dated this June 1, 201-

12

13

14                                    _____
                                      BARBARA M. JOHNSON
15                                    NEWTON & JOHNSON
                                      Attorney for Defendants
16                                    JONATHAN MOVERS and
                                      LAUREL DELIVERIES
17

18

19

20

21

22

23

24

25

26


                           Notice of Deposition - 2
```

DECIMAL TABS

Decimal tabs can be used to align numbers containing decimals in a column as shown in column A in the table below. A decimal tab can also be used to right-align numbers in a column. You have used the Align Text Right button to right-align the numbers in the column. Using the Align Text Right button produces the result shown in column B. Column C shows the numbers right-aligned using a decimal tab. Setting a decimal tab allows you to keep the numbers right-aligned and make them appear centered in the column.

If the tab for the column needs to be moved, you must first select all the numbers in the column before moving the tab. Otherwise the change will only take place in the cell where the insertion point is positioned.

Numbers with Decimals	Use Align Text Right Button	Use Decimal Tab
2.1	56	56
10.75	100	100
325.333	2,050	2,050

To set decimal tab:

1. Key the table with the numbers left-aligned in the column. Select the column or the cells in the column where the decimal tab will be used.

2. Click the tab selector at the left edge of the Ruler until the decimal tab displays.

3. Click the Horizontal Ruler where you want to set the tab. The numbers immediately align to the decimal tab.

4. If you need to move the decimal tab, first select the column or the necessary cells before moving the tab marker on the Ruler.

DRILL 1   DECIMAL TAB AND COLUMN WIDTH

1. Create the table shown above (*Numbers with Decimals,* etc.). Bold and center the column headings.

2. Select cells A2–A4 and set a decimal tab at 1" on the Horizontal Ruler. The numbers automatically align with the decimal tab.

3. Select cells B2–B4 and click the Align Text Right button.

4. Select cells C2–C4 and set a decimal tab at 5.5".

5. Select cells C2–C4; move the decimal tab on the Ruler to 5.25".

6. Move the mouse over the border between columns A and B. When the mouse changes to a double-headed arrow, hold down the ALT key and click the column border to display the column width. Drag the border until the Ruler displays a width of 1.95" for column A. Do the same with column B. Adjust the width of column C to 1.7".

7. Center the table horizontally.

8. Proofread and check; click Next to continue. (*65-drill1*)

```
 1  NEWTON & JOHNSON
    15 Civic Center Drive, Suite 200
    Santa Ana, CA 92701-3821
 2
    Telephone:  714-555-0134
 3
    Attorneys for Defendants
 4  JONATHAN MOVERS and
    LAUREL DELIVERIES
 5

 6

 7
                   SUPERIOR COURT OF THE STATE OF CALIFORNIA
 8
                        FOR THE COUNTY OF ORANGE
 9

10
                                      ) Case No.: SO C 87321
11  HENRY HURT, et al.,               )
                                      ) NOTICE OF DEPOSITION AND REQUEST FOR
12            Plaintiff,              ) PRODUCTION OF DOCUMENTS AT DEPOSITION
                                      )
13       vs.                          )
                                      )
14  JONATHAN MOVERS, et al.,          )
                                      )
15  _____) 
             Defendant                )

16

17  TO:  ALL PARTIES AND THEIR ATTORNEYS OF RECORD

18

19       PLEASE TAKE NOTICE that defendants will take the deposition of

20  plaintiff Henry Hurt on July 7, 201-, at 2:00 p.m., at the offices of

21  Newton & Johnson, 15 Civic Center Drive, Suite 200, Santa Ana, CA 92701-3821,

22  before a notary public authorized to administer oaths in the State of

23  California.  The deposition will continue from day to day, excluding

24  Saturdays, Sundays, and holidays, until completed.

25  ///

26  ///


                         Notice of Deposition - 1
```

CHANGE TEXT DIRECTION

Text is traditionally displayed horizontally in a table cell. At times, it is preferable to display the text vertically in a cell. Typically, text is displayed vertically when a number of narrow columns are included in a table. The Text Direction button rotates text in a cell 90 degrees each time you click the button. Rotated text will be easier to read if it is centered in the table cell.

To change text direction:

Table Tools Layout/Alignment/Text Direction

1. Click in the cell where the text will be rotated.
2. Click the Text Direction button to rotate the text. Continue clicking Text Direction until the text displays in the desired direction.
3. Use Align Center to center the text in the cell.

DISTRIBUTE ROWS OR COLUMNS

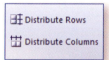

When a table has many columns or rows, it may be a tedious task to set each column width or height to make the columns the same dimensions. The Distribute Rows and Distribute Columns commands will distribute the columns and rows evenly.

To distribute rows or columns:

Table Tools Layout/Cell Size/Distribute Rows or Columns

1. Select the rows or columns that are to be distributed evenly.
2. Click Distribute Rows or Distribute Columns.

GUIDELINES FOR KEYING TABLES

1. When main and secondary headings are used in a document, make the main heading larger than the secondary heading. Column headings may be centered and boldfaced. If styles are applied to main and secondary headings, adjust spacing as needed.
2. Adjust column width attractively, and center the table horizontally.
3. When a table is within a document, the same amount of blank space should display before and after the table as between paragraphs.

DRILL 2 | TEXT DIRECTION AND DISTRIBUTE text direction

1. In the open document, click the Text Direction button two times in each cell for cells B1–H1. The text will read from bottom to top.
2. Select all the cells in row 1.
3. Click Align Center to center all the text in the cells horizontally and vertically.
4. Select rows 2–4. Change the row height to 0.3".
5. Use Align Center Left to center the text vertically in the cells.
6. Bold the column heads in row 1.
7. Select columns B–H and use Distribute Columns to make the columns equal width.
8. Click in row 4 and change row height to 0.6".
9. Select rows 2–4; then click the Distribute Rows button.
10. Proofread and check; click Next to continue. (65-drill2)

3. Click the Download button to display the pleading on the screen.

4. Once the template is downloaded, it is saved in My templates by default. Remember that in a classroom environment, however, you may need to save it to a flash drive or another location.

Keyboarding Pro DELUXE 2 users: Pleadings will open automatically as a data file. You will not download templates.

To use the Legal Pleading template:

If saved to the hard drive:

1. Click the File tab and select New. The Available Templates screen displays.

2. Select My templates; then select Pleading form with 26 lines. Click OK to display the template.

-or-

If saved to a flash drive:

1. Click the File tab, select Open, and browse to your flash drive.

2. Select Pleading form with 26 lines. Click OK to display the file. Save the file using a new name.

Applications

97-d1

Download Legal Pleading Template

Keyboarding Pro DELUXE 2 users: Skip this exercise.

1. Click File and select New.

2. Search for **Pleadings** on www.Office.com.

3. Download the Pleading form with 26 lines.

4. Scroll through the document; then close it without saving it.

5. Click the File tab and select New. Select Pleading form with 26 lines. Save as a template.
Note: If you are using a flash drive, select New from existing. Browse to your flash drive.

6. Proofread and check; click Next to continue. (*97-d1*)

97-d2

Notice of Deposition and Request for Production of Documents at Deposition

A deposition is the testimony of a witness taken under oath in question-and-answer form. It has the same legal effect as open court testimony.

1. Open *97-d1*, the template file you saved in Application 1. (*Keyboarding Pro DELUXE 2:* The Pleadings template will open automatically.)

2. Key the document as shown on the next two pages. Align your text with the line numbers shown in the illustration. Text that is shown in uppercase should be keyed in uppercase.

3. Click on the bracketed text and key the new text.

4. Key / / / on lines 25 and 26; this shows that the lines were left blank by the writer. Key **Notice of Deposition** in the footer of the document.

5. To key the second page, place the insertion point on the ¶ at the end of line 26. Tap ENTER to move the insertion point to line 1 on the second page.

6. Key the enumerations on the second page using the Numbering feature. Then select all the enumerations and drag the left Indent marker on the ruler to .75".

7. Check and close. (*97-d2*)

65-d1

Table with Decimal Tab

TIP

Remember to change to left alignment and 11-point font, and turn off bold before inserting the table.

1. Center the main heading using all caps, 14-point font, and bold.
2. Create the table. Bold and center the column headings.
3. Adjust column widths, and center the table horizontally.
4. Center column B; align columns C and D with a decimal tab.
5. Proofread and check; click Next to continue. (65-d1)

LAUREL CANYON ENTERPRISES

Employee	I.D.	Hardware	Software
Alexander, J.	R492	$105,134,384	$1,868,553
Courtenay, W.	R856	79,364,091	1,384,219
Holsonback, E.	C845	27,386,427	1,098,237
Rajeh, C.	M451	82,665,900	1,052,564

65-d2

Insert and Delete Columns and Rows

1. Open *65-d1*.
2. Insert a column between columns B and C. Insert the following information in the new column. Remove the decimal tab in the new column.

   Department | Public Relations | Maintenance | Accounting | Engineering
3. Delete the row containing *Holsonback*.
4. Insert two additional rows and key the names and accompanying information below in correct alphabetical order. Adjust column widths as necessary.

Baxter, L.	K511	Accounting	44,296,101	971,360
Talbert, S.	P053	CFO	82,091,433	985,201
5. Proofread and check; click Next to continue. (65-d2)

65-d3

Merge Cells and Rotate Text

TIP

After keying the text in column C, tap TAB twice to return to column B.

1. Center the main heading, **NBA EASTERN CONFERENCE**, in all caps and 14-point, bold font.
2. Create a 3-column, 6-row table. Select the entire table and change the row height to 0.25".
3. Merge the cells in column A. Key **Southeast Division**; rotate the text so that it reads from bottom to top. Center the text and apply bold.
4. Key columns B and C of the table. Bold column heads. Align Center Left columns B and C.
5. Adjust the width of column A to 0.5". Adjust widths of columns B and C to 1.9".
6. Center the table horizontally on the page.
7. Proofread and check; click Next to continue. (65-d3)

	Team	City
Southeast Division	Atlanta Hawks	Atlanta, Georgia
	Charlotte Bobcats	Charlotte, N. Carolina
	Miami Heat	Miami, Florida
	Orlando Magic	Orlando, Florida
	Washington Wizards	Washington, D. C.

Lesson 97 | *Legal Pleadings*

Document Design

97b

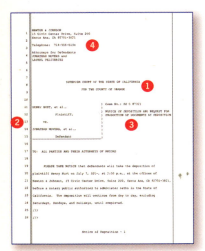

LEGAL DOCUMENTS

Legal documents that are presented for filing in court must follow specific guidelines and be keyed on pleading paper. Most documents today are keyed on standard 8.5" x 11" paper; some lawyers may still use legal-size paper (8.5" x 14"). Legal documents contain a double ruling, from top to bottom, at the left margin; a single ruling displays at the right margin. Legal pleading forms contain line numbers in the left margin. The pleading form contains either 25, 26, 28, or 32 lines per page.

The margins for legal documents can be 1.25" on the left and 1" on the right. Some lawyers will use a 1.5" left margin and a 0.5" right margin. Top and bottom margins are usually 1".

Review the document on pages 511 and 512. The key identifying components of the legal pleading are described below. Each pleading begins with a **caption** to identify the action. The styles of captions vary, depending on the state; however, all captions include the **jurisdiction**—the name of the court that has authority to rule with reference to specific persons or subject matter. The name of the county and the state in which the court is located is usually included with the jurisdiction ❶.

The pleading also contains a box, which is formed with symbols. The box shows the names of the individuals or corporations involved in the lawsuit ❷. The title of the pleading is located to the right of the box ❸.

The name, address, and telephone number of the attorney originating the paper precedes the caption ❹. In some states, this information is placed at the end of the pleading.

The www.Office.com website contains legal pleading forms that can be downloaded. The forms are preformatted to include vertical rulings, line numbers, and the box.

To download the Legal Pleading template:

File/New

1. Click File and select New. Click in the Search Office.com for templates box and key **Pleadings** ❶; tap ENTER.
2. Choose Pleading form with 26 lines.

> ★ **NOTE**
>
> The Legal Pleading templates available from Microsoft are not *Word 2010* templates.

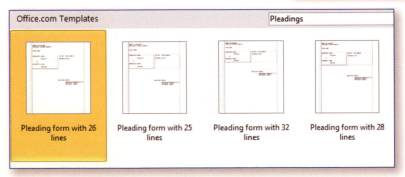

Pleading form with 26 lines | Pleading form with 25 lines | Pleading form with 32 lines | Pleading form with 28 lines

65-d4

Insert Column

1. Open *65-d3*.
2. Insert a column to the right of the table. Key the following information in column D.

   Arena

   Philips Arena

   Charlotte Bobcats Arena

   American Airlines Arena

   Amway Arena

   Verizon Center
3. Change the alignment of the text in column D to Align Center Left to match the rest of the table.
4. Proofread and check; click Next to continue. (*65-d4*)

65-d5

Merge and Split Cells

 TIP

Key the numbers in columns D and E using left alignment. Then select the numbers and set the decimal tab. Numbers will automatically align at the decimal point.

1. Create a 3-column, 7-row table.
2. Merge the cells in the first row. Change the row height to 0.6".
3. Key the main heading in 14-point uppercase font, and the secondary heading in 12-point title case font. Apply bold to both headings.
4. Select cells B3–B7 and split the cells into 2 columns and 5 rows; do the same with cells C3–C7.
5. Merge cells A2–A3. Center the column head, **Description**, using Align Center.
6. Key the table shown below. Adjust column widths and center the table horizontally. Bold and center all headings vertically and horizontally.
7. Center the numbers in cells B4–B7 and cells C4–C7. Use a decimal tab to align the numbers in columns D and E.
8. Click in the last row in the table. Change the row height to 0.5". Select rows 4–7 and distribute row heights. Center the copy vertically in the cells.
9. Check and close. (*65-d5*)

OUTPATIENT PROSPECTIVE PAYMENT SYSTEM Unadjusted National Medicare Reimbursement				
Description	Code		Insurance	
	CPT	APC	Medicare	Coinsurance
Immobilization	77341	0303	91.08	69.28
Basic Dosimetry	77300	0304	388.52	498.26
Daily IMRT Treatment	60174	0302	7,625.19	8,662.14
Physical Therapy	77336	0311	270.48	253.26

TIP

Remember to return to left alignment; turn off bold and all caps before creating the table.

1. Center and bold each line of the heading as shown, beginning at about 2". Remove space after paragraph as per illustration. Tap ENTER.

2. Create a 4-column, 7-row table.

3. Key the table. At the bottom of the table key **TOTAL PROPERTY ON HAND**, tap ENTER, press CTRL+TAB, and key **JUNE 30, 201-**. Use the SUM formula to add the totals in columns B and C. Display the total with a dollar sign and two decimal places.

4. Bold and center-align column heads.

5. Adjust column width and center table horizontally. Decimal-align columns C and D.

6. Insert a blank row after each row except the last.

7. Click the Table Move handle to select the table and remove all borders. Underline the date in the column heads and the 325,000.00 in columns C and D.

8. Check and close. (*96-d3*)

SCHEDULE 2

Conservatorship of Jacob Brian Saldana
For period July 1, 201- through June 30, 201-

PROPERTY ON HAND
AS OF JUNE 30, 201-

		Carry Value 6/29/201-	**Market Value 6/30/201-**
1.	Bank of Huntington Pointe Brookhurst Branch Savings Account No. 578-1234	$ 21,050.00	$ 21,050.00
2.	National Federal Credit Union Santa Ana, California Checking Account No. 21-00037	7,500.00	6,573.64
3.	1,000 shares, Unocal Corp., common stock	78,000.00	71,000.00
4.	Furniture and furnishings	2,000.00	2,000.00
5.	Condominium residence located at 3522 Sea Breeze Way, Huntington Beach, CA	325,000.00	325,000.00
	TOTAL PROPERTY ON HAND JUNE 30, 201-		

Tap the spacebar once following the $ to align it with the $ that will appear in the total line.

Lesson 66 | *Format and Sort Tables*

New Command

- Sort Data in Tables

Skill Building

66b **Timed Writing**

Key one 2' timed writing at your control rate.

	gwam	2'
Little things do contribute to success in keying.	6	53
Take our work attitude, for example. It's a little thing; yet	12	59
it can make quite a lot of difference. Demonstrating patience	18	66
with a job or a problem, rather than pressing much too hard for a	25	72
desired payoff, often brings better results than we expected.	31	79
Other "little things," such as wrist and finger position, how we	38	85
sit, size and location of copy, and lights, have meaning for	44	91
any person who wants to key well.	47	94

| 1   2   3   4   5   6 |

Review Commands

66c

KEYBOARDING PRO DELUXE 2

References/Word 2010
Commands/Lessons 38–40

ENHANCE TABLE APPEARANCE

Once you have created a table, a variety of tools are available on the Table Tools Design tab that can enhance the appearance of the table. The Design tab is divided into three groups: Table Style Options, Table Styles, and Draw Borders. Review the following design options.

Shade Cells, Columns, or Rows

Table Tools Design/Table Styles/Shading

Shading adds emphasis to cells. Frequently, header rows or rows containing totals are shaded. Select the cell(s), column, or row to be shaded. Click Shading to display the color palette. Click the desired color. To remove the shading, select the cell(s), column, or row, and click No Color.

Change Border Appearance

Table Tools Design/Table Styles/Borders

The Borders command allows you to choose various border options. For example, you can choose to have borders on the outside of the table or only on the top or bottom of certain cells. You can also choose to remove the borders. Select the cell(s) or table in which the border will be altered. Click the Borders drop-list arrow to display the border options. Click the desired borders or click No Border.

Change Line Style, Weight, and Color

Table Tools Design/Draw Borders/Line Style, Line Weight, or Pen Color

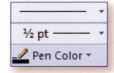

The Line Style, Line Weight, and Pen Color features are often used in combination with the Borders options. Use these options to apply dashed or double lines, make borders heavier or lighter, and change border color.

Mail Merge Articles of Incorporation

★ NOTE

Articles of Incorporation contain information regarding the name, address, and purpose of the company, as well as the share structure. Articles of Incorporation may differ for medical, nonprofit, professional, and municipal corporations.

1. Tap ENTER five 5 times to leave an approximate 3" top margin for the Secretary of State to place the filing stamp. Key **ARTICLES OF INCORPORATION**; apply Heading 1 style.

2. Create the data source using the fields and data shown in the table; save the data file as *96-d2data*. Key the Articles of Incorporation, inserting the fields as shown below. Tap ENTER twice before keying the underscore for the signature. Key the Incorporator's name, right-aligned below the line; remove space after paragraph.

3. Merge the data source and the main document.

4. Proofread and check; click Next to continue. (*96-d2*)

Field Name	Entry 1	Entry 2
Corporate Name	Quality Care Medical Center	Gourmet Food Shops
Profession	providing medical care	providing retail sales
Name	Andrew Wainscott	Jeannette Smith
Street Address	5561 Golden Lantern Drive	1521 Mack Avenue
City	Laguna Niguel	Orange
ZIP Code	92677-1234	92865-2214
Amount	Ten Thousand (10,000)	Five Thousand (5,000)

ARTICLES OF INCORPORATION

I

The name of this corporation is «Corporate_Name».

II

The purpose of the corporation is to engage in the profession of «Profession» and any other lawful activities (other than the banking or trust company business) not prohibited to a corporation engaging in such profession by applicable laws and regulations.

III

The corporation is a professional corporation within the meaning of Part 4, Division 3, Title I, California Corporation Code.

IV

The name and address in the State of California of this corporation's initial agent for service of process are:

 Name: «Name»

 Street Address: «Street_Address»

 City: «City» California ZIP Code: «ZIP_Code»

V

The corporation is authorized to issue only one class of stock; and the total number of shares which the corporation is authorized to issue is «Amount».

_____

David M. Smith, Incorporator

To change the line style, line weight, or pen color:

1. Click the Line Style drop-list arrow and choose a line style.

2. Click the Line Weight drop-list arrow and select from a variety of line weights or thicknesses.

3. Click the Pen Color drop-list arrow and select the desired color from the color palette.

4. Select the cells to be changed and then click the appropriate borders option.

DRILL 1   APPLY SHADING AND BORDER   shading

1. In the open document, add a row below the table by clicking in the last cell and tapping TAB.

2. Key **Total** in cell A6. Key **482,271,983** in cell C6.

3. Select the cells in the row containing the total. Apply Red, Accent 2, Lighter 80% shading to the row.

4. Change the line style to a double line.

5. Change the line weight to ¾ pt. Select the entire table.

6. Click the Borders drop-list arrow and choose Outside Borders.

7. Proofread and check; click Next to continue. *(66-drill1)*

TABLE STYLES

Word includes a gallery of preformatted table styles that you can use to make tables more attractive. The styles contain font attributes, color, shading, and borders to enhance the appearance of a table. Display additional styles by clicking the More button to show the entire gallery. Move the mouse over each style to see your table formatted in that style. The name of the style also displays.

More

The Table Style Options group allows you to make changes to the table style to suit your needs. As you select and deselect these options, the styles in the gallery display those options. For example, if your table has a total row, select the Total Row option. Table styles in the gallery change to show emphasis on this row.

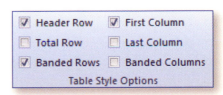

To add, change, or remove a table style:

Table Tools Design/Table Styles

1. Click in the table where the style is to be applied. Follow the path to view table styles.

2. Click the desired table style. To see the entire style gallery, click the More button.

3. To change to another style, click in the table and choose a different style.

4. To remove a style, click the table; then click the More button. Below the gallery of styles, click Clear.

5. If you wish to make a change to the style, click in the table; then click the option you wish to change in the Table Style Options group.

1. Use the Mail Merge Wizard and advance to step 4. Place the insertion point on the first left parenthesis, (Field: County), in step 4, and click More items. Insert the field name, **County**, and then delete the parentheses and the text inside them. Insert the remaining two field codes in the same manner.

2. Non-*Keyboarding Pro DELUXE 2* users will need to save the main document using a name that identifies it as being the main, such as *power of attorney main*.

3. In step 5, choose Next: Complete the merge. In step 6, click Edit individual letters. When the Merge to New Document box displays, click OK.

4. Proofread and check; click Next to continue. (*96-drill2*) Non-*Keyboarding Pro DELUXE 2* users will need to save the merged document.

Applications

96-d1

Mail Merge Letter

Non-*Keyboarding Pro DELUXE 2* users will need to save the main document.

1. In the open document (*96-d1main*), create the data source using the field names shown in the table below. Save as *96-d1data*.

2. Key the following letter with open punctuation as a main document for a mail merge. Apply bold to each of the field names. Insert the merge fields in the main document.

3. Merge the data source and the main document.

4. Proofread and check; click Next to continue. (*96-d1*)

Current date | Secretary of State | State of California | P.O. Box 12345 | Sacramento, CA 96814-2591 | Dear Secretary

Please reserve the following name to be used by a California corporation proposed to be formed in the near future:

Field: Name   Center field

If the name is not available for corporate use, the following names are listed as alternatives:

First: Field: First
Second: Field: Second   Use default tabs
Third: Field: Third

An envelope is enclosed for returning the Certificate of Reservation of Name. A check for $750 to cover the processing fee is also enclosed.

Thank you for your attention in this matter.

Sincerely | Armando J. Reynoza | Attorney | xx | Enclosure

Field Name	Letter 1	Letter 2
Name	LO-CARB MEALS, INC.	NEW IMAGE SURGERY CENTER
First	LO-CARB MEALS ARE US, INC.	A-1 PROFESSIONAL SURGERY CENTER
Second	LO-CARB DIETS, INC.	IDEAL SURGERY CENTER
Third	LO-CARB PASTA, INC.	A-1 LASER SURGERY CENTER

1. Open *66-drill1*. Remove the shading from the last row (select cells, click Shading, and click No Color).

2. Apply Medium Shading 2 – Accent 3 table style. Bold the heading in cell A2.

3. Click the Total Row checkbox in the Table Style Options group to add emphasis to the last row.

4. Center the table horizontally. Center the main heading vertically in the row.

5. Proofread and check; click Next to continue. (*66-drill2*)

POSITION A TABLE IN A DOCUMENT

When inserting a table into a document, care must be taken to provide the same amount of space below the table as above the table. *Word*'s default Normal style inserts a 10-point space after a paragraph and uses 1.15 line spacing. However, *Word* defaults to single spacing in a table with no spacing after a paragraph. Therefore, when a table is keyed within a document, extra spacing needs to be inserted below the table to match the spacing above the table. The extra space can easily be inserted by clicking on the paragraph below the table, clicking the Line Spacing drop-list arrow, and choosing Add Space Before Paragraph.

New Commands

66d

SORT IN TABLES

One of the advantages of keying data in a *Word* table is that you can sort the data. The sort can be performed in three ways:

- **Text sort.** Text is sorted alphabetically. Numbers sorted in a text sort are based purely on the first digit. If the numbers 1, 7, and 100 are sorted, the resulting list will be in this order: 1, 100, 7.

- **Number sort.** Numbers are sorted numerically. For example, a list of 1, 100, 7 would be sorted as 1, 7, 100.

- **Date sort.** When dates are involved; text is sorted based on date chronology.

To sort data in a table:

Table Tools Layout/Data/Sort

1. Click in the table; then follow the path to display the Sort dialog box.

2. When row 1 contains column headings, it is called the *header row*. Click the appropriate button indicating whether the table contains a header row ❶.

3. Click the drop-list arrow next to Sort by ❷. (**Note:** Sort by tells *Word* how to arrange the information.) Select the header that you will sort by.

4. Select Ascending to sort the list from A to Z. Descending sorts from Z to A ❸.

5. If the first-level sort cannot establish the sort order (this will be true if several cells are identical in the first column), then you will need to establish a second-level sort in the first Then by section ❹. You can also enter a third-level sort in the subsequent Then by section ❺.

Legal and Medical Documents

LEARNING OUTCOMES

- Format legal office applications.
- Format medical office applications.
- Skillbuilding.

Lesson 96 | Legal Documents

WARMUP

KEYBOARDING PRO DELUXE 2

Lessons/96a Warmup

Document Design

96b

LEGAL AND MEDICAL DOCUMENTS

This module is an introduction to legal and medical word processing. You will be using word processing features that you learned in previous modules to create medical and legal documents. You will work with a variety of documents, including Power of Attorney, Articles of Incorporation, Conservatorship table, Notice of Deposition, Notice of Motion, Notary form, medical reports and SOAP notes.

DRILL 1   CREATE DATA FILE   power of attorney

1. In the open document, turn on Show/Hide. Use the Mail Merge Wizard to create the data source. *Mailings/Start Mail Merge/Step by Step Mail Merge Wizard*

2. In step 1, select Letters. Step 2, choose Use current document. Step 3, Type a new list and then Create.

3. Click Customize Columns; delete the fields in the Field Names box and add the field names listed below.

4. Key the data information for each recipient.

5. Save data file as *power of attorney data*. Proofread and check; click Next to continue. Non-*Keyboarding Pro DELUXE 2* users may leave the document on screen and continue with Drill 2.

Field Name	Recipient 1	Recipient 2
County	Orange	San Diego
Date	June 6, 201-	June 15, 201-
Name	Lawrence Rodriguez	James Thompson

Table Tools Layout/Data/Sort

1. In the open document, sort the table by Dish in ascending order. (Sort by Dish; Ascending.)

2. Sort the table by Cost in descending order. (Sort by Cost; Number; Descending.)

3. Sort the table by Nationality in ascending order and then by Dish in descending order. (Sort by Nationality; Text; Ascending; Then by Dish; Text; Descending.)

4. Your sorted table should look like the one at the right.

5. Proofread and check; click Next to continue. (66-drill3)

INTERNATIONAL FOODS

Dish	Nationality	Cost
Hamburger	American	6.50
Sweet and Sour Pork	Chinese	8.95
Hong Kong Steak	Chinese	15.95
Veal Marsala	Italian	18.75
Shrimp Tempura	Japanese	11.50
Fish Burrito	Mexican	6.96

Applications

66-d1

Table with Border and Style Options

 TIP

For all tables in this lesson, adjust column width and center table horizontally.

1. Insert a 3-column, 7-row table at 2". Apply the Civic theme.

2. Merge rows 1 and 2 in column A; select rows 2–7 in column B and split in two columns. Do the same for column C.

3. Key the table. Align numbers with decimal tabs. Adjust column widths.

4. Insert a row above the table; merge the cells.

5. Center **WEXMARK COLLEGE** in 14-point, all caps. Tap ENTER and key **201- Enrollments** in 12-point font.

6. Apply Light Grid – Accent 2 table style. Deselect Header Row in the Table Style Options.

7. Change the height of rows 2–8 to 0.25". Center the copy vertically in the cells.

8. Change the height of row 1 to 0.6". Bold and center vertically and horizontally all headings.

9. Center the table horizontally on the page.

10. Apply a double-line Orange, Accent 6, Darker 25% border to the outside of the table.

11. Proofread and check; click Next to continue. (66-d1)

College	Semester		Division	
	Fall	Spring	Upper	Lower
Business Administration	1,296	677	395	1,586
Computer Science	945	322	124	1,143
Allied Health Sciences	3,925	2,650	4,500	7,125
Arts and Sciences	98	76	29	108
Engineering Technology	179	156	32	96

4. Turn Track Changes on. Check to see that your name and initials are in the User name and Initials boxes.

5. Make the following changes.

   a. In the first paragraph under *Call to Order*, insert a comma after the year.

   b. In the paragraph under *Conflict of Interest*, add **Policy** in the last sentence so that it reads "...complete the Conflict of Interest Policy Acceptance Form."

   c. Under *New Business*, insert **Portfolio Review** between the first and second paragraphs and apply Heading 2 style.

   d. Under *New Business*, insert **Review of Managers** before the last paragraph and apply Heading 2 style.

   e. Move the content under the heading *Portfolio Review* and position it under the heading *Review of Managers*.

   f. Move the paragraph about the review of the portfolio under the heading *Portfolio Review*.

   g. Change the adjournment time from *11:00 a.m.* to **11:15 a.m.**

6. Use a Motion Even Page header to add the title and page number to the second page only.

7. Review the document to ensure that all of the changes were made.

8. Accept all changes.

9. Check and close. (*95-d2*)

BOOKMARK

www.collegekeyboarding.com
Module 15 Practice Quiz

66-d2

Create and Format Table

1. Key the table below. Center the main heading, **NATIONAL TEAM LEADERS**, in 14-point, bold, and caps above the table.
2. Apply the Light List – Accent 2 style to the table and center horizontally.
3. Center columns D and E, including the column heads.
4. Proofread and check; click Next to continue. (*66-d2*)

Last Name	First Name	City	State	ZIP
Louie	Martin	Seattle	WA	98101-1075
Palms	Lorraine	Minneapolis	MN	55455-8415
Straus	Patricia	Omaha	NE	68105-4398
Soey	Ellen	San Francisco	CA	94107-0357
Zampich	Christina	Hayden Lake	ID	83835-2735
Le	Trinh	Oxnard	CA	93033-4890
Pham	Chinh	San Francisco	CA	94107-6592
Kumar	Lauren	Durham	NC	27703-5283
Williams	James	New Bern	NC	28562-7963
Toyota	Janice	Del Rio	TX	78840-3122
Carpenter	Roger	Laredo	TX	78040-2361
Garcia	Pena	Bellevue	WA	98005-9407

66-d3

Sort Table and Apply Style

1. Open *66-d2*. Sort the table in ascending order by last name. (*Hint:* Check to see that Header row is selected.)
2. Sort the table in descending order by ZIP Code. (The Sort by entry you will see is ZIP.)
3. Apply the Light Grid – Accent 2 style to the table.
4. Proofread and check; click Next to continue. (*66-d3*)

66-d4

Multiple Sort and Apply Style

1. Open *66-d3*. Sort the table in ascending order by state, then by city, and then by last name.
2. Apply the Light Grid – Accent 1 style to the table.
3. Proofread and check; click Next to continue. (*66-d4*)

95-d2

continued

Approval of Minutes

Mr. Lettsworth noted that all members had received copies of the minutes prior to the meeting, and copies are also in the meeting packet. The minutes were approved as presented.

Open Issues

Two open issues came before the Committee.

Conflict of Interest (Heading 2 style)

The Conflict of Interest Policy was reviewed. No changes were made in the existing policy. Committee members were asked to complete the Conflict of Interest Acceptance Form and return it to the office.

Investment Policy (Heading 2 style)

The Investment Policy was reviewed in detail. After considerable discussion, the Committee recommended that the Alternative Investments allocation be increased from a maximum of 10 percent of the portfolio to a maximum of 20 percent of the portfolio.

New Business

Mr. Jeffery Harsh, our investment consultant, presented both the portfolio performance report and the evaluation of eight portfolio managers.

Mr. Harsh recommended that Beckwith Investment Services be terminated immediately and that the funds managed by Beckwith be split between the large cap growth and value managers. The motion passed unanimously.

Mr. Harsh reviewed the report on portfolio performance for the previous calendar year. The written report is attached. Total returns were 24 percent. All segments of the portfolio exceeded the benchmarks except the core segment which underperformed the benchmarks all four quarters.

Adjournment

Chairman Bennett adjourned the meeting at 11:00 a.m.

Minutes submitted by

Roger Lettsworth   Tap ENTER twice to allow space for each signature.

Minutes approved by

John Bennett

(continued)

1. Key the following memo according to memo formatting guides.

2. Insert the table after the first paragraph; adjust column widths using AutoFit contents; apply 0.3" row height and Medium Shading 2 – Accent 2 style. Center data vertically in the cells. Center table horizontally.

3. Use decimal tabs to right-align the numbers in the columns.

4. Check and close. (66-d5)

TO: Parents | FROM: Lynn Marshall | DATE: May 15, 201- | SUBJECT: Tuition

The Board of Directors has reviewed our financial statements, the proposed budget for next year, and our current tuition plan. Although we have tried to maintain tuition at the current rate, it is not possible to do so. Our costs for utilities, food, supplies, and gasoline for the buses have increased substantially. Therefore, we have applied a 2.5% increase in tuition for next year. The following table summarizes our new weekly rates.

Age Group	Single-Child Rate	Multi-Child Rate	Half-Day Rate
Infant/Toddler	$268	$245	$150
Preschool 2	$253	$233	$140
Preschool 3	$240	$230	$125
Preschool 4	$237	$228	$122
Preschool 5	$235	$225	$122

The new rates take effect on July 1 and will be guaranteed not to change for one full year. The Children's Center will continue to accept credit cards and personal checks as it has always done. Tuition may be paid weekly, monthly, and annually.

If you wish to pay the annual tuition at one time prior to July 1, you may pay the current rates rather than these new rates with the 2.5% increase shown in the table. If you have any questions about tuition or other financial issues, please check with our business manager at the Children's Center.

We look forward to seeing all of you at the annual picnic next week.

Agenda

1. Key the title and subtitle shown below. Use the default Office theme.
2. Use Title style for the title and Subtitle for the location, time, and date. Set a center tab at 3.25" and a right-align tab at 6.5".
3. Change tabs to 1" left tab and 6.5" right-aligned leader tab; key the remainder of the agenda.
4. Proofread, preview, and continue to the next document. (*95-d1*)

Agenda—Investments Committee

Boardroom   9:30 AM   January 19, 201-

9:30	Call to Order	John Bennett
	Approval of Minutes	John Bennett
9:35	Open Issues	
	Conflict of Interest Policy	Roger Lettsworth
	Investment Policy	Kevin Vickers
10:05	New Business	
	Portfolio Performance Review	Jeffery Harsh
	Investment Manager Performance	Jeffery Harsh
11:00	Adjournment	

95-d2

Minutes

1. Use the same document theme and heading that you used for the agenda in *95-d1*; change Agenda to **Minutes**.
2. Key the minutes shown below. Note that two levels of headings are used. Use Heading 1 style except where noted to use Heading 2 style.
3. After you complete the minutes, follow the additional directions on page 504 to make changes with Track Changes.

Call to Order

Chairman John Bennett called the meeting of the Investments Committee to order at 9:30 a.m. on January 19, 201- in the Boardroom.

The following members were present: Mr. John Bennett, Ms. Carla Greene, Mr. Marquez Garcia, Mr. Roger Lettsworth, Ms. Makayla Parker, Ms. Akira Surabaya, Mr. Kevin Vickers, Ms. Alexis Weaver, Mrs. Kiele Wong, and Mr. Quinn Young.

(continued)

Lesson 67 | Calculations in Tables

New Commands
- Use Formulas in Tables
- Write Formulas in Tables
- Use Paste Functions

WARMUP

Lessons/67a Warmup

LA | ALL LETTERS

Skill Building

67b Timed Writing
1. Key a 1' timed writing on each paragraph, working for speed.
2. Key a 3' timed writing, working for control.

	gwam	1'	3'
Do you need a different vacation? A cruise is a wonderful way to	13	4	39
get away from it all. Think how long you would like to be away and	26	9	44
start planning your vacation today. Then, begin relaxing.	38	13	48
It is the opinion of many travelers that the food alone is worth	13	17	52
the trip. You'll have a huge selection, excellent quality, and all you	27	22	57
can eat.	29	22	57
Better get started on the fun and try to cross as many time zones	13	27	62
as possible. The quality of your vacation will be better and you'll have	28	32	67
a million great experiences. Have a great time.	37	35	70

1'	1	2	3	4	5	6	7	8	9	10	11	12	13
3'		1			2			3			4		

New Commands

67c

FORMULAS

Microsoft Word can perform basic mathematical calculations, such as addition, subtraction, multiplication, and division, when numbers are keyed in a table. *Word* can also recalculate answers when the numbers in a table change. While *Word* is excellent for working with basic formulas, more complex calculations are better performed in a spreadsheet, such as *Excel*.

SUM FUNCTION

TIP

Formulas cannot be entered directly in a table cell; they must be keyed in the Formula dialog box.

SUM is the default formula that appears if you click in a cell below a column of numbers or to the right of a row of numbers. If you click the cell below a column of numbers, =SUM(ABOVE) appears in the Formula dialog box as the formula. If you click a cell at the right of a row of numbers, =SUM(LEFT) appears in the dialog box as the formula.

To total a column or row of numbers:

Table Tools Layout/Data/Formula

1. Position the insertion point in the empty cell that is to contain the answer.
2. Follow the path to display the Formula dialog box. The SUM formula appears in the Formula box ❶ with either ABOVE or LEFT depending if you clicked below a column or at the end of a row.
3. Select the number format desired ❷.

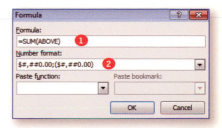

Lesson 95 | Assessment

A   **ALL LETTERS**

Skill Building

95b   Timed Writing

Key two 3' timed writings. Work at your control rate.

	gwam	3'	5'
Something that you can never escape is your attitude.	4	2	44
It will be with you forever. However, you decide whether your	8	5	47
attitude is an asset or a liability for you. Your attitude	12	7	49
reflects the way you feel about the world you abide in and	16	9	52
everything that is a part of that world. It reflects the way you	20	12	54
feel about yourself, about your environment, and about other peo-	25	15	57
ple who are a part of your environment. Oftentimes, people with	29	17	59
a positive attitude are people who are extremely successful.	33	20	62
At times we all have experiences that cause us to be	36	22	64
negative. The difference between a positive and a negative per-	41	24	66
son is that the positive person rebounds very quickly from a bad	45	27	69
experience; the negative person does not. The positive person is	49	30	72
a person who usually looks on the bright side of things and	53	32	74
recognizes the world as a place of promise, hope, joy, excite-	58	35	77
ment, and purpose. A negative person generally has just the	62	37	79
opposite view of the world. Remember, others want to be around	66	40	82
those who are positive but tend to avoid those who are negative.	70	42	84

```
3' |    1    |    2    |    3    |    4    |
5' |      1      |      2      |      3      |
```

Applications

95c

Assessment

 Continue

 Check

When you complete a document, proofread it, check the spelling, and preview for placement. When you are completely satisfied, click the Continue button to move to the next document. Click the Check button when you are ready to error-check the test. Review and/or print the document analysis results.

sum

1. In the open document, position the insertion point in the last cell and tap TAB to add a row at the bottom.

2. Key **TOTAL** in cell A8.

Table Tools Layout/Data/Formula

3. Insert the total for column C in cell C8. Insert the total for column D in cell D8. Verify the number format is the same as the numbers in the column.

4. Insert a column at the right of the table.

5. Key **Total per Employee** in cell E1; it will wrap to a second line. Center the column head vertically and horizontally in the cell.

6. Add the numbers in columns C and D, and place the total for each row in column E; you do not need to insert a sum for the total row. If the formula displays as SUM(ABOVE), replace the word ABOVE with LEFT. Center the numbers vertically in the cells to match the other columns.

7. Proofread and check; click Next to continue. (*67-drill1*)

WRITE FORMULAS

You can write your own formulas directing *Word* to add, subtract, multiply, divide, or average numbers in a table. A formula always begins with an equal sign and then is followed by the cell address and the mathematical operation. For example, =B2-C2 means "cell B2 minus cell C2." Formulas use the standard mathematical symbols shown below.

Operation	Symbol	Example
Addition	+	=B2+C2
Subtraction	- (hyphen)	=B2-C2
Multiplication	*	=B2*C2
Division	/	=B2/C2

To write a formula:

Table Tools Layout/Data/Formula

1. Place the insertion point in the cell that is to contain the calculation.
2. Follow the path to display the Formula dialog box.
3. Delete the existing formula if necessary.
4. Key the formula in the Formula text box, beginning with =.
5. Choose a number format if desired.
6. Repeat steps 1–5 for each formula.

RECALCULATE

When a change is made to a number that was part of a calculation, *Word* can recalculate the answer. By default, *Word* automatically updates fields when a document is opened. Fields can also be updated by right-clicking a field and then clicking Update Field or by clicking a field and then tapping F9. Note that fields will not update the moment numbers are changed, the way they do in a spreadsheet.

94-d3

Draft Agenda

1. Apply Apex theme. Tap ENTER three times and key the agenda title and subtitle. Use Title and Subtitle styles; shrink the title to fit on one line. In the subtitle line, set a center tab at 3.25" and a right-align tab at 6.5".

2. Change tabs to a 0.5" left tab and a 6.5" right-align leader tab and key the remainder of the agenda as shown below.

3. Remove the space after the paragraph between the subitems under the four headings with no name.

4. Proofread and check; click Next to continue. (*94-d3*)

Agenda—Moorman Children's Home Board of Directors Meeting

Board Room   8:00 a.m.   April 16, 201-

Welcome and Call to Order ....Carol Trotter

Approval of Minutes...Carol Trotter

Finance

         Audit... Jerry McAlister

         Quarterly Statements .... Mary Morales

Development

         Moorman Charity Golf Tournament .... Bill Mann

         Moorman Annual Barbecue........................ Wayne Lipscomp

Infrastructure

         Building Update .... Ken Price

         Perimeter Drive .... Fred Simmons

Programs Update

         Accreditation Review .... Keith Knight

         Review of Each Program......................... Sharon Washburn

---

94-d4

Final Agenda

 agenda revisions

1. In the open document, review the changes by each reviewer separately and accept each change. Remember to remove the space after paragraph for the subitems under the four headings.

2. Save the agenda heading as a Quick Part with **Moorman Heading** as the name and description.

3. Proofread and check; click Next to continue. (*94-d4*)

94-d5

Minutes

 moorman minutes

1. In the open document with Track Changes turned on, insert the *Moorman Heading* and change Agenda to **Minutes**. Check to see that your name appears in the User name box.

2. Review the changes and comments made by the reviewers. Insert the headings suggested; use Heading 1 style and make other suggested corrections. Delete all comments after you have finished the revisions. Turn Track Changes off. Accept the changes made when inserting headings.

3. Add the closing lines: Key **Respectfully submitted** and tap ENTER twice to leave space for the handwritten signature, and key **Gregg Parrish**.

4. Check and close. (*94-d5*)

1. In the open document, calculate Net Profits by subtracting Expenses from Income (B2 – C2). Display the answer in $#,##0.00 format.

2. Adjust column widths and center the numbers and the column heads in all the columns.

3. Change the height of all the rows to 0.25". Center the text vertically in the cells. Center the table horizontally.

4. Change the number in B2 to **$165,000.00.**

5. Recalculate the answers in D2 by placing the insertion point in D2 and tapping F9.

6. Insert a blank row above the table and merge the cells. Key **BRANDONMORE, INC.** as the main heading in bold, 14-point font. Key **Projected Income and Expense Statement** as the secondary heading in bold, 12-point font.

7. Change the height of row 1 to 0.6"; center the headings vertically and horizontally in the row.

8. Proofread and check; click Next to continue. (*67-drill2*)

PASTE FUNCTION

Additional mathematical functions are in the Paste function box. You have worked with SUM. Some of the Paste functions you will work with include:

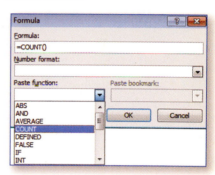

AVERAGE()	Calculates the average of the numbers in the cells indicated in parentheses such as cells above or to the left of the current cell.
MAX()	Locates the highest number in the cells indicated in parentheses.
MIN()	Locates the lowest number in the cells indicated in parentheses.
COUNT()	Counts the number of numeric values in the cells indicated in parentheses.

You can use directions such as ABOVE, BELOW, LEFT, or RIGHT with the Paste functions just as you did with SUM. For example, COUNT(ABOVE) or MAX(LEFT).

To use Paste functions:

Table Tools Layout/Data/Formula

1. Place the insertion point in the cell where the calculation will be made.
2. Follow the path to display the Formula dialog box.
3. Delete the existing formula, but not the = sign.
4. Click the Paste function drop-list arrow.
5. Choose the new function, and then key the cell references (such as A1:A3) between the parentheses or the direction (LEFT, RIGHT, ABOVE) to which the function should apply.

---

1. In the open document, click in cell E1.

2. Use the Paste function COUNT to total the number of cells that contain information. Key **LEFT** between the parentheses ( ). The answer is 4.

3. Repeat the function with the remainder of the cells in column E.

4. Proofread and check; click Next to continue. (*67-drill3*)

Sun Property and Casualty Insurance Company

1592 S. Plaza Way | Flagstaff, AZ 86011-7155

Telephone: 928-555-0174 | Solana.Rodriquez@spci.com | Fax: 928-555-0136

NEWS RELEASE   **Contact Person:** **Solana Rodriquez**

Current date

For Release: Immediately

SUN RECEIVES NATIONAL AWARD

FLAGSTAFF, AZ—The Sun Property and Casualty Insurance Company announced today that it received the *American Family-Friendly Work Environment Award* presented by the American Council on Insurance. Only one award is given each year to an insurance company for a unique contribution to improving the work environment for families.

Sun was cited for the unique partnership it established with Century Medical University and Sunbelt Child Development Centers to create a state-of-the-art Sun Child Development and Research Center. The center is in its first year of operation. The first floor of the center provides facilities for approximately two hundred children, and the second floor research center focuses on health and development issues impacting preschool children. Children receive medical screenings, and special isolated facilities are available for sick children at the center. Sun provides partial scholarships to employees and to low-income families.

Sun is the only insurance company to ever receive this prestigious award more than once. Five years ago, Sun received the award for its creative *Surrogate Grandparents Mentoring Program* in partnership with Central Academy to mentor children from low-income families after school. That program is still in effect today and is very successful. More than forty "grandparents" mentor over a hundred students each year.

Sun has offices throughout the Southwest and has 1,274 employees—430 of whom are in the Flagstaff area.

###

KEYBOARDING PRO DELUXE 2

*References/Communication
Skills/Semicolons*

SEMICOLONS

1. Create the table shown below.

2. Merge row 1 and key the main heading in 16-point font. Change the row height to 0.5". Change the height of row 2 to 0.3" and key the column headings.

3. Key the table.

4. Review the rules in the left column regarding the use of semicolons; review the example in the right column. Apply the rule and key a corrected copy of the sentence labeled *Application*.

5. Apply Medium Shading 1 – Accent 2 table style. Bold and center vertically and horizontally all headings.

6. Adjust the width of column A to 2.25". Apply a Red, Accent 2, 2¼-point border to the outside of the table.

7. Check and close. (67d)

Use a Semicolon	
Rule	**Example and Application**
To separate independent clauses in a compound sentence when the conjunction is omitted.	**Example:** Please review the information; give me a report by Tuesday. **Application:** The citizens voted to recall the mayor an election will be held in November.
To separate independent clauses when they are joined by conjunctive adverbs (however, nevertheless, consequently, etc.).	**Example:** The traffic was heavy; consequently, I was late. **Application:** Mr. Smith refused to increase our travel expense budget furthermore he suggested that we decrease it by 10 percent.
To separate a series of elements that contain commas.	**Example:** The new officers are: Fran Pena, president; Harry Wong, treasurer; and Muriel Williams, secretary. **Application:** We will be driving this summer to Las Vegas Nevada Phoenix Arizona Austin Texas and Chicago Illinois.

Lesson 94 | News and Meeting Documents

Document Design

94b

NEWS RELEASE

A news release disseminates information that an organization wishes to publish. Typically, the information is sent to newspapers, radio stations, television stations, and other media outlets. Well-prepared news releases stand a good chance of getting published when the information contained in the release is newsworthy and easy to publish. Media outlets may publish only a portion of a news release; therefore, the release should be designed to present the most important information first and the least important news last.

The release can be prepared using a form, a template, or building blocks. The news release heading generally contains the same information that would be on a letterhead. In addition, it is labeled a news release, provides the name of a contact person to reach for additional information, contains the date the information may be released, and includes a short subject line that could serve as a news headline. Typically, ### or *-30-* is used to indicate the end of the article.

If the news release is more than one page long, the word *more* is usually centered in a footer on the first page to indicate additional news is contained on the next page. The second and subsequent pages should contain a header (often called a *slug line*) with a short heading and the page number.

Applications

94-d1

News Release

 news release

1. In the open document, select the heading of the news release form and save it as a building block in the Quick Parts Gallery. Use **Sun News** for the name and description.
2. Key the news release shown on the next page.
3. Proofread and check; click Next to continue. (*94-d1*)

94-d2

News Release

 sun ceo

1. Insert the *Sun News* building block for the heading of a news release and key the first paragraph shown below. The news will be released immediately.
2. Insert the data file *sun ceo* after the first paragraph.
3. Then key the following closing paragraph: **Ledbetter is married to Kirk T. Parham, a nationally known pediatrician. They have two teenage children—a son, Joseph, and a daughter, Caitlyn.**
4. Indicate the end of the release.
5. Proofread and check; click Next to continue. (*94-d2*)

SUN NAMES NEW PRESIDENT AND CHIEF EXECUTIVE OFFICER

FLAGSTAFF, AZ—The Sun Property and Casualty Insurance Company announced today that its Board of Directors unanimously approved Amy T. Ledbetter as its new chief executive officer. Ledbetter replaces Mark R. Daff, who served as chief executive officer for the past eight years.

67–d1

Format and Total

⭐ **TIP**

Adjust column width and center all tables horizontally on the page.

⭐ **TIP**

Insert the formula including the number format in cell B8 to obtain the total. Click in cell C8 and press CTRL + Y to repeat the command.

1. Create a 4-column, 7-row table. Merge row 1 and change the height of row 1 to 0.7". Key the main heading in bold, 14-point font, and caps. Key the secondary heading in bold, 12-point font.

2. Apply the Sketchbook theme. Decimal-align columns B–D.

3. Add a row at the bottom of the table. Key the word **TOTAL** in cell A8. Calculate and insert the total expenses for each month; use the number format with a dollar sign, comma, and two decimal places.

4. Apply Light Grid – Accent 2 style. Select Total Row in the Table Style Options. Deselect Banded Rows and select Banded Columns.

5. Center and bold the headings in rows 1 and 2. Note the directions at the left regarding table position.

6. Proofread and check; click Next to continue. (67-d1)

EXPENSES FOR LAURA PEREZ First Quarter, 201-			
Expenses	**January**	**February**	**March**
Rent	$800.00	$850.00	$850.00
Food	$270.50	$255.25	$295.00
Transportation	$140.00	$125.00	$675.00
Clothing	$180.00	$110.50	$225.00
Miscellaneous	$125.00	$130.00	$120.00

67–d2

Average Calculation

1. Open 67-d1. Insert a column to the right of the table. Select all the cells in row 1 and click Merge Cells. Key **Average** in cell E2.

2. Using the Paste function AVERAGE, calculate the average for each expense and place the answers in column E. Average the total row by calculating averages to the left. The answers should contain a dollar sign and two decimal places.

3. Format column E to match the rest of the columns.

4. Proofread and check; click Next to continue. (67-d2)

67–d3

Recalculate

1. Open 67-d2. Change the February rent to **$900.00** and the March rent to **$975.00**.

2. Recalculate the average rent in cell E3, and then recalculate the totals in row 8. Reapply formatting to the cells that were recalculated.

3. Proofread and check; click Next to continue. (67-d3)

67–d4

Sort within Table

1. Open 67-d1. Select cells A3–A7 (*Rent – Miscellaneous*).

2. Sort column 1 in ascending order. (Sort by Column 1; Text; Ascending.)

3. Apply Orange, Accent 2, Lighter 40% shading to the Total row.

4. Proofread and check; click Next to continue. (67-d4)

93-d3

Return to Defaults

1. Reset the Track Changes Options to the default: **Insertions**—Underline and Color by Author; **Deletions**—Strikethrough and Color by Author.

2. Key on the first line: **I have returned the Track Changes Options to the defaults as a courtesy to other users of my computer.**

3. Proofread and check; click Next to continue. (*93-d3*)

93-d4

Itinerary in a Table

1. Tap ENTER three times and then apply Aspect document theme.

2. Key the itinerary shown below using a two-column table. Apply Medium Shading 1 – Accent 3 table style. Deselect First Column in the Table Style Options. Adjust the width of the first column to 2".

3. Use 1" row height for the first row; apply 14-point bold font and Align Center to the heading.

4. Bold the information in the three rows with the dates. Adjust row height to 0.4" and apply Align Center Left to those three rows. Leave a blank row between days of the trip.

5. Check and close. (*93-d4*)

ITINERARY FOR LAURIE HAMMER July 14 – 16, 201-	
Wednesday, July 14	**Columbia to Cincinnati**
4:40 p.m.	Leave Columbia on non-stop Flight 5173 and arrive in Cincinnati at 5:55 p.m.; Metro Rental Car (Confirmation #67540912); Riverside Hotel (Confirmation #34898732)
8:15 p.m.	Picked up at hotel by Dave Calhoun and Jack Shaut; dinner at Royal Mason
Thursday, July 15	**Cincinnati**
8:00 a.m.	Leave for Natorp Publishing Center; 6319 Natorp Boulevard, Mason, Ohio
9:00 a.m.	Meet with President and Editor-in-Chief; President's office—Suite 600
9:45 a.m.	Meet with the Editorial Team, Fifth Floor Conference Room
11:45 a.m.	Break
12:00 noon	Working lunch, Fifth Floor Conference Room
2:00 p.m.	Meet with book designers, Fifth Floor Conference Room
2:30 p.m.	Break
3:00 p.m.	Meet with the Production Team, Fifth Floor Conference Room
5:30 p.m.	Return to hotel
7:30 p.m.	Meet Project Team for dinner; Chez Ruby; 644 Walnut Street; map in Travel folder
Friday, July 16	**Cincinnati to Columbia**
8:15 a.m.	Return rental car; Flight 6754 departs at 9:20 a.m. and arrives in Columbia at 10:40 a.m.

Paste MAX Function

1. Create a 6-column, 7-row table. Rotate the text in cells B1–E1.
2. Select columns B–E and adjust the width of columns to 0.6". Change the width of column A to 2.6". Adjust the width of column F until the heading fits on one line.
3. Calculate the average for each test and place in row 7. Display the answer as a whole number (Number format, 0).
4. Use the MAX function to find the maximum score for each student. Place the answers in column F.
5. Center-align columns B–F. Center and bold all column heads.
6. Proofread and check; click Next to continue. (67-d5)

Name	Test 1	Test 2	Test 3	Test 4	Maximum Score
Appleton, Jonathan	87	73	85	87	
Carey, Elizabeth Marie	88	92	93	91	
Palembo-McCormick, Vanessa	72	69	70	71	
Valenzuela, Roberto	92	95	97	96	
Zacariaha, Timothy J.	92	90	88	93	
Average per Test					

67–d6

Calculate Net Profits

1. Key the table, aligning all numbers at the left. Adjust the height of the first row to approximately 0.75". Apply 14-point bold to the title and 12-point bold to the subtitle.
2. Insert totals for each column in row 7. Calculate net profits in column D (*Gross Revenue – Expenses*). Display the answers with a dollar sign and two decimal places.
3. Align the numbers in columns B, C, and D with a decimal tab.
4. Change the height of rows 2–7 to 0.25"; center the copy vertically in the cells.
5. Apply Medium Shading 1 – Accent 3 table style. Select Total Row in Table Style Options. Insert an Olive Green – Accent 3, Darker 25% ½ point, double-line outer border.
6. Check and close. (67-d6)

RICHMOND INDUSTRIES INCORPORATED			
Eastern Region			
Quarter	Gross Revenue	Expenses	Net Profits
First	$980,000.00	$375,000.00	
Second	$1,877,000.00	$620,000.00	
Third	$95,000.00	$31,000.00	
Fourth	$991,000.00	$420,000.00	
Total			

Applications

93-d1

**Itinerary Formatted
with Tabs**

1. Apply Aspect document theme, and key the headings shown on the previous page. Apply Title and Subtitle styles to the headings; set a right-align tab at 6.5" for the date.

2. Set a 2.25" left tab with a hanging indent and key the trip information as shown. Do not format the internal headings for each day until after you have keyed the entire document.

3. Apply Heading 3 style to the internal headings. After each heading, use the Add Space After Paragraph command to insert additional space after each heading to make the document easier to read.

4. Proofread and check; click Next to continue. (93-d1)

93-d2

Modified Itinerary

Several items have changed on Mr. Winn's itinerary. Make all changes using Track Changes.

1. Open 93-d1 and turn Track Changes on.

2. Change the Track Changes Options as follows: **Insertions**—Underline and Dark Red color; **Deletions**—Strikethrough and Dark Blue color.

3. Make the following changes in the itinerary.

   a. On Wednesday, October 9, add:

      7:00 p.m. | **Dinner at Pat's Buckhead Café with Rhett Brown, Joyce Downy, and Hudson Davis.**

   b. Change the time on the return flight to Chicago to **11:40 a.m.** with arrival at **1:15 p.m.**

   c. Click at the end of the entry and insert the comment: **Southern Express Airlines called with the flight schedule change.**

4. Preview in both Final and Final: Show Markup views.

5. Proofread and check; click Next to continue. (93-d2)

! WORKPLACE SUCCESS

Fear of Failure

TOM GRILL/AGE FOTOSTOCK/PHOTO LIBRARY

Many employees—particularly young employees—limit their success because they have an unfounded fear of failure. They often confuse failing with being a failure. If they take on a project and it fails, they think of themselves as failures and avoid taking on similar projects. This type of behavior is often referred to as a self-fulfilling prophecy. If you think you can do something, you are likely to, but if you do not think you can do something, you are not likely to do it. The attitude that leads to success is to view failed projects as something that did not work, to try to learn why, and to move to something that might work. The owner and chef of a great restaurant had a total failure with his first restaurant, then took a job as a chef and was fired; his next venture was a resounding success—arguably the leading restaurant in the country. Baseball home-run kings often also have high strikeout numbers. Successful people are persistent—when something does not work, they try alternatives and learn from each trial until they reach success.

Lesson 68 | Convert Text and Tables

WARMUP

KEYBOARDING PRO DELUXE 2

Lessons/68a Warmup

Review Commands

68b

INSERT BULLETED AND NUMBERED TEXT IN TABLE CELLS

Home/Paragraph/Bullets or Numbering

To emphasize portions of table text, bulleted or numbered paragraph formatting can be applied to the text. Apply these formats just as for any paragraph: Click in the table paragraph and click either the Bullets command or the Numbering command. You may want to decrease the indent on bulleted or numbered items so they are not indented in the table cell.

The bullet symbol can be changed by clicking the Bullets drop-list arrow and making a selection from the Bullet Library. You can also create a custom bullet by choosing Define New Bullet.

The numbering style for a numbered list can be changed by clicking the Numbering drop-list arrow and making a selection from the Numbering Library. A custom style can be created by choosing Define New Number Format.

New Commands

68c

CONVERT TEXT TO TABLE

Text that has been keyed as paragraphs or in a list can be converted to a table. The table will consist of one column, and each paragraph will be in its own row. Text can be placed in more than one column if it is properly delimited. Delimited text is divided into sections by a consistently used symbol. Tabs and commas are most commonly used as delimiter characters.

To convert text to a table:

Insert/Tables/Table/Convert Text to Table

1. Select the text to be converted to a table.
2. Follow the path to display the Convert Text to Table dialog box.
3. Indicate the number of columns for the table ❶.
4. Select an AutoFit behavior for the table ❷. These are the same options as when creating a table using Insert Table.
5. Under Separate text at ❸, select the delimiter character.
6. Click OK to convert the text to a table.

Itinerary for Landon Winn *Title Style*

Chicago to Atlanta   2.25" tab   *October 9-11, 201-*

Wednesday, October 9   ↓ **Chicago to Atlanta**

| 8:45 a.m. | Leave Chicago Midway Airport (MDW) on Southern Express Flight 1387 and arrive at Atlanta Hartsfield (ATL) at 11:20 a.m.; take MARTA to Buckhead Station (N-7). Taxi to the Buckhead Inn (Confirmation #204857) 260 Pharr Road, NE. (45 minutes) |
| 2:30 p.m. | Meeting with Rhett Brown, Joyce Downy, and Hudson Davis in Conference Room A of the Buckhead Inn. Refreshments ordered. |

Thursday, October 10   **Atlanta**

| 9:45 a.m. | Picked up at the hotel by Michael Jones; drive to Dunwoody Conference Center. Full-day meeting with Pearce Sports Equipment Company. |
| 7:00 p.m. | Dinner with Michael Jones, Kevin Pearce, and Trinity Jenkins. Restaurant to be determined by hosts. Return to hotel by 10:00 p.m. |

Friday, October 11   **Atlanta to Chicago**

| 8:30 a.m. | Breakfast at hotel with Trey Meyer, Travis Smoak, and Drew Dyson. |
| 9:45 a.m. | Leave for airport (ATL) with Trey Meyer. Southern Express Flight 1436 departs at 11:35 a.m. and arrives at Chicago (MDW) at 1:10 p.m. |

CONVERT TABLE TO TEXT

A table can be converted to regular paragraph text. Again, you will be asked to identify a delimiter character that will substitute for the column breaks. Tabs and commas are traditionally used, but you can select any character.

To convert a table to regular text:
Table Tools Layout/Data/Convert to Text

1. Click the insertion point in the table.
2. Follow the path to display the Convert Table to Text dialog box.
3. Select the delimiter character to be used.
4. Click OK to convert the table to text.

DRILL 1   CONVERT TEXT TO TABLE

1. Key the text at the right. Turn on Show/Hide.
2. Select only the text; do not select any ¶ markers above or below the text.

Insert/Tables/Table/Convert Text to Table

3. Convert the text to a 2-column table using fixed column width.
4. Proofread and check; click Next to continue. (68-drill1)

Employee, Department

Lambert C. Harrington, Accounting

Justin A. Rodriguez, Information Technology

Hillary M. Anderson, Project Planning

Irma J. Kuar, Human Resources

DRILL 2   CONVERT TABLE TO TEXT

1. Open *68-drill1*. Click the insertion point in the table. Convert the table to text, separating the text with tabs.

2. Check and close. (*68-drill2*)

NICK DOLDING/PHOTODISC/JUPITER IMAGES

! WORKPLACE SUCCESS

High-Tech Etiquette

Many offices use an open office layout. The cubicle work environment encourages collaboration, but the lack of doors and ceilings also requires basic consideration for others. Respect others' privacy. Do not take items from other peoples' workstations without asking, or hover over their shoulder while they finish a phone call. Do not use another person's computer without permission. If you share a cubicle, remember to clean up after yourself.

If you listen to music while you work, wear a headset. If you keep your cell phone on, set it on vibrate.

If you eat at your desk, choose "silent" foods. Think twice about foods that have strong odors—remember that other people will have to smell those odors all afternoon. Dispose of banana peels in the kitchen; do not place them in a cubicle wastebasket.

1. Key your name and initials in the User name box. With the document open, turn Track Changes on.

2. Change the default Track Changes Options to those shown at the right.

3. With the defaults changed, make the changes you made in steps 2–4 of Drill 1.

4. Observe carefully how all of the changes displayed using the options you set.

5. Proofread and check; click Next to continue. (93-drill2)

- **Insertions**—Color only; **Deletions**—Strikethrough.

- **Moved from**—Bold and Dark Yellow color; **Moved to**—Underline and Dark Yellow color.

- **Formatting**—Bold; keep in balloon.

- **Balloons**—change width to 2" and display in left margin.

DRILL 3   RETURN OPTIONS TO DEFAULT

1. In the open document, change the Track Change Options back to the defaults shown at the right.

2. Then key on the first line: **For this document, the Track Changes Options were returned to the default setting.**

3. Proofread and check; click Next to continue. (93-drill3)

- **Insertions**—Underline; **Deletions**—Double strikethrough.

- **Moved from**—Double strikethrough and Green color; **Moved to**—Double underline and Green color.

- **Formatting**—(none).

- **Balloons**—Width: 3"; Margin: Right.

Document Design

93d

ITINERARY

An itinerary is a detailed plan for a trip. Itineraries for work-related trips provide details about the business activities as well as the travel information. Normally, when people are working in their offices, they have various types of information available to them. When they are out of the office, a comprehensive itinerary provides a quick summary of all the logistical information needed to function effectively. Typically, an itinerary includes the following information:

- Heading with name and dates of trip.
- Transportation information—maps and route information for driving trips; or airline flight numbers and times, ticket information, passport or other identification, visa requirements, rental car or ground transportation for air travel.
- Hotel information—name and address, confirmation number, special requests made.
- Restaurant information—name and address, reservation information, participants.
- Meetings or appointments—individual and company names, times, addresses, and transportation information if needed.
- Leisure-time information.

Generally, itineraries are formatted using tabs or a table. Fragments are used rather than complete sentences.

Review the itinerary on the next page; pay particular attention to the way the content is presented. Also review the format.

68-d1

Create Table and Convert to Text

1. Key the table and apply Light Shading – Accent 3 design.
2. Adjust column widths and center the table horizontally.

Form	Name of File	Path and Subdirectory
Invoice	Invoice	C:\Business Forms
Purchase Order	PurchaseOd	C:\Business Forms\Purchasing
Medical Leave of Absence	Medleave	C:\HR\Medical
Cash Reimbursement	Reimburse	C:\HR\Business Forms
Dental Insurance	Dental	C:\HR\Medical

3. Convert the table to text using tabs to separate text.
4. With the converted text still selected, use Remove Space After Paragraph to remove extra space after all paragraphs.
5. Apply bold to the column headings.
6. Proofread and check; click Next to continue. (68-d1)

68-d2

Memo with Table

 form list

1. Key the following memo; insert necessary memo parts.
2. Insert the data file *form list* where indicated below the first paragraph.
3. Select rows 2–6 of the inserted list and sort the paragraphs in ascending alphabetical order by form name (Field 1).
4. Proofread and check; click Next to continue. (68-d2)

★ DISCOVER

Sort Paragraphs

Home/Paragraph/Sort

Use the Sort Text dialog box to sort paragraphs the same way you learned to sort table data.

TO: Royal Canadian Employees

FROM: Mary Nottingham, Administrative Assistant

DATE: Current date

SUBJECT: Company Forms

The IT Department has downloaded the most widely used forms onto the hard drive of your computer. Below is a list of the forms, the filename under which the form is stored, and the path and subdirectory in which the form is saved.

[Insert *form list* here]

If you need additional help in retrieving these forms, please call me at extension 617.

Review/Tracking/Track Changes/Change User Name

1. Turn on Track Changes; check to see that you are listed in the User name box.

2. Change all headings to Heading 1 style; then make the changes in the first two sections as shown below.

3. Change the name and initials in the User name box from your name to **Lynn West** and **lw**.

4. Make the changes shown in the remainder of the document; observe how the changes display.

5. Proofread and check; click Next to continue. *(93-drill1)*

Changes by Student

Nursing Partnerships

~~Demand for Nurses Exceeds Supply~~

~~As we all know,~~ the demand for nurses far exceeds the supply of nurses in ~~this~~ *the entire* *central* region of the state. Local ~~colleges~~ *educational institutions* are unable to prepare an adequate supply of nurses to meet this growing demand. *The result is that healthcare facilities are unable to meet workforce demand.*

Partnership Proposed

The ~~four~~ *five* local hospitals, the local technical college, and the local university in the *central* region ~~has~~ *have* developed a ~~strong~~ comprehensive ~~and~~ viable plan to increase the supply of both licensed practical nurses and registered nurses, *over the next ten years*

Hospitals

~~Four~~ *Five* area hospitals will contribute $1,000,000 each to the Nursing Partnership this year. Of the $~~4~~*5*,000,000, the university will be allocated $~~3~~*4*,000,000, and the technical college will be allocated $1,000,000. In addition, the hospitals each pledged to invest $50,000 a year in the Nursing Partnership for the next five years. These annual funds will be split ~~50/50~~ *equally* between the technical college and the university.

Changes by Lynn West

The attached table summarizes the five-year funding plan for the hospitals and the five-year spending plan for the educational institutions.

Program Implementation

The agreement will be finalized and signed within three weeks, and the funds will be made available within three months. Other potential partners are being contacted to determine their willingness to participate in the program.

Convert List to Table

 power options

1. In the open document, turn on Show/Hide. Place the insertion point on the first letter in the list (A). Tap ENTER to place a blank line above the list.

2. Click in the paragraph above the list. Center the main heading in all caps, bold, 14-point font.

3. Select the list and convert it to a 1-column, 7-row table.

4. Apply Medium List 1 – Accent 4 table style. Deselect Header Row in Table Style Options.

5. Change the width of the table to 4". Center the table horizontally on the page.

6. Change the bullets to numbers. Click Decrease Indent to move the enumerations to the left edge of the table.

7. Key the text in the table.

8. Check and close. (*68-d3*)

POWER OPTIONS PROPERTIES

1.	Advanced—Change user power options.
2.	Alarms—Change settings for low battery notification alarms (available on most laptop computers).
3.	APM—Turn on or turn off Advanced Power Management (APM) support to reduce overall power consumption.
4.	Hibernate—Turn on and off hibernation. If the Hibernation option is turned on, you can select it when you shut down your computer.
5.	Power Meter—Display power usage details for each battery in your computer.
6.	Power Schemes—Change power settings for your monitor and hard disks.
7.	UPS—Select and configure an Uninterruptible Power Source.

⭐ **TIP**

If you change options on a computer that is used by others, you should change the options back to the default as a courtesy to them.

TRACK CHANGES OPTIONS

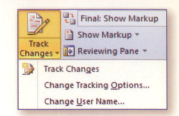

Users have the option of using the default Track Changes Options or changing the tracking options. Options can be changed in a variety of ways that involve the type of markup, type style, color, and whether or not to track certain changes such as formatting.

Tracking options are designed to identify which reviewer made each suggested change. In order for *Word* to recognize different reviewers, each reviewer must have his or her name keyed in the User name box that can be accessed on the Options of the File menu or from the Track Changes Options. If a reviewer keys initials in the Initials box, the initials are used in designating who made the change; if not, the full name is used.

It is important to note that not all computers display colors in the same way. The color one reviewer has displayed on a computer may be different from the color another reviewer sees when he or she is reviewing the document. As noted in the last lesson, the Show Markup command lists the reviewers and identifies the color for each reviewer.

To display and change default tracking options:
Review/Tracking/Track Changes

1. Select Change Tracking Options to display the Track Changes Options dialog box.
2. Click the drop-list arrow of the option you wish to change, and select the option you wish to use from the list. Note that (*none*) is an option—you can choose to display or not display that option. Also note the variety of colors and style options that can be used. When you have completed all changes, click OK.

Markup—controls how insertions, deletions, and comments display. Changed lines alert the reviewer to changes made. A punctuation or one-letter change may be difficult to see; lines point out where the changes were made.

Moves—controls how changes in repositioned text display.

Table cell highlighting—controls the color used to show cells inserted, deleted, merged, or split.

Formatting—controls whether or not formatting is tracked and provides display options.

Balloons—controls what balloons are used for and their size and position.

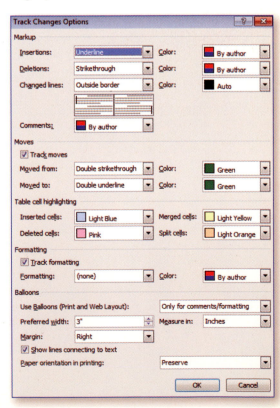

Lesson 69 | Create Documents with Tables

Skill Building

69b Timed Writing
1. Key one 3' writing.
2. Key one 5' writing.

	gwam	3'	5'
Eating is often the solution to any and all problems for many people. Our society has been known to use food as a tranquilizer. Many times if a child expresses unhappiness, someone will try soothing the child with a cookie.

Food cravings may mean that a person is hungry. But for emotional eaters, it may mean that they need something else. For some people, it may be a sign of boredom, frustration, or loneliness. It is important to understand the reason for eating and then try confronting those issues.

You can control your eating by changing the way you do things. Work on a hobby during commercials rather than going to get something to eat. Special events do not need to be centered around food. Celebrate a special occasion by going dancing rather than going out for dinner.

gwam	3'	5'
4	3	35
9	5	38
13	8	40
15	9	41
20	12	44
24	14	46
29	17	49
33	20	52
35	21	53
39	24	56
43	26	58
48	29	61
52	31	63
54	32	64

3' | 1 | 2 | 3 | 4
5' | 1 | 2 | 3

Applications

69-d1

Flyer with Table and Graphics

power foods

You will be creating the flyer that is shown at the left. The major points of the flyer are keyed in a table.

1. In the open document, create the main heading:
   a. Use WordArt style Fill – Olive Green, Accent 3, Outline – Text 2 to key **Power-Packed Foods May Save Your Life**.
   b. Change the font to Calibri and the font size to 26 points so the WordArt fits on one line. Adjust the graphic to about 7.1" wide. Center the WordArt text.
   c. Change the shape of the WordArt by applying the Chevron Up style on the Text Effect/Transform gallery.
   d. Position the WordArt at the top of the page as shown at left.

2. Insert a 2-column, 5-row table below the second paragraph of text. Change the width of column A to 1.55", and the width of column B to 3.75". Center the table horizontally on the page. Key the text on the next page in the table; tap ENTER after each item. Search for and insert appropriate clip art of each item in column A; size to fit in row.

3. Sort the table so that the items in column B display in alphabetical order. Choose to sort by column 2, using the Text Type, and Ascending.

(continued)

Lesson 93 | Itinerary and Tracking Options

New Commands
- Track Changes Options

93b Timed Writing

1. Key a 1' writing on each paragraph; work to increase speed.
2. Key a 5' timing on both paragraphs.

	gwam	3'	5'

What do you think about when you hear individuals being · · · 4 · · · 8 · · · = 4 | 2 | 50

called student-athletes? Many people think only of the very = 8 | 5 | 52

visible football or basketball players who attract a lot of = 12 | 7 | 55

attention and often get special treatment on campus. Few people = 16 | 10 | 57

think about the large numbers of young men and women who put in = 20 | 12 | 60

long hours working and training to be the very best they can be = 25 | 15 | 62

in a wide variety of sports. These students may never receive = 29 | 17 | 65

any type of recognition in the news media, and they do not = 33 | 20 | 67

attract large crowds to watch them perform. They frequently = 37 | 22 | 70

excel in both academic and athletic performance. = 40 | 24 | 72

What does a student-athlete in one of the less visible = 44 | 26 | 74

sports with very little opportunity to become a professional = 48 | 29 | 76

athlete gain from the significant investment of time and = 52 | 31 | 79

effort in a sport? To be successful in a sport, a student must = 56 | 34 | 81

be organized, be an effective time manager, and have self- = 60 | 36 | 83

confidence. An athlete learns that teamwork, ethical conduct, = 64 | 38 | 86

and hard work are a major part of success in any type of = 68 | 41 | 88

endeavor. The skills do not apply just to sports; they also apply = 72 | 43 | 91

to your job and your life. Most important of all, these individuals = 77 | 46 | 93

are doing what they really enjoy doing. = 79 | 47 | 95

69-d1

continued

▶▶ **REVIEW**

Sort Table Data

Table Tools Layout/Data/Sort

4. Select the table and remove all borders.

5. Proofread and check; click Next to continue. (*69-d1*)

	Carrots are rich in beta carotene. Eating two carrots every other day will provide enough beta carotene to reduce stroke risk by half for men who already display symptoms of heart disease.
	Spinach contains vitamins A and C, folic acid, and magnesium. Spinach may help control cancer, reduce heart disease and stroke risk, and may help prevent osteoporosis.
	Garlic may lower cholesterol and blood pressure. Garlic may also contain chemicals capable of destroying cancer cells.
	Oat bran can help lower cholesterol and blood pressure and may also reduce risk of colon cancer. Eating oat bran for breakfast will keep you from getting hungry mid-morning.
	Mangos contain bioflavonoids that can aid the immune system. Mangos are also rich in fiber.

69-d2

Create Form with Graphics and WordArt

▶▶ **REVIEW**

Adjust Brightness

Picture Tools Format/Adjust/ Corrections

✱ **DISCOVER**

To move the picture around after it has been inserted behind the text: Click inside the document, follow the path Home/Select/Select Objects, then click the picture and move it.

You will be creating a form in which the table provides a grid to key text and insert graphics. The form is shown on the next page with the table grid displayed to help you arrange the document. The table grid will be removed when the text is complete.

1. Create a 2-column, 16-row table. Merge the cells in row 1. Using *dog grooming* as keywords, search for and insert the clip art shown. Change the height of the clip art to 1".

2. Use WordArt to insert the main heading in row 1 as shown. Choose the Gradient Fill – Orange, Accent 6, Inner Shadow style. Change the font to Maiandra GD or Lucida Calligraphy.

3. Merge the cells in row 2. Use the Arial Rounded MT Bold font and center alignment and key **Grooming Form**. Change font size to 18 point. Tap ENTER.

4. Select the remaining rows and change the row height to 0.4". Key the text as shown and center it vertically in the cells. Change the font to Arial, bold, and 12 point.

5. Insert checkboxes under *Services to be performed* (Insert/Symbols/Symbol/ More Symbols/Wingdings/Wingdings 114).

6. Merge the cells in the row below *Special Instructions*. Change the height of the row to 2".

7. Merge the cells in the row containing the dashed line. Key the line using the hyphen key. Insert the scissors symbol at the left of the line (Insert/Symbols/ Symbol/More Symbols/Wingdings).

8. Merge the cells in the row containing *Receipt of Sale*. Change the heading to 14 point.

9. After you are finished keying the form, select the entire table and choose No Border.

10. Insert a clip art similar to the one shown (search for the clip art *dog*). Center the picture vertically and horizontally on the table. Change the picture height to 7.16".

11. Adjust the brightness of the picture to Brightness: +20% contrast: -40% so that the text will be visible. Change the text wrapping on the picture to Behind Text.

12. Proofread and check; click Next to continue. (*69-d2*)

Minutes—Nursing Partnership Board

Hospital Atrium   *10:30 AM*   *1/15/201-*

The Nursing Partnership Board met on January 15, 201- at 10:30 AM in the Hospital Atrium. Team members present were Lester Caldwell, team leader; Mary Freeman, team facilitator; Jane Metze, technical college representative; Wanda Stewart, project coordinator; Student's Name, project assistant; and Tyler Walker, hospital representative.

Proposal

Mary Freeman presented the agreement with the markup showing all changes in it. She pointed out that these changes were made in the last meeting. The team agreed that the revised version reflected the discussion of the previous meeting. Mary Freeman was asked to revise the final agreement with the changes noted.

Terms

(Student's Name) presented the changes reflecting the additional $1,000,000 committed by the fifth area hospital. The hospital also committed to the $50,000 annual contribution. The team decided to use the same distribution formula for the funds contributed by the other hospitals. Mary Freeman was asked to revise the final agreement to reflect the additional funds, and she agreed to finalize all documents within two weeks.

Hospital Perspective

Tyler Walker presented the attached funding plan submitted by the hospitals. The team approved the plan.

Technical College Perspective

Jane Metze presented the attached fund usage plan submitted by the technical college. The team approved the plan.

University Perspective

Lester Caldwell presented the attached fund usage plan submitted by the university. The team approved the plan.

Approval

After considerable discussion of how plans would be implemented, the team gave approval to the entire project.

Adjournment

The meeting adjourned at 12:05 PM.

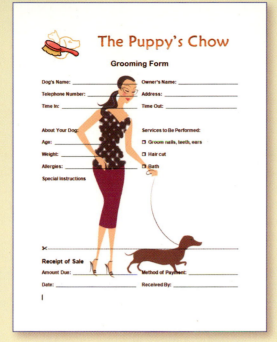

Finished copy with picture inserted behind text.

Key the text in the table cells using this illustration as a guide.

69-d3

Table with Merged Cells

 ★ TIP

Move the bullets to the left edge of the cell by clicking the Decrease Indent button.

1. Insert a 3-column, 8-row table to create the table shown on the following page.

2. Merge the cells in row 1. Center the main heading as shown on the next page in 14 point, bold, and all caps; tap ENTER and adjust font formats to the default; tap ENTER again. Key the paragraph below the heading.

3. Key the column heads in row 3. Change the row height to 0.3".

4. Key the table in rows 4, 6, and 8. Leave rows 5 and 7 blank. Decrease the indent for the bulleted items in column C to set them at the left margin of the column.

5. Apply Light List – Accent 2 style to the table. Bold and center the column heads vertically and horizontally.

6. Adjust the width of column A to approximately 1.65". Adjust column C to approximately 1.9". Column B should be about 2.6" wide.

7. Change the height of row 1 to 1.25". Center the text vertically in the row.

8. Check and close. (69-d3)

1. Open *92-drill1* and display the Reviewing Pane vertically. Note the number and types of changes made in this document.

2. Accept each change in sequence until you get to the comment; delete the comment.

3. Click Accept All Changes in Document to accept the remainder of the changes.

4. Proofread and check; click Next to continue. (*92-drill3*)

Document Design

92c

TIP

For minutes that are more than one page long, include an appropriate header on all pages except the first one. Generally, the header would include the meeting name and the page number.

MINUTES

Minutes provide a record of what occurred in a meeting. Typically, minutes are prepared relatively soon after a meeting and distributed to all participants. Minutes may vary significantly depending on the type of meeting. In some cases, only a brief summary of the action taken is recorded. In other cases, a verbatim transcript of everything said in a meeting is recorded. Most organizations prefer to record only the essential or very important information that needs to be preserved for future reference. These minutes are usually called *action minutes* because they capture the decisions that are made and the actions that take place. Some minutes are very formal; others are very informal using first names and a casual writing style.

Typically, minutes contain the following information:

1. Heading information—*Minutes*, meeting name, date, time, and location.
2. Name of presiding officer or meeting leader and names of attendees.
3. Introduction of topics or outcomes expected.
4. Summary of decisions and actions.
5. Handouts and meeting materials may be attached to be part of the record.

Applications

92-d1

Draft Minutes

1. In a new document, insert the *NPB Agenda Heading* from the Quick Parts Gallery.
2. Select the Agenda title and modify it to **Minutes—Nursing Partnership Board**, and save the selection as a building block in the Quick Parts Gallery. Use **NPB Minutes Heading** as the name and description.
3. Key the meeting date **1/15/201-**.
4. Key the minutes from the draft version on the next page, using normal margins. Your document will be two pages long. This draft will be reviewed by several reviewers. Use Heading 1 style for all headings.
5. Proofread and check; click Next to continue. (*92-d1*)

92-d2

Final Minutes

 draft minutes

1. Make sure Track Changes are turned on. In the first paragraph, delete the first sentence; delete student's name, and key your name. Also replace (*Student's Name*) in the paragraph below with your name.
2. Add a second-page header using Motion Even Page and the title from the first page; do not show the header on the first page.
3. Review the summary in the Reviewing Pane. Then review changes by each reviewer separately. Accept all changes shown for each reviewer.
4. View your changes and accept all changes in the document.
5. Check and close. (*92-d2*)

MOBILE PHONE: JACK OF ALL TRADES		
Cell phones have the capability of doing more than just calling people. New technology is now producing faster chips, bigger and brighter screens, and more applications for the cell phone. A hand-held computer may be a more appropriate name for the future cell phone.		
Additional Services	**Description of Service**	**Service Provider**
Obtain Driving Directions	Several services have added Wi-Fi "hotspot" finders to their mobile mapping service so that you can get driving directions on your cell phone for just a couple of extra dollars per month.	• StreetFinder just launched its mobile version called StreetFinder Navigator • Telecomm • PhoneNav
Get Extra Money	You can now turn your cell phone into a digital wallet. Some banking systems allow you to use your cell phone to transfer money from your bank account to a credit or debit card.	• International Express • AmeriCard
Access Computer Files	If you left a file on a home or work computer, you can remotely access that computer and get the file. Software is being developed that will also allow you to access computers that are not turned on.	• Computer Transcender • Hitch Hiker Express

Review/Tracking/Track Changes

1. In the open document, turn Track Changes on and make the changes shown below.

Review/Tracking/Show Markup

2. Review the document by selecting Final: Show Markup and then by selecting Final.

3. Proofread and check; click Next to continue. (92-drill2)

The first on site meeting is scheduled for November 10. We plan to meet at the main entrance at 10:30 o'clock **a.m.** to tour the property and review the procedures that NatureLink plans to use in designing the trails ~~close to~~ **near** the red cockaded woodpecker (RCW) habitat. Since the RCW is an endangered species, we want to balance the wishes of ecotourists to observe these birds and the need to ~~preserve~~ **protect** them.

REVIEWING PANE

The Reviewing Pane provides a summary of the tracked changes and comments in a document. Vertical and Horizontal options are available.

To view a summary of tracked changes and comments:

Review/Tracking/Reviewing Pane

- Follow the path and select either Reviewing Pane Vertical or Reviewing Pane Horizontal.

REVIEW CHANGES AND COMMENTS

Changes and comments can be reviewed in sequence, and each change can be accepted or rejected. Comments should be rejected or deleted after they have been read and appropriate action has been taken. Comments do not convert to text. All changes can also be accepted or rejected at one time.

To accept or reject changes:

Review/Changes/Previous or Next

1. Click Previous or Next to move to a change.

2. To accept a change, click Accept and Move to Next; to reject a change, click Reject and Move to Next.

3. To accept all changes at once, click Accept and then Accept All Changes in Document; to reject all changes, click Reject and then Reject All Changes in Document.

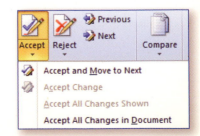

Lesson 70 | Assessment

Skill Building

A | ALL LETTERS

gwam | 3' | 5'

70b Timed Writing

Key two 3' writings.

		3'	5'
How are letters and other documents produced in the modern		4	2	52
office? They are prepared in a number of ways. Just a few years		8	5	54
ago, with rare exceptions, a document was composed by a manager		13	8	57
who either wrote it in longhand or dictated it. Then, one of the		17	10	60
office staff typed it in final form. Today, the situation is		21	13	62
quite different. Office staff may compose and produce various		25	15	65
documents, or they may finalize documents that were keyed by		29	18	67
managers. In some cases, managers like to produce some or all of		34	20	70
their documents in final form.		36	22	71

Many people question how this dramatic change in the way documents are prepared came about. Two factors can be cited as the major reasons for the change. The primary factor is the extensive use of computers in offices today. A manager who uses a computer for a variety of tasks may find it just as simple to key documents at the computer as it would be to prepare them for office personnel to produce. The other factor is the increase in the ratio of office personnel to managers. Today, one secretary is very likely to support as many as six or eight managers. Managers who share office staff find that they get much quicker results by finalizing their own documents when they compose them.

40 | 24 | 73
44 | 26 | 76
48 | 29 | 78
52 | 31 | 81
57 | 34 | 83
61 | 37 | 86
65 | 39 | 89
70 | 42 | 91
74 | 44 | 94
78 | 47 | 96
82 | 49 | 99

```
3'  |    1    |    2    |    3    |    4    |
5'  |      1      |      2      |      3      |
```

Applications

70c

Assessment

 Continue

 Check

When you complete a document, proofread it, check the spelling, and preview for placement. When you are completely satisfied, click the Continue button to move to the next document. Click the Check button when you are ready to error-check the test. Review and/or print the document analysis results.

DISPLAY FOR REVIEW

Options are available to view a document with tracked changes from several different perspectives. Note the difference in the displays with the four options shown below.

❶ Final: Show Markup: Shows the document with all proposed changes included.

❷ Final: Shows the document as it would look if all changes are accepted.

❸ Original: Show Markup: Shows document with all proposed changes except formatting changes.

❹ Original: Shows the document before changes were made.

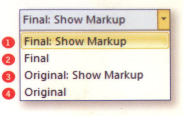

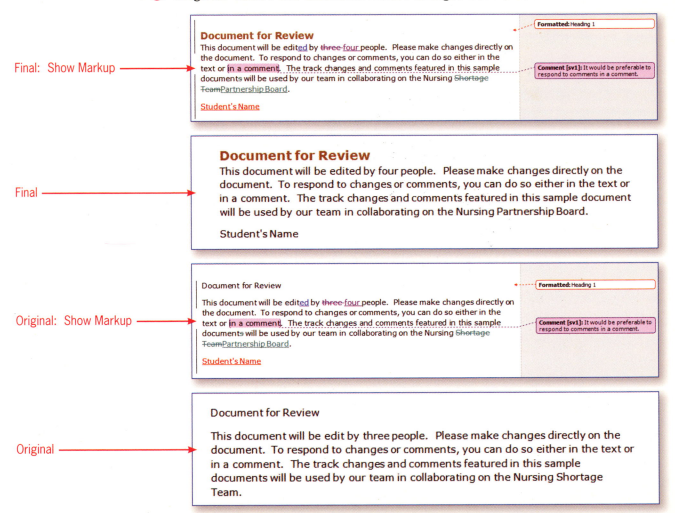

Final: Show Markup

Final

Original: Show Markup

Original

DRILL 1   DISPLAY FOR REVIEW   track changes

1. In the open document, note that the document opens in the default view, Final: Show Markup. Hover the mouse above each change and review the information provided.

2. Turn on Track Changes. Key your name below the last line of text.

3. View the document in each of the four options for review.

4. Check to see that your name is listed as a reviewer. Then turn Track Changes off.

5. Proofread and check; click Next to continue. (*92-drill1*)

70-d1

Create Table, Rotate Text, and Calculate

1. Create the 6-column, 7-row table shown below. Merge the cells in column A.

2. Key the main heading **MONTHLY DEDUCTIONS** in bold, 14-point caps. Rotate the text and apply White, Background 1, Darker 15% shading. Change the width of the column A to 0.5".

3. Change the height of row 1 to 1". Key the column headings in bold, 12-point font; center them vertically and horizontally in the cells.

4. Key the table, adjust column widths, and center table horizontally.

5. Insert the totals in the last row and last column. Totals should contain a comma and two decimal places. Use a decimal tab to align numbers. Change the height of rows 2–7 to 0.25"; center text vertically in the cells.

6. Change Bennet's Disability Insurance to **55.00** and Fraser's Tax Shelter Annuity amount to **375.00**. Update the totals to reflect the changes.

7. Proofread the document carefully. Continue to the next document. (70-d1)

MONTHLY DEDUCTIONS	Employee	Tax Shelter Annuity	Health Insurance	Disability Insurance	Total Deduction
	Bennet, Susan	500.00	355.00	25.00	
	Carillo, Marlan	175.00	685.00	25.00	
	Fraser, Elisol	100.00	320.00	0.00	
	Jones, Barbara	300.00	220.00	25.00	
	Tanaka, Ellen	200.00	375.00	25.00	
	Total				

70-d2

Sort in Table

1. Center the main heading in 14-point bold font and caps. Center the secondary heading in 12-point bold font.

2. Key the table below and apply Medium Shading 2 – Accent 4 table style.

3. Adjust column width and center table horizontally. Center column D.

4. Sort the table according to *Founded*, then *Arena*, then by *Team* in ascending order.

5. Adjust the height of all rows to 0.25". Center the text vertically in the cells.

6. Proofread carefully. When you are satisfied, continue to the next document. (70-d2)

WESTERN CONFERENCE
Pacific Division

Team	City, State	Arena	Founded
Golden State Warriors	Oakland, CA	Oracle Arena	1946
Los Angeles Clippers	Los Angeles, CA	Staples Center	1970
Los Angeles Lakers	Los Angeles, CA	Staples Center	1946
Phoenix Suns	Phoenix, AZ	US Airways Center	1968
Sacramento Kings	Sacramento, CA	ARCO Arena	1945

Lesson 92 | Minutes with Track Changes

New Commands   • Track Changes   • Show Markup   • Reviewing Pane

New Commands

92b

TRACK CHANGES

On   **Off**

The Track Changes feature shows suggested revisions or changes in a document. Tracked changes enable a reviewer to make suggestions in the form of insertions, deletions, and formats to the text of a document without the document itself changing. Each suggested change can be viewed and accepted or rejected. Once changes are accepted, the document is actually changed. Comments differ from tracked changes in that suggestions are offered, but they cannot be accepted and made a part of the document. Comment text would have to be copied or keyed to integrate it in the document.

To turn Track Changes on or off:
Review/Tracking/Track Changes

1. Click Track Changes to turn tracking on. When tracking is turned on, the button turns orange.
2. To turn tracking off, click the orange Track Changes button.

MARKUP

Markup provides options for viewing changes that have been tracked. Some reviewers prefer to focus on insertions and deletions and deal with other revisions separately. Others prefer to review the suggestions of one reviewer at a time.

❶ **Display for Review:** Choose how to view proposed changes to the document.

❷ **Show Markup:** Choose the type of markup to show in the document.

❸ **Reviewing Pane:** Show revisions in a separate window.

❶ Final: Show Markup
❷ Show Markup ▾
❸ Reviewing Pane ▾

To show markup:
Review/Tracking/Show Markup

1. Display the markup options.
2. Check options that you wish to display and deselect options that you do not wish to display.

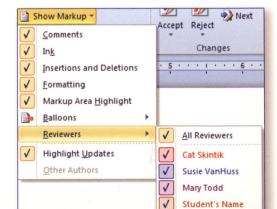

70-d3

Convert Table to Text

1. Open *70-d2*. Delete the main heading, secondary heading, and row 1 of the table.
2. Click in the table and convert it to text. Separate the text with tabs. With the text selected, click the Center button.
3. Continue with the next document. (*70-d3*)

70-d4

Merge and Split Cells, Use Formulas

1. Key the table below. Change the height of row 1 to 0.7"; change the height of all other rows to 0.2". Key the main heading in 14 point, bold, and all caps. Key the secondary heading in 12-point, bold font.
2. Bold and center all headings. Adjust column width and center table horizontally on the page. Center the *Hours* columns.
3. Write a formula that will calculate the amount of both regular and overtime earnings. Display the answer in the *Amount* columns with a dollar sign and two decimal places. Decimal-align the *Amount* and *Rate* columns.
4. Add a column to the right of the table; select row 1 and click Merge Cells. Select cells H2 and H3 and click Merge Cells; key **Total Earnings** in the merged cell. Write a formula that will calculate total earnings; place the answer in dollar format with two decimal places in the *Total Earnings* column. Decimal-align the column.
5. Add a row at the bottom of the table; key **Total** in cell A9. Use SUM(ABOVE) to place the total for the *Amount* columns and *Total Earnings* in row 9.
6. Proofread carefully and verify the totals. Check and close. (*70-d4*)

PAYROLL REGISTER For Week Ending January 19, 201-						
Name	Regular Earnings			Overtime Earnings		
	Hours	Rate	Amount	Hours	Rate	Amount
Oldfield, Cary	40	22.75				
Weingard, Susan T.	40	12.50		2	18.75	
Thompson, William	40	14.50		4	21.75	
Morrison, Carl	40	16.50		6	24.75	
Pham, Vo	38	18.00				

◆ BOOKMARK

www.collegekeyboarding.com
Module 11 Practice Quiz

91-d1

Agenda with Comments

1. Prepare the agenda illustrated on the previous page, formatting it as indicated below.
2. Key the title and subtitle and apply Title and Subtitle styles. Format the subtitle:
   a. Position the standard meeting location at the left margin.
   b. Set a 3.25" center tab to position the standard meeting time at the center.
   c. Set a 6.5" right tab to key the variable meeting date at the right margin.
3. Change the tabs to 1" left tab and 6.5" right-aligned dot leader tab and key the agenda on the previous page.
4. Add and edit the following comments to the agenda:
   a. Select *Call to Order* and add Comment 1: **Please confirm your attendance.**
   b. Select *Proposal* and add Comment 2: **Copies will be distributed at least three days prior to the meeting.**
   c. Select *Approval* and key Comment 3: **If the Board is not ready to finalize the decision, another meeting will be scheduled.**
   d. Edit Comment 1 as follows: **Please confirm your attendance and indicate any additional items you wish to add to the agenda.**
5. Select the heading (title and subtitle) and save it for future use as a building block with the name and description **NPB Agenda Heading**.
6. Proofread and check; click Next to continue. (*91-d1*)

91-d2

Revised Agenda

1. Open *91-d1* and make the following revisions to the preliminary agenda.
2. **Approval of Minutes** needs to be added to the agenda. Mary Freeman does not require additional time for that item. Position after *Call to Order* and do not list a time.
3. The speakers giving the three perspectives—hospital, technical college, and university—indicated that 10 minutes would be adequate for their comments. Reduce their times to 10 minutes each and add the 15 minutes saved to the discussion time.
4. Delete all comments.
5. Proofread and check; click Next to continue. (*91-d2*)

91-d3

Agenda Formatted in Table

 training agenda

1. In the open file, select the date and replace it with **5/14/201-**.
2. Key the response to Comment 2 made by Mary Todd: **I agree. The Bradford, Eastman, and McAlexander proposals should be reviewed separately.**
3. Select *Discussion* and add a new comment: **I think we should allow 10 minutes for each proposal and 20 minutes for discussion.**
4. Delete the first comment by Jason Tapp.
5. Proofread and check; click Next to continue. (*91-d3*)

91-d4

Revised Agenda

1. Open *91-d3* and make the following revisions to the agenda.
2. Add two rows below row 4 (2:50 time slot). Add the following information:

Row 5:	**3:00**	**Review of Eastman Proposal**	**Mary Todd**
Row 6:	**3:10**	**Review of McAlexander Proposal**	**Your Name**

3. In row 4, modify the text in column B to **Review of Bradford Proposal**.
4. Change times: Discussion **3:20**; Recommendations **3:40**; and Adjournment **4:00**.
5. Delete all comments.
6. Check and close. (*91-d4*)

Reports

Lesson 71 | Review Reports

Lesson 71 *Review Reports*
Lesson 72 *Report with Built-in Headers and Footers*
Lesson 73 *Report with Preliminary Pages*
Lesson 74 *Table of Figures and Index*
Lesson 75 *Report with Citations and Bibliography*
Lesson 76 *Edit Citations and Manage Sources*
Lesson 77 *Assessment*

LEARNING OUTCOMES

- Format reports with cover page and footnotes.
- Insert page numbers in report with preliminary pages.
- Format report using Citations command.
- Generate table of contents, index, and bibliography.
- Use navigation tools.

Lesson 71 | Review Reports

Review Commands
- Page numbers
- Sections
- Footnotes

KEYBOARDING PRO DELUXE 2

WARMUP

Lessons/71a Warmup

A | ALL LETTERS

Skill Building

71b Timed Writing
1. Key a 3' timed writing on each paragraph. Work to increase speed.
2. Key a 5' timed writing on both paragraphs.

	gwam	3'	5'
Do you ever "goof off" for an hour or more with a television		4	3
program or a visit on the telephone and realize later that you		9	5
haven't actually enjoyed your leisure? Each nagging little vision		13	8
of homework or chores to be completed always seems to result in		17	10
taking the edge off your pleasure. And then you must hurriedly		22	13
complete whatever you postponed. Why do so many people end up		26	15
rushing around in a frenzy, trying to meet their deadlines?		30	18
First, do not waste time feeling guilty. Check with your		34	20
friends who always seem ready for a good time but are also ready		38	23
for unexpected quizzes. Learn their secrets to managing time.		43	26
Knowing that there are sixty seconds in every minute and sixty		47	28
minutes in each hour, you can schedule your activities into the		51	31
time available. Second, learn to set priorities. You can achieve		55	33
your plans and enjoy your leisure as well.		58	35

```
3' |    1    |    2    |    3    |    4    |
5' |      1      |      2      |      3      |
```

AGENDA

An agenda is a plan for conducting a meeting. Typically, the agenda is distributed to participants prior to the meeting and contains four or five types of information:

1. A heading that usually contains the general topic of the meeting, the time, the date, and the location.

2. A list of specific topics to be discussed in the meeting.

3. The individual or group responsible for leading the discussion on each topic.

4. Time allocated for the discussion of each topic, -or- the beginning and ending time of the meeting. Time allocation depends on company philosophy.

5. Attachments that provide information about some of the discussion topics. In some cases, this information is distributed separately from the agenda.

Agendas may be prepared using a traditional format, a template, a table, or building blocks. For a short agenda, the heading should be positioned at 2". If the agenda goes to a second page, the heading should be positioned at 1.5". If it still goes to a second page, position the heading at 1". Generally, a preliminary agenda is sent out to all participants, and they are asked to review the agenda and respond with additional items.

2"

Agenda—Nursing Partnership Board

Hospital Atrium		10:30 AM		1/15/201-
10:30	Call to Order			Mary Freeman
	Approval of Minutes			Mary Freeman
10:35	Proposal			Mary Freeman
10:45	Terms of the Agreement			Student's Name
11:00	Hospital Perspective			Tyler Walker
11:10	Technical College Perspective			Jane Metze
11:20	University Perspective			Lester Caldwell
11:30	Discussion and Approval			All
12:00	Adjournment			

71c

PAGE NUMBERS

Multiple-page documents such as reports require page numbers. Suppress the page number from displaying on the first page by selecting Different First Page.

To insert page numbers:

Insert/Header & Footer/Page Number

1. Follow the path to display a list of page number positions and formatting options.
2. Click an option such as Top of Page ❶ to display a gallery of page number styles.
3. Click the down scroll arrow to browse the various styles ❷. **Note:** To remove page numbers, click Remove Page Numbers ❸.

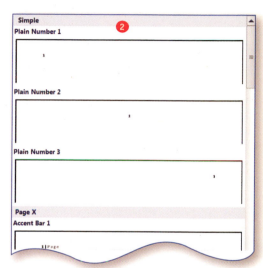

Double-click in the body of the document to close the header. Double-click in the header area to open the header.

To remove the page number from the first page:

Header & Footer Tools Design/Options/Different First Page

Follow the path and click Different First Page. The page number does not display on the first page.

DRILL 1   **PAGE NUMBERS**   benefits

1. In the open document, insert page numbers at the top right using the Plain Number 3 page numbers style.

2. Click Different First Page to suppress the page number from displaying on the first page.

3. Proofread and check; click Next to continue. (*71-drill1*)

QUICK ✔

Answer the questions below to check your solution.

1. Does page 2 include the number 2 positioned at the top right in the header position?
2. Is the page number suppressed on page 1?

New Commands

- New Comment
- Delete Comment
- Edit Comment

WARMUP

KEYBOARDING PRO DELUXE 2

Lessons/91a Warmup

New Commands

91b

COMMENTS

New Comment   Delete   Previous   Next

Comments

Comments enable multiple reviewers to critique a document and insert remarks or annotations. Comments are generally displayed in balloons positioned in the right margin.

f text

> **Comment [svh1]:** This comment demonstrates how comments are displaying in a balloon in the right margin.
>
> **Comment [jm2R1]:** Note that a response has an R in the label to indicate the it is a response to a comment.

To insert a comment:

Review/Comments/New Comment

1. Select the text or click at the end of the text on which you wish to comment, and follow the path to display the Comment balloon.
2. Key the comment you wish to make.

To respond to a comment:

Review/Comments/New Comment

1. Click the balloon containing the comment to which you want to respond.
2. Click New Comment to display a new comment balloon with a dotted line to the comment to which you are responding and with an R in the label to indicate a response.
3. Key your response in the New Comment balloon.

To delete a comment:

Review/Comments/Delete

1. Click in the balloon containing the comment you want to delete.
2. Click Delete. -or-

1. Right-click the balloon containing the comment you want to delete.
2. Click Delete Comment.

DRILL 1   COMMENTS   comments

1. In the open document, note each section that is highlighted and view the comment that is attached to it.
2. Select *add a new comment* in the first line of the last paragraph; then click New Comment.
3. Key the following comment: **Adding a new comment is very easy to do.**
4. Click in *Comment [svh3]*, which is attached to *Respond to a comment.* Click New Comment.

5. Key **Responding to a comment is also very easy to do.**
6. Click in the comment attached to *Delete a comment* and read it; then delete it.
7. Click in your response to *Comment [svh3]* and edit it, adding the following: **Editing is very simple, too.**
8. Proofread and check; click Next to continue. (*91-drill1*)

SECTIONS

Mastering section breaks is very important as you advance to more complex documents. In this lesson, you will review inserting a section break after the cover page and then number the pages of the report, beginning it on page 1. Later in this module you will add additional preliminary pages and number the preliminary pages as well as the report page.

To enter a section break:

Page Layout/Page Setup/Breaks

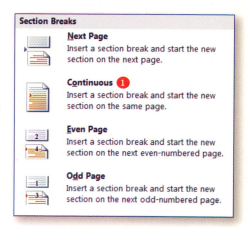

1. Follow the path to insert the section break.

2. From the Section Breaks category, click the desired section break ❶, and then click OK.

   Next Page: Begins a new page at the point the section break is entered.

   Continuous: Begins a new section on the same page.

   Even Page: Begins a new section on the next even-numbered page.

   Odd Page: Begins a new section on the next odd-numbered page.

In Draft View, section breaks appear as a dotted line with the type of break indicated. *Word* displays the current section number on the status bar.

Refer to the status bar to determine the section in which your insertion point is located. If you do not see the section number, place the insertion point on the status bar and right-click. Click Section.

Section: 1   Page: 1 of 5   At: 2"

To delete a section:

1. In Draft View, select the section break to be deleted.

2. Tap DELETE.

90c Textbook Keying

1. Key each line once, concentrating on good keying techniques. Tap ENTER twice after each 2-line group.
2. Repeat if time permits.

1st row
1 Zack and Max became exercise advocates, but they ate many pizzas.
2 Max Mizel verbalized his excessive love for throwing curve balls.

home row
3 Ada Hall's class was at a lake in Dallas; Kala Klass had a salad.
4 Sally's glass flask was full of salt; Sal also saw a glass flask.

3rd row
5 Terry or Peter saw Perry at the polo tryout; you were there, too.
6 Trey, a poet, wrote the quote for Peter; we were there with Trey.

4th row
7 10487 24680 31579 90642 35179 86210 38764 21430 79538 24680 97315
8 63829 87321 90543 28645 80902 21354 87654 23890 27480 46572 89340

balanced hand
9 pens turn fur slam pay rifle worn pan duck ham lap slap burn girl
10 Andy Clancy, a neighbor, may visit at the lake and at the island.

one hand
11 read ploy create kiln crate plum were pony cats jump severe hump
12 Phillip, as you are aware, was a reader on deferred estate cases.

combination
13 did you we spent pony street busy jump held severe pant exert due
14 Were profits better when we were on Main Street than Duck Street?

| 1 | 2 | 3 | 4 | 5 | 6 | 7 | 8 | 9 | 10 | 11 | 12 | 13 |

Communication

90d

pronoun agreement

KEYBOARDING PRO DELUXE 2

References/Communication Skills/Pronoun Agreement

PRONOUN-ANTECEDENT AGREEMENT

1. Review the following guides and those in *Keyboarding Pro DELUXE 2*. In the *pronoun agreement* data file, follow the specific directions provided.
2. Check and close. (*90d*)

1. The antecedent is the word in the sentence to which the pronoun refers. In the examples, the antecedent is bold and the pronoun is in italics.
    Players must show *their* birth certificates.
    The **boy** lost *his* wallet.

2. The antecedent must agree with the pronoun in **person** (first, second, third).
    I am pleased that *my* project placed first. (Both are first person.)
    You must stand by *your* display at the science fair. (Both are second person.)
    He has lost *his* watch. (Both are third person.)

3. The antecedent must agree with the pronoun in **gender** (neuter when gender of antecedent is unknown).
    Gail said that *she* preferred the duplex apartment.
    The adjustable **chair** sits firmly on *its* five-leg base.
    The **dog** looked for *its* master for days.

4. The antecedent must agree with the pronoun in **number**. If the antecedent of a pronoun is singular, use a singular pronoun. If the antecedent is plural, use a plural pronoun.
    All **members** of the class paid *their* dues.
    Each of the Girl Scouts brought **her** sleeping bag.

BREAK LINK BETWEEN SECTIONS AND INSERT PAGE NUMBERS

To be successful on the first attempt every time in breaking the link between sections and number the pages of the report, follow the directions on the next page in the exact order. However, should the first attempt not work, follow the troubleshooting tips on page 347.

Step 1: To break the links in Section 2:

1. Move the insertion point to the top ½" of the page ❶ and double-click to position the insertion point in what is called the header section. Note the Header – Section 2 label displays at the left of the header and the Same as Previous label at the right.

Header & Footer Tools Design/Navigation

2. Follow the path above and click the Link to Previous button ❷ to break the link for the header. Note the Go to Header button is dimmed, meaning the insertion point is in the header.

3. In the Navigation group, click Go to Footer to move to the footer of Section 2. Click the Link to Previous button ❸ to break the link for the footer.

   Note: The Link to Previous button will display in gold until the link is successfully broken.

Step 2: To insert page numbers in Section 2:

4. Click Go to Header to return to the header section where the page number is to be inserted (Header & Footer Tools Design/Navigation/Go to Header).

5. In the Header & Footer group, click Page Number. Click Top Right and select a page number style that displays numbers at the top right.

6. From the Options group, click Different First Page ❹ to select the option to suppress page numbers on the first page.

Step 3: To start number at page 1:

Insert/Header & Footer/Page Number/Format Page Numbers

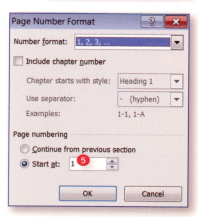

7. Follow the path above and click Format Page Number. Click the Start at up arrow until the number 1 displays ❺.

8. Check the numbers in Section 2. No number should appear on page 1, and remaining pages should be numbered at the top right.

Meeting, Travel, and News Documents

LEARNING OUTCOMES

- View, insert, modify, and delete comments.
- Apply and manage track changes.
- Format meeting management documents.
- Build keyboarding skills.

Lesson 90 | *Skill Building*

KEYBOARDING PRO DELUXE 2

WARMUP

Lessons/90a Warmup

A **ALL LETTERS**

Skill Building

90b   Timed Writing

1. Key two 1' writings on each paragraph; work at your top speed.
2. Key a 3' timing on both paragraphs; work at your control rate.

	gwam	1'	3'
An effective job search requires very careful planning and a	13	4	71
lot of hard work. Major decisions must be made about the type of	26	9	76
job, the size and the type of business, and the geographic area.	39	13	80
Once all of these basic decisions have been made, then the complex	53	18	84
task of locating the ideal job can begin. Some jobs are listed in	66	22	89
what is known as the open job market. These positions are listed	79	26	93
with placement offices of schools, placement agencies, and they are	93	31	98
advertised in newspapers or journals.	101	34	100
The open market is not the only source of jobs, however.	12	38	105
Some experts believe that almost two-thirds of all jobs are in	25	42	109
what is sometimes called the hidden job market. Networking is	38	46	113
the primary way to learn about jobs in the hidden job market.	50	50	117
Employees of a company, instructors, and members of professional	63	55	121
associations are some of the best contacts to tap the hidden job	76	59	126
market. Much time and effort are required to tap these sources.	89	63	130
But the hidden market often produces the best results.	100	67	134

```
1' |  1  |  2  |  3  |  4  |  5  |  6  |  7  |  8  |  9  | 10  | 11  | 12  | 13  |
3' |        1        |        2        |        3        |        4        |
```

Troubleshooting Tips

Were your pages numbered correctly? If not, try these suggestions.
1. Remove all page numbers in header and footer.
2. Be sure the Different First Page command is not selected when you begin.
3. Check the Break the Link buttons in the header and footer to be sure the link is broken. Remember the Link to Previous button will display in gold until the link is successfully broken. The Same as Previous label will also display when there is a link between sections.

DRILL 2   SECTIONS

 sections

Page Layout/Page Setup/Breaks

1. In the open document, position the insertion point at the beginning of page 2, which is page 1 of the report. *Hint:* Click Show/Hide and click on the first paragraph marker at 1".

2. Insert a Continuous section break.

3. Double-click in the header on page 1 of the report. Deselect Different First Page if it is selected.

4. Click Link to Previous to break the links between the headers in both sections. **Note:** This button should not display in gold if the link is correctly broken.

5. Click Go to Footer and click Link to Previous to break the links between the footers in both sections.

Insert/Header & Footer/Page Number

6. Click Page Number and Top of Page and select the Rounded Rectangle 3 page number style.

7. Click Different First Page. You should now have a check mark in that option. This suppresses the page number from displaying on the first page of the report.

8. Click Page Number and Format Page Numbers. Change the page number format to begin with page 1.
   Note: Use the troubleshooting tips above if you have problems.

9. Proofread and check; click Next to continue. (*71-drill2*)

QUICK ✔

Check your document against the illustration below.

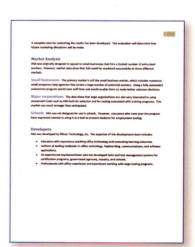

89-d1

continued

panel may consist of fifty or sixty people, but only twelve jurors and one or two alternates may be selected to serve on the jury for a particular case.

The judge asks a series of questions to the randomly selected panel of jurors to determine if any of them have cause for not serving. Usually individuals are excused for cause by the judge if they are related to or know well individuals participating in the case on either side. The judge attempts to determine if each individual can serve fairly and impartially to both sides.

Attorneys representing each side of the case then question the potential jurors and can eliminate from the panel a specified number who they believe would not be beneficial to their client. The jurors who will hear and judge the facts are then randomly selected from the remaining members of the panel.

Tipping the Scale (Sidebar heading and text)

Juror selection is both an art and a science based on extensive psychological research. Potential jurors bring to the situation attitudes, experiences, and beliefs that influence their view of a situation even though they make a conscious effort to be objective and fair.

The judge in a case excuses for cause individuals who may not be objective and fair in the decision-making process. Attorneys for both sides use the peremptory challenges (excuse without explaining the reason) they are given to try to select jurors whose profile might make them more sympathetic to the individual they represent.

Much time, effort, and money is spent reviewing the panel of potential jurors who have been summoned to appear. Attorneys representing both sides are provided with a profile of each person in the panel. Additional research is done to learn more about each potential juror.

In some cases, juror consultants who have done extensive psychological research on jury selection are hired to help select individuals who might be beneficial to their side. More importantly, they try to eliminate jurors who might be negative to their side.

BOOKMARK

www.collegekeyboarding.com
Module 14 Practice Quiz

FOOTNOTES

Insert Footnote

References cited in a report are often indicated within the text by a superscript number (. . . story.[1]) and a corresponding footnote with full information at the bottom of the same page where the reference was cited. Additionally, content footnotes supplement the information included in the body of the report.

To insert and edit footnotes:

References/Footnotes/Insert Footnote

1. Switch to Print Layout view and position the insertion point in the document where the footnote reference is to be inserted.

2. Follow the path to insert the footnote. The reference number and the insertion point appear at the bottom of the page. Key the footnote ❶.

   A footnote divider line ❷ is automatically added above the first footnote on each page. Tap ENTER once to add one blank line between footnotes.

3. Click anywhere above the footnote divider line to return to the document.

To edit a footnote, click in the footnote at the bottom of the page and make the revision. To delete a footnote, select the reference number in the text and tap DELETE. To move a footnote, select the reference number in the text and drag to the desired location in the text.

DRILL 3	FOOTNOTES	footnote

1. In the open document, insert the first footnote after the first sentence, the second footnote after the second sentence, and so forth. Tap ENTER between each footnote.

2. Delete the second footnote.

3. Proofread and check; click Next to continue. (*71-drill3*)

Footnotes

[1]Marshall Baker, *High School Athletic Records* (Seattle: Sports Press, 2011), p. 41.

[2]Lori Guo-Patterson, "Top Ten Athletes," *Sports Journal,* Spring 2011, www.tsj.edu/athletes/topten.htm (accessed June 25, 2011).

[3]Payton Devaul, pdevaul@mail.com "Basketball Scholarship," January 9, 2011, e-mail to Kirk Stennis (accessed April 15, 2011).

1. In a new document, apply Narrow margins. Make sure Show/Hide is turned on.
2. Key the title **Juror Information**. Apply 48-point Cambria heading font and Gradient Fill – Blue, Accent 1, Outline – White text effect.
3. Use *justice* as the keyword to search for scales that represent justice or the legal system; select an unbalanced scale and size the clip 1" high. Position in Top Left with Square Text Wrapping. Tap ENTER and change to the default text size and style and clear the text effect.
4. Tap ENTER again and insert an Annual sidebar. Position it on the right with the top even with the second blank paragraph symbol. Size it 2.7" wide by 8.4" high. See illustration below.
5. Key the text shown below for the main document and for the *Tipping the Scale* sidebar.
6. Insert a Conservative Quote on the left side of the first paragraph below the third line. Key: **Serving on a jury when called is an obligation of every qualified citizen.** Reduce the text size to 12 points. Size the quote 1" high by 1.8" wide.
★7. Apply Heading 3 style to the heading in the main document.
8. Apply Cambria 14-point bold to the title of the sidebar and center the title. Key the body of the sidebar using 10-point Calibri font.
9. Preview to ensure the document fits on one page.
10. Proofread; use Spelling and Grammar; correct all errors.
11. Check and close. (*89-d1*)

★ DISCOVER

If Heading 3 is not displayed in your styles, apply Heading 2; then Heading 3 will display. Change the heading to Heading 3 style.

A cornerstone of the American judicial process is the right of each individual to have legal issues heard by a jury of his or her peers. Peers serve as the "judge" of the facts of a case. Individuals called to serve as jurors have an obligation to serve unless they are excused by the judge presiding over the case. Generally, individuals younger than 18 years of age and individuals who have been convicted of a crime for which they have not been pardoned are not eligible to serve on a jury. Individuals with legal custody of young children and who cannot arrange adequate care for the children and individuals over 65 years of age may elect to be exempted from jury duty. Individuals who have schedule problems may be granted a transfer to serve on a different date.

Jury Selection

Typically, potential jurors are randomly selected and are notified to appear at the appropriate jury room at a specified date and time. Most courts bring together a pool of individuals who may be selected to serve on any of four or five cases that are being tried in different courtrooms at approximately the same time. The number of individuals called for jury duty far exceeds the number of jurors actually selected to serve on a case—for example, the jury

(continued)

REPORT FORMAT—UNBOUND AND LEFTBOUND REPORTS

71d

Report Format Guides

KEYBOARDING PRO DELUXE 2

References/Document
Formats/Reports

Review the formatting guides for preparing unbound and leftbound reports that you learned previously. Study the illustration of a two-page unbound report shown below and on pages 350–351. In the following lessons in this module you will learn more advanced report formatting.

Margins: Use the default side margins and bottom margin in an unbound report. In a leftbound report, set the left margin at 1.5", allowing 0.5" for the binding.

Font size: Use the 11-point default font size.

Spacing: Use the default 1.15 line spacing for all reports.

Page numbers: ❶ Insert page numbers at the top right. Suppress the page number on the first page. The illustration shows the Rounded Rectangle 3 page number style.

Enumerated or bulleted items: ❷ Use the default 0.25" indention of bulleted and numbered items. Tap ENTER once after each item.

Explanatory footnote: ❸ Superscript appears in report text and reference displays at the bottom of the page where the reference was cited.

Headings: Headings should reflect a hierarchy of importance.

Title: ❹ Tap ENTER three times to position title at about 2". Apply Title style. Capitalize the first letter of all main words. Shrink the font so the title fits on one line. Tap ENTER once after the heading.

Side heading: ❺ Key at the left margin; apply Heading 1 style. Capitalize the first letter of all main words. Tap ENTER once after the heading.

Paragraph heading: ❻ Key at the left margin. Capitalize the first word and follow the heading with a period. Apply Heading 2 style.

Use the Keep with Next command if necessary to keep side headings from displaying alone at the bottom of the page. (Home/Paragraph Dialog Box Launcher/Line and Page Breaks tab)

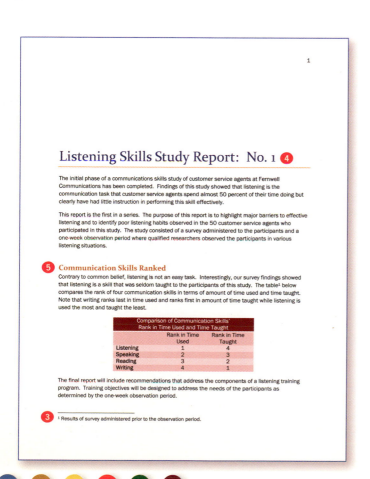

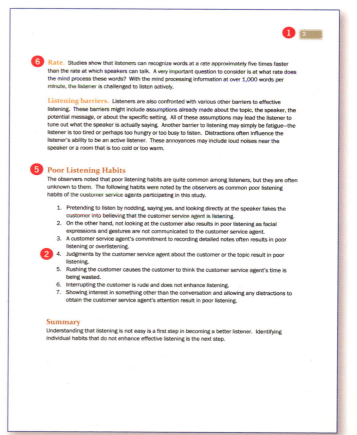

Lesson 89 | Assessment

WARMUP

Lessons/89a Warmup

A   ALL LETTERS

Skill Building

89b   Timed Writing

Key one 5' timed writing.

	gwam	3'	5'

Employees who work together as a team are more effective   4 | 2 | 39
than those who work solo. This concept is known as synergy.   8 | 5 | 42
Synergy simply means that the joint action exceeds the sum of   12 | 7 | 44
individual actions. The results are not just in the quantity of   16 | 10 | 47
work; major increases in quality result when people work together as   21 | 12 | 49
a team. Teamwork is critical for success.   24 | 14 | 51

What characterizes an excellent team member? An excellent   28 | 17 | 53
team member understands the goals of the team and will place team   32 | 19 | 56
values above her or his individual objectives. An excellent team   36 | 22 | 59
member helps to determine the most effective way to reach the   40 | 24 | 61
goals that were set by the group and will help to make each   44 | 27 | 63
decision that affects the group. Above all, an excellent team   49 | 29 | 66
member will support a decision made by the team. Each member   53 | 32 | 68
must understand her or his role and respect the roles of others.   57 | 34 | 71
Every member of a team must share in both victory and defeat.   61 | 37 | 74

3' | 1 | 2 | 3 | 4
5' | 1 | 2 | 3

Applications

89c

Assessment

Continue

Check

When you complete a document, proofread it, check the spelling, and preview for placement. Click the Check button when you are ready to error-check the test. Review and/or print the document analysis results.

1

2"

Title style

Listening Skills Study Report: No. 1

The initial phase of a communications skills study of customer service agents at Fernwell Communications has been completed. Findings of this study showed that listening is the communication task that customer service agents spend almost 50 percent of their time doing but clearly have had little instruction in performing this skill effectively.

This report is the first in a series. The purpose of this report is to highlight major barriers to effective listening and to identify poor listening habits observed in the 50 customer service agents who participated in this study. The study consisted of a survey administered to the participants and a one-week observation period where qualified researchers observed the participants in various listening situations.

Heading 1 style

Communication Skills Ranked

Contrary to common belief, listening is not an easy task. Interestingly, our survey findings showed that listening is a skill that was seldom taught to the participants of this study. The table[1] below compares the rank of four communication skills in terms of amount of time used and time taught. Note that writing ranks last in time used and ranks first in amount of time taught while listening is used the most and taught the least.

Comparison of Communication Skills' Rank in Time Used and Time Taught		
	Rank in Time Used	Rank in Time Taught
Listening	1	4
Speaking	2	3
Reading	3	2
Writing	4	1

Adjust spacing after table

The final report will include recommendations that address the components of a listening training program. Training objectives will be designed to address the needs of the participants as determined by the one-week observation period.

---

[1] Results of survey administered prior to the observation period.

Crown Lake SportsPlex

Executive Summary

The Crown Lake SportsPlex concept and conceptual drawing of the campus plan has been approved by the Board of Directors. The plan will be unveiled at a special seminar for potential investors on March 15.

Concept

The SportsPlex is envisioned as a three-tiered venue. The tiers match users and type of sports offered. The tier structure is based on revenue-generating potential, with the individual and corporate users expected to produce the bulk of the revenue. Students, competitive athletes, and the general public are expected to produce the highest volume of use but the lowest level of revenue.

The SportsPlex will be divided into three component venues—the Aquatics Center, the Golf Center, and the Olympics Center—based on the type of sporting venue. Supporting facilities, including restaurants, pro shops, boutiques, and family-oriented activities, will be provided with each of three venues.

Venues

Each of the three venues is designed to appeal to the three types of users. Venues will be carefully segmented to ensure that conflicts among users will not exist. The lake is located in the center of the 265 acres of property. High usage areas are located on the north side of the lake, and the upscale private-membership facilities are located on the south side of the lake.

> Venues will be carefully segmented to ensure that conflicts among users will not exist.

Aquatics Center

Adequate frontage on the lake is available to have three completely different segments of the Aquatics Center. The Swim Center is designed to be a family-friendly area with a lakefront swimming area, a large swimming pool, a competitive swimming pool, and a wading pool for children. Boats and jet skis are not allowed in this area.

The Sailing Club is the upscale area of the Aquatics Center. Boats are limited to sail boats and pontoon or party boats. Both an indoor and an outdoor facility are available for special events, including weddings, parties, and corporate functions. An upscale restaurant with indoor seating and an outdoor patio is planned.

The Marina is designed to meet the needs of individuals with large boats, fishing boats, power boats, jet skis, kayaks, and canoes. Areas are designed for each type of boat and for water skiing. The Anchor restaurant, which is designed to appeal to the casual boater, has a large dock to accommodate boat docking for clientele.

Golf Center

The Golf Center features a beautiful 18-hole, 72-par, Nero-designed golf course with an adjacent driving range and practice area. Walking trails are located around the perimeter of the golf course. Amenities include the 19th hole grill, a clubhouse with a pro shop and a restaurant, a gazebo and outdoor patio, and the Crown Lake Special Events Center shown below that was part of the property purchased.

This 10,000-square-foot facility is located on the lake and has a beautiful back lawn with a 60' x 60' cloverleaf pool. The facility has a full kitchen with an 8' x 6' granite-top island that is ideal for buffet-service functions. The planned use is for upscale parties, corporate events, and weddings.

Olympics Center

The Olympics Center features tennis courts, handball courts, racquetball courts, a volleyball court, a soccer field, a multipurpose field, and a track. This family-friendly area is designed primarily for students, competitive athletes, and the general public.

Estimated Project Costs

Land and existing facilities, including the Crown Lake Special Events Center, have been purchased by the Crown Lake SportsPlex founders at a cost in excess of $20 million. The estimated costs of the facilities are shown in the following table.

Total Estimated Cost by Facility		
Venue and Facility	**Facility Costs**	**Venue Costs**
Aquatics Center		
Sailing Club	1,275,000	
Swim Center	225,000	
Marina	265,000	
Total		1,765,000
Golf Center		
Golf Course	5,250,000	
Practice Areas	250,000	
Walking Trails	195,000	
Clubhouse	1,600,000	
Total		7,295,000
Olympics Center		
Courts	1,175,000	
Fields	1,325,000	
Track	290,000	
Total		2,490,000
Total Costs		11,850,000

The total cost is projected to be $11,850,000. Detailed costs of each facility and venue are provided in the comprehensive report. Conceptual designs are also available.

Investment Opportunities

Qualified investors are being offered the opportunity to invest in the Crown Lake SportsPlex. Extensive proformas have been prepared, and investment professionals will attend the March 15 seminar to explain the investment opportunities and offer professional opinions about the project. They will discuss the projected return on investment and other benefits associated with the project. In addition to the return on the investment, all levels of investment include private club membership benefits.

The reward provided with this investment opportunity is significant, but it is important to understand that the risk involved in this project is also significant.

This document contains confidential and proprietary information that is provided only to investors and potential investors of the Crown Lake SportsPlex. Do not copy, distribute, or share this information.

> Level-One Investor
> Minimum investment of $250,000 but less than $500,000.

> Level-Two Investor
> Investment is larger than $500,000 but less than $1,000,000.

> Level-Three Investor
> Investment of $1,000,000 or more.

2

Heading 2 style   **Rate.** Studies show that listeners can recognize words at a rate approximately five times faster than the rate at which speakers can talk. A very important question to consider is at what rate does the mind process these words? With the mind processing information at over 1,000 words per minute, the listener is challenged to listen actively.

Listening barriers. Listeners are also confronted with various other barriers to effective listening. These barriers might include assumptions already made about the topic, the speaker, the potential message, or about the specific setting. All of these assumptions may lead the listener to tune out what the speaker is actually saying. Another barrier to listening may simply be fatigue—the listener is too tired or perhaps too hungry or too busy to listen. Distractions often influence the listener's ability to be an active listener. These annoyances may include loud noises near the speaker or a room that is too cold or too warm.

Heading 1 style

Poor Listening Habits

The observers noted that poor listening habits are quite common among listeners, but they are often unknown to them. The following habits were noted by the observers as common poor listening habits of the customer service agents participating in this study.

1. Pretending to listen by nodding, saying yes, and looking directly at the speaker fakes the customer into believing that the customer service agent is listening.
2. On the other hand, not looking at the customer also results in poor listening as facial expressions and gestures are not communicated to the customer service agent.
3. A customer service agent's commitment to recording detailed notes often results in poor listening or overlistening.
4. Judgments by the customer service agent about the customer or the topic result in poor listening.
5. Rushing the customer causes the customer to think the customer service agent's time is being wasted.
6. Interrupting the customer is rude and does not enhance listening.
7. Showing interest in something other than the conversation and allowing any distractions to obtain the customer service agent's attention result in poor listening.

Summary

Understanding that listening is not easy is a first step in becoming a better listener. Identifying individual habits that do not enhance effective listening is the next step.

Total Estimated Cost by Facility		
Venue and Facility	Facility Costs	Venue Costs
Aquatics Center		
Sailing Club	$1,375,000	
Swim Center	225,000	
Marina	165,000	
Total		
Golf Center		
Golf Course	5,350,000	
Practice Areas	250,000	
Walking Trails	195,000	
Clubhouse	1,600,000	
Total		
Olympics Center		
Courts	1,275,000	
Fields	1,325,000	
Track	890,000	
Total		
Total Costs		

The total cost is projected to be $12,650,000. Detailed costs of each facility and venue are provided in the comprehensive report. Conceptual designs are also available.

Apply Heading 1 style. Insert three linked text boxes in the right margin. Key the text from the instructions on the previous page. See illustration on page 477 for position.

Investment Opportunities

Qualified investors are being offered the opportunity to invest in the Crown Lake SportsPlex. Extensive proformas have been prepared, and investment professionals will attend the March 15 seminar to explain the investment opportunities and offer professional opinions about the project. They will discuss the projected return on investment and other benefits associated with the project. In addition to the return on the investment, all levels of investment include private club membership benefits.

The reward provided with this investment opportunity is significant, but it is important to understand that the risk involved in this project is also significant.

This document contains confidential and proprietary information that is provided only to investors and potential investors of the Crown Lake SportsPlex. Do not copy, distribute, or share this information.

(continued)

71-d1
Unbound Report

1. Key the model report on pages 350–351. Apply the Pushpin theme. Tap ENTER three times to position the title at about 2". Use default side margins.
2. Inert the table shown below and apply the Colorful List – Accent 2 style to the table. Center the title of the table. Select the cells that contain numbers and center. Center the table horizontally. Adjust the space after the table.
3. Insert the explanatory footnote as marked in the report.
4. Create a cover page using the Pinstripes cover page. Use the information in the report and that follows:

   Document title: **Listening Skills Study Report**

   Document subtitle: **No. 1**

   Author: Student's Name

   Date: Select the current year

5. Insert a Continuous section break at the top of the first page of the report.
6. Position the insertion point in the header of Section 2. Deselect Different First Page if it is selected. Break the links between the headers for both sections. Go to the footer of Section 2. Break the link between the footers for both sections.
7. Go the header of Section 2 and number the pages of the report at the top right using the Rounded Rectangle 3 page number style. Change the page number format to begin with page 1. Click Different First Page to suppress the page number on the first page of the report.
8. Show the Navigation pane. Click Browse headings to display the headings in the report. Click the various headings to move to the heading in the report. Click Browse pages and click on the various pages in the report. **Note:** Use this shortcut to move quickly in reports as you complete this module.
9. Proofread and check; click Next to continue. (*71-d1*)

> **▶▶ REVIEW**
>
> **Navigate Documents**
> View/Show/Navigation Pane
>
> Click the first button to browse headings in the document and the second button to browse pages in the document.

71-d2
Edit Report

1. Open *71-d1*.
2. Change the margins to convert this unbound report to a leftbound report.
3. Select the reference number in the text and drag the footnote to display after the word *survey* in the second sentence of that paragraph.
4. Double-click in the header and change the page number style to Accent Bar 2.
5. Proofread and check; click Next to continue. (*71-d2*)

71-d3
Edit Report

 progress report

1. Double-click in the header of the open document. (*Hint:* Double-click the center tab and change to 4" left underline tab.) At the left margin, key **Name** and tap the Space Bar once, followed by an underline tab that ends at 4". Tap TAB and key **Fall 201-** at the right margin. Do not suppress the header on the first page.
2. Insert a page number at the bottom of the page; select the Accent Bar 4 page number style. Do not suppress the footer on the first page.
3. Position the insertion point after the title *Technique Rating Sheet and Progress Report* and insert the following footnote:

   Technique rating sheet used with permission of Cengage Learning—South-Western from the keyboarding textbook *College Keyboarding: Microsoft 2010 Keyboarding & Word Processing*, 18th edition.
4. Check and close. (*71-d3*)

d. Use the appropriate formula to total the cost of each venue and place the results in the *Total* row of the *Venue Costs* column.

e. Use the appropriate formula to obtain the total costs of the three venues. Position the results in the last row of the *Venue Costs* column.

11. Create three linked text boxes.

a. Draw a text box; size it 1" by 2" and position in the right margin as shown in the illustration.

b. Copy two more text boxes and position them directly below the first text box; link the boxes.

c. Key the following text. (Press SHIFT + ENTER after each level of investor.)

> **Level-One Investor**
>
> **Minimum investment of $250,000 but less than $500,000.**
>
> **Level-Two Investor**
>
> **Investments larger than $500,000 but less than $1,000,000.**
>
> **Level-Three Investor**
>
> **Investments of $1,000,000 or more.**

d. Apply Tight text wrapping, red shape fill, and white text color.

12. Preview, check, and close. (*88-d1*)

The Crown Lake SportsPlex concept and conceptual drawing of the campus plan has been approved by its Board of Directors. The plan will be unveiled at a special seminar for potential investors on March 15.

Apply Heading 1 style ⟶ Concept

The SportsPlex is envisioned as a three-tiered venue. The tiers match users and type of sports offered. The tier structure is based on revenue-generating potential, with the individual and corporate users expected to produce the bulk of the revenue. Students, competitive athletes, and the general public are expected to produce the highest volume of use but the lowest level of revenue.

Insert Pyramid List SmartArt graphic here ⟶

The SportsPlex will be divided into three component venues—the Aquatics Center, the Golf Center, and the Olympics Center—based on the type of sporting venue. Supporting facilities, including restaurants, pro shops, boutiques, and family-oriented activities, will be provided with each of three venues.

Insert Converging Radial SmartArt graphic here ⟶

Apply Heading 1 style; insert the *venues* data file after the heading; position the Braces Quote 2 on the right side of the first paragraph under the Venues heading; copy the second sentence and place it in the text box. ⟶ Venues

Estimated Project Costs ⟵ Apply Heading 1 style

Land and existing facilities, including the Crown Lake Special Events Center, have been purchased by the Crown Lake SportsPlex founders at a cost in excess of $10 million. The estimated costs of the facilities are shown in the following table.

(continued)

© IMAGE COPYRIGHT STOCKLITE, 2009. USED UNDER LICENSE FROM SHUTTERSTOCK.COM

What Is Your Listening Grade?

Isn't it interesting that students are not required to complete a course in listening when 80 percent of our time each day is spent listening? To perform well in organizations, a keen listening skill is essential. Evaluate yourself on the following areas and start today working on a listening improvement plan in those areas. Search for excellent listening quizzes to assist you.

BODY LANGUAGE:

Do you ... sit with your arms closed?

stand with your hand on the door as you listen to someone?

doodle while listening or play with a pen or some other object?

look at your watch while others are talking?

continue checking your e-mail while listening to someone on the phone or someone face to face?

MINDSET

Do you ... think you already know what the speaker has to say?

think the speaker is wasting your time?

tune out anything boring? or too long?

disregard anything being said if you do not agree with it?

judge the speaker before he/she begins to speak?

RESPONSES TO THE SPEAKER

Do you ... finish the speaker's sentence because you know what he/she is going to say?

think about what you will say while the speaker is talking?

interrupt the speaker so you can start talking sooner?

look ridiculous sometimes when you respond in a manner that tells others that you were not listening?

Lesson 88 | *Advanced Documents with Graphics*

Applications

88-d1

Report Summary

venues
events

This document summarizes a large, comprehensive report that can be used as a promotion piece. Review the Quick Check on page 477 before you begin preparing the document. The document must fit on four pages, and each page should contain the content shown.

1. Develop the CLSP (Crown Lake SportsPlex) custom theme:

   a. **Colors:** Note all are Standard colors. **Text/Background Dark 2:** Red; **Accent 1:** Blue; **Accent 2:** Yellow; **Accent 3:** Green; **Accent 4:** Red; **Accent 5:** Orange; **Hyperlink:** Light Blue; **Followed Hyperlink:** Purple.

   b. **Fonts: Heading:** Consolas; **Body:** Constantia.

   c. **Effects:** Concourse.

2. Tap ENTER twice to key the title **Crown Lake SportsPlex** at 1.7" and apply Title style; key the subtitle **Executive Summary** and apply Subtitle style.

3. Key the document shown on the next pages. Number pages using Plain Number 3 at the top of the page. Apply Different First Page. Follow instructions in callouts.

4. Apply a dropped cap to the C in the *Concept* heading; drop the cap four lines.

5. Insert a Pyramid List SmartArt graphic where indicated. Change colors to Dark 2 Fill from the Primary Theme Colors. Add text:

   a. Top shape: **Students and General Public**

   b. Middle shape: **Competitive Athletes**

   c. Bottom shape: **Individual and Corporate Users**

6. Insert a Converging Radial SmartArt graphic at the top of page 2. Change colors to Colorful Range – Accent Colors 4 to 5. Add text:

   a. Left shape: **Aquatics Center**

   b. Center top shape: **Golf Center**

   c. Right shape: **Olympics Center**

   d. Bottom shape: **Crown Lake SportsPlex**

7. Insert the *venues* data file below the *Venues* heading. Apply Heading 2 style to all headings in the data file.

8. Insert a Braces Quote 2 where shown in the Quick Check; copy the second sentence under *Venues* to the pull quote; select Keep Source Formatting paste option. Apply white text color and Red, Text 2 fill. Size the pull quote about 1.1" high and 2.5" wide.

9. Insert the *events* picture from the data files where indicated in the *Golf Center* section. Crop about 0.25" from the top and 0.5" from the bottom of the picture. Finished height should be 4". Compress the picture.

10. Key and format the table using Medium Shading 2 – Accent 4.

    a. Merge cells in the top row; increase row height to 0.4"; center the title vertically and horizontally; bold and center columns B and C headings.

    b. Set a 0.25" left tab in the first column to indent the items as shown.

    c. Select column B and set a right-align tab at 1.4" in the Tabs dialog box. Repeat this procedure for column C.

TIP

You may have to rotate the Braces pull quote to size it properly.

Lesson 72 | *Reports with Built-in Headers and Footers*

New Commands
- Built-in headers and footers
- Multilevel list
- Split panes
- View Side by Side and Arrange all

New Commands

72c

BUILT-IN HEADERS AND FOOTERS

Header Footer Page Number

Header & Footer

In this module, you will insert and edit headers and footers from Quick Parts, and you will create custom headers and footers.

To insert a header or footer:

Insert/Header & Footer/Header or Footer

1. Follow the path to display the Built-In gallery of header or footer styles.
2. Click the down scroll arrow to browse the various styles. Click the desired header or footer style.
3. Click [*Type the document title*] and key the desired text for the header.
4. From the Options group, click Different First Page to remove the page number from the first page if desired.

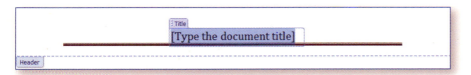

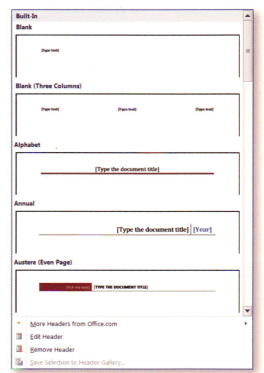

To create a header or footer not using Quick Parts:

Double-click in the header or footer area. Key the header or footer, including page numbers if desired. You may suppress the header or footer on the first page.

To remove a header or footer:

Insert/Header & Footer/Header or Footer

Follow the path and click Remove Header or Remove Footer.

Crown Lake News and Views

Current date

Newsletter Staff

Eric Burge
Editor

Nancy Suggs
Christopher Hess
Anne Reynolds
Associate Editors

Wayne Martin
Editorial Assistant

Crown Lake News and Views is a weekly newsletter compiled by the staff of the Human Resources Department, and it is sent to all employees.

New Development Project

Crown Lake won the bid to develop and construct the new multimillion dollar Business Center adjacent to Metro Airport. Connie McClure, one of the three senior project managers, has been named as the Business Center project manager. The project is expected to take more than two years to complete. Approximately fifty new permanent employees will be hired to work on this project. All jobs will be posted within the next two weeks. The recruiting referral program is in effect for all jobs. You can earn a $100 bonus for each individual you recommend who is hired and remains with Crown Lake for at least six months. You may pick up your recruiting referral forms in the Personnel Office.

Blood Drive Reminder

The Crown Lake quarterly blood drive is set for next Friday in the Wellness Center. The Community Blood Bank needs all types of blood to replace the supplies sent to the islands during the recent disaster caused by Hurricane Lana. Employees in all divisions are being asked to participate this quarter because of the current supply crisis. All three donation sites will be used. Several volunteers will be needed to staff the two additional sites. The regular division rotation will resume next quarter.

Lee Daye Honored

The Community Foundation honored Lee Daye of the Marketing Department with the Eagle Award for outstanding service this year. The Eagle Award is presented each year to three citizens who have made a significant impact on  the lives of others. The Community Foundation recognized Lee for his work with underprivileged children, the Community Relations Task Force, the Abolish Domestic Violence Center, and the Community Transitional Housing Project. Congratulations, Lee. You made a difference in the lives of many citizens in our community. Your award was richly deserved.

New Training Program

The pilot test of the new Team Effectiveness training program was completed last month, and the results were excellent. Thanks to all of you who participated in the development and testing of the program. Your input is vital to its success. The training schedule will be announced shortly.

DRILL 1   HEADER AND FOOTER

1. In the open document, insert the Alphabet header. The report title automatically displays in the header. Suppress the header on the first page.

2. Insert the Alphabet footer. Key **Zeigler Productions, Inc**.

3. Proofread and check; click Next to continue. (*72-drill1*)

MULTILEVEL LIST

 A multilevel list shows the list items at different levels rather than at one level that is created when bullets and numbering commands are used.

To format items in a multilevel list:

Home/Paragraph/Multilevel List

1. Select the items to be formatted.
2. Click the Multilevel List button.
3. Use the Increase or Decrease Indent button to promote or demote item in the list.

DRILL 2   MULTILEVEL LIST

1. Study the two lists below. Key the first list and then follow the instructions to format it as shown in the second list.

2. Select the items below each heading in the list you key and click the Multilevel List button. Select the second item in the List Library.

3. Use the Increase Indent command to demote the second, third, and fourth items under Phase 1. Use the Decrease Indent command to promote Review plan.

4. Proofread and check; click Next to continue. (*72-drill2*)

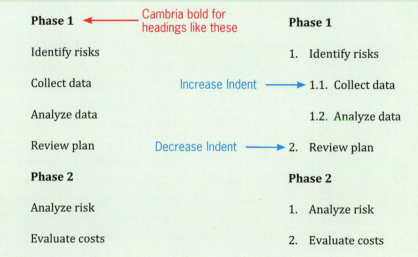

Phase 1 ← Cambria bold for headings like these

Identify risks

Collect data

Analyze data

Review plan

Phase 2

Analyze risk

Evaluate costs

Phase 1

1. Identify risks

    Increase Indent ⟶ 1.1. Collect data

    1.2. Analyze data

    Decrease Indent ⟶ 2. Review plan

Phase 2

1. Analyze risk

2. Evaluate costs

87-d2

Newsletter with Unequal Columns

business center

1. Key the newsletter shown on the next page as a one-column document; apply Opulent theme, Heading 2 style for all headings, and Narrow margins. Remove the space after the paragraph between the staff names and positions as illustrated on the next page.

2. At the top of the newsletter, tap ENTER once and key the title; apply 36-point Trebuchet Heading font and Pink, Accent 1, Darker 25% font color. Center the title.

3. Tap ENTER once after the title and change the font size to 11 point and alignment to Left. Change the font color to Automatic.

4. Tap ENTER and insert a Continuous section break. Begin keying in the paragraph below the section break.

5. Select the text of the newsletter and format it using three unequal columns with the following settings in the Columns dialog box:

   Column 1: 1.5" | Space between columns: 0.3" |

   Columns 2 and 3: 2.7" | Check Line between

6. Insert a Column break after the *Crown Lake News and Views* information.

7. Insert the *business center* picture from the data files; use Tight text wrapping, size it 2.2" high, and position it as shown on the next page.

8. Insert an eagle from the clip art gallery; use Tight text wrapping, size it 1.1" high, and position it after the Eagle Award has been mentioned.

9. Preview, check, and close. (87-d2)

WORKPLACE SUCCESS

MEL YATES/PHOTOLIBRARY

Role Models and Mentors

Role models and mentors are very different, but both can be helpful to young people beginning their careers. Role models are individuals who are admired and emulated by others for who they are, the positions they hold, the behavior they exhibit, or specific skills they have. Role models may be positive, or they may be negative. Many young people look up to athletes and celebrities. Some athletes and celebrities are outstanding role models who exhibit exemplary behavior, while others may be highly successful in their career pursuits but exhibit behavior that should not be emulated.

In the workplace, it is wise to select many role models because of specific traits that are outstanding. One person may be excellent at conducting meetings; another may command attention when delivering presentations. You can learn from many male and female role models. A role model does not even have to know that she or he is serving as your role model.

Mentors take an active role in a person's career. Mentors agree to counsel or coach an individual. In addition, behind the scenes they may be strong advocates of their mentees. Mentors can work directly with the individual being mentored, or they can be total outsiders. Relying on mentors too heavily can have negative implications—especially if the mentor falls out of favor in the company. Having more than one mentor is helpful.

SPLITTING PANES

In long documents, it can be very useful to view two parts of the document at the same time. To do so, you must first split the window into two panes. Each pane will have its own ruler bar and scroll bars.

To split panes:

<mark>View/Window/Split</mark>

1. Follow the path above to display the split bar.

2. Drag the split bar to the desired location and click to position it ❶. Note that you have two panes, with each having a ruler bar and scroll bars.

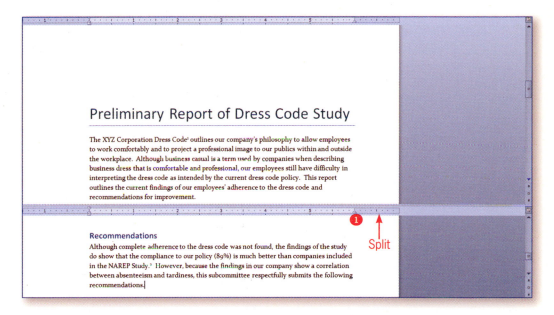

Alternate method:

1. Point to the split box at the top of the top vertical scroll bar. The pointer changes to a resize pointer.

2. Drag the split bar to the desired position in the document. Note that you have two panes with each having a ruler bar and scroll bars.

Once the screen is split, you can arrange the panes by dragging the split bar to any desired location. The pane becomes active when you click in it. Position the insertion point at one part in the document. Then click in the second pane and position the insertion point at another place. To move or copy text or a graphic from one pane to another, just select and drag the text or graphic across the split bar.

To return to a single window, double-click the split bar.

COLUMNS OF UNEQUAL WIDTH

Columns may be of equal or unequal width. When newsletters include organization information, they are often formatted with that information in a narrow first column.

To format columns of unequal width:

Page Layout/Page Setup/Columns

1. Click More Columns at the bottom of the drop-list options to display the Columns dialog box.

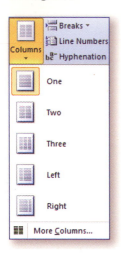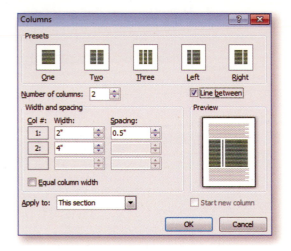

2. Select the number of columns desired and remove the check from the Equal column width box.

3. Use the spin arrows to set the width of each column and the spacing between columns.

4. Click Line between if a line is desired between columns.

DRILL 2 COLUMNS OF UNEQUAL WIDTH   litter

1. In the open data file *litter*, use WordArt Fill – Olive Green, Accent 3, Powder Bevel to key the title: **Are You a Litter Bug?** Apply In Line with Text wrapping and then center the paragraph in which the WordArt is inserted.

2. Position the insertion point at the first line of text and insert a Continuous section break.

3. Display the Columns dialog box and select two columns. Remove the check from the Equal column width box.

4. Use the spin arrows to set the width of the first column to 2" and spacing to 0.5". The second column will be 4" wide.

5. Check Line between and click OK.

6. After the Staff information, insert a Column break.

7. Preview the document to ensure that it fits properly on the page.

8. Proofread and check; click Next to continue. (*87-drill2*)

Applications

87-d1

Remove Background

 statue

1. Insert the *statue* data file in a new document.

2. Compress the picture, size it 4" high, and position it in Top Center with Square Text Wrapping.

3. Remove the background that surrounds the statue.

4. Proofread and check; click Next to continue. (*87-d1*)

View/Window/Split

1. In the open document, point to the split box at the top of the vertical scroll bar. Drag the split bar and drop just before #3.

2. In the bottom pane, scroll to #9.

3. In the top pane select the second numbered item. *Hint:* Do not select the automatic number 2.

4. Drag the selection across the split bar. Drop to the left of the word *fewer* (item #9). **Note:** If you did not drop the text correctly, you may have to make minor spacing and numbering adjustments.

5. Double-click the split bar.

6. Proofread and check; click Next to continue. (*72-drill3*)

VIEW SIDE BY SIDE AND ARRANGE ALL

In the workplace, a user may have two or more documents open and be working with all of them. View Side by Side and Arrange All Windows are explained below.

To view side by side:
View/Window/View Side by Side

1. Open both files to be viewed.
2. Follow the path to display Compare Side by Side dialog box. If not automatically activated, click Synchronous Scrolling to scroll both documents at the same time. If you prefer to scroll one document at a time, deselect Synchronous Scrolling.

To arrange all windows:
View/Window/Arrange All

1. Open the files to be viewed.
2. Follow the path and note each window has its own vertical scroll bars for moving within the document.

To move to different windows, click in the document and that window becomes active.

To return to one window, click the Maximize button on the document you wish to open in full view.

Do not use *Keyboarding Pro DELUXE 2* for this job. Launch *Word* and follow the directions below.

1. Open the following files: *document 1* and *document 2*.

2. Click View Side by Side. Click OK. Click in each document to make it active.

3. Click the scroll bar and note that both documents scroll at the same time. Click the Synchronous Scrolling button to turn this feature off. Click in *document 1* and scroll. Note *document 2* does not move now.

4. Maximize *document 1*.

5. Open *document 3*. Click Arrange All so that all these files display on the screen.

6. Click in each document to make it active. Scroll in each one.

7. Click in *document 1* and maximize the screen to display only one window, and then close all three files.

Not all foregrounds can be isolated so that the entire background can be removed. In those cases, the Background Removal tools can be used to refine the background removal.

To remove the picture background using Background Removal tools:

Picture Tools Format/Adjust/Remove Background

1. Select the picture and click Remove Background to display the Marquee and the Background Removal tools.

2. Adjust the Marquee to surround the foreground you wish to keep.

3. Mark the areas you wish to keep (**1**) and/or the areas you wish to remove (**2**) by drawing a line through the area with the appropriate tool.

4. If you mark an area in error, click Delete Mark (**3**).

Move the Marquee as close to the foreground as possible.

Click out of picture; a little background was left on the back and the antlers were cut short.

Mark areas on antlers to keep and mark areas on the back to remove.

Picture with top of antlers added and background removed.

DRILL 1   REMOVE BACKGROUND   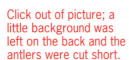 helliconia, antelope

1. Insert the *helliconia* picture in a new document and adjust the Marquee to surround the flower closely.

2. Click out of the picture to remove the background.

3. Compress the picture; size it 3" high and position in Top Center with Square Text Wrapping. After moving the picture, you may have to remove additional background.

4. Insert the *antelope* picture below the *helliconia* and adjust the Marquee to remove the background.

5. Click the Mark Areas to Remove tool and draw lines in the areas where you need to remove background. Note that they are shown with the minus (−) sign.

6. Click the Mark Areas to Keep tool and draw lines to keep the top of the antlers. Note they are shown with the plus (+) sign.

7. Click out of the picture to remove the background. Compress the picture and size it 4" high.

8. Proofread and check; click Next to continue. (*87-drill1*)

LEFTBOUND REPORT WITH BUILT-IN HEADERS AND FOOTERS

Reports prepared with binders are called leftbound reports. The binding takes 0.5" of space. Therefore, set the left margin at 1.5" to accommodate a left binding.

Built-in headers and footers are available in *Word 2010* in a gallery of preformatted headers and footers. The illustration below shows a leftbound report with the Sideline header and footer inserted. Click on the Header from Top and Footer from Bottom spin arrows to increase or decrease the header and footer margins from the default .5" margins.

Note the header contains the title of the report and the footer includes the page number. Other styles will include the page number in the header. Remember a page number must display either in the header or the footer of a multiple-page document.

The use of color and graphics enhances the professional design of this report, and it was completed quickly and easily using the built-in headers and footers.

KEYBOARDING PRO DELUXE 2

*References/Document Formats/
Reports*

2"

1.5"

Guidelines to Escape Computer-Related Injuries

Repetitive stress injuries (RSI), cumulative trauma disorder (CTD), and carpal tunnel syndrome (CTS) have mushroomed to afflict everyone from administrative assistants to executives with hurting muscles, tendons, and nerves. Hand-arm alignment is one of the causes of keyboard repetitive stress injuries. Misalignment causes muscles to become overworked, causing stress and fatigue in the hands, arms, neck, and shoulders. Improper use of the mouse causes stress injuries as well.

To avoid computer-related injuries, all computer users can benefit from understanding the basic guidelines for proper positioning at the computer and effective workstation design that are presented in this report.

Position Yourself Properly
Preventing tired wrists and hands is really a matter of taking charge of your posture and computer work environment. Awkward posture while keying and failure to change your keying or sitting position can add to wear and tear on your wrists and hands.

Hand position. Keep your wrists and hands straight. When you work with straight wrists and fingers, the nerves, muscles, and tendons stay relaxed and comfortable. Therefore, they are less likely to develop the strains and pains that are often associated with keying.

Posture. Your posture at the computer affects the position of your wrists and hands. If you lean your body forward (flexion) or backward (extension) or if you slouch, your wrists and hands also adapt by becoming flexed or extended. Slouching causes the nerves, muscles, and tendons that support your wrists and hands to become tense and strained. Study the guides that follow to position yourself properly at the computer.

- Sit up straight; face the computer straight-on.
- Hold your head at a slight downward tilt to avoid straining muscles in your neck and shoulders.
- Keep hands and wrists straight while keying.
- Keep arms naturally close to your body; do not reach for the mouse.
- Touch your keys lightly; this keeps your wrists and fingers relaxed.
- Keep your feet flat and pointed toward the workstation.

Guidelines to Escape Computer-Related Injuries ← Header

Adjust Your Workstation
Your goals in adjusting your computer furniture are to be able to maintain a straight wrist, hand, and back posture and to position items at an appropriate level and reach.

- Adjust keyboard tray to desk height so that your wrists and hands are straight while keying. Position your keyboard so that your wrists and forearms are straight.
- Place the mouse close to you. Your arm should be naturally close to your body; do not raise your arm to reach the mouse. Suggestions for mouse placement include placing the mouse on the same level as and parallel to the keyboard, on a bridge that sits over the numeric keypad, in between the split keyboard that contains two separate pieces, and on a specially designed kneepad.
- Adjust screen height so that the top of the screen is at your eye level. Then move the monitor 16 inches away from your face. Increase the zoom setting if a closer view of the screen is required.
- Adjust chair height and seat back so that you can key with straight wrists and hands.

Check Your Ergonomic Practices
All computer users should complete a self-analysis of their practices that could result in ergonomic ramifications. Answer each question below comparing your response to the desired response in parentheses. Study the guides that follow to position yourself properly at the computer; use a technique rating sheet to track your progress.

1. Do you strike the computer keys hard? (No)
2. Do you reach for your mouse? (No)
3. Is your chair adjustable? (Yes)
4. Is your computer screen the proper distance from your eyes? (Yes)
5. Are your wrists and hands straight while keying? (Yes)
6. Do you tilt your neck backward to see the computer screen? (No)
7. Do you take two 5-minute breaks and one 15-minute break in the morning and afternoon? (Yes)
8. Do you vary your activities to break the repetitive motion? (Yes)
9. Do you drink plenty of water to lubricate your joints? (Yes)

For each of your responses that do not match the desired response, please accept the challenge today to correct the undesired practice and avoid computer-related stress injuries.

Footer

Lesson 87 | *Graphic Applications*

New Commands
- Remove Picture Background
- Uneven Columns

New Commands

87b

REMOVE PICTURE BACKGROUND

Background removal separates a picture into the *foreground* and the *background*, which is the portion to remove. More emphasis is placed on the picture when the background is removed. With some pictures, the background can be removed by adjusting the Marquee.

Marquee (outlines area to keep)

Background (portion to remove)

Foreground (portion to keep)

Marquee (size adjusted to foreground)

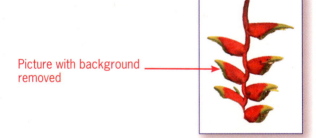

Picture with background removed

To remove the picture background:

Picture Tools Format/Adjust/Remove Background

1. Select the picture and adjust the Marquee so that it surrounds the foreground that you wish to keep.
2. Click outside the picture to remove the background.

72-d1

Leftbound Report

    injuries

→ **REVIEW**

Insert File

Insert/Text/Object down list arrow/Text from File

1. Key the leftbound report that follows. Tap ENTER three times to position the title at about 2". Change the left margin to 1.5".

2. Apply the Flow document theme. Apply appropriate styles to the title and side headings. Shrink title font to fit on one line.

3. Format the bulleted list with square bullets.

4. Insert the Sideline cover page. Key the following information:

   Company: **Galey Financial, LLC**

   Document title: Refer to report title for 72-d1.

   Document subtitle: Click the subtitle text box; click the Subtitle control above the text box, and tap DELETE.

   Author: Student's Name

   Date: Current date

5. Insert a Continuous section break at the top of the first page of the report.

6. Position the insertion point in the header of Section 2. Deselect Different First Page if it is selected. Break the links between the headers for both sections. Go to the footer of Section 2. Break the link between the footers for both sections.

7. Go to the header of Section 2 and insert the Sideline header. Go to the footer of Section 2 and insert the Sideline footer. Change the page number format to begin with page 1. Click Different First Page to suppress the header and footer on the first page of the report.

8. Proofread and check; click Next to continue. (*72-d1*)

Guidelines to Escape Computer-Related Injuries

Repetitive stress injuries (RSI), cumulative trauma disorder (CTD), and carpal tunnel syndrome (CTS) have mushroomed to afflict everyone from administrative assistants to executives with hurting muscles, tendons, and nerves. Hand-arm alignment is one of the causes of keyboard repetitive stress injuries. Misalignment causes muscles to become overworked, causing stress and fatigue in the hands, arms, neck, and shoulders. Improper use of the mouse causes stress injuries as well.

To avoid computer-related injuries, all computer users can benefit from understanding the basic guidelines for proper positioning at the computer and effective workstation design that are presented in this report.

Position Yourself Properly

Preventing tired wrists and hands is really a matter of taking charge of your posture and computer work environment. Awkward posture while keying and failure to change your keying or sitting position can add to wear and tear on your wrists and hands.

Hand position. Keep your wrists and hands straight. When you work with straight wrists and fingers, the nerves, muscles, and tendons stay relaxed and comfortable. Therefore, they are less likely to develop the strains and pains that are often associated with keying.

Insert file **injuries;** format like the rest of the report.

Client Companies (Sidebar heading and text)

SMS employees frequently perform work for client companies whose policies may differ from SMS policies. Therefore, employees should assume the most conservative position and avoid using client company technology for any personal use whatsoever.

SMS Policies – E-Mail and Internet Abuse (Document title)

Effective (Current date) (Subtitle)

Spurrier Medical Systems attempts to strike a balance between meeting the needs of employees, protecting the privacy of employees, and protecting the company's interest. However, it is imperative that employees understand that the computer technology provided by SMS is the property of SMS and its contents may be inspected at any time without notice to the employee. It is important to remember that items deleted from the system may be recovered and reviewed. Although SMS has the technology to monitor e-mails, block spam, check for viruses, and limit access to certain sites, it does not routinely monitor the work of employees. However, occasional monitoring of system usage should be expected.

SMS expects ethical and professional behavior of its employees and based on that expectation permits the limited and judicious use of e-mail and access to the Internet for personal use. The following specific guides should be followed.

1. Personal telephone calls, e-mails, and Internet surfing must be reasonable and limited so that productivity is not negatively impacted.

2. Employees are responsible for the content of personal e-mails and attachments they receive and send.

3. E-mails that contain solicitations, chain letters, religious, political, racial, or sexual content are unacceptable and will not be tolerated. Legal precedent exists to show that these types of messages may create a hostile work environment.

4. SMS has a zero tolerance policy for surfing, downloading, or distributing content from sites that contain obscene language or pornographic images, and disciplinary action may be as severe as termination of employment. Remember that many of these sites trace visitors to the site and identify SMS for future contacts. This activity could be damaging to SMS's image.

5. Confidential company documents should not be distributed over the Internet to protect SMS's intellectual property.

6. Do you tilt your neck backward to see the computer screen? (No)

7. Do you take two 5-minute breaks and one 15-minute break in the morning and afternoon? (Yes)

8. Do you vary your activities to break the repetitive motion? (Yes)

9. Do you drink plenty of water to lubricate your joints? (Yes)

For each of your responses that do not match the desired response, please accept the challenge today to correct the undesired practice and avoid computer-related stress injuries.

72-d2

Edit Report

1. Open *72-d1*.

2. Double-click in the header and change the header style to Annual.

3. Double-click in the footer and change the footer style to Annual.

4. Split the window into two panes. In the top pane, scroll so you can see the header on the second page of the document. In the bottom pane, scroll to view the footer on the second page of the document. Note that the Annual style selected for both the header and the footer match in design.

5. Double-click the split bar to return to a single pane.

6. Proofread and check; click Next to continue. (*72-d2*)

72-d3

Outline

 outline, guidelines, notes

Do not use *Keyboarding Pro DELUXE 2* for this job. Launch *Word* and follow the directions provided.

1. Open the following files: *guidelines* and *outline*.

2. Use the View Side by Side command to display both documents on the screen. Click to deactivate the synchronous scrolling.

3. Click in the data file *outline* and position the insertion point below the title. Key an outline using the headings in guidelines. Use the multilevel list with Roman numerals (I., A., 1.)

4. Maximize the screen displaying the outline.

5. Open notes and click Arrange All to view all three documents in this lesson.

6. Check and close. (*72-d3*)

QUICK ✔

Check your document against the illustration below.

> ### Guidelines to Escape Computer-Related Injuries
>
> **I. Position Yourself Properly**
>
>   A. Hand position
>
>   B. Posture
>
> **II. Adjust Your Workstation**
>
> **III. Check Your Ergonomic Practices**

Collaborative Writing

A Key Component of Teamwork

Teamwork is the norm in modern-day organizations. The team concept is critical because many projects are complex and require more and different kinds of expertise than one person is likely to have. Teams usually consist of members from different departments of an organization because employees from different areas tend to view a project from different perspectives.

Team Writing

Collaborative writing is a skill that must be developed. Writing as a team is far more challenging than writing as an individual. An effective team begins by developing a strategy for writing the documentation required for most projects.

Collaborating with People of Different Cultures

Collaborative writing is challenging within a culture and even more challenging across cultures. Consider the following six keys to successful team writing across cultures:

1. Good listening skills
2. Good interpersonal skills
3. Respect for the ideas of others
4. Patience in trying to understand differences
5. A willingness to help others understand differences
6. Courtesy

Most people respond positively to those who show that they are interested in the ideas of others. Working with people from other cultures provides a great learning opportunity to those who will take advantage of it.

86-d2

Policy with Pull Quote and Sidebar

 TIP

If numbered item 2 breaks across pages, use Keep Lines Together to make sure the whole item stays together.

1. Apply Aspect theme; key the report shown on the next page.
2. Apply Title and Subtitle styles to the first two lines; shrink font to fit title on one line.
3. Select the first sentence of the second paragraph and copy to an Alphabet Quote. Position on the left side of the second paragraph. Size the pull quote 2.3" high and 3" wide.
4. Add an Alphabet sidebar; position it in the right margin even with the first line of text. Shorten the sidebar to 6.8" high and key the text shown on the next page in it.
5. Number pages at the top using Plain Number 3 and Different First Page.
6. Preview, check, and close. *(86-d2)*

Lesson 73 | Report with Preliminary Pages

WARMUP

KEYBOARDING PRO DELUXE 2

Lessons/73a Warmup

New Commands

73b

KEYBOARDING PRO DELUXE 2

TABLE OF CONTENTS

The Table of Contents command enables a table of contents to be created automatically if the built-in heading styles are used. You may also create a table of contents from custom styles, using outline levels, or by marking entries to be included in the table of contents. A table of contents can also be modified manually or automatically after it has been created.

In Web Layout View, the entries in the table of contents are hyperlinks. Clicking on an entry moves the insertion point to the appropriate page in the document. In Print Layout view, tapping CTRL plus clicking on an entry moves the insertion point to the appropriate page in the document.

TABLE OF CONTENTS

References/Table of Contents/Table of Contents

To create a table of contents using built-in heading styles:

1. Position the insertion point in the completed document where the table of contents is to be created (normally on a blank page at the beginning of the report). **Note:** Styles have already been applied to the document headings.

2. Follow the path above to display the Built-In gallery of table of contents styles.

3. Choose the Automatic Table 2 style. The table of contents automatically displays at the insertion point. The title Table of Contents is also automatically generated as a part of the table of contents.

4. Position the title Table of Contents at approximately 2".

To remove a table of contents, click Remove Table of Contents.

Built-In

Automatic Table 1

Contents
Heading 1 1
   Heading 2 1
     Heading 3 1

Automatic Table 2

Table of Contents
Heading 1 1
   Heading 2 1
     Heading 3 1

Manual Table

Table of Contents
Type chapter title (level 1) 1
   Type chapter title (level 2) 2
     Type chapter title (level 3) 3
Type chapter title (level 1) 4

More Table of Contents from Office.com ▸
Insert Table of Contents...
Remove Table of Contents
Save Selection to Table of Contents Gallery...

4. Note the Create Link command on the Drawing Tools Format tab is replaced by the Break Link command. To break the link between the text boxes, click Break Link.

5. Apply a text wrap option and any other format desired.

6. Key the text in the first box; when it is full, the text will flow to the next box.

DRILL 3 **LINK TEXT BOXES** 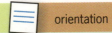 orientation

1. In the open document, draw a text box in the right margin next to the first bullet point under *Core Values*. Size it to 1.2" high and 2" wide.

2. Copy the text box and position it next to the first paragraph on page 2.

Drawing Tools Format/Text/Create Link

3. Select the first text box and click Create Link. When the cursor turns to an upright pitcher, move it over the second text box. When the pitcher tilts, click the mouse to create the link. Apply Square text wrapping to the first text box.

4. Key the text shown at the right in the first text box. After *Success Tips*, press SHIFT + ENTER to move to the next line without the 10 points space after paragraph. Note when the text flows to the second text box.

5. Apply Square text wrapping to the second box and move it up to the position shown at right.

6. Apply 11-point bold Cambria to *Success Tips*. Apply Light 1 Outline, Colored Fill – Blue, Accent 1 Shape Style to both text boxes.

7. Proofread and check; click Next to continue. (*86-drill3*)

Success Tips

Learn your organization's core values and how you can contribute to them.

Always be well prepared so you can demonstrate competence to the leaders of your company.

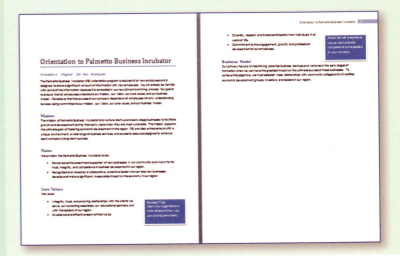

Applications

86-d1

Report with Linked Text Boxes

1. Apply Aspect theme, and key the report on the next page. Apply Title and Subtitle styles to the first two lines. Apply Heading 1 style to the two headings.

2. Draw a text box and position it in the right margin as shown; size it 1.5" high by 2" wide. Copy the box and position the second text box below the first one.

3. Create a link between the two text boxes.

4. Click in the first text box and key the Success Tips shown below.

5. Apply Square text wrapping and Subtle Effect – Tan Accent 6 shape style.

6. Proofread and check; click Next to continue. (*86-d1*)

Success Tips (Verdana 12-pt bold; press SHIFT + ENTER)

Learning to work effectively with team members is a critical career skill. (Tap ENTER)

Good problem-solving skills and good interpersonal skills are required to be an effective team member.

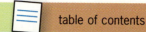
1. In the open document, position the insertion point on the second page at 2".

2. Generate a new table of contents using the Automatic Table 2 style.

3. Point to the selection area to the left of the title and click to select the heading *Table of Contents*. Apply Title style. If the appropriate Title with the underline does not display, click undo and follow the directions again.

4. Proofread and check; click Next to continue. (*73-drill1*)

MODIFY TABLE OF CONTENTS

 A table of contents is often modified after it has been created, such as updating changes in the headings and page numbers, choosing another format, or adding text.

To update a table of contents:

1. At the top of the generated table of contents, click Update Table ❶. The Update Table of Contents dialog box displays.

2. Select Update page numbers only or Update entire table, and click OK.

To change the format:

1. Click the Table of Contents button ❷ and select another table of contents style.

– or –

References/Table of Contents/Table of Contents

2. For additional styles, follow the path above and click Insert Table of Contents to display the Table of Contents dialog box.

   a. Accept the defaults to show page numbers, right-align page numbers, and use leaders; or click the arrow next to Formats and select the desired format, such as Formal.

   b. Indicate the number of heading levels to be included in the table of contents in the Show Levels box (up to nine). Click OK.

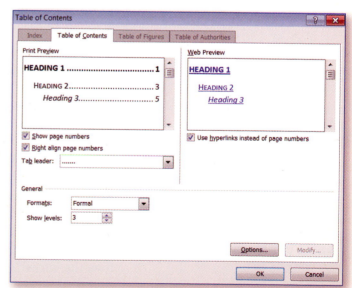

To draw a text box and format it:

Insert/Text/Text Box

1. Follow the path to display the Text Box gallery and click Draw Text Box at the bottom of the gallery.

2. When the mouse pointer changes to a crosshair, drag to draw a text box of the size desired. Release the mouse button to display the text box.

3. Click in the text box and key the text.

4. Use the tools on the Drawing Tools Format tab to format the text box. Note that these formatting tools are the same basic tools that you used to format shapes and other types of graphics. You can also modify the text box with these tools.

DRILL 2 — DRAW TEXT BOX

1. Click Draw Text Box and draw a new text box; size it 2.5" high and 3.5" wide.

2. Key the text shown at the right. Tap ENTER after each line. Center and grow the font to fill the text box.

3. Apply Intense Effect – Blue, Accent 1 Shape style.

4. Position in Top Center with Square Text Wrapping.

5. Proofread and check; click Next to continue. *(86-drill2)*

Jan M. Hawkins

Computer Lab Manager

Lab Hours

8:30 a.m. to 6:30 p.m.

Monday through Friday

LINK TEXT BOXES

ᴦᴩ Create Link   Many articles and newsletters begin on one page and are continued several pages later. Text boxes are used to place the information at the desired position. Text boxes are a fixed size. When a text box is filled, the text that does not fit disappears unless the text box is expanded. Multiple text boxes can be drawn and linked so that when one text box is filled, the text flows to the next box. The boxes can be positioned and linked on different pages. Only empty text boxes can be linked because they must be available to receive the overflow text.

To link text boxes:

Insert/Text/Text Box

1. Draw a text box and position it as desired. Then copy the text box and position the second text box on the same or another page.

Drawing Tools Format/Text/Create Link

2. Select the first text box. On the Drawing Tools Format tab, click Create Link. The cursor turns to an upright pitcher.

3. Move the cursor over the second text box that will be linked; the pitcher tilts. Click the mouse to create the link.

✱ DISCOVER

Drawing Tools Format/
Arrange/Align

Showing gridlines is helpful in adjusting the position of text boxes. Select the text box and click View Gridlines on the Align options. To remove the gridlines, deselect View Gridlines.

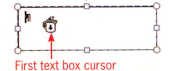

First text box cursor

Second text box cursor

To add text to the table of contents:

References/Table of Contents/Add Text

1. Select the text to be added to the table of contents.
2. Follow the path above and click Add Text.
3. Choose the desired level of heading.
4. Click in the table of contents and click Update Table.

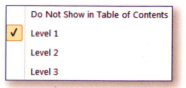

Note: You may also key text directly in a table of contents. Use the Format Painter to copy the format of the entry; then key the correct page number.

DRILL 2   REVISE TABLE OF CONTENTS   modify toc

1. In the open document, click in the selection area left of the generated table of contents to display the Table of Contents controls. Change the style to Automatic Table 1.

References/Table of Contents/Table of Contents

2. Click Insert Table of Contents and change to the Formal style. Click Yes to the prompt to replace the selected table of contents.

3. Modify the report as follows and update the table of contents. Click Update entire table.

   a. Select the Market Analysis section on page 1 of the report. Be sure to also select the three paragraphs with paragraph headings. Move this section to page 2 of the report just before the side heading *Developers*. This section is now on page 2.

   b. In the paragraph heading *Small Businesses*, change *Businesses* to lowercase.

4. Select the Appendix title on the last page of the report and click Add Text to add this text to the table of contents. Select Level 1. Click Update Table button to update the contents page.

5. Click the selection area to the left of the title Contents and apply Title style. If the appropriate Title with the underline does not display, click Undo and follow the directions again.

6. Verify that the page numbers were updated, the heading was changed, and the Appendix was added to the table of contents. See the illustration on the next page to check.

7. Proofread and check; click Next to continue. (*73-drill2*)

NUMBER PRELIMINARY PAGES

 Preliminary pages are numbered with lowercase Roman numerals. Change the number format when inserting the page number in this report.

To change page number format:

Insert/Header & Footer/Page Number

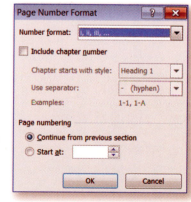

1. Follow the path above and click Page Number format.
2. Click the down list arrow and select the desired page number format. If necessary, set the starting page number.

TEXT BOXES

Text boxes enable you to position text at any location on a page. Since you can move them around, they are often called *floating boxes*. Text boxes can also be linked so that text can flow from one to another. Two types of text boxes are used—Built-In (preformatted) text boxes and text boxes that you draw and format yourself. You have already converted many shapes into text boxes by adding text to them. Many of the Built-In text boxes are used to format pull quotes and sidebars in newspapers, magazines, reports, brochures, or newsletters.

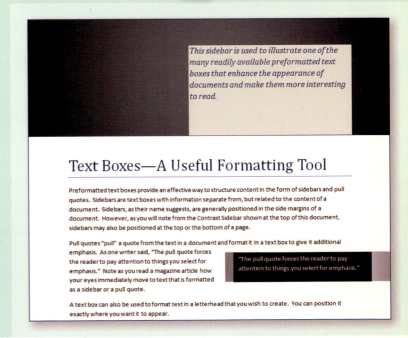

To insert a Built-In text box:

Insert/Text/Text Box

1. Display the gallery of Built-In text boxes.
2. Scroll through the thumbnails and click the text box you wish to insert.
3. Select the text in the placeholder and key your text, or copy and paste text in the placeholder.

★ TIP

The document theme used affects the format of the text box selected. Apply the theme; then select the text box.

DRILL 1   TEXT BOXES   text boxes

1. In the open document, read to learn about sidebars and pull quotes. Position the insertion point at the top of the page.

2. Display the Text Box gallery. Scroll down to locate and insert the Contrast sidebar.

3. Select the sidebar text and key the following text in the placeholder.

   This sidebar is used to illustrate one of the many readily available preformatted text boxes that enhance the appearance of documents and make them more interesting to read.

4. Position the insertion point on the right side of the second paragraph containing the quote. Insert the Contrast Quote text box.

5. Select the quote in the second paragraph; copy and paste it in the placeholder. Drag the text box to position it on the right side of the paragraph as shown at the right.

6. Proofread and check; click Next to continue. (*86-drill1*)

1. In the open document, insert a page break after the cover page to insert a blank page for the table of contents.

2. Position the insertion point at the top of the first page of the report (1") and insert a Continuous section break.

3. Go to the header of page 2 of Section 1. Deselect Different First Page if selected. Break links between headers and footers if a link displays. Insert a page number at the bottom of the page using the Plain Number 2 style. Change the page number format to lowercase Roman numerals. Change Start at to i.

4. Click Next and go to the header of Section 2. Deselect Different First Page if selected. Break the links between the headers and footers. Delete the number in the footer of section 2.

5. Go to the header of Section 2 and insert a page number at the top right using the Plain Number 3 style. Change the page number format to Arabic numerals (1, 2, 3). Change Start at to 1. Click Different First Page. If necessary, reposition the title on the first page to about 2".

6. On the blank page after the cover page, generate a table of contents using the Automatic Table 1 style. Position the title at 2" and apply Title style. *Hint:* Position insertion point at 2" before you generate the table of contents.

7. Verify that the page numbers are correct in each section. If necessary, refer to the troubleshooting tips below.

8. Proofread and check; click Next to continue. (*73-drill3*)

Troubleshooting Tips

Were your pages numbered correctly? If not, try these suggestions.

1. Remove all page numbers in header and footer in both sections. Follow the steps exactly as shown in the application.
2. Be sure the Different First Page command is not selected when you begin.
3. Check the Break the Link buttons in the header and footer to be sure the link is broken.
4. Do not forget to delete the incorrect page number that automatically displays in the footer of Section 2 after you break the links.

Document Design

TABLE OF CONTENTS

73c

A table of contents contains a list of the headings in a document, along with the page number on which each heading appears.

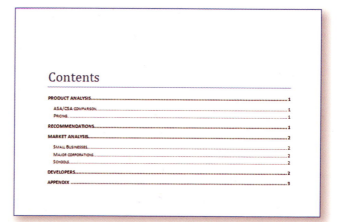

Lesson 86 | Text Boxes

New Commands   • Insert Text Boxes   • Format Text Boxes   • Link Text Boxes

86b Timed Writing

1. Key a 1' writing on each paragraph; work to increase speed.
2. Key a 3' timing on all paragraphs.

	gwam	1'	3'	5'
Americans tend to have a different view of vacation than		12	4	2
citizens of many other countries. In this country, companies usually		26	9	5
provide employees with a maximum of two or three weeks of vacation		40	13	8
each year. Many companies wait to award the second week of vacation		54	18	11
until employees have five years of tenure with them. Those who earn		67	22	13
more than three weeks of vacation typically do so by staying with the		81	27	16
same company for many years.		87	29	17
In many other countries, the case is quite different. Employees		14	34	20
typically receive four to six weeks of vacation each year. It is		27	38	23
also awarded much earlier in their tenure with the company. Vacation		41	43	26
is thought of as just another benefit that has value to the company		54	47	28
as well as to the employee. Employees often spend a whole month on		68	52	31
holiday as they call vacation time.		75	54	32
While some individuals think how wonderful and luxurious it		13	58	35
would be to have extra days or weeks of vacation, the fact is that		26	63	38
a large percentage of Americans do not take the vacation time they		40	67	40
are allotted by their companies. The American culture is such that		53	72	43
many employees feel they cannot be away from their positions for		66	76	46
more than two weeks at one time.		73	78	47

73-d1

Cover Page

1. Create a cover page using the Alphabet style.
2. Key the following:

   Document title: **Forms Design and Management**; shrink font to fit on one line.

   Subtitle: **Summary of Three-Year Implementation**

   Date: Current

   Author: **Student's Name, Forms Design Consultant**
3. Proofread and check; click Next to continue. (*73-d1*)

73-d2

Report

 forms

1. Open *73-d1*.
2. Position the insertion point on page 2. Insert the data file *forms*.
3. Key the remainder of the report on the next page below the file you inserted. Format the title and side headings appropriately.
4. Insert a blank page after the cover page for the table of contents. *Hint:* Position the insertion point immediately after the Page Break marker on the cover page. Be sure the Show/Hide button is turned on. Insert a manual page break.
5. Position the insertion point at the top of the first page of the report and insert a Continuous section break.
★ 6. Position the insertion point in the header of page 2 of Section 1. Deselect Different First Page if it is selected. Click Go to Footer and insert a page number at the bottom of the page using the Plain Number 2 page number style. Change the page number format to lowercase Roman numerals. Click Different First Page to suppress the page number on the cover page.
7. Click Next and position the insertion point in the header of Section 2. Deselect Different First Page if it is selected. Break the links between the headers for both sections. Go to the footer of Section 2. Break the link between the footers for both sections. Delete the page number in the Section 2 footer.
8. Go to header of Section 2 and number the pages of the report at the top right using the Plain Number 3 page number style. Change the page number format to begin with page 1. Click Different First Page to suppress the page number on the first page of the report.
9. Position the insertion point on the blank page left for the table of contents (not in the header section). Generate the table of contents using the Automatic Table 2 style. Position the heading at approximately 2" and apply Title style.
10. Move the section Conversion from Paper to Electronic Forms to appear below the Existing System section. Add the word **Implementation** after the heading *Forms Inventory*. Update the table of contents.
11. Proofread and check; click Next to continue. (*73-d2*)

1. Apply landscape orientation.
2. Use WordArt Fill – Red, Accent 2, Matte Bevel for the title; apply Text Effects Transform: Chevron Up.
3. Key the invitation shown below using Calibri 28 point.
4. Insert the *river camp* picture watermark.
5. Proofread and check; click Next to continue. (*85-d1*)

River Camp Experience

Join the Leisure Travelers Club

for an exciting video report of the

River Camp Experience

Friday, March 24 at 5:30 p.m.

at the Westside Center

Refreshments provided

QUICK ✓

Check your document against the one shown below.

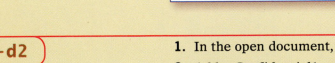

Texture 4x4

1. In the open document, use Fill Effects to add a Stationery background.
2. Add a Confidential1 watermark to the document.
3. Add a ½-point page border using the Dark Red, Accent 1 theme color.
4. Check and close. (*85-d2*)

Forms Inventory

A perpetual forms inventory system was designed and maintained online for all company-wide forms. Employees were encouraged to add their individual or departmental forms to the inventory system so that they could be shared with others.

Goal of the System

The goal of the system was to convert 70 to 75 percent of the forms to an electronic format within a three-year time period. This goal was considered to be ambitious because a wide range of computers were used in the various departments, and some departments did not have access to the central network. During this same time frame, the company planned to upgrade computers and make the network available to all employees except warehouse and delivery personnel.

Follow-Up Study

This phase of the study was authorized to determine the effectiveness of the program that was implemented. The following table shows the progress made since the program was instituted.

Copy the table on page 1 of the report and paste here. Edit the percentages as shown here.

Employee—Paper, 8%

Company—Paper, 5%

Vendor—Paper, 3%

External—Paper, 4%

Company—Electronic, 48%

Employee—Electronic, 32%

Results

Currently, 80 percent of all forms are in electronic format, and 20 percent are paper based. The four forms that are currently purchased from vendors are being redesigned so that they can be made available electronically. The remaining paper-based forms are used primarily by warehouse and delivery personnel. However, the Technology Committee has recommended providing these employees with handheld computers to perform their work. As soon as this recommendation is implemented, the forms they use can be converted to electronic format.

The new system has resulted in a 20 percent cost savings over the previous system. In addition, more than 80 percent of the employees indicated that the new system improved their efficiency and effectiveness.

73-d3

Executive Summary

1. Open *73-d2*.
2. In Draft View, position the insertion point at the end of the table of contents just before the section break line, but not in the table of contents area. Insert a manual page break.
3. Change to Print Layout view and key the executive summary on the next page. Begin the title at 2" and apply Title style.

PAGE COLORS

A color page background is used predominantly in Web browsers; however, the subtle use of page color and particularly fill effects can enhance the appearance of a document. The use of page color needs to be tactful and should be appropriate for the type of document. More formal documents should be limited to page color using fill effects, such as parchment or stationery. Less formal documents may be formatted using a background with more color.

To apply page color and fill effects:

Page Layout/Page Background/Page Color

1. Follow the path to display the color palette.

2. To apply a color, click the desired theme or standard color. Custom colors (often used to match company brand colors) can be accessed by clicking More Colors.

3. To apply an effect, click Fill Effects to display the gallery of effects. Click the appropriate tab (Gradient, Texture, Pattern, or Picture) to display the effect desired. To display the name of the effect, click it.

DRILL 4   PAGE COLOR

invitation

1. In the open document, remove the watermark.

2. Apply Light Blue Standard color to the document.

Page Layout/Page Background/Page Borders

3. Add a ½-point Orange, Background 2 page border.

4. Proofread and check; click Next to continue. (*85-drill4*)

DRILL 5   FILL EFFECTS

roswell

1. In the open document, display the Fill Effects dialog box.

2. Click each tab and preview the options.

3. Click the Texture tab, select Parchment (column C, row 4), and then click OK. Do not edit the body of the letter.

4. Proofread and check; click Next to continue. (*85-drill5*)

---

4. Verify that page iii displays at the bottom center of the page. Remember the preliminary pages were numbered in Document 2.

5. Proofread and check; click Next to continue. (73-d3)

Executive Summary

Approximately three years ago, a forms design, management control, and conversion program was instituted at Hess and Glenn, Inc. A survey of forms showed that 74 percent of all forms were paper-based forms and only 26 percent of the forms were electronic. The goal of the program was to convert 70 to 75 percent of the paper-based forms to an electronic format.

The current survey shows that 80 percent of the forms used at Hess and Glenn, Inc. are in electronic format. The only company forms currently in paper format are those that are filled in with pen or pencil and that are used as checklists for warehouse and delivery personnel.

The new system has reduced costs and has improved efficiency and effectiveness. In addition, employees are extremely pleased with the new forms program.

73-d4

Transmittal Letter

1. Open 73-d3. In Draft View, position the insertion point at the end of the cover page just before the table of contents. Change to Print Layout view.

2. Compose a transmittal letter from you to **Mr. Patrick Hess**, President, Hess and Glen, Inc., 1598 Harmon Road, Hopkins, SC 29061-3498. Thank Mr. Hess, state the report is attached, and offer to answer any questions.

3. Verify that page ii displays at the bottom center of the page.

4. In the table of contents, key **Letter of Transmittal** as the first entry and **Executive Summary** as the second entry. Use the Format Painter to copy the format of the entries and key the appropriate page numbers. If necessary, remove the underline and blue font color.

5. Proofread and check; click Next to continue. (73-d4)

73-d5

Edit Report

1. Open 71-d1. Insert a blank page after the cover page for the table of contents.

2. Insert the Plain Number 2 page number style at the bottom of the page in Section 1. Format page numbers appropriately.

3. Verify that page numbers are correct in Section 2.

4. Generate a table of contents using the Formal style with dashed tab leaders. Add the title Table of Contents. Position appropriately and apply Title style. *Hint:* Apply black font if white font is selected.

5. Check and close. (73-d5)

DRILL 1   TEXT WATERMARK

recruitment

1. In the open document, display the Watermark gallery.
2. Click DO NOT COPY 1.

3. Preview the watermark.
4. Proofread and check; click Next to continue. (*85-drill1*)

★ TIP

If you format a multiple-page document with a watermark and page number or other header information, the watermark will not display on the first page if you choose Different First Page to suppress the page number or header.

To insert a watermark with custom text:

Page Layout/Page Background/Watermark

1. Follow the path to display the gallery of built-in watermarks.
2. Click Custom Watermark at the bottom of the gallery to display the Printed Watermark dialog box.
3. Select Text watermark and then key the desired text in the Text box. Select font and layout.
4. Click Apply and Close.

DRILL 2   CUSTOM TEXT WATERMARK

 team writing

1. In the open document, display the Watermark gallery and click Custom Watermark at the bottom of the gallery.
2. Select Text watermark and then key **GREAT JOB!** in the Text box. Use Arial font and Diagonal layout.

3. Click Apply and Close. Preview the watermark to ensure that it displays on both pages.
4. Proofread and check; click Next to continue. (*85-drill2*)

✱ DISCOVER

To remove a watermark, click Remove Watermark at the bottom of the Watermark gallery.

To insert a picture watermark:

Page Layout/Page Background/Watermark

1. Display the gallery of built-in watermarks.
2. Click Custom Watermark at the bottom of the gallery to display the Printed Watermark dialog box.
3. Select Picture watermark and click Select Picture to browse, select, and insert the desired picture.
4. Click Apply and Close.

DRILL 3   PICTURE WATERMARK

 picnic, lake house

1. In the open document, remove the *ASAP* watermark.
2. Insert a custom watermark, click Picture watermark, and then click Select Picture.

3. Browse data files, select *lake house*, and click Insert.
4. Click Apply and Close.
5. Proofread and check; click Next to continue. (*85-drill3*)

Lesson 74 | Table of Figures and Index

New Commands
- Table of Figures
- Index
- Bookmarks
- Hyperlinks

WARMUP

Lessons/74a Warmup

New Commands

74b

TABLE OF FIGURES

A table of figures is a list of all of the captions for tables, charts, pictures, graphics, and equations in a document. Captions can be added automatically or manually to an existing object. See the illustration below. Generally, tables are labeled above the table, and figures are labeled below the figure.

Table of Figures

To insert a caption

References/Captions/Insert Caption

1. Select the item to be captioned. In the caption text box, space once after the number and key the caption.

2. Follow the path and from the Label list, click the drop-list arrow and select the desired label, e.g., Figure, Table, Equation.

3. From the Position list, click the drop-list arrow and select Above selected item or Below selected item.

4. Click the Numbering button to choose the desired number format, e.g., 1, 2, 3. Click OK.

5. Click New Label to create a new label group, such as Sports Photos. Click OK.

Note: Click AutoCaption to select the objects for which you want captions created automatically, e.g., *Microsoft Word* Table.

Lesson 85 | *Document Backgrounds*

New Commands   • Watermarks   • Page Colors

WARMUP

Lessons/85a Warmup

Skill Building

85b   Textbook Keying

1. Key each line once, concentrating on using good keying techniques. Tap ENTER twice after each 3-line group.

2. Repeat the drill if time permits.

direct reaches

1 red much brief hunt bred zany check jump decrease music many brat
2 polo excel munch brake junk swim wreck lunch curve kick dazed bed
3 Cec and Kim enjoy a great hunting trip in June after school ends.

adjacent reaches

4 were guy sad junior tree trio fast point rest joint walk gas join
5 opt crew going port backlog poster web suit few folder buy porter
6 Porter saw two important guys after we walked past Union Station.

double letters

7 bell look deed glass upper inn odd committee cabbage effect inner
8 add spell pool happy jazz mass scurry connect office fall setting
9 Debbie Desselle called a committee meeting at noon at the office.

| 1 | 2 | 3 | 4 | 5 | 6 | 7 | 8 | 9 | 10 | 11 | 12 | 13 |

New Commands

85c

WATERMARKS

Watermarks are text or pictures that display behind document text in a light or washed-out version. They display in Print Layout and Full Screen Reading views and on printed documents. Watermarks are grouped in three categories: Confidential, Disclaimers, and Urgent. Picture watermarks and watermarks with custom text can also be used. The logo of a business is often displayed as a watermark.

To insert a text watermark:

Page Layout/Page Background/Watermark

1. Follow the path to display the gallery of built-in watermarks.

2. Scroll down and click the desired option, such as DO NOT COPY 1, to insert it. Note that watermarks are typically positioned either horizontally or diagonally on the page.

To create a table of figures:

References/Captions/Insert Table of Figures

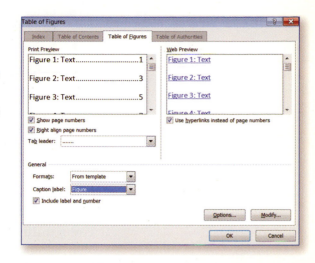

1. Position the insertion point where the table of figures is to be positioned.

2. Follow the path above to display the Table of Figures dialog box.

3. Click the down list arrow beside the

   a. Tab leader box and select the leader type.

   b. Formats box and select the format.

   c. Caption label box and select the caption label , e.g., Table. Click OK.

DRILL 1   TABLE OF FIGURES    guide

1. Insert captions below the figure for the three figures in this file. Label as follows:

   • **Figure 1 Caption Dialog Box**

   • **Figure 2 Caption Numbering Dialog Box**

   • **Figure 3 New Label Dialog Box**

2. Create a table of figures on the first page using the Formal format and the Figure caption label. Choose the dot leaders.

3. Proofread and check; click Next to continue. (*74-drill1*)

QUICK ✓

Check your table of figures and captions from the illustration below.

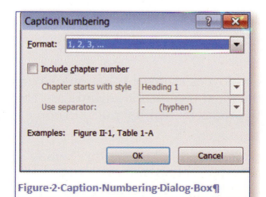

Table of Figures

Figure·1·Caption·Dialog·Box¶

Figure·2·Caption·Numbering·Dialog·Box¶

Figure·3·New·Label·Dialog·Box¶

1. Apply Aspect theme and then customize the theme as follows:

   a. **Colors: Accent 1:** Tan, Accent 6; **Accent 5:** Yellow Standard color; **Accent 6:** Orange, Accent 1; **Hyperlink:** Light Blue Standard color. Name color theme: **Rex**.

   b. **Fonts: Heading:** Verdana; **Body:** Cambria. Name font theme: **Rex**.

   c. **Effects:** Module

   d. Save theme as **Rex**.

2. Key report below. Apply Title and Subtitle styles to title and subtitle. Apply heading styles indicated. Shrink the font so that the title fits on one line.

3. Check and close. (*84-d1*)

Trevor Bradwell—Instant Messaging

Corporate Sur...

The results of t...ent Bradwell corporate survey on communication technologies re...some very interesting findings. When employees were asked to check...technologies enhanced their internal communications most, more tha... ...rcent wrote instant messaging in the Other category. Further research...ed that this percentage is typical in many companies. A significant num...f employees use instant messaging on the job without the employer's kn...ge.

Heading 1 style → Uses of Instant M...ng

An e-mail follow-up survey produced additional information on the ways that instant messages are being used in our company. Some of the uses are summarized in this report.

Heading 2 style → Presence

Results of the e-mail indicated that the use of instant messaging to determine if someone was in the office and available for a quick online chat, a quick call, or a meeting was one of the best uses of instant messaging. If three or four were available, they could get together immediately to solve a problem that might otherwise take days to resolve.

Heading 2 style → Information Requests

The second most frequent use of instant messaging was for conveying quick requests for information needed from others. Usually a response was provided immediately.

Heading 1 style → Advantages and Disadvantages of Instant Messaging

Trevor Bradwell employees reported both advantages and disadvantages of using instant messaging in the business environment.

Heading 2 style → Advantages

Most employees indicated that quick responses to requests for information were the most significant advantage. They reported that instant messaging usually produced results quicker than e-mail or voice mail.

Heading 2 style → Disadvantages

Most people reported that if the "buddy" list was too long, instant messaging became a distraction and interrupted work being done. Instant messages tend to be abbreviated and very casual.

New Commands

- Table of Figures
- Index
- Bookmarks
- Hyperlinks

KEYBOARDING PRO DELUXE 2

WARMUP

Lessons/74a Warmup

New Commands

74b

TABLE OF FIGURES

A table of figures is a list of all of the captions for tables, charts, pictures, graphics, and equations in a document. Captions can be added automatically or manually to an existing object. See the illustration below. Generally, tables are labeled above the table, and figures are labeled below the figure.

Table of Figures

To insert a caption

References/Captions/Insert Caption

1. Select the item to be captioned. In the caption text box, space once after the number and key the caption.

2. Follow the path and from the Label list, click the drop-list arrow and select the desired label, e.g., Figure, Table, Equation.

3. From the Position list, click the drop-list arrow and select Above selected item or Below selected item.

4. Click the Numbering button to choose the desired number format, e.g., 1, 2, 3. Click OK.

5. Click New Label to create a new label group, such as Sports Photos. Click OK.

Note: Click AutoCaption to select the objects for which you want captions created automatically, e.g., *Microsoft Word* Table.

Lesson 85 | Document Backgrounds

New Commands • Watermarks • Page Colors

WARMUP

Lessons/85a Warmup

Skill Building

85b Textbook Keying

1. Key each line once, concentrating on using good keying techniques. Tap ENTER twice after each 3-line group.

2. Repeat the drill if time permits.

direct reaches	1	red much brief hunt bred zany check jump decrease music many brat
	2	polo excel munch brake junk swim wreck lunch curve kick dazed bed
	3	Cec and Kim enjoy a great hunting trip in June after school ends.
adjacent reaches	4	were guy sad junior tree trio fast point rest joint walk gas join
	5	opt crew going port backlog poster web suit few folder buy porter
	6	Porter saw two important guys after we walked past Union Station.
double letters	7	bell look deed glass upper inn odd committee cabbage effect inner
	8	add spell pool happy jazz mass scurry connect office fall setting
	9	Debbie Desselle called a committee meeting at noon at the office.

| 1 | 2 | 3 | 4 | 5 | 6 | 7 | 8 | 9 | 10 | 11 | 12 | 13 |

New Commands

85c

WATERMARKS

Watermarks are text or pictures that display behind document text in a light or washed-out version. They display in Print Layout and Full Screen Reading views and on printed documents. Watermarks are grouped in three categories: Confidential, Disclaimers, and Urgent. Picture watermarks and watermarks with custom text can also be used. The logo of a business is often displayed as a watermark.

To insert a text watermark:

Page Layout/Page Background/Watermark

1. Follow the path to display the gallery of built-in watermarks.

2. Scroll down and click the desired option, such as DO NOT COPY 1, to insert it. Note that watermarks are typically positioned either horizontally or diagonally on the page.

To create a table of figures:

References/Captions/Insert Table of Figures

1. Position the insertion point where the table of figures is to be positioned.

2. Follow the path above to display the Table of Figures dialog box.

3. Click the down list arrow beside the

   a. Tab leader box and select the leader type.

   b. Formats box and select the format.

   c. Caption label box and select the caption label , e.g., Table. Click OK.

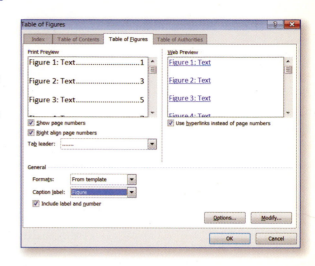

DRILL 1   TABLE OF FIGURES    guide

1. Insert captions below the figure for the three figures in this file. Label as follows:

   • **Figure 1 Caption Dialog Box**

   • **Figure 2 Caption Numbering Dialog Box**

   • **Figure 3 New Label Dialog Box**

2. Create a table of figures on the first page using the Formal format and the Figure caption label. Choose the dot leaders.

3. Proofread and check; click Next to continue. (*74-drill1*)

QUICK ✔   Check your table of figures and captions from the illustration below.

Table of Figures

Figure·1·Caption·Dialog·Box¶

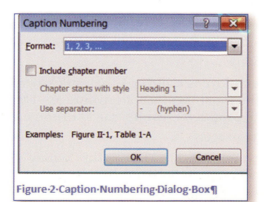

Figure·2·Caption·Numbering·Dialog·Box¶

Figure·3·New·Label·Dialog·Box¶

84-d1

Report with Custom Theme

1. Apply Aspect theme and then customize the theme as follows:
   a. **Colors:** **Accent 1:** Tan, Accent 6; **Accent 5:** Yellow Standard color; **Accent 6:** Orange, Accent 1; **Hyperlink:** Light Blue Standard color. Name color theme: **Rex**.
   b. **Fonts: Heading:** Verdana; **Body:** Cambria. Name font theme: **Rex**.
   c. **Effects:** Module
   d. Save theme as **Rex**.

2. Key report below. Apply Title and Subtitle styles to title and subtitle. Apply heading styles indicated. Shrink the font so that the title fits on one line.

3. Check and close. (*84-d1*)

Trevor Bradwell—Instant Messaging

Corporate Survey

The results of the recent Bradwell corporate survey on communication technologies revealed some very interesting findings. When employees were asked to check which technologies enhanced their internal communications most, more than 30 percent wrote instant messaging in the Other category. Further research showed that this percentage is typical in many companies. A significant number of employees use instant messaging on the job without the employer's knowledge.

Heading 1 style → **Uses of Instant Messaging**

An e-mail follow-up survey produced additional information on the ways that instant messages are being used in our company. Some of the uses are summarized in this report.

Heading 2 style → **Presence**

Results of the e-mail indicated that the use of instant messaging to determine if someone was in the office and available for a quick online chat, a quick call, or a meeting was one of the best uses of instant messaging. If three or four were available, they could get together immediately to solve a problem that might otherwise take days to resolve.

Heading 2 style → **Information Requests**

The second most frequent use of instant messaging was for conveying quick requests for information needed from others. Usually a response was provided immediately.

Heading 1 style → **Advantages and Disadvantages of Instant Messaging**

Trevor Bradwell employees reported both advantages and disadvantages of using instant messaging in the business environment.

Heading 2 style → **Advantages**

Most employees indicated that quick responses to requests for information were the most significant advantage. They reported that instant messaging usually produced results quicker than e-mail or voice mail.

Heading 2 style → **Disadvantages**

Most people reported that if the "buddy" list was too long, instant messaging became a distraction and interrupted work being done. Instant messages tend to be abbreviated and very casual.

To modify the format:

References/Captions/Insert Table of Figures

1. Follow the path above to display the Table of Figures dialog box.

2. Click Modify.

3. In the Style dialog box, click Modify. The Modify Style dialog box displays.

4. Change the format of the table of figures entries, e.g., font, font size, font color, alignment, and spacing.

5. Click OK.

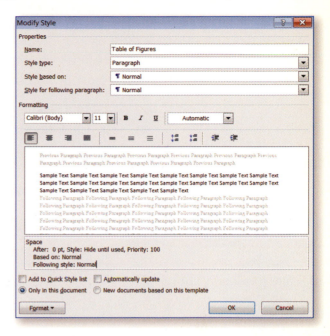

DRILL 2   **TABLE OF FIGURES**   pictures

1. In the open document, create a new label named **May 2011 Photo.** Insert a caption for the pictures as follows:

   a. May 2011 Photo 1: **Maggie and the Bradford Pear**

   b. May 2011 Photo 2: **Our Morning Visitors at the Beach House**

   c. May 2011 Photo 3: **Andy to the Rescue**

2. Create a table of figures using a modified style. Modify the format of the entries as follows: 12 point, bold, Purple Accent 4, and 1.5 line spacing.

3. Proofread and check; click Next to continue. (*74-drill2*)

To update a table of figures:

1. Make changes as desired in the captions.

2. Click in the table of figures. From the Captions group, on the References tab, click Update Table. (*Shortcut:* F9.)

3. Select Update page numbers only or Update entire table. Click OK.

TIP

In an academic setting, you should not change the default theme and leave your workstation before changing the default theme back to Office.

SAVE THEMES AS DEFAULT

The Office theme is set as the default in the Normal template that is used to create new blank documents. You can customize a theme and save it as the default. If a company creates a custom theme, it is usually set as the default theme.

To set a new default theme:

Home/Styles/Change Styles

1. In a new document, display the Change Styles options.
2. Click the right arrow on Colors and select the desired color set, such as My Colors.
3. Click Change Styles again, click the right arrow on Fonts, and select the desired font set, such as My Fonts.
4. Click Change Styles and then click Set as Default.

DRILL 3 | **SET DEFAULT THEME**

1. Click Change Styles and then Colors. From the Custom group, select My Colors.

2. Click Change Styles and then click Fonts; from the Custom group, select My Fonts.

3. Click Change Styles and then Set as Default.

4. Key the heading and paragraph below. Apply Heading 1 style and note that both the font and colors have changed to the new default you set.

5. Proofread and check; click Next to continue. (84-drill3)

Heading 1

My colors and fonts are now set as the default document theme.

DRILL 4 | **CHANGE DEFAULT THEME**

1. Change the color set back to Office.

2. Change the font set back to Office.

3. Set as default.

4. Key the heading and paragraph below. Apply Heading 1 style and note that both the font and colors have changed to the Office default.

5. Proofread and check; click Next to continue. (84-drill4)

Heading 1

My default has now been changed back to Office.

Communication

84c   pronouns

KEYBOARDING PRO DELUXE 2

References/Communication Skills/Pronoun Case

1. Review the following guides and those in *Keyboarding Pro DELUXE 2*. In the *pronouns* data file, key the correct pronoun in the first column next to each sentence.

2. Proofread and check; click Next to continue. (84c)

Nominative case: Use the nominative case (*I, you, we, she, he, they, it, who*) when the pronoun acts as the subject of a verb or when the pronoun is used as a predicate pronoun. (The verb *be* is a linking verb; it links the noun/pronoun to the predicate.)

Objective case: Use the objective case (*me, you, us, her, him, them, it, whom*) when the pronoun is used as a direct or indirect object or is an object of the preposition.

1. Open *74-drill2*. Edit the captions as follows:

   a. May 2011 Photo 1: Add **in Full Bloom**

   b. May 2011 Photo 2: Delete Morning

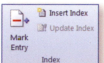
Picture Tools Format/Size

2. Tap ENTER twice at the end of the last caption. Insert the data file *giraffes*. Right-click the picture and select Size. Change height to 2.66" and accept the adjusted width. Click Close.

3. Using the May 2011 Photo label, add the caption **Giraffes Seen on Last Day of Safari.**

4. Update the table of figures. Reapply the format if necessary.

5. Proofread and check; click Next to continue. (*74-drill3*)

INDEX

An index is a list of topics in a document and the page numbers on which they appear. The index is created after the document has been completed and is positioned as the last page of a report.

An index entry can consist of a word, phrase, or symbol. A cross-reference, which refers the reader to other text, can be added at the time an entry is marked.

The process of creating an index involves marking the text that will be included as entries, selecting the format, and then creating the index. *Word* automatically eliminates duplicate entries. Modifying an index is also quite simple. An example of an Index page using the Format style is shown here.

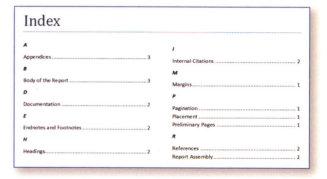

To mark index entries:

References/Index/Mark Entry

1. Select the text to be marked as an index entry.

2. Follow the path to display the Mark Index Entry dialog box. The selected word displays in the Main entry box. Make any edits. (If needed, drag the dialog box to position it so you can see the text.)

3. To add a cross-reference, key the text after See in the Cross-reference entry box ❶.

4. Click Mark to mark the one entry or click Mark All to mark the entry each time it occurs. **Note:** Use Find (CTRL + F) to locate entries if marking one at a time.

5. Close when all index entries are marked.

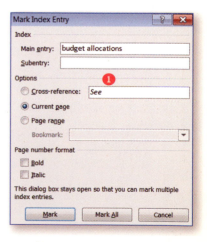

To create new theme colors:

Page Layout/Themes/Colors

1. Follow the path to display the Colors gallery; click Create New Theme Colors at the bottom of the gallery to display the Create New Theme Colors dialog box.

2. Click the drop-list arrow on each theme color you wish to change to display the theme, standard, or custom colors that can be selected.

3. Select the desired color and repeat the step until all colors that you want to change have been changed. Key the name for the new color set and click Save.

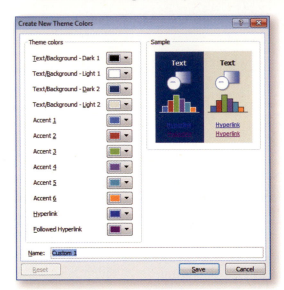 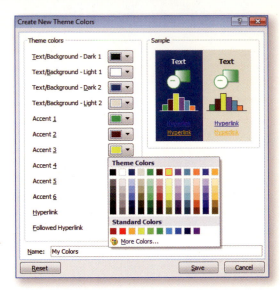

To create a new custom theme:

Page Layout/Themes/Themes

1. In a new document, create and name custom fonts and custom colors.

2. Select the desired effects.

3. Follow the path and click Save Current Theme to save as a new document theme with the name of your choice.

DRILL 2　　CUSTOM THEME

Page Layout/Themes/Fonts

1. Create new theme fonts using Century Schoolbook as the Heading font and Century as the Body font. Save the font set as **My Fonts**.

2. Create new theme colors: Change Accent 1 to Green from the Standard colors. Change Accent 2 to Red, Accent 2, Darker 50%, and change Accent 3 to Yellow from the Standard colors.

3. Change the Hyperlink to Standard color Orange. Save the theme colors as **My Colors**.

4. Apply Executive effects to your document.

5. Save the theme as **My Theme**.

6. Key the paragraph below, tapping ENTER after the period; apply Heading 1 to *Contact Information*.

7. Proofread and check; click Next to continue. (*84-drill2*)

Contact Information

All officers can be contacted using the following e-mail address: officers@bradwell.com.

To create an index:

References/Index/Insert Index

1. Position the insertion point where you want to create the index. Generally, an index is positioned on a new page at the end of the document. Key the heading **Index** at the top of the page at about 2" so that the heading will be positioned above the index. Apply Title style.

2. Follow the path above to display the Index dialog box.

3. For Type, select either Indented or Run-in. Indented is commonly used.

4. Click the Columns spin arrow to select the desired number of columns.

5. From the Formats list, select the desired format, e.g., Classic or From template. Click OK.

Note: You may also modify the format of the index in the same way you modified the table of figures. Click the Modify button.

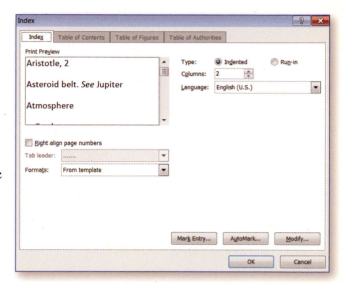

DRILL 4 INDEX

1. Open *73-drill2*.

2. Position the insertion point on page 1 of the report. Mark the index entries in the column below and click Mark All to mark all occurrences.

   Administrative Skills Assessment

   Comprehensive Skills Assessment

   budget allocations

   Discounts

   large organizations

   marketing allocations

   small business market

3. Use Keep with next to keep table caption and table together.

4. Click Mark Entry and key **ASA** as the main entry. Select the option Cross-reference and key **Administrative Skills Assessment**.

5. Repeat step 3 for **CSA** (main entry) **Comprehensive Skills Assessment** (cross reference).

6. Begin a new page as the last page of the report. Begin the main heading *Index* at 2" and apply Title style. (*Hint:* Turn off bullets before you begin.)

7. Create an index using the Fancy format, Indented type, and two columns.

8. Use the Add Text feature to add the index to the table of contents; update the table of contents.

9. Proofread and check; click Next to continue. (*74-drill4*)

To create a new theme using built-in sets:

Page Layout/Themes/Colors, Fonts, and Effects

1. In a new document, click the Colors button and select the desired color set.
2. Click Fonts and select the desired heading and body font set.
3. Click Effects and select the desired effect set.
4. Click Themes to display the gallery of Built-In themes, and then click Save Current Theme at the bottom of the gallery to display the Save Current Theme dialog box.
5. Key the name of the theme and click Save.

DRILL 1   CUSTOM THEME FROM BUILT-IN SETS

1. Apply Clarity theme.
2. Click Colors and then select Hardcover colors.
3. Click Fonts and then select Black Tie.
4. Click Effects and then select Angles.
5. Click Themes and then click Save Current Theme.

6. Key **Officers** as the filename and click Save.
7. Click Themes and check to see that *Officers* is now listed as a Custom theme.
8. Key **Officers** on the first line of the document and apply Title style.
9. Proofread and check; click Next to continue. (*84-drill1*)

CREATE CUSTOM THEMES

Most companies create logos and letterhead with the company colors, fonts, and various effects as part of their identity or branding. Companies like to create document themes that match their company identity. Each font set consists of a heading and a body font. Each theme color consists of 12 components—four text/background colors, six accent colors, and two hyperlink colors.

To create new theme fonts:

Page Layout/Themes/Fonts

1. Follow the path to display the Fonts gallery; click Create New Theme Fonts at the bottom of the gallery to display the Create New Theme Fonts dialog box.

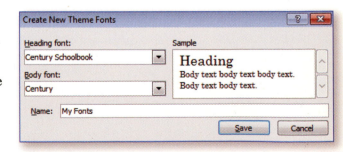

2. Click the Heading font drop-list arrow and select the heading font.
3. Click the Body font drop-list arrow and select the body font.
4. Key the name for the new font set and click Save. The fonts you selected appear as a new custom font set.

UPDATE INDEX

To update an index:

References/Index/Update Index

1. Mark the additional index entries.
2. Click in the index. Follow the path above. The update automatically takes place.

DRILL 5   **UPDATE INDEX**

1. Open *74-drill4*.
2. Add the following index entries:

   Recommendations (mark on page 1 only).

   Development team (mark all)

3. Delete the entry for *budget allocations*. (*Hint:* Delete the code {XE "budget allocations"} in the text on page 1.)
4. Position the insertion point in the index and update the index.
5. Proofread and check; click Next to continue. (*74-drill5*)

NAVIGATION TOOLS

Lengthier and more complex documents require use of two convenient navigation tools—bookmarks and hyperlinks.

BOOKMARKS

 A bookmark is inserted in a document to mark a specific location.

To insert and name a bookmark:

Insert/Links/Bookmark

1. Place the insertion point where the bookmark is to be inserted or select a block of text.
2. Follow the path above to display the Bookmark dialog box.
3. In the Bookmark name box, key a name for the bookmark. Click Add.

Important Naming Rules: (1) Must begin with a letter, (2) No spaces, and (3) Can contain numbers.

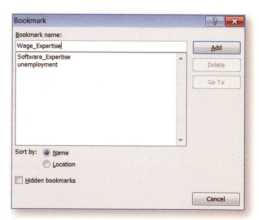

To navigate with a bookmark:

Insert/Links/Bookmark

1. Follow the path above to display the Bookmark dialog box.
2. From the Bookmark name box, select the desired bookmark. Bookmarks can be in alphabetical order or by location in the document.
3. Click Go To.

Shortcut: CTRL + G. Click Bookmark, click the down arrow, and select the desired bookmark. Click Go To.

New Commands

- Custom Themes from Built-In Sets
- Custom Themes
- Set Custom Themes as Default
- Restore Default Theme

New Commands

84b

CUSTOM THEMES FROM BUILT-IN SETS

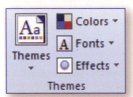

You have already applied Built-In document themes to many documents you have prepared. In this lesson, you will customize document themes, set themes as the default, and restore the Office default. The Themes group contains a gallery of 40 Built-In or preformatted color themes. Each Built-In theme consists of three elements—colors, a set of heading and body fonts, and effects as shown below. Colors and fonts affect the appearance of text. Effects affect the appearance of graphics. The same themes are available in other *Microsoft Office* suite applications so that documents can be formatted consistently. Office is the default theme for all applications. You can mix and match colors, fonts, and effects to create new themes. Note the Create New Theme Colors and Create New Theme Fonts commands at the bottom of these galleries. You can also download themes from Office.com.

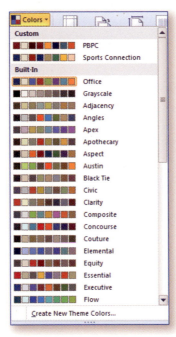

To delete a bookmark:

1. Select the desired bookmark in the dialog box.
2. Click Delete.

To show bookmarks:

1. Click the File button and Options.
2. In the left pane, click Advanced and select Show bookmarks. Click OK.

DRILL 6	BOOKMARKS	project

1. In the open document, select the words *Time Limit* under the column *Criteria* in the rubric table. Create a bookmark named **Time_Limit**.

2. Select the word *Time* on page 1 under the title *Training Team Project* and create a bookmark named **Time**. Delete the *Time* bookmark.

3. Select the words *Delivery Schedule* on page 3. Create a bookmark named **Delivery_Schedule**.

4. Show the bookmarked items.

5. Proofread and check; click Next to continue. (*74-drill6*)

HYPERLINK

 A hyperlink is text that when clicked will navigate the user to a specific location. You will learn to link to existing files or Web pages or to a place in the current document.

To create a hyperlink to an existing file or Web page:

Insert/Links/Hyperlink

1. Select the text or object to be hyperlinked.
2. Follow the path above to display the Insert Hyperlink dialog box.
3. In the Link to pane, click Existing File or Web Page.
4. In the Look in pane, browse to locate the desired file. Use the Current Folder, Browsed Pages, or Recent Files options to assist in locating the file. Click OK.

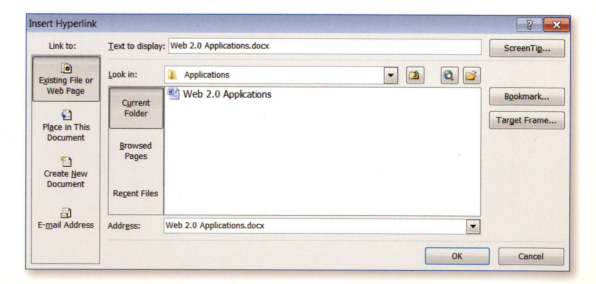

83-d1

continued

⭐ TIP

The flowchart has the same shapes as the one you created in Drill 1. Recreate it using the same directions given in Drill 1.

4. Number the pages at the top of the page using Plain Number 3 and Different First Page.

5. Apply a dropped cap to the first letter; change the color to Red, Accent 1, and increase distance from the text to 0.1".

6. Create the flowchart shown below following the second paragraph, using the directions from Drill 1, and add the text:

Fountain delivered

Prepare setting sketch

Is the sketch approved?   No   Yes

Modify sketch   Begin planning

Install fountain and landscaping

7. Insert the *gate fountain* picture at the end of the document; format as follows:

    a. Crop as shown.

    b. Apply Bevel Rectangle style; size 5.5" wide.

    c. Make the following adjustments: Sharpen 25%; apply 200% Saturation; compress the picture.

8. Proofread and check; click Next to continue. (*83-d1*)

QUICK ✔

Check your documents against the illustration below.

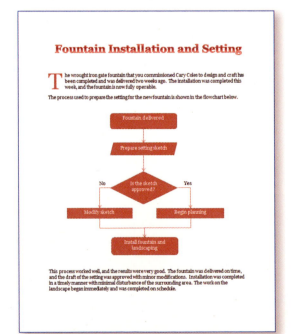

To create a hyperlink to a place in the document:

1. Select the text or object to be hyperlinked.

2. Follow the path above to display the Insert Hyperlink dialog box.

3. In the Link to pane, click Place in This Document.

4. In the Select a place in this document pane, click on the desired location in the document. Note you may click on Headings or a bookmark. Click OK.

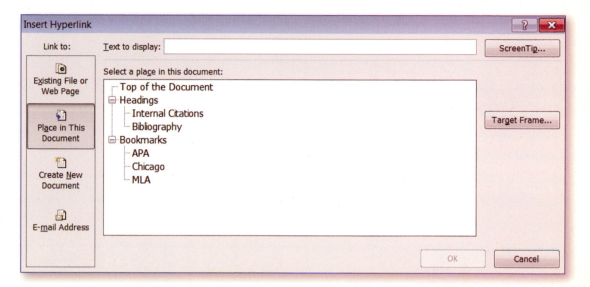

DRILL 7 — HYPERLINKS

 evaluation

1. Open *74-drill6*. Revise the title by adding the words **Directions and Rubric**. Select the word *Rubric* and insert a hyperlink to the Heading *Training Project Rubric*.

2. Select the word *Time* at the top of the document and hyperlink to the bookmark *Time_Limit*.

3. Select the text Delivery Dates. Hyperlink to the bookmark *Delivery_Schedule*.

4. Select the word *here* in the Evaluation text box. Hyperlink to the data file *evaluation*.

5. Proofread and check; click Next to continue. (*74-drill7*)

Applications

74-d1

Edit Report

1. Open *73-d4*. Add the captions to the two tables as shown below. Position the caption above the table and number with Arabic numbers.

   Table on first page: **Table 1 Form Sources—2008 Survey**

   Table on second page: **Table 2 Form Sources—2011 Survey**

2. Insert a blank page after the page break on the table of contents page. Remember to click Show/Hide so you can see the Page Break. Be sure to position the insertion point to the left of the section break.

3. Generate the table of figures using the default format. Key the title appropriately and apply Title style.

4. Edit both table captions as follows. Update the table of figures.

   Table 1 **Sources of Company Forms—2008 Survey**

   Table 2 **Sources of Company Forms—2011 Survey**

   (continued)

Dropped caps can be modified by changing the style, the color, the number of lines to drop, and the distance from the text.

To modify a dropped cap:

- To change the color, select the dropped cap and click the desired color on the Font Color gallery.
- To change the style, select the dropped cap, click Drop Cap, and change to style desired.
- To change the number of lines or the distance from the text, click Drop Cap and select Drop Cap Options. Use the spin arrows to increase or decrease the number of lines to drop or the distance from the text.

DRILL 6	DROP CAP	architecture

1. In the open document, click in the first paragraph and apply an In margin drop cap.

2. Select the drop cap and change the color to Orange, Accent 1.

3. Select the drop cap and change the style to Dropped.

4. Increase the number of lines dropped to 4 and the distance from the text to 0.1".

5. Proofread and check; click Next to continue. (83-drill6)

Applications

Report with Graphics

 gate fountain

1. In a new document, apply the Civic theme.

2. Insert Gradient Fill – Red, Accent 1 WordArt at 1.3". Key the title shown below. Shrink the font to 26 points so that it fits on one line.

3. Key the report shown below; insert and format the graphics as noted after the report.

Fountain Installation and Setting

The wrought iron gate fountain that you commissioned Cary Coles to design and craft has been completed and was delivered two weeks ago. The installation was completed this week, and the fountain is now fully operable.

The process used to prepare the setting for the new fountain is shown in the flowchart below.

This process worked well, and the results were very good. The fountain was delivered on time, and the draft of the setting was approved with minor modifications. Installation was completed in a timely manner with minimal disturbance of the surrounding area. The work on the landscape began immediately and was completed on schedule.

Ms. Coles is a gifted artist who created a beautiful work of art that will be cherished for many years. The fountain has substantially exceeded our expectations. All of the specifications were met, and the fountain fit perfectly into the area designed for it, as you will note from the picture below.

Ms. Coles requested that we notify you that the project has been completed to our satisfaction so that you will release the final payment for the work. We are delighted to convey this information to you, and we highly recommend Cary Coles for future projects.

5. Insert a blank page at the end of the report for the index. Mark the phrases *paper-based* and *electronic format*. Create the index using the Formal style. Format and position the title appropriately. Add the index to the table of contents as Level 1.

6. Change the document theme to Aspect.

7. Proofread and check; click Next to continue. (*74-d1*)

 progress report

1. Open *72-d2*. Use the Navigation pane to browse to go to the side heading *Adjust Your Workstation*. Add the following sentence to the last bullet: **The chair shown here illustrates an excellent adjustable chair for any user.**

2. Search the Internet using the keywords *picture adjustable computer chair*. Insert the picture to the right of the sentence you just inserted. Use Square text wrapping. Record the Web address of the picture for step 7 below.

3. Use the Find command to go to the paragraph heading *Posture*. Select the text *position yourself properly at the computer*. Create the bookmark **computer_position**.

4. Go to the numbered list at the bottom of page 2. Click at the beginning of the first item. Name the bookmark **practices**.

5. Delete the *practices* bookmark. Create it again and name it **my_practices**.

6. Create the hyperlinks in the following steps.

7. Select the picture of the adjustable chair you inserted in step 2. Insert a hyperlink to link to the Web page recorded in step 2.

8. Use the Navigation pane to browse to go to the heading *Posture*. Insert a clip art using the keywords *hands computer*. Insert the clip with hands in correct position on a laptop. Use Square text wrapping. Select the clip art and insert a hyperlink to link to the Web address: *http://community.cengage.com/SWKeyboarding/blogs/forde/archive/2010/01/08/assessment-strategies-positive-coaching-and-technique-rating-sheet.aspx.*

9. Select the text *technique rating sheet* found in the *Check Your Ergonomic Practices* section. Insert a hyperlink to the data file *progress report*.

10. Proofread and check; click Next to continue. (*74-d2*)

★ TIP

Browsed Pages

From your browser open the Web address at the right to ensure it is the correct Web address. Then insert the hyperlink by clicking Browsed Pages. Select the link you just opened.

1. Open *74-d1*.

2. Delete the table of figures.

3. Generate a new table of figures and modify the format as follows: 12 point, bold, Red Accent 2, and 1.5 line spacing.

4. Format the title and position appropriately.

5. Add the following words to the index: *conversion* and *inventory*. Update the index.

6. Check and close. (*74-d3*)

WORDART

WordArt consists of decorative text that can be added to documents such as announcements, flyers, and newsletters to make them more interesting. Styles and visual effects can be added. You will also learn how to modify WordArt.

To insert WordArt:

Insert/Text/WordArt

1. Follow the path to display the WordArt gallery; preview and select the desired option.
2. Select the text in the text box that displays and replace it with your text.
3. Size and position the WordArt as desired.

Use the tools on the Drawing Tools Format tab to format and modify WordArt. You can change the appearance of WordArt by changing the style; by using Text Fill to add color or change the color of the interior of the letters; by using Text Outline to change color, style, or weight of the lines of the exterior border of the letters; and by applying Text Effects such as Shadow, Reflection, Glow, Bevel, 3-D Rotation, or Transform to emphasize or change the shape of the text.

To apply or modify WordArt formats:

Drawing Tools Format/WordArt Styles/WordArt Styles, Text Fill, Text Outline, or Text Effects

- To change to a new WordArt style, click the WordArt Style gallery, preview, and click the desired style.
- To change Text Fill, Text Outline, or Text Effects, select the text, click the appropriate drop-list arrow, and select the desired color, line, or effect.
- To change the font size, select the text and apply the desired font size from the Font group on the Home tab.

DRILL 5 WORDART

1. Select the Fill – Olive Green, Accent 3, Powder Bevel WordArt style; select the text if necessary; key **Bon Voyage!**

2. Position at Top Center with Square Text Wrapping. Select the text and increase the font size to 72 points.

3. Change the WordArt style to Fill – Olive Green, Accent 3, Outline – Text 2. Click the Text Effects drop-list arrow; select Transform; then click Double Wave 2 to apply it.

4. Proofread and check; click Next to continue. (*83-drill5*)

CREATE A DROP CAP

A drop cap is a large capital letter at the beginning of a text block that is used to draw the reader's attention. The dropped cap usually extends from the top of the paragraph down two or three succeeding lines of the paragraph. The text of the paragraph can wrap around the dropped cap or extend to the right of it.

To create a dropped cap:

Insert/Text/Drop Cap

1. Click in the paragraph that you want to begin with a dropped cap.
2. Click Drop Cap and select Dropped or In margin.

Lesson 75 | Report with Citations and Bibliography

New Commands   • Insert citations   • Generate bibliography   • Edit citations

New Commands

75b

KEYBOARDING PRO DELUXE 2

*References/Word 2010
Commands/Lesson 75*

CITATIONS

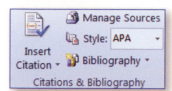

The Citation feature allows the user to key in a dialog box the various pieces of information needed for a citation. The software uses this data to enter the internal citation automatically in the report and then create the reference page or bibliography at the end of the report. In the previous lessons in this book, you have learned to key internal citations and to key the reference page at the end of the report. You will be amazed in this lesson as you simply enter the data and the software does the rest. **Caution:** Always proofread carefully that all style rules have been applied according to your specific requirements.

Simple requirements of the user:

1. Choose the manuscript style from a list of ten styles, including APA, Chicago, MLA, and Turabian.

2. For each citation in the document, select the type of source from a list of 16 choices in addition to miscellaneous, e.g., book, journal article.

   Note: When the citation is entered, it becomes a part of the user's master list of sources and can easily be selected for any future document the user creates.

3. Generate the reference page or bibliography at the end of the report.

Bibliography

Kwon, C. (2011, May). *What Should I Weigh?* Retrieved from Medical Notes: www.doctorsandnurseshi-energy.com/whatshouldiweigh.html

Livingston, S. (2011). A Study of Diseases Related to Diet. *Medical Journal, 47*(2), 51-69.

Sanchez, R. (2011, May 2011). Did You Get Your Water Today? *Nutrition Journal,* 58-60.

Wright, D. (2011, November 4). Nurse Practitioner. (D. Young, Interviewer)

APA Style

Works Cited

Kwon, Chien. "What Should I Weigh?" May 2011. <u>Medical Notes.</u> 23 July 2011 <www.doctorsandnurseshi-energy.com/whatshouldiweight.html>.

Sanchez, Rosa. "Did You Get Your Water Today?" <u>Nutrition Journal</u> (2011): 58-60.

Wright, Dona. <u>Nurse Practitioner</u> Dean Young. 4 November 2011.

MLA Style

DRILL 3 — PICTURES

Insert/Illustrations/Picture

1. Insert the three pictures *great wall*, *sandy beach*, and *fishing boats*; position each picture at the horizontal center with Square text wrapping. The second picture should be about 1" below the first picture, and the last picture will be on page 2. Size pictures 5.5" wide and compress them.

Picture Tools Format/Adjust/Corrections, Color, or Artistic Effects

2. To format the *great wall* picture, select Sharpen 50%, Brightness +20%, and Contrast +40%.

3. To format the *sandy beach* picture, select Saturation 300% in the Color Saturation category and Temperature 6500 K in the Color Tone category.

4. To format the *fishing boats* picture, select the Paint Brush artistic effect.

5. Proofread and check; click Next to continue. *(83-drill3)*

SMARTART

In this activity, you will apply skills reviewed in Lesson 57, and you will also learn how to add bullets to shapes, to promote or demote text, and to reorder the shapes.

To modify a SmartArt graphic:

SmartArt Tools Design/Create Graphic/Add Bullet; Promote or Demote; Move Up or Move Down

- To add bullets, select shape and click Add Bullet. Tap ENTER after each line to add additional bullets.
- To promote or demote text, click in a bulleted item, and then click Promote or Demote.
- To reorder shapes, click in the shape and then click Move Up or Move Down until the shape is in the desired position in the graphic.

DRILL 4 — SMARTART

1. Insert a Vertical Box List layout; add another shape at the bottom; size the layout 5" high and 6.5" wide. Click each shape and key the text shown below.

2. Add bullets to each shape and demote the text as shown. Promote *Conceptual Skills*. Reorder the shapes to move *Relevant Work Experience* to be the last shape.

3. Proofread and check; click Next to continue. *(83-drill4)*

Relevant Work Experience
- Preferred for all levels; required for higher-level positions
  - Past performance is an indicator of future performance

Technical Skills
- Required for entry-level positions
  - Content knowledge
  - Ability to do the job

Human Relations Skills
- Required for positions at all levels
  - Ability to get along with others
  - Is an effective team member
- Conceptual Skills
- Required for upward mobility
  - Ability to see the big picture
  - Know how your job fits within the company

To insert citations:

References/Citations & Bibliography

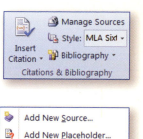

1. Switch to Print Layout view if not already in it.

2. Position the insertion point in the document where the reference is to be inserted.

3. Follow the path above. Click the down list arrow in the Style box and select the desired style, e.g., APA Fifth Edition, Chicago Fifteenth Edition, MLA Sixth Edition, etc. This example will illustrate the MLA style.

4. Click Insert Citation. From the drop list, select Add New Source. The Create Source dialog box displays.

5. Click the down arrow in the Type of Source box. Select one of the choices, e.g., book, journal article, etc. The following example illustrates the book type.

6. Key in the fields that are displayed from your type of source choice. Click OK.

7. Note the report text where the citation has been created. To edit the citation, click it and then click the down arrow.

8. Select Edit Citation from the drop-down list. The Edit Citation dialog box displays.

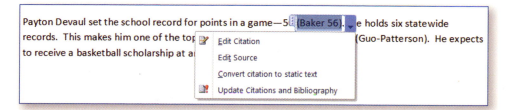

9. Make the needed corrections to the current citation, e.g., add page number where a direct quotation was lifted. Click OK.

CLIP ART

Clip art is provided with *Office* software. *Office 2010*'s clip art files include illustrations (created by hand or computer software), photographs, and audio and video clips. Clip art can be located by using keywords that describe the type of clip you are trying to find. Tools on the Picture Tools Format tab can be used to format clip art. If you do not check Include Office.com content **1**, a limited number of clips will display. If you check Include Office.com content, clips from the Microsoft online gallery will display. To locate even more clips, click Find more at Office.com **2**.

For example, a search using the keyword *temple* without checking Include Office.com content produced only the first clip shown in the illustration at the right. When Include Office.com content was selected, over a hundred clips were displayed. When Find more at Office.com was clicked and *temple* was used as the keyword to search for clips, more than a thousand clips were located. Clips found at this location can be copied and pasted in the document or can be downloaded to your computer.

Note: If you do not have Internet access, you will only complete the first two steps in the next drill and then check and close the document.

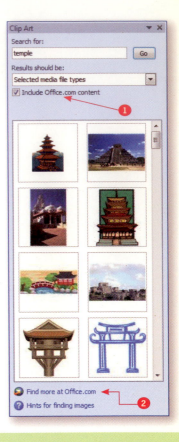

DRILL 2   CLIP ART

Insert/Illustrations/Clip Art

1. Display the Clip Art task pane and search for a clip of a temple. Do not check Include Office.com content.

2. Select the first clip that displays and insert it in the document. Apply Square text wrapping to the clip and size it 2.5" high.

3. Check Include Office.com content and search again, this time using *Beijing temple* as the keywords.

4. Select the second clip on the right side of the pane and insert it in the document below the previous clip.

5. Apply Square text wrapping to the clip and size it 2.5" high.

6. Click Find more at Office.com and search using *temple* as the keyword. Note the number of clips that were located. Select one clip and copy and paste it in the document.

7. Apply Square text wrapping to the clip and size it 2.5" high.

8. Proofread and check; click Next to continue. (*83-drill2*)

PICTURES

In this activity, you will apply skills reviewed in Lesson 57, and you will also learn how to adjust pictures by applying Corrections, Color, and Artistic Effects tools.

To adjust pictures:

Picture Tools Format/Adjust/Corrections, Color, or Artistic Effects

- Select the picture; click Corrections; then select the Soften or Sharpen picture option desired and the Brightness and Contrast option desired.

- Select the picture; click Color; then select the Color Saturation and Color Tone option desired or select Recolor to change the color of the picture.

- Select the picture; click Artistic Effects; then select the Artistic Effect desired.

To create the bibliography or reference page:
References/Citations & Bibliography/Bibliography

1. Position the insertion point below the last line of the report and insert a manual page break. Position the insert point at about 2".

2. Follow the path above to display the Built-In gallery of bibliography styles.

3. Select Bibliography (APA) or Works Cited (MLA).

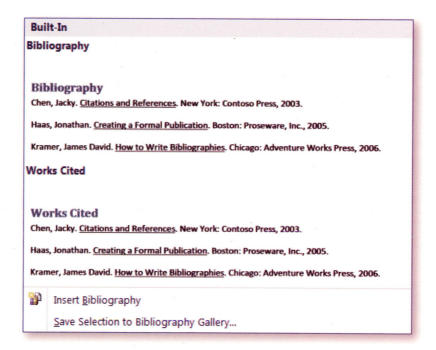

4. Select the title and apply Title style. Check that the position is at 2".

5. Verify that the list of references is formatted in the hanging indent style. **Note:** When creating a document, refer to the manuscript style manual to determine appropriate formatting for the reference list. The hanging indent command was applied automatically to the bibliography shown below.

Bibliography

Baker, M. (2011). *High School Athletic Records*. Seattle: Sports Press.

Devaul, P. (2011, January 9). (K. Dennis, Interviewer)

Guo-Patterson, L. (2011, Spring). *Top Ten High School Athletes*. Retrieved June 25, 2011, from Sports Journal: www.tsj.edu/athletes/topten.htm

KEYBOARDING PRO DELUXE 2

*References/Word 2010
Commands/Lesson 83*

DISCOVER

Insert Drawing Canvas

Insert/Illustrations/Shapes/
New Drawing Canvas

REVIEW

Rotate Tool

Drawing Tools Format/
Arrange/Rotate

If you used *Keyboarding and Word Processing Essentials, Lessons 1–55,* you will be familiar with most of the commands that are reviewed and applied in this review lesson. You will apply these commands and use additional features to enrich the graphics you prepare. The path for the commands will be provided in the drills as a quick reminder of how to create or insert and format the illustrations.

SHAPES

Add individual shapes to a document, or combine a number of shapes to create a more complex drawing. When working with a number of shapes, you can organize them using a drawing canvas. A drawing canvas is a frame inside which shapes can be drawn and formatted. The canvas can be aligned, positioned, and resized as desired. When connectors are used to connect shapes inside a drawing canvas, the connector ends snap to red connection points ➊ that appear on each side of the object. Another useful tool in working with flowcharts is the Rotate tool, which can be used to flip connectors vertically or horizontally.

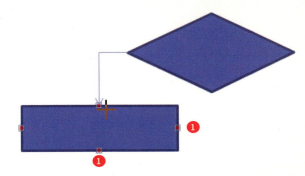

DRILL 1   SHAPES

Insert/Illustrations/Shapes

1. In a new document, insert a new drawing canvas and adjust its height to 5".

2. Create the flowchart shown at the right inside the drawing canvas using the shapes from the Flowchart category. Position shapes in the approximate vertical position shown.

3. Use the Arrow and Elbow Arrow connectors to connect shapes, and snap ends to connection points when possible.

Drawing Tools Format/Size

4. Size each shape 2.2" wide. Size the rounded rectangles and parallelogram about 0.5" high, the diamond about 1" high, and the remaining rectangles about 0.3" high.

5. Key the text shown in the shapes at the right.

6. Insert small text boxes on the left and right sides of the diamond shape indicating a decision is needed. Key **No** in the left text box and **Yes** in the right text box. Remove the borders and fill from the text boxes and position as shown.

Drawing Tools Format/Arrange/Position

7. Click the drawing canvas border to select the canvas. Position the drawing canvas in Top Center with Square Text Wrapping.

8. Proofread and check; click Next to continue. (*83-drill1*)

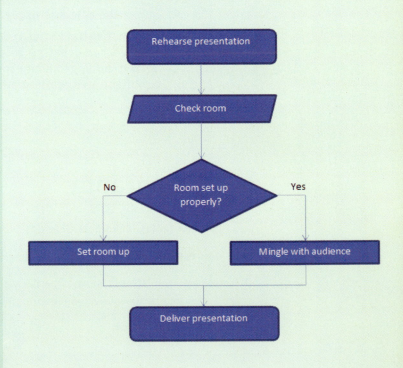

1. Key the paragraph shown below. Insert the MLA citations as indicated in the paragraph. The data for the three citations are shown in the three Create Source dialog boxes below.

2. Edit the Baker citation to add page 56 as the page where this reference appeared. Note the citation in the report displays as (Baker 56).

3. Position the insertion point below the paragraph and generate the bibliography page. Remember to choose Works Cited since the manuscript style is MLA.

4. Position title at 2". Select the title *Works Cited* and apply Title style.

5. Select the list of references and format as a hanging indent.

6. Proofread and check; click Next to continue. (*75-drill1*)

Payton Devaul set the school record for points in a game—50 (Citation 1). He holds six statewide records. This makes him one of the top ten athletes in the school's history (Citation 2). He expects to receive a basketball scholarship at an outstanding university (Citation 3).

Citation 1: Book

Citation 2: Document from Website

Citation 3: Interview

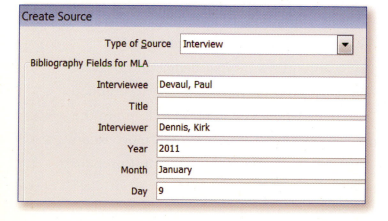

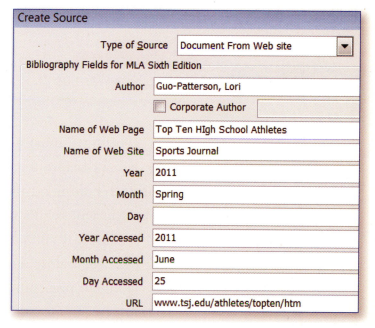

Documents with Graphics

LEARNING OUTCOMES

- Review, create, and format graphics.
- Enhance documents with graphics.
- Create advanced documents with columns and graphics.
- Build keyboarding skills.

Lesson 83 | Graphics Review

Review Commands

- Shapes
- Clip Art
- Pictures
- SmartArt
- WordArt
- Drop Cap

KEYBOARDING PRO DELUXE 2

WARMUP

Lessons/83a Warmup

A   ALL LETTERS

Skill Building

83b   Timed Writing

1. Key a 1' timing on each paragraph; work to increase speed. Use wordwrap.
2. Key a 3' timing on both paragraphs.

	gwam	1'	3'
You have most likely heard it said that people would rather die	14	5	58
than speak before a group. To assist in overcoming this fear, many	27	9	62
experts recommend preparation. Spending a large amount of time	40	13	66
preparing will result in big dividends. Select a topic that you like	54	18	71
and research it completely, know your purpose and your audience,	67	22	75
and practice before a mirror and in front of a group of friends.	80	27	79
Finally, presenting with ease requires an excellent knowledge of	14	31	84
technology. Come to the room early to open the show and to practice	28	36	89
in the presentation room. Determine which key to press to jump to the	42	40	93
next slide or to move to a previous position. Know how to move to an	55	45	98
exact position in the show. Practice these success skills and prepare	69	50	103
your next presentation with zeal and confidence.	79	53	106

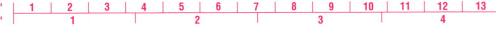

1' | 1 | 2 | 3 | 4 | 5 | 6 | 7 | 8 | 9 | 10 | 11 | 12 | 13 |
3' | 1 | 2 | 3 | 4 |

1. Open *75-drill 1*.

2. Change the manuscript style to APA Fifth Edition. Note the change in the internal citations.

3. On the last page, change the title to Bibliography. Check for any changes in the bibliography.

4. Proofread and check; click Next to continue. (*75-drill2*)

DELETE A CITATION FROM THE DOCUMENT

Writers sometimes find it necessary to delete a citation from the report. This task involves editing the report text, the source manager that contains all the references, and finally updating the bibliography if it has already been generated.

To delete a citation:

<mark>References/Citations & Bibliography</mark>

1. Click the citation and then the down arrow.

2. Click Convert citation to static text. Select the unneeded text and tap the DELETE key.

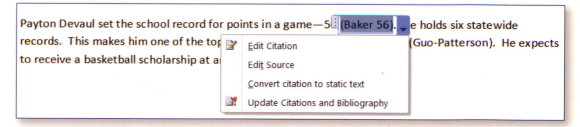

3. Click Manage Sources. The Source Manager displays.

4. In the Current List shown at the right in the Source Manager, click the citation to be deleted. Click Delete. Click Close.

Note: If you wish to delete from the Master List, click the citation in the Master List on the left side of the dialog box, and click Delete.

5. In the document bibliography, click Update Citations & Bibliography. Check that the citation does not appear in the updated bibliography.

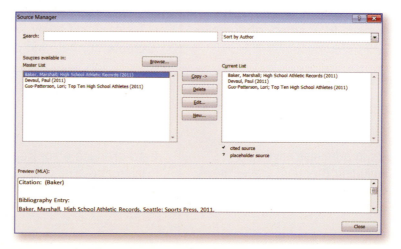

ADVANCED DOCUMENT PROCESSING

Level 4

Learning Outcomes

Document Design Skills

+ To apply effective designs to a variety of complex documents.

+ To organize content effectively with graphics.

+ To improve document quality using review and collaboration tools.

+ To design documents in administrative and specialized areas, including meeting, travel, news, employment, legal, and medical documents.

Word Processing Skills

+ To learn and apply *Word 2010* commands to create, format, and customize complex documents.

Communication Skills

+ To review and improve basic communication skills.

+ To produce error-free documents and apply language arts skills.

Keyboarding

+ To improve keyboarding speed and accuracy.

1. Open *75-drill1*. Delete the second citation. Update the reference page.

2. Click Manage Sources and delete from the Current List.

3. In the bibliography of the document, click Update Citations & Bibliography.

4. Proofread and check; click Next to continue. (*75-drill3*)

Applications

75-d1

Leftbound Report

1. Key the leftbound report below.

2. Insert the citations in the APA manuscript style as directed in the text below. The citations are shown at the end of the text. Review the citation to determine which data to enter in each Create Source entry box. Click Show All Bibliographic Fields if additional data fields are needed.

3. Position the title at approximately 2" and apply Title style. Format the side headings as Heading 1 style and paragraph headings as Heading 2 style.

4. Number the pages at the top right using the Plain Number 3 page style; suppress the page number on the first page.

5. Edit the Sanchez citation in the report by suppressing the author's name and title and adding page 59.

6. Generate the bibliography page as the last page of the report. Position the title at approximately 2"; apply Title style. The reference list should be formatted in the hanging indent format.

7. Proofread and check; click Next to continue. (*75-d1*)

Nutrition Guides for Good Health

Good health is a high priority for most people. Yet many individuals know relatively little about nutrition and make dietary choices that are detrimental to their health. Studies show that at least one-third of all cancer and heart attack deaths are directly related to diet (Citation 1). This report presents valuable guides to eating and drinking as well as weight guides.

Guides for Eating and Drinking

Diet consists of both the foods and beverages consumed daily. The foods and beverages consumed should be selected carefully to ensure good nutrition as well as healthy guides for preparing and making wise food choices.

Food. A wide variety of foods should be eaten each day since no one food contains all of the nutrients needed. Foods that are rich in vitamins and high in dietary fiber should be eaten daily. Fruits, vegetables, and whole-grain breads are particularly good sources of vitamins and fiber.

A good diet also avoids harmful foods. Sodium, saturated fat, high-fat dairy products, salt, and sugar should be eaten in moderation.

Selecting the proper food and beverages is only one part of a healthy diet. The quantity consumed and the manner in which foods are prepared are equally important. A person's diet should be planned carefully to maintain a desirable

Writing 53

We are living in a wonderful period of history. This is a   12
time when historians are recording many exciting changes in our   25
world. The past two decades have shown that all inhabitants of   37
this planet must learn to exist together. We no longer are able   50
to isolate ourselves from other countries. The action of one   63
nation has a direct effect on nearly every other nation in the   75
world. We must quickly recognize and adjust to peaceful solutions.   89

| 1 | 2 | 3 | 4 | 5 | 6 | 7 | 8 | 9 | 10 | 11 | 12 | 13 |

Writing 54

gwam 3' | 5'

Traffic jams, deadlines, problems at work, and squabbles at   4 | 2 | 52
home are some ways in which tension is created. When our tension   8 | 5 | 54
is about to reach the boiling point, what do people usually tell   13 | 8 | 57
us? In most cases, they urge us to relax. But relaxing is not   17 | 10 | 60
always easy to accomplish. We frequently think we cannot find the   21 | 13 | 62
time for this important part of our daily activity.   25 | 15 | 64

To understand how relaxation works for us, we must realize how   29 | 17 | 67
the stress of contemporary existence works against us. Developed   33 | 20 | 69
for survival in a challenging world, the human body reacts to a   38 | 23 | 72
crisis by getting ready for action. Whether we are preparing for a   42 | 25 | 75
timed writing or for an encounter in a dark street, our muscles   47 | 28 | 77
tighten and our blood pressure goes up. After years of this type   51 | 31 | 80
of response, we often find it difficult to relax when we want to.   55 | 33 | 83

Now think about the feeling which is the opposite of this tur-   59 | 36 | 85
moil. The pulse slows down, the breath comes slowly and calmly,   64 | 38 | 88
and the tension leaves the body. This is total relaxation. And if   68 | 41 | 90
it sounds good, consider how good it must actually feel. Our bod-   72 | 43 | 93
ies are already prepared to relax; it is an ability all indivi-   77 | 46 | 95
duals have within themselves. What we have to practice is how to   81 | 49 | 98
use this response.   82 | 49 | 99

```
3' |   1   |   2   |   3   |   4   |
5' |     1     |     2     |     3     |
```

weight for the body size. Obesity increases the risk of many diseases. Being underweight can also create problems.

Foods should also be prepared in a manner that does not add fat to the food. Baking, steaming, poaching, roasting, and cooking in a microwave are the best ways to prepare foods.

Wise food choices are important for a healthy diet. Many health-conscious individuals have learned to make the following substitutions for foods that are high in fat and calories (Citation 2).

- Diet soda for regular soda
- Skim, 1%, or 2% milk for whole milk (begin with 2% and work down to skim milk)
- Egg whites for whole egg
- Low-fat cheese for full-fat cheese

Drinks. The body needs a significant amount of fluids. The daily minimum of water is eight glasses per day. Rosa Sanchez (Citation 3), a well-known nutritionist, states, "Increase the minimum requirement of water when exercising briskly, when weather temperatures are hot, and when dieting to burn fat." Consider creative ways to consume the daily requirement of water, such as drinking water at all meals, keeping a measured container of water in your work area, and substituting water for a snack.

If alcoholic beverages are consumed, they should be consumed in moderation. Alcoholic beverages are high in calories and low in food value. In addition, excessive drinking can lead to major health problems.

Weight Guides

A person's body frame helps to determine the desirable weight for that person. Desirable weight for a person with a small frame is less than for a person with an average or large frame. For example, the desirable weight for a 6'0" male with a large frame is 195-205 pounds, while weight for a 6'0" male with a medium frame is 180-190. On the other hand, the desirable weight for a 5'4" female with a medium frame is 118-130 and a female with a small frame is 110-120 (Citation 4). Desirable weights based on body frame size are helpful to guide individuals in healthy body weight.

Summary

Health-conscious individuals make wise choices daily related to foods and drinks realizing that health issues can become problematic. Maintaining the desirable weight level for the size frame is equally important.

Writing 51

gwam 1'

　　Educated people have learned that they can find important 12
details just through the simple act of listening. The secret, 24
however, as is well known, is to listen with discretion. Our 37
usual ability to hear forces us to hear many thousands of noises, 50
while our amazing listening ability lets us select only what we 63
think is important from what is minutiae. Often our only contri- 75
bution is a question; and if our listening area is an exciting 88
television show, we are not required to reply. 98

| 1 | 2 | 3 | 4 | 5 | 6 | 7 | 8 | 9 | 10 | 11 | 12 | 13 |

Writing 52

gwam 1' | 3' | 5'

　　People spend far more time listening than they spend communi- 12 | 4 | 2
cating in any other way, but only a very few people have developed 26 | 9 | 5
good listening skills. There is a big difference between hearing 39 | 13 | 8
and listening. Hearing does not require major effort, but listen- 52 | 17 | 10
ing is hard work. One of the problems with listening is that we 65 | 22 | 13
can listen about three times faster than most people speak. We 78 | 26 | 16
are able to hear what the speaker is saying and still have extra 91 | 30 | 18
time for our minds to wander to other things. 100 | 33 | 20

　　An active listener utilizes the difference between the 11 | 37 | 22
listening and the speaking rates to make mental summaries of the 24 | 41 | 25
conversation. One way to listen actively is to try to anticipate 37 | 46 | 27
the next point that the individual will make. It is also impor- 50 | 50 | 30
tant to clarify in your own mind what is being said. Generally, 63 | 54 | 32
people try to assume too much. A good listener will let the per- 76 | 58 | 35
son explain in her or his words exactly what he or she would like 89 | 63 | 38
to say. Paraphrasing is a good way to confirm that the message is 102 | 67 | 40
understood. 104 | 68 | 41

　　A person who has developed good listening skills will not 12 | 72 | 43
interrupt the person who is speaking. The problem is that more 24 | 76 | 46
people prefer to speak than to listen. Sometimes it takes a con- 37 | 80 | 48
siderable amount of effort to give the person an opportunity to 50 | 85 | 51
get the message across. Showing that you are interested in what 63 | 89 | 53
is being said helps to put the speaker at ease. It is not enough 76 | 93 | 56
just to listen; you also have to look like you are listening. The 90 | 98 | 59
effective use of body language enhances listening. 100 | 101 | 61

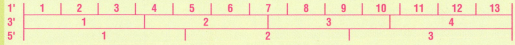

1'	1	2	3	4	5	6	7	8	9	10	11	12	13
3'		1			2			3			4	
5'		1			2			3		

Data for APA Citations:

1 Journal Article

Livingston, Steven
A Study of Diseases Related to Diet
Medical Journal
2011
Volume 47, Issue 2
pp. 51 – 69.

2 Interview

Wright, Dona (Interviewee)
Nurse Practitioner (Title)
Young, Dean (Interviewer)
November 4, 2011.

3 Journal Article

Sanchez, Rosa
Did You Get Your Water Today? (Title)
Nutrition Journal (Journal Name)
May 2011
pp. 58 – 60

4 Document from Web site

Kwon, Chien.
What Should I Weigh? (Name of Web Page)
Medical Notes (Name of Web Site)
2011 (Year)
May (Month)
www.doctorsandnurseshi-energy.com/whatshouldiweigh.html
2011 (Year Accessed)
July (Month Accessed)
23 (Day Accessed)

75-d2

Edit report

1. Open *75-d1*.
2. Change the manuscript to MLA.
3. Delete the Livingston citation from the report by converting to static text and deleting. Click Manage Sources and delete the source from the current list.
4. Update the bibliography. Change the title to **Works Cited**.
5. Check and close. (*75-d2*)

DRILL 27

Number Review

Key each line once at a comfortable rate; practice difficult lines.

1 On June 11 and July 11, 11 men and 11 women worked 11 hours each.
2 Al received Invoice 22RC22 on May 22 and paid $225.22 on June 22.
3 The 33 boys visited 3 girls at 3:30 p.m. on May 3 at 33 Oak Road.
4 The 44 men found 44 sections of 4' pipe required before 4:44 p.m.
5 On June 15, 55 women ran over 25 miles in 2 hours and 55 minutes.
6 The 66 players shot 6,666 free throws in 66 minutes and made 666.
7 The 7 rooms were 17' 7" wide and 7' 7" long with 17' 7" ceilings.
8 Those 8 coaches made 88 trips averaging 88 miles each in 88 days.
9 The 9 boys packed 9 boxes weighing 99 pounds in 9 hours on May 9.
10 Was the value listed at $10,000,000 or $20,000,000 on October 20?

| 1 | 2 | 3 | 4 | 5 | 6 | 7 | 8 | 9 | 10 | 11 | 12 | 13 |

A   ALL LETTERS

Writing 50

	gwam	3'	5'

The kinds of leisure activities you choose constitute   4 | 2 | 62
your life style and, to a great extent, reflect your personality.   8 | 5 | 65
For example, if your daily activities are people oriented, you   12 | 7 | 67
may balance this by spending your free time alone. On the other   17 | 10 | 70
hand, if you would rather be with people most of the time, your   21 | 13 | 72
socialization needs may be very high. At the other end of the   25 | 15 | 75
scale are people who are engaged in machine-oriented work and   29 | 18 | 77
also enjoy spending leisure time alone. These people tend to be   33 | 20 | 80
rather quiet and reserved.   35 | 21 | 81

Every individual needs a certain amount of relaxation to   39 | 23 | 83
remain physically and mentally alert. However, what one person   43 | 26 | 86
finds relaxing may be just the opposite for another person. For   48 | 29 | 89
example, one person may like to read a good book; another may   52 | 31 | 91
find that reading causes nervousness and fatigue. The same holds   56 | 34 | 94
true for the person who enjoys sports. Studies have shown that   61 | 36 | 96
jogging may be quite good for a person who enjoys it but may be   65 | 39 | 99
detrimental to another person who does not enjoy it.   69 | 41 | 101

Experts have noted that the proper balance of leisure,   72 | 43 | 103
relaxation, and recreation is almost essential for individuals   76 | 46 | 106
who live and work in a highly automated world. This balance is   81 | 48 | 108
necessary if each person is to be productive in handling the   85 | 51 | 111
everyday pressure and stress of life. Because every person has   89 | 53 | 113
unique needs that are met in a variety of ways, one must properly   93 | 56 | 116
assess all of the day's activities if the maximum benefit is to   98 | 59 | 118
be gained from each day of life.   100 | 60 | 120

3' | 1 | 2 | 3 | 4 |
5' | 1 | 2 | 3 |

Lesson 76 | Edit Citations and Manage Sources

New Commands

- Edit citation source
- Document properties

WARMUP

Lessons/76a Warmup

Communication

76b

1. Complete the Other Internal Punctuation pretest, rules, and posttest in *Keyboarding Pro DELUXE 2.*
2. Key the sentences, correcting punctuation errors related to the apostrophe, colon, parenthesis, hyphen, and dash. Use the Numbering command to number the sentences.
3. Proofread and check; click Next to continue. (76c)

KEYBOARDING PRO DELUXE 2

*References/Communication Skills/
Other Internal Punctuation*

1. Youre to pick up Dr. Thames gift at the registration table.

2. The three speakers credentials are included in the head coordinators information packet.

3. Concurrent sessions are scheduled for 50 while computer sessions are scheduled for 90. (Denote time in minutes.)

4. Exhibit booths measuring 10 x 20. (Denote measurements in feet.)

5. The resort amenities illustrated on the website are: two golf courses, three pools, exercise room, and activity room.

6. The layout of the condominium shows the following rooms master bedroom with bath, guest bedroom with bath, kitchen, dining room, and laundry room.

7. Registration opened at 7 30 a.m. and closed at 4 30 p.m.

8. Exhibit space includes space rental, standard pipe and drape, two chairs, wastebasket, and general security. (Denote items with parentheses.)

9. Thirty five volunteers staffed the busy convention registration area during the three day conference.

10. The officers not the committee chairs are seated at the head table.

DRILL 26

Response Pattern

Key each line once;
DS between groups.

★ **TIP**

Use top speed for easy words and phrases and lower speed for words that are more difficult to key. Key phrases marked with a line as a unit.

1 it to the us me you so go now we my he two in can her by of do no
2 it is | it is the | is it | is it you | he can | can he | he can go | can he go
3 who is | who is it | is it you | you can go | can you go | you can go to it

4 car mail two you may just can lake ask sail sign his form her who
5 who can sail | you can sail | you may sign | can you sign | sign his form
6 sign the form | mail the form | sign and mail | sign and mail that form

7 it was | was it so | if she can go to | can he go to the | can she go to the
8 she can | she may not | she may not go | can you go to the | so we may go
9 sign the | sign the form | they may sign that | they may sign that form

---

KEYBOARDING PRO DELUXE 2 | **Timed Writings**

A ALL LETTERS

Writing 49

| | gwam | 3' | 5' |

An essential part of analyzing a career option is to de- 4 | 2 | 65
termine the type and extent of education that are required for a 8 | 5 | 67
selected career. A main factor to consider about an education is 12 | 7 | 70
how long it will take to get the skills that are needed to com- 17 | 10 | 73
pete successfully for a job. This factor includes any other 21 | 12 | 75
training that may be essential at the outset of employment. Be- 25 | 15 | 78
cause jobs change, also assess how an educational program is 29 | 17 | 80
structured to meet work changes. 31 | 19 | 81

Many people choose a career without considering how well 35 | 21 | 84
they may be suited for it. For example, a person who is outgoing 39 | 24 | 86
and enjoys being around people probably should not select a 43 | 26 | 89
career that requires spending long hours working alone. A job 48 | 29 | 91
that requires quick, forceful action to be taken probably should 52 | 31 | 94
not be pursued by a person who is shy and contemplative. Just 56 | 34 | 96
because one has an aptitude for a specific job does not mean he 60 | 36 | 99
or she will be successful in that job. Thus, be sure to weigh 65 | 39 | 101
individual personality traits before making a final career 69 | 41 | 104
choice. 69 | 42 | 104

Money and inner satisfaction are the two leading reasons 73 | 44 | 106
why most people work. For most persons, the need for money 77 | 46 | 109
translates into food, shelter, and clothing. Once the basic 81 | 49 | 111
needs of a person are met, satisfaction is the greatest motivator 85 | 51 | 114
for working. To the average person, a job is satisfying if he or 90 | 54 | 117
she enjoys the work, likes the people associated with the work, 94 | 56 | 119
and feels a sense of pride in a job well done. Because you may 98 | 59 | 122
not be the average person, analyze yourself to discover what will 103 | 62 | 124
provide job satisfaction. 104 | 63 | 125

3' | 1 | 2 | 3 | 4
5' | 1 | 2 | 3

MANAGE SOURCES

Writers working on various manuscripts find it helpful to use the Source Manager that maintains a master list of all references keyed in *Word*. Using this list, the writer may copy references from the Master List to the Current List (new document), and delete and edit sources from the Master List.

To copy a reference (or source) from the Master List:
References/Citations & Bibliography/Manage Sources

1. Follow the path above to display the Source Manager dialog box.
2. Select the reference (or source) to be copied in the Master List on the left side of the Source Manager.
3. Click Copy. Note the reference now displays in the Current List on the right side of the dialog box.
4. Click Close.
5. At the appropriate place in the document, click the Insert Citation button. At the top of the drop-down menu, choose the reference you just copied to the current document.

To delete a source from the master source:
1. From the Source Manager dialog box, select the reference to be deleted from the Master List.
2. Click Delete. The source does not display in the Master List of sources and cannot be used in later manuscripts.
3. Click Close.

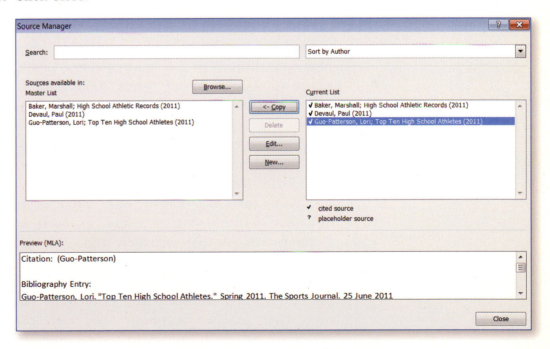

Note: If you wish the source to be deleted from the Current List, delete the citation in the document first and then delete it in the Source Manager dialog box. See page 381 for review.

DRILL 25

Opposite-Hand Combinations

Key each line once; repeat four-line groups.

★ **TIP**

Key fluently, without rushing.

br/rb	1	break barb brawn orbit brain carbon brakes barbecue brazen barber
	2	Barbara Brady brought us a new brand of barbecue to eat at break.
ce/ec	3	cease decide cent collect cell direct cedar check center peck ice
	4	Cecil recently received a check for his special barbecue recipes.
mu/um	5	mull dumb must human mud lumber mulch lump mumps slump music fume
	6	Bum Muse must have dumped too much muddy mulch on the bumpy lawn.
nu/un	7	nut sun fun nurse gun sinus number punch nuzzle pound lunch until
	8	Uncle Gunta, a nurse, was uneasy about numerous units unionizing.
gr/rg	9	grade merge grand purge great large grab organ green margins gray
	10	Margo, our great grandmother, regrets merging those large groups.
ny/yn	11	Wayne any shyness many agony balcony Jayne lynx penny larynx myna
	12	Wayne and Jayne fed many skinny myna birds on that sunny balcony.

KEYBOARDING PRO DELUXE 2 | **Timed Writings**

A **ALL LETTERS**

Writing 48

	gwam 1'	5'
The job market today is quite different than it was a few	12	2
years ago. The fast track to management no longer exists.	24	5
Entry-level managers find that it is much more difficult to	36	7
obtain a promotion to a higher-level position in management than	49	10
it was just a few years ago. People who are in the market for	61	12
new jobs find very few management positions available. In fact,	74	15
many managers at all levels have a difficult time keeping their	87	17
current management positions. Two factors seem to contribute	99	20
heavily to the problem. The first factor is the trend toward	112	22
self-managed teams. The second factor is that as companies	124	25
downsize they often remove entire layers of management or an	136	27
entire division.	140	28
Layoffs are not new; but, what is new is that layoffs are	12	30
affecting white-collar workers as well as blue-collar workers.	24	33
Coping with job loss is a new and frustrating experience for many	38	35
managers. A person who has just lost a job will have concerns	50	38
about personal security and welfare, and the concerns are com-	63	40
pounded when families are involved. The problem, however, is	75	43
more than just an economic one. Job loss often damages an in-	87	45
dividual's sense of self-worth. An individual who does not have	100	48
a good self-concept will have a very hard time selling himself	112	50
or herself to a potential employer.	120	52

```
1' |  1  |  2  |  3  |  4  |  5  |  6  |  7  |  8  |  9  |  10  |  11  |  12  |  13  |
5' |        1        |        2        |        3        |
```

1. In a new document, copy the Baker, Devaul, and Guo-Patterson sources in the Master List.

2. Rekey the paragraph in *75-drill1* on page 380 in APA style. Insert the three citations by choosing the sources that have already been keyed.

3. Edit the Baker citation to add page 56 as the page where this reference appeared. Delete the Guo-Patterson source from the Master List only.

4. Generate the bibliography and format appropriately.

5. Proofread and check; click Next to continue. (*76-drill1*)

EDIT CITATION SOURCE

Writers often find errors in the citation source, and editing is required.

To edit a citation source:

References/Citations & Bibliography/Manage Sources

1. Follow the path above to display the Source Manager dialog box. In the sources listed in the Master List (left pane), select the source to be edited.

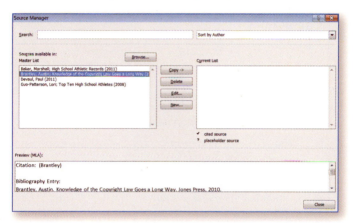

2. Click Edit to display the Edit Source dialog box. Key the edits. Click Show All Bibliography Fields if more fields are needed.

3. Click OK. Click Close. A *Microsoft Word* prompt automatically displays. Click Yes to update both the Master List and the Current List with these changes.

DRILL 24

Specific Rows

Key each line once; DS between groups.

⭐ **TIP**

Reach to the first and third rows with a minimum of hand movement; keep hands quiet; don't bounce on the keys.

Rows 3, 2, 1

1 you we quip try pot peer your wire put quit wet trip power toy to
2 salad fad glad lass lag has gall lash gas lad had shall flag half
3 comb zone exam man carve bun oxen bank came next vent zoo van cab

4 we try to; you were; put up your; put it there; you quit; wipe it
5 Gail asked Sissy; what was said; had Jake left; Dana sold a flag
6 Zam came back; can Max fix my van? a brave man, Ben came in a cab

7 Peter or I will try to wire our popular reports to Porter or you.
8 Ada Glass said she is glad she had half a kale salad with Dallas.
9 Zack drove a van to minimize expenses; Ben and Max came in a cab.

KEYBOARDING PRO DELUXE 2 | **Timed Writings**

A ALL LETTERS

Take two 3' or one 5' writing; key with fluency and control.

Writing 47

	gwam	3'	5'

Sports are very big business today; that is, those sports competitions in which men participate are very big business. What about sports for women? At the professional level, women have made real progress in golf and tennis; they, as well as their sponsors, can make big money in both of these events. The other sports for women still are not considered to be major revenue sports. The future may be much better, however, because sports for women at all levels are gaining in popularity. Programs that are designed to help young girls develop their athletic skills and interest are having an impact. The result is that girls now expect to play for organized clubs as well as in school programs just as boys do. Club sports often will lead to varsity teams.

Many people wonder how much impact the current emphasis on gender equity will have on sports at the college level. Most people agree that this new emphasis is very positive for women. Some people feel, though, that it either has had or could have a negative impact on sports for men. They believe that resources that would have been spent on sports such as football, basketball, and baseball for men are now being spent on the Olympic sports for women. Overall, most people believe that both men and women who have the ability to excel in an athletic event as well as in the classroom should have the opportunity and should be encouraged to do so. Success for both women and men is better than success for either.

gwam 3'	5'
4	3	62
9	5	65
13	8	67
18	11	70
22	13	73
26	16	75
31	19	78
35	21	81
40	24	83
44	26	86
48	29	88
51	31	90
55	33	92
59	35	95
63	38	97
68	41	100
72	43	103
77	46	105
81	49	108
85	51	111
90	54	113
94	56	116
98	59	118
99	59	119

3' | 1 | 2 | 3 | 4
5' | 1 | 2 | 3

1. In the open document, edit the Brantley citation as follows:

    a. Change city to **Portland**.

    b. Change year to **2011**.

2. Click Close and then Yes to update both the Master List and the Current List.

3. Edit the Jones citation as follows:

    a. Change volume to **55** and issue to **5**.

    b. Change pages to **11–16**.

4. Close and agree to update both the Master List and the Current List.

5. Proofread and check; click Next to continue. (*76-drill2*)

Advanced Properties

Click the Properties drop-list arrow, Advanced Properties, and Summary tab. Key the information in the appropriate boxes.

DOCUMENT PROPERTIES

Details that help to identify a document are called Document Properties. Some information is entered and updated automatically while other information must be keyed by the user.

To view and modify document properties:

File/Info

1. Open the document that you wish to view and edit properties.

2. Follow the path above and the document information panel displays in the right pane. Note the properties in the far right side of the pane that displays automatically, e.g., Size, Words, Date Created, Date and Time Modified, etc.

3. Key additional information in the appropriate text boxes.

Title:	Click Add a title and key the document title.
Tags:	Click Add a tag and key one or more words that describe the document separated by a semicolon. Can be used to search for the document.
Comments:	Click Add comments and key an abstract of contents.
Author:	Click Add an author and key additional author names. Additional author

4. Click Save.

Note: Tags are very helpful when searching for related documents. In *Windows* 7, key the tag in the Search program and files box. In *Word* key the tag in Search Documents box in the Open dialog box.

1. Go to the Document Information Panel. Key the following properties:

Author:	**Student's Name**
Title:	**Styles**
Tags:	**style usage**
Comments:	**Final Draft Approved 3/21/201-**

2. Check to identify the following properties of the file you have open.

    Words:

    Size of file:

    Date and time modified:

    Date created:

3. Proofread and check; click Next to continue. (*76-drill3*)

DRILL 23

Specific Fingers

Key each line once;
DS between groups.

1st
1 fun gray vent guy hunt brunt buy brunch much gun huge humor vying
2 buy them brunch; a hunting gun; Guy hunts for fun; try it for fun

2nd
3 cite decide kick cider creed kidded keen keep kit idea ice icicle
4 keen idea; kick it back; ice breaker; decide the issue; sip cider

3rd
5 low slow lax solo wax sold swell swollen wood wool load logs doll
6 wooden dolls; wax the floor; a slow boat; saw logs; pull the wool

4th
7 quip zap Zane zip pepper pay quiz zipper quizzes pad map nap jazz
8 zip the zipper; jazz at the plaza; Zane quipped; La Paz jazz band

---

KEYBOARDING PRO DELUXE 2 **Timed Writings** **A ALL LETTERS**

1. Take three 1' writings on each paragraph.
2. Take one 5' or two 3' writings.

Option: Practice as a guided writing.

1/4'	1/2'	3/4'	gwam 1'
8	16	24	32
9	18	27	36
10	20	30	40
11	22	33	44
12	24	36	48
13	26	39	52
14	28	41	56
15	30	45	60
16	32	48	64
17	34	51	68
18	36	54	72

Writing 46

gwam 3' | 5'

How much power is adequate? Is more power always better | 4 | 2 | 50
than less power? People often raise the question in many differ- | 8 | 5 | 52
ent instances. Regardless of the situation, most people seem to | 12 | 7 | 55
seek more power. In jobs, power is often related to rank in an | 17 | 10 | 57
organization, to the number of people reporting to a person, and | 21 | 13 | 60
to the ability to spend money without having to ask someone with | 25 | 15 | 63
more power. Most experts indicate that the power a person has | 30 | 18 | 65
should closely match the responsibilities (not just duties and | 34 | 20 | 68
tasks) for which he or she can be held accountable. | 37 | 22 | 70

Questions about power are not limited to jobs and people. | 41 | 25 | 72
Many people ask the question in reference to the amount of power | 45 | 27 | 75
or speed a computer should have. Again, the response usually | 50 | 30 | 77
implies that more is better. A better approach is to analyze how | 54 | 32 | 80
the computer is to be used and then try to match power needs to | 58 | 35 | 82
the types of applications. Most people are surprised to learn | 62 | 37 | 85
that home computer buyers tend to buy more power than buyers in | 67 | 40 | 87
offices. The primary reason is that the computers are used to | 71 | 43 | 90
play games with extensive graphics, sound, and other media appli- | 75 | 45 | 93
cations. Matching the needs of the software is the key. | 79 | 47 | 95

3' | 1 | 2 | 3 | 4
5' | 1 | 2 | 3

76-d1

Edit Report

1. Open *75-d2*.
2. Edit the Kwon source. Change *Medical Notes* to **Nutrition Notes**. Click Yes to update the Master List and the Current List.
3. Edit the Sanchez source. Insert volume number **10** and issue **1**. Click Yes to update the Master List and the Current List. Update the bibliography page.
4. Double-click in the header and insert the Alphabet built-in header. Key the report document as the document title. **Note:** The header overrides the plain page number already inserted.
5. Double-click in the footer and insert the Alphabet built-in footer. At the left margin in the Text textbox, key **Revised** followed by a space. Insert the date command using the 00/00/0000 style; deselect the option to update automatically.
6. Edit the document properties as follows:

   Author: Add your instructor's name

   Tags: **nutrition; weight guides**

   Comments: Final
7. Proofread and check; click Next to continue. (*76-d1*)

76-d2

Report

DISCOVER

Move Citation

Click the move handle in the upper-left corner of citation and drag it to the new location.

1. In a new document, select APA as the manuscript style.
2. Copy the Wright citation from the Master List to the Current List.
3. Key the text below. Format the title Interview with Dona Wright appropriately.
4. Move the Wright citation to display after *Ms. Wright* at the beginning of the second sentence. Edit the citation to suppress the author's name. Suppress the title as well.
5. Search the Internet to list at least five food substitutions for high-calorie food choices. One example is given for you. Reference your sources in the body of the report.
6. Key the information from your research in the two tables shown below. Apply the Colorful List – Accent 1 table style. Adjust the column width appropriately and center the table horizontally.
7. Create a bibliography page.
8. Proofread and check; click Next to continue. (*76-d2*)

On November 4, 2011, I met with Dona Wright, nurse practitioner with the Foundation Nutrition Center in (Student's Home Town). Ms. Wright suggested beginning my weight management program by (1) reviewing my food choices and substituting high-calorie choices with low-calorie choices and (2) listing ways to increase my daily physical activity (insert Wright citation).

My goals are as follows:

Replace High-Calorie Food Choices	Substitute with Low-Calorie Choices
Regular soda	Diet soda

Increase Physical Activity
Park away from the front door of the office and shopping mall.

DRILL 20

Adjacent Keys

Key each line once; repeat entire drill. DS between groups.

Goal: To eliminate persistent errors on side-by-side keys.

as/sa
1 has sale fast salt was saw vast essay easy say past vast mast sap
2 We saw Sam; Sal was sad; Susan has a cast; as Sam said; as I said

er/re
3 were there tree deer great three other her free red here pert are
4 we were there; here we are; there were three; here are three deer

io/oi
5 point axiom prior choir lion boil toil billion soil action adjoin
6 join a choir; prior to that action; millions in a nation rejoiced

op/po
7 polo drop loop post hope pole port rope slope power top pony stop
8 rope the pony; drop the pole; power at the top; hope for the poor

rt/tr
9 trail alert train hurt tree shirt trap smart trim start tray dirt
10 trim the tree; start the train; dirt on the shirt; alert the trio

ew/we
11 few we stew were pew went dew web sew wept crew wear brew wet new
12 we were weak; few were weeping; the crew went west; we knew a few

gh/ui
13 sight quit laugh suit might ruin ghost guide ghastly guilt ghetto
14 a ghastly suit; quit laughing; recruit the ghost; might be guilty

DRILL 21

Outside Reaches

Key each line once. DS between groups.

Goal: To key with a maximum of one error per line. (Letters are often omitted in outside reaches—concentrate.)

a/p
1 tapioca actual against casual areas facial equally aware parallel
2 impower purpose people opposed compute pimple papyrus pope puppet
3 Perhaps part of the chapter page openers can appear on red paper.

s/w
4 class sash steps essential skills business discuss desks insisted
5 wow wayworn away awkward wrong awaits wildwood waterworks wayward
6 The snow white swan swayed as the waves swept the swelling shore.

z/l
7 hazard zip zero zeolite freezer zoom zealous z-axis zodiac sizing
8 likely indelibly, laurel finally leaflet regularly eloquently lily
9 A New Zealand zoologist was amazed as a zebra guzzled the zinnias.

x/?
10 fax oxford exert excite examples xylan exercise oxygen exact taxi
11 When? Where? Which? For her? How much? What color? To whom?
12 After examining the x-rays, why did Dr. Ax exempt an exploratory?

DRILL 22

Alphabetic Sentences

Key each line once with good rhythm. Keep fingers curved and upright over the keys. DS between groups.

1 Judge McQuoy will have prizes for their next big track meet.
2 Jack may provide some extra quiz problems for the new group.

3 Gary Quazet mended six copies of books and journals we have.
4 Jack quibbled with a garrulous expert on Zoave family names.

5 Jake will study sixty chapters on vitamins for the big quiz.
6 Max asked Quin to provide a jewel box for the glossy zircon.

7 This judge may quiz the Iowa clerks about extensive profits.
8 Meg Keys packed and flew to Venezia to acquire her next job.

76-d3

Challenge

1. Open *76-d1*.

2. Insert a Next page break at the beginning of page 1.

3. Click at the top of Section 1 and generate a table of contents using the Automatic Table 1 style. Format the title appropriately and position at 2".

4. Insert a cover page using the Alphabet cover page style. Key the following information:

   Title: Document title

   Subtitle: **A Daily Choice**

   Date: Current date

   Author's name: **Student's Name**

5. Position the insertion point in the header of Section 2. Deselect Different First Page if it is selected. Break the links between the headers and footers for both sections.

6. Position the insertion point in the header of Section 1. Delete the Alphabet header. Go to the footer and delete the Alphabet footer. Insert a page number at the bottom of the page using the Plain Number 2 page number style. Change page format to lowercase Roman numerals and start numbering at ii.

7. Click Next and position the insertion point in the header of Section 2. Click Different First Page to suppress the header from the first page. Format page number to begin numbering at 1.

8. Verify that both sections are numbered correctly.

9. Check and close. (*76-d3*)

Troubleshooting Tips

Were your pages numbered correctly? If not, try these suggestions.

1. Remove all page numbers in header and footer in both sections. Follow the steps exactly as shown in the application.

2. Be sure the Different First Page command is not selected when you begin numbering each section.

3. Check the Break the Link buttons in the header and footer to be sure the link is broken. Remember the Link to Previous button will display in gold until the link is successfully broken. The Same as Previous label will also display when there is a link between sections.

4. Do not forget to delete the incorrect header and footer that automatically displays in Section 1. Delete before you insert the page number at the bottom center.

5. Remember to start the page number at ii for Section 1 and start at 1 for Section 2.

Writing 43: 85 *gwam*

	gwam	1'	3'

Business letters can be defined by their goals; for example, a letter of inquiry, a reply letter, a promotion letter, a credit letter, or other specialized letter. While you learn to compose these letters, just keep each letter's individual goals always in front of you. If you fix in your mind a theme, pattern, and ideal for your writing, composing good business letters may emerge as one of the best tricks in your bag.

Competent business writers know what they want to say—and they say it with simplicity and clarity. Words are the utensils they use to convey ideas or to convince others to accomplish some action. The simple word and the short sentence usually are more effective than the big word and the involved sentence. But don't be afraid of the long or unusual word if it means exactly what you intend to say in your business letter.

Writing 44: 90 *gwam*

Although many of us are basically comfortable with sameness and appear to dislike change, we actually prize variation. We believe that we are each unique individuals, yet we know that we are really only a little different; and we struggle to find "sense of self" in how we think and act. Our cars, too, built on assembly lines are basically identical; yet when we purchase one, we choose model, color, size, and style which suits us individually.

Also many people expect to find security by buying things that are in keeping with society's "image" and "status." But what we think of as "status" always changes. The wise buyer will buy those items that give most in utility, comfort, and satisfaction. Status should just be a thing we create in ourselves, not a thing created for us. Common sense should guide us in making good decisions—and if our "status" is increased thereby, well, why not?

Writing 45: 95 *gwam*

Normally, customers do not abandon a firm because of a mistake. All firms will make mistakes at one time or another. The way a problem is resolved is far more crucial than the fact that a problem existed. More customers leave a firm and take their business to a competitor because they get upset with an employee than for any other reason. The key qualifications for a customer service employee are superb human relations skills and knowledge of the product or service.

Lesson 77 | Assessment

Skill Building

77b Timed Writing

Take two 5' timed writings.

gwam | 3' | 5'

What characterizes the life of an entrepreneur? Those who | 4 | 3
have never owned their own businesses may think owning a business | 9 | 5
means being your own boss, setting your own hours, and making a | 13 | 8
lot of money. Those who have run their own businesses are quick | 17 | 10
to report that owning a business may be exciting and challenging, | 22 | 13
but it also requires hard work, long hours, and personal sacrifice. | 26 | 16
A good idea is not the only prerequisite for a successful business. | 31 | 19
A little luck even helps. | 33 | 20

Many small businesses are operated as businesses from the | 37 | 22
initial stages. However, some small businesses that turn out to be | 41 | 25
successful are just hobbies in the early stages. The entrepreneur | 46 | 27
has a job and uses the income from it to support the hobby. When | 50 | 30
the hobby begins to require more and more time, the entrepreneur | 55 | 33
has to choose between the job and the hobby. The decision is | 59 | 35
usually based on finances. If enough money can be made from the | 63 | 38
hobby or can be obtained from another source, the hobby is turned | 67 | 40
into a business. | 68 | 41

3' | 1 | 2 | 3 | 4
5' | 1 | 2 | 3

Applications

77c

Assessment

 Continue

 Check

When you complete a document, proofread it, check the spelling, and preview for placement. When you are completely satisfied, click the Continue button to move to the next document. Click the Check button when you are ready to error-check the test. Review and/or print the document analysis results.

Writing 40: 70 *gwam*

gwam 1' 3'

    Foreign study and travel take extra time and effort, but 11 | 4 | 50
these two activities quickly help us to understand people. Much 24 | 8 | 55
can be learned from other cultures. Today, business must think 37 | 12 | 59
globally. Learning about the culture of others is not a luxury. 50 | 17 | 63
Even the owner of a small business realizes that he or she cannot 64 | 21 | 68
just focus on the domestic scene. 70 | 23 | 70

    Many examples can be used to show how a local business may 11 | 27 | 74
be influenced by global competition. A hair stylist may be re- 24 | 31 | 78
quired to learn European styles because customers may want to try 38 | 36 | 83
a style just like they saw on their travels. Or salons may want 51 | 40 | 87
to offer other services such as facials that people have tried 63 | 44 | 91
while they were traveling abroad. 70 | 47 | 93

Writing 41: 75 *gwam*

gwam 1' 3'

    Getting a job interview is certainly a triumph for the job 12 | 4 | 54
seeker. Yet anxiety quickly sets in as the applicant becomes 24 | 8 | 58
aware of the competition. The same attention to details that was 37 | 12 | 62
used in writing the successful resume will also be needed for the 51 | 17 | 67
interview. Experts often say that the first four minutes are the 64 | 21 | 71
most crucial in making a strong impact on the interviewer. 75 | 25 | 75

    First, people focus on what they see. Posture, eye contact, 12 | 29 | 79
facial expression, and gestures make up over half of the message. 26 | 33 | 84
Next, people focus on what they hear; enthusiasm, delivery, pace, 39 | 38 | 88
volume, and clarity are as vital as what is said. Finally, 51 | 42 | 92
people get to the actual words that are said. You can make a 63 | 49 | 96
good impression. But, realize, you have just four minutes. 75 | 50 | 100

Writing 42: 80 *gwam*

gwam 1' 3'

    Would a pitcher go to the mound without warming up? Would 12 | 4 | 57
a speaker go to the podium without practice? Of course not! These 25 | 8 | 62
experts have spent many long hours striving to do their best. 38 | 13 | 66
Similarly, the performance of business employees is rated. The 51 | 17 | 70
manager's evaluation will include a record of actual performance 64 | 21 | 75
and a list of new goals. A good mark in these areas will demand 77 | 26 | 79
much hard work. 80 | 27 | 80

    Many work factors can be practiced to help one succeed on 12 | 30 | 84
the job. Class attendance and punctuality can be perfected by 24 | 35 | 88
students. Because work is expected to be correct, managers do 37 | 39 | 92
not assign zeros. Thus, students must learn to proofread their 49 | 43 | 96
work. A project must also be completed quickly. Students can 62 | 47 | 101
learn to organize work and time well and to find ways to do their 75 | 52 | 105
work smarter and faster. 80 | 53 | 107

1'	1	2	3	4	5	6	7	8	9	10	11	12	13
3'		1			2			3			4		

77-d1

Cover Page

1. Create a cover page using the Cubicles style. Key the following information:
   a. Company: **Marcus Employment Services**
   b. Document Title: **Regional Employment Analysis**. Shrink the font to fit on one line.
   c. Subtitle: **Three Market Regions**
   d. Author: **Student's Name**
   e. Year: Current

2. Continue to the next document. (77-*d1*)

77-d2

Leftbound Report

TIP

Remember to proofread and preview each document for placement before you move to the next one.

1. Open 77-*d1*.

2. Key the leftbound report on pages 393 and 394. Apply appropriate styles to the title and headings.

3. Key the two tables using the Medium List 2 – Accent 1 table style. Center the tables horizontally. Add the captions shown above each table and center. Adjust the space appropriately after the tables.

4. Choose the APA manuscript style. Insert the two citations where shown in the report. Use the citation shown below to create each source.

5. Edit the second citation (Falgoust) to suppress the author's name and publication title. Add page 339.

6. Generate the bibliography as the last page of the report. Format the title appropriately.

7. Insert a blank page after the cover page for the table of contents you will generate in step 13.

8. Position the insertion point at the top of the first page of the report and insert a Continuous section break.

9. Position the insertion point in the header of page 2 of Section 1. Deselect Different First Page if it is selected. Click Go to Footer and insert a page number at the bottom of the page using the Plain Number 2 page number style. Change the page number format to lowercase Roman numerals. Start number at ii. Suppress the page number on the cover page.

10. Position the insertion point in the header of Section 2. Deselect Different First Page if it is selected. Break the links between the headers for both sections. Go to the footer of Section 2. Break the link between the footers for both sections. Delete the page number in the Section 2 footer.

11. Go to header of Section 2 and number the pages of the report at the top right using the Puzzle (Odd Page) header style. Change the page number format to begin with page 1.

12. Go to footer of Section 2 and insert the Puzzle (Odd Page) footer style. Click Different First Page to suppress the header and footer on the first page of the report.

13. Position the insertion point on the blank page left for the table of contents (not in the header section). Generate the table of contents using the Automatic Table 2 style. Position the heading at approximately 2" and apply Title style.

14. Continue to the next document. (77-*d2*)

Writing 37: 55 *gwam*

		gwam	1'	3'

A crucial life skill is the ability to put things in proper   12 | 4 | 41
perspective.   Individuals often fail to realize that many things   25 | 8 | 45
are just not worth fighting about. A quick way to know whether   38 | 13 | 50
an issue is worth fighting for is to look at the situation from a   51 | 17 | 54
long-term perspective.   55 | 18 | 55

If you will care five or six years from now that you de-   11 | 22 | 59
fended an issue, it is a principle worth defending.   If you will   24 | 26 | 63
not even remember, the situation does not justify the effort   36 | 31 | 67
required for defending it.   The odds of winning are also impor-   49 | 35 | 72
tant. Why fight a losing battle?   55 | 37 | 74

Writing 38: 60 *gwam*

		gwam	1'	3'

Why do we remember some things and forget others? Often,   12 | 4 | 44
we associate loss of memory with aging or an illness such as   24 | 8 | 48
Alzheimer's disease.   However, the crux of the matter is that we   37 | 12 | 52
all forget various things that we prefer to remember. We tend to   50 | 17 | 57
remember things that mean something special to us.   60 | 20 | 60

For many people, recalling dates is a difficult task; yet   12 | 24 | 64
they manage to remember dates of special occasions, such as anni-   25 | 28 | 68
versaries.   Processing requires one not only to hear but to   36 | 33 | 72
ponder and to understand what has just been said. We recall   49 | 37 | 77
things that we say and do longer than things we hear and see.   60 | 40 | 80

Writing 39: 65 *gwam*

		gwam	1'	3'

Humor is very important in our professional and our personal   12 | 4 | 47
lives. Fortunately, we realize that many things can and do go   25 | 8 | 52
wrong.   If we can learn to laugh at ourselves and with other   37 | 12 | 56
people, we will get through the terrible times. Adding a little   50 | 17 | 60
extra laughter can help put the situation in proper perspective   63 | 21 | 64
much quicker.   65 | 22 | 65

Maintaining our sense of humor lets us enjoy our positions   12 | 26 | 69
to a greater degree. No one is perfect, and we cannot expect   24 | 30 | 73
perfection from ourselves. However, the quality of our perfor-   37 | 34 | 77
mance is greater when we do the things we like. We realize our   50 | 38 | 82
prime time is devoted to work.   Thus, it is important that we   62 | 42 | 86
enjoy this time.   65 | 43 | 87

1'	1	2	3	4	5	6	7	8	9	10	11	12	13
3'		1			2			3			4		

Citation data:

1 Journal Article—Michael W. Cummings, "Predictions for Unemployment Remain Stable," Employment Outlook Journal, Volume 45, Issue 1, 2011, p. 105. *Hint:* Do not key the quotation marks in the article title.

2 Book—Brandon Falgoust, *The Economic Outlook and Job Expertise.* Philadelphia: Farrell, Inc., 2011, p. 339.

Regional Employment Analysis

The Executive Committee of Marcus Employment Services requested an analysis of the labor market in three service regions. Previous studies show that these three regions are representative of the total market Marcus serves.

Economic Conditions

Similar economic conditions exist in the three market regions. Leading economic indicators in all three regions support the conclusion that the economy is growing slowly and at a sustainable rate. The unemployment rate in the three areas ranges from 4.1% to 4.4% explaining the gradual increase in wages in all three areas. Demand for temporary services remains strong. Demand may even increase as employers hesitate to fill permanent positions until the economy improves significantly. Unemployment is predicted to remain under 5% for the next six to twelve months (Citation 1).

Wage Survey

The wage survey focused on the three broad categories of jobs that Marcus specializes in providing temporary workers—computer specialists, office assistants, and healthcare services. Table 1 shows median weekly wages for the two positions of greatest demand for Marcus employees in each category.

Table 1 Median Weekly Wages ← Caption

Positions	Region 1	Region 2	Region 3
Computer scientists	960	1,025	997
Computer programmers	923	975	951
Office assistants	525	618	573
Legal assistants	605	679	655
Health technicians	575	648	612
Healthcare assistants	495	550	535

Approximately fifty separate job titles were analyzed as part of this study. Complete data for all of the specific jobs that were analyzed can be accessed from the detailed report that is available on the human resources website. The standard access restrictions apply to these data.

JAMIE GRILL/TETRA IMAGES/
JUPITER IMAGES

KEYBOARDING PRO DELUXE 2 | **Timed Writings**

A **ALL LETTERS**

1. Key a 1' writing on each paragraph.
2. Practice each ¶ in a set until you can complete it in 1' with no more than one error.
3. Take a 3' writing; strive to maintain your 1' rate.
4. Move onto the next set. Notice that each set progresses by 5 words.

Writing 34: 40 *gwam*

	gwam	1'	3'

"An ounce of prevention is worth a pound of cure" is really `12 | 4 | 31` based on fact; still, many people comprehend this statement more `25 | 8 | 35` for its quality as literature than on a practical, common-sense `38 | 12 | 39` philosophy. `40 | 13 | 40`

Just take health, for example. We agonize over stiff costs `12 | 17 | 44` we pay to recover from illnesses; but, on the other hand, we give `25 | 22 | 48` little or no attention to health requirements for diet, exercise, `38 | 26 | 53` and sleep. `40 | 27 | 53`

Writing 35: 45 *gwam*

	gwam	1'	3'

Problems with our environment show an odd lack of foresight. `12 | 4 | 34` We just expect that whatever we may need to support life will be `25 | 8 | 38` available. We rarely question our comforts, even though they may `38 | 13 | 43` abuse our earth, water, and air. `45 | 15 | 45`

Optimism is an excellent virtue. It is comforting to think `12 | 19 | 49` that, eventually, anything can be fixed. So why should we worry? `25 | 23 | 53` A better idea, certainly, is to realize that we don't have to fix `38 | 28 | 58` anything we have not yet broken. `45 | 30 | 60`

Writing 36: 50 *gwam*

	gwam	1'	3'

Recently, a friend of mine grumbled about how quickly papers `12 | 4 | 37` accumulated on her desk; she never seemed able to reduce them to `25 | 8 | 42` zero. She said some law seemed to be working that expanded the `38 | 13 | 46` stack today by precisely the amount she reduced it yesterday. `50 | 17 | 50`

She should organize her papers and tend to them daily. Any `12 | 21 | 54` paper that needs a look, a decision, and speedy, final action `24 | 25 | 58` gets just that; any that needs closer attention is subject to a `37 | 29 | 62` fixed completion schedule. Self-discipline is the key to order. `50 | 33 | 67`

1'	1	2	3	4	5	6	7	8	9	10	11	12	13
3'		1		2		3			4				

Careful analysis of the data is needed to determine if the rates Marcus charges employers need to be adjusted in any of the specific job categories. Falgoust stated, "Wages for positions requiring expertise in using the entire suite of office software increased more than 10% as compared to the study Marcus conducted about eighteen months ago" (Citation 2).

Virtually all of the office assistant and legal assistant positions required knowledge of word processing, spreadsheet, presentation, database, and personal information management software. The few positions that did not list this requirement had significantly lower pay rates.

Job Growth

The predicted growth of jobs in many positions in which Marcus supplies employees is much higher than previously estimated. Table 2 shows predicted job growth for the two positions of greatest demand for Marcus employees in each category.

Table 2 Predicted Job Growth ←——— Caption

Positions	Region 1	Region 2	Region 3
Computer scientists	102%	118%	104%
Computer programmers	88%	94%	91%
Office assistants	60%	68%	61%
Legal assistants	54%	62%	56%
Health technicians	56%	58%	49%
Healthcare assistants	55%	61%	69%

The current plan for hiring workers will not meet the predicted demand in any of the three market areas. Further analysis of the data collected is warranted before making any adjustments in the hiring plan. Although the data collection design matches the design used in the previous surveys, the changing market situation may require some modification in the data collection methodology to verify these high growth rates.

Conclusions

Market conditions make it feasible to raise the hourly rates Marcus charges employers in many categories. However, it is also evident that Marcus will have to increase the wages paid to its staff of temporary workers in order to retain the quality of worker required to meet market demand.

If further analysis supports the job growth data presented, significant changes must be made in the strategic plan for all regions. The current strategic plan for Marcus is based on a much lower growth rate than this study shows.

5. Format the table as follows:

   a. Apply Medium Shading 2 – Accent 2 table style.

   b. Increase the height of row 1 to 0.3"; apply Align Center Left to column A; apply Align Center to columns B and C.

   c. Use the Formula command to sum the Total Annual Revenue. Use the whole number format, but add the $ sign.

   d. Add the following caption below the table: Figure 1 **Projected Monthly and Annual Revenue**; add space before the paragraph.

6. Format the SmartArt graphic as follows:

   a. Change the design to a Diverging Radial layout.

   b. Change the colors to Colorful – Accent Colors; then apply SmartArt style White Outline.

   c. Add the following caption to the graphic: Figure 2 **Projected Revenue Sources**

COMPLETE THE REPORT

1. Number the preliminary pages using lowercase Roman numerals centered in footer and select Different First Page.

2. Use a right-aligned header with a plain Arabic number to number the report body; use a different first page. Remember to break the link with the previous section for both the header and footer.

3. On the second preliminary page, generate the table of contents using Automatic Table 2. Apply Title style to the title. Position the title at 2".

4. On the third preliminary page, key the title **Table of Figures** at 2" and apply Title style. Generate the table of figures.

5. Preview the document; check to ensure that pages are formatted and numbered correctly.

6. Check and close. (*proj2-d10*)

 # WORKPLACE SUCCESS

Click Fraud

Buyer or user beware is an appropriate term to remember anytime you use the Internet. Many companies advertise on the Internet and agree to pay the host an advertising fee based on the number of clicks or hits on their ad. To increase advertising fees and to make buyers believe the advertising is being viewed by numerous visitors, many unscrupulous hosts pay individuals to do nothing but click on the ad as quickly as they can. Some individuals are in foreign countries and some sites even have robots to click on the ads. The scam could have a very serious effect on the future of advertising on the Internet. Most buyers are willing to pay for legitimate prospects to view their ad, but not for scams.

© MIKKEL WILLIAM NIELSEN / iSTOCKPHOTO

77–d3

Edit Report

1. Open *77-d2*.
2. Apply the Apex document theme.
3. Add **Prediction** to the Job Growth heading. Use the Add Text feature to add Bibliography to the table of contents.
4. Insert a blank page after the table of contents. Create a table of figures and format using the Formal 1 style with dot tab leaders. Add the table of figures to the table of contents.
5. Insert a blank page at the end of the report for the index. Mark the following words: unemployment rate, temporary services, and market conditions. Create the index using the Formal style. Format and position the title appropriately. Add the index to the table of contents.
6. Go to the footer of Section 2 and delete the word *Confidential*.
7. Edit the bibliography as follows: Change the capitalization of the journal article and the book to capitalize first word only. You have just learned this is a requirement of APA. *Hint:* Select the title and click Change Case.
8. Check and close. (*77-d3*)

BOOKMARK

www.collegekeyboarding.com
Module 12 Practice Quiz

Document 9
Labels

1. In the open document (*proj2-d9 labels*), prepare address labels for the recipients of the form letter prepared in Document 8. Use Avery US Letter 5162 labels.
2. Preview and proofread.
3. Complete the merge and check; click Next to continue. (*proj2-d9*)

Document 10
Report

pbpc theme
business plan

Dr. Faulk and Mr. Schmidt asked you to work with a small team of analysts to put together the preliminary data needed to complete the Palm Beach Pet Center Business Plan. You have decided to prepare a very professional report with a cover, table of contents, table of figures, graphics, and footnotes to present the data requested.

PRELIMINARY PAGES

1. Open the *pbpc theme* template and then insert a Tiles cover page. Complete the placeholders by keying **Palm Beach Pet Center** in the company name at the top; key **Business Plan** as the title; and **Preliminary Data** as the subtitle. Use your name as author; click Today to insert the year. Key the PBPC address at the bottom of the cover sheet; separate the street address from the city, state, and Zip Code with a vertical bar (|).
2. Leave two blank pages for the table of contents and the table of figures. Do not number any of the pages until you complete the entire report.

BODY OF THE REPORT

1. Insert a Continuous section break at the top of the first page of the body of the report.
2. Insert the data file *business plan*, which was drafted for this report. Apply Title and Subtitle styles. Select all text below the subtitle and apply Justify.
3. Apply Heading 1 style to all headings except for the five market segment headings after the *Revenue Potential Analyzed* heading, which should be formatted using Heading 2 style.
4. Insert the following footnotes. (Reminder: Tap ENTER once after each footnote.)
   a. Insert the Reference number for footnote 1 at the end of the first sentence in the second paragraph of the market segment *Veterinary Clinic*. Key footnote 1: **Revenues were $750,000 for last year and $725,000 for the prior year.**
   b. Insert the Reference number for footnote 2 at the end of the first paragraph in the *Luxury Suite Boarding* market segment. Key footnote 2: **Data were analyzed on six luxury facilities in six different states.**
   c. Insert the Reference number for footnote 3 at the end of the second sentence in the second paragraph in the *Luxury Suite Boarding* market segment. Key footnote 3: **More than 95 percent of those surveyed indicated they would use Palm Beach Pet Center for boarding their pets at least three days a month, and approximately 80 percent said they preferred luxury accommodations to standard units. A table of comparative costs was provided to participants prior to answering the questions.**
   d. Insert the Reference number for footnote 4 at the end of the third sentence in the *Doggie Day Camp* market segment. Key footnote 4: **Day camps are more popular in resort areas than in other areas.**

Mail Merge

LEARNING OUTCOMES

- Merge form letters.
- Merge envelopes and labels.
- Edit the data source and sort and filter records.
- Merge using *Word*, *Access*, and *Excel* as the data source.

Lesson 78 | Mail Merge

New Commands

- Mail Merge Wizard

KEYBOARDING PRO DELUXE 2

WARMUP

Lessons/78a Warmup

A   ALL LETTERS

Skill Building

78b   Timed Writing

1. Key a 3' timed writing on each paragraph. Work to increase speed.
2. Key a 5' timed writing on all paragraphs.

	gwam	3'	5'

One of the major trends in the workplace today is telecommuting. In fact, over fifty million workers own home-based businesses or work for a business from home. This number of workers grows each year with companies of all sizes hiring workers who will work from home offices.

Why do workers choose to telecommute? Reasons include reducing stress of rush hour traffic, being flexible to balance family and work time, and being able to work when they work best. Workers often find an increase in work done because of fewer stops to answer the telephone or talk to another person.

Working successfully from home requires new considerations. Of course, it is obvious that technology needs must be in place in the home office. Yes, the worker must have a home office, one that is separate from the rest of the house. He or she must set a daily routine and request that family respects the new freedom and knows the work performance that is expected to be achieved.

gwam 3' / 5' values:
5 | 3 | 42
9 | 6 | 45
14 | 8 | 48
19 | 11 | 50
23 | 14 | 53
28 | 17 | 56
32 | 19 | 59
37 | 22 | 61
39 | 24 | 63
44 | 26 | 65
48 | 29 | 68
52 | 31 | 71
57 | 34 | 73
61 | 37 | 76
65 | 39 | 78

3' 1   2   3   4
5' 1   2   3

Field Names	Record 1	Record 2	Record 3	Record 4
Title	Mr. and Mrs.	Mr. and Mrs.	Mr. and Mrs.	Mr. and Mrs.
First Name	Tommy	Pat	Ed	John
Last Name	Suggs	VanHuss	Skintik	Forde
Address Line 1	410 Seabreeze Avenue	190 S. Ocean Boulevard	300 Barton Avenue	206 Dunbar Road
City	Palm Beach	Palm Beach	Palm Beach	Palm Beach
State	FL	FL	FL	FL
ZIP Code	33480-4107	33480-6105	33480-6166	33480-3715
Pets	Lizzie and Molly are	Andy is	Sadie is	Fred is

3. Key the main document shown below and insert the merge fields in it.
4. For the closing lines, use **Sincerely** and your name and title (**Intern**).
5. Sort by ZIP Code in ascending order. Preview and proofread the document.
6. Merge the data source and the main document.
7. Check; click Next to continue. (*proj2-d8*)

«AddressBlock»

«GreetingLine»

We are currently preparing a new newsletter that will be sent to all of our clients, including the resorts in the area that refer their guests needing pet services to us. When you receive the newsletter, you will note that «Pets» featured in it. The online version will be published within the next two weeks. We hope you enjoy reading it.

The response to our announcement in the last newsletter that pbpc now provides services for cat owners as well as dog owners has been very positive. Many of our current clients and several new clients have brought their cats in for professional care services, and a number of them have made reservations for boarding their pets.

The newsletter summarizes all of our services that are currently available for both dogs and cats. The veterinary clinic currently offers the highest level of pet care available. The clinic will be enlarged over 50 percent when the new facilities are completed. In addition, state-of-the-art technology will be installed. The number of luxury units available for boarding will be expanded, and the Boutique will feature many more items.

We look forward to seeing you at pbpc soon.

TIP

Remember to remove the extra space after the paragraphs in the letter address.

MAIL MERGE

Creating personal form letters, printing labels, and addressing envelopes to a large number of individuals are tasks done easily using the Mail Merge feature. Mail merge is creating a new (merged) document by combining information from two other documents—the main document and the data source.

The **main document** contains the text and graphics that remain the same for each version of the merged document. Within the main document, **merge fields** are inserted as placeholders in locations where you want to merge names, addresses, and other variable information that comes from the data source file.

The **data source** is a file that contains the names, addresses, and other variables to be merged with the main document. All the variables for one individual are called a **record**. The separate variables for each record are called **fields**.

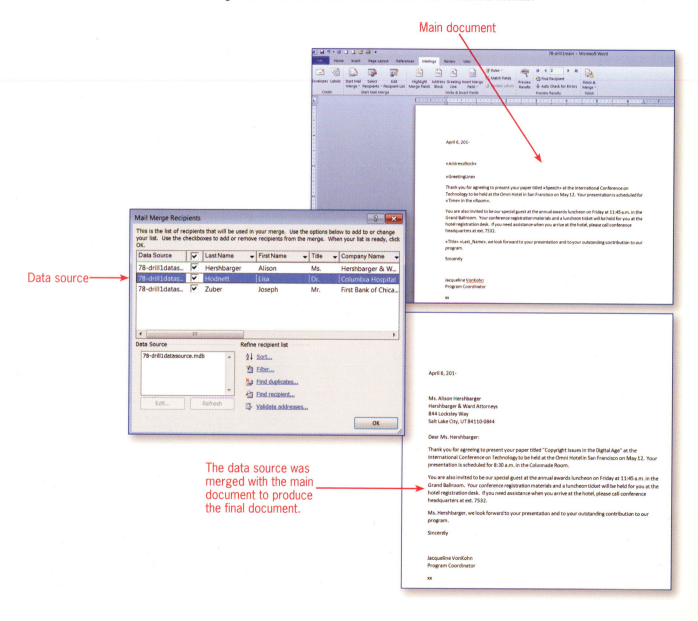

Main document

Data source

The data source was merged with the main document to produce the final document.

services for cats:

- Total professional care provided by board-certified veterinarians and highly trained technicians.

- Luxury pet boarding.

- Boutique that provides one-stop shopping to meet your cat's needs and desires.

The architects and construction team met and agreed that we could finish an expansion area of the new facility and have a nice area to meet the demand for accommodations for cats. This expansion will not impact the construction completion dates. Space in the veterinary clinic and the boutique is already available.

QUICK ✔

Check your document against the illustration below.

PBPC News and Views

Palm Beach Pet Center now provides full-service luxury pet care to dog owners. Recently, we have been inundated with requests from current clients and from a number of the resorts in our area to expand our services to cat owners. Providing services to cat owners has always been a part of our long-range business plan; therefore, we decided to survey all of our clients and resorts whose guests use our services.

Client Survey

First, we asked current clients if they had any objections to adding cats to the facilities. None of our current clients objected to having cats in the facility. More than 20 percent of our current clients have both dogs and cats. Resorts also indicated that approximately 25 percent of their guests with pets need services for cats.

What was even more surprising were responses from clients who only have dogs, but who indicated many of their friends would like to use our services for their cats. Several sent pictures of their friends' cats. They all indicated we could publish their names and pictures in our newsletter. Sadie Skiratk shown above is one that would likely be a frequent boarder at Palm Beach Pet Center

Some of our clients even sent pictures of their dog with cats that belonged to their friends who want to use our services. Andy VanHuss is pictured below with his friend Charlie Turnquist and two Turnquist kittens—Henry and Choo Choo.

Action Plan

We will begin with a pilot project immediately that will include three types of services for cats:

- Total professional care provided by board-certified veterinarians and highly trained technicians.
- Luxury pet boarding.
- Boutique that provides one-stop shopping to meet your cat's needs and desires.

The architects and construction team met and agreed that we could finish an expansion area of the new facility and have a nice area to meet the demand for accommodations for cats. This expansion will not impact the construction completion dates. Space in the veterinary clinic and the boutique is already available.

Document 8
Mail Merge

proj2-d8 main

Prepare a form letter that will be sent to the owners of pets that will be featured in the next newsletter.

1. In the open document (*proj2-d8 main*), insert the current date at 2".

2. Create the data source using the records shown on the next page. Customize the field names to include those shown in the first column. Save as *proj2-d8 data*.

MAIL MERGE WIZARD

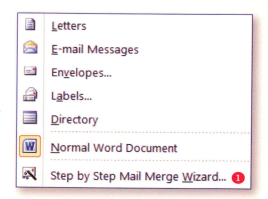

The Mail Merge Wizard is a straightforward way to produce a merged document such as the form letters you will create in this lesson.

To start the Mail Merge Wizard:

Mailings/Start Mail Merge/Start Mail Merge

1. The main document automatically opens and is saved by *Keyboarding Pro DELUXE 2*.
2. Follow the path above to display a list of mail merge options.
3. Click Step by Step Mail Merge Wizard ①.

DRILL 1   MAIL MERGE WIZARD

1. The open document (*78-drill1main*) is the main document. Follow the path above to display a list of mail merge options. Click Step by Step Mail Merge Wizard.

2. Follow the six steps of the Mail Merge Wizard explained below and on the next few pages. To move from one step to the next, click Next located at the bottom of the pane. This drill will lead you through the steps for using the Mail Merge Wizard.

Step 1: Select document type
- Choose Letters ①.
- Click Next: Starting document to go to step 2 of the Wizard.

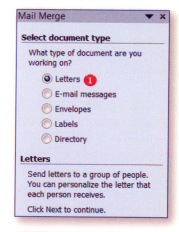

Step 2: Select starting document
- Click Use the current document ② to create a new form letter in the active window.
- Click Next: Select recipients. (**Note:** You may click Previous: Select document type to return to the previous step.)

Step 3: Select recipients
- Click Type a new list ③.
- Under Type a new list, click Create ④ to display the New Address List dialog box.

Document 7
Newsletter

pbpc theme
sadie skintik
andy and friends

★ TIP

If *Word* AutoCorrects PBPC to spell out Palm Beach Pet Center, reverse the correction to keep the initials.

1. Open *pbpc theme* from the data files. This file contains a blank page with a custom document theme applied. Apply Moderate margins to the document.

2. Tap ENTER twice (position 1.7") and insert a Continuous section break in the third paragraph marker. (The section break will appear in the second blank paragraph.)

3. Click the paragraph marker below the Continuous section break and key the text shown below. Apply Heading 2 style to both headings. Use square bullets.

4. Select the text and apply two-column layout with equal-width format.

5. Insert the picture *sadie skintik* from the data files in the paragraph in which she is mentioned. Crop the picture so that only the cat is shown; compress the picture and size it 2.5" high. Apply Tight text wrapping and position the picture at the right side of the column.

6. Insert the picture *andy and friends* below the paragraph in which he is mentioned. Compress the picture and size it 1.8" high. Tap ENTER once to leave space below the picture. (Format the blank paragraph with Heading 2 style if necessary.)

7. Insert Gradient Fill – Dark Red, Accent 1, Outline – White, Glow – Accent 2 WordArt at the paragraph marker at the top of the page. Key **PBPC News and Views**; center the text horizontally.

8. Compare your document to the Quick Check shown on the next page.

9. Proofread and check; click Next to continue. (*proj2-d7*)

Palm Beach Pet Center now provides full-service luxury pet care to dog owners. Recently, we have been inundated with requests from current clients and from a number of the resorts in our area to expand our services to cat owners. Providing services to cat owners has always been a part of our long-range business plan; therefore, we decided to survey all of our clients and resorts whose guests use our services.

Client Survey

First, we asked current clients if they had any objections to adding cats to the facilities. None of our current clients objected to having cats in the facility. More than 20 percent of our current clients have both dogs and cats. Resorts also indicated that approximately 25 percent of their guests with pets need services for cats.

What was even more surprising were responses from clients who only have dogs, but who indicated many of their friends would like to use our services for their cats. Several sent pictures of their friends' cats. They all indicated we could publish their names and pictures in our newsletter. Sadie Skintik, shown above, is one that would likely be a frequent boarder at Palm Beach Pet Center.

Some of our clients even sent pictures of their dog with cats that belonged to their friends who want to use our services. Andy VanHuss is pictured below with his friend Charlie Turnquist and two Turnquist kittens—Henry and Choo Choo.

Action Plan

We will begin with a pilot project immediately that will include three types of

(continued)

- In the New Address List dialog box, click Customize Columns ⑤ to edit the default field names provided in the Wizard. The Customize Address List dialog box displays.

   a. To delete a field name, select the field and click Delete ⑥. Click Yes to confirm the deletion of each field. For this drill, delete Address Line 2, Country or Region, Home Phone, Work Phone, and E-mail Address.

   b. To add a field name, select a field name and click Add ⑦. The Add Field dialog box displays. Add three fields: Time, Room, and Speech.

   c. To position the new fields correctly, select the field to be moved. Click Move Up or Move Down ⑧ as appropriate. Move the field names so they are positioned as shown at the right. Click OK.

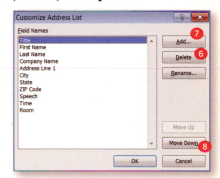

- Key the variables for Record 1 in the New Address List dialog box. Click New Entry to begin a new record, and key the variables for Record 2. Repeat for Record 3. Click OK after keying all of the records.

Field names	Record 1	Record 2	Record 3
Title	Ms.	Dr.	Mr.
First Name	Alison	Lisa	Joseph
Last Name	Hershbarger	Hodnett	Zuber
Company Name	Hershbarger & Ward Attorneys	Columbia Hospital	First Bank of Chicago
Address Line 1	844 Locksley Way	303 Park Circle Road	1106 Whispering Pines Road
City	Salt Lake City	Milwaukee	Chicago
State	UT	WI	IL
ZIP Code	84110-0844	53221-0303	60650-1106
Speech	"Copyright Issues in the Digital Age"	"Creating Interactive Presentations"	"Creating a Web Presence for Your Organization"
Time	8:30 a.m.	9:30 a.m.	10:30 a.m.
Room	Colonnade Room	Diplomat Room	Laurel Suite

Document 5
Convert Table to Text

1. Open the table you created in Document 4.
2. Convert the table to text; separate text with tabs.
3. Adjust tabs to align the values appropriately under headings.
4. Apply Title style to the main heading and Subtitle style to the column heads.
5. Proofread and check; click Next to continue. (*proj2-d5*)

Document 6
Organization Chart

TIP

To remove the space after paragraph for each name, use the shortcut SHIFT + ENTER.

1. Prepare the organization chart for the Retail and Service Operations shown below using a Name and Title Organization Chart from the Hierarchy category of SmartArt diagrams. Use Landscape orientation.
2. Add your name to the chart.
3. Size the chart to 6.8" high and 9" wide; expand shapes if necessary so that the text can be keyed as shown below. Use Corbel font for all text.
4. Apply the following font sizes:
   a. Use 24-point font for all names; remove space after each name.
   b. Use 14-point font for the second lines in each shape, such as *Retail and Service Operations*.
   c. Use 18-point font for all titles.
5. Change colors to Colored Fill – Accent 2. Position the chart at Top Center with Square Text Wrapping.
6. Add a shape below each manager.
7. Key each name and title from the left shape to the right: **Mark Jones**, **JoAnn Jameson**, and **Jan Marcus**. Each has the title **Assistant Manager**. Use Corbel font for the new shapes.
8. Proofread and check; click Next to continue. (*proj2-d6*)

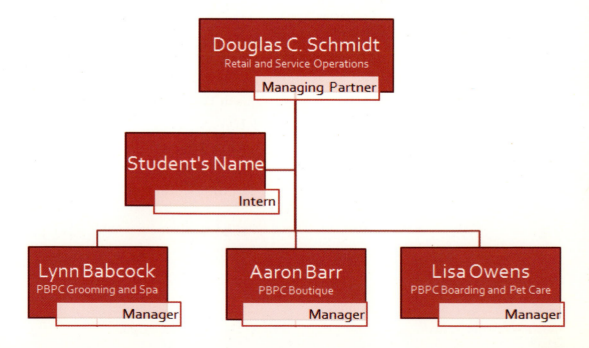

- The Save Address List dialog box displays. Key a filename (*78-drill1datasource*) in the File name box and click Save. (**Note:** By default, data files are saved to the folder My Data Sources under the My Documents folder.) In the Save in box, choose the appropriate folder for saving this file.

- The Mail Merge Recipients dialog box now displays and shows the variables in table format. Click OK.

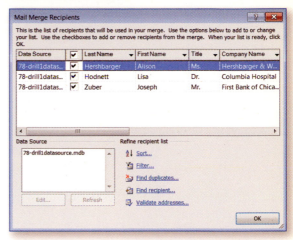

- **Note:** To move within the Mail Merge Recipients dialog box, click the desired row. Use the scroll bar to navigate in the record. With a long recipient list, click Find recipient to search for the desired recipient.

- Click Next: Write your letter from the Mail Merge task pane.

Step 4: Write your letter

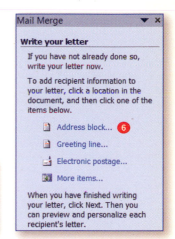

- Begin keying the main document at approximately 2". In this drill, key **April 6, 201-** as the date. Normally you would insert the current date. Tap ENTER two times.

- From the right pane, click Address block ⑥ (or from the Write & Insert Fields group, on the Mailings tab, click the Address Block button). The Address Block dialog box displays. Click OK to accept the default settings for recipient's name, company name, and postal address.

- Tap ENTER one time.

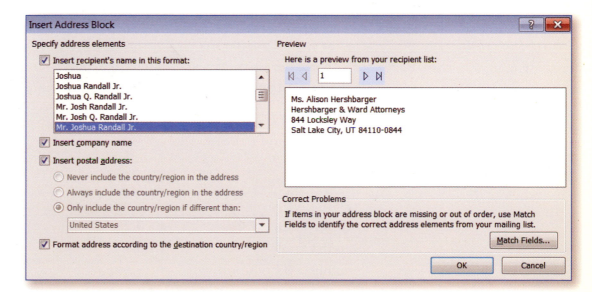

Document 4
Table

Design a table for pet boarding fees.

1. Create a 4-column, 8-row table; apply Landscape orientation, and key the information shown below.

2. Change the text direction for the *Daily Cost* and *Weekly Cost* columns to vertical with text aligned at the bottom as shown.

3. Sort the data in the *Daily Cost* column in ascending order.

4. Fill in the *Weekly Cost* column by using a formula to multiply the daily cost by 5. (The weekly discount is equal to five days with two free days.)

5. Delete the *Doggie Day Camp* column.

6. Insert one column to the left of the *Weekly Cost* column and one column to the right of it; key **Multiple Pets in Same Unit** for both column heads. Change the text direction back to horizontal. Adjust the width so that the heading fits on one line.

7. Select the first three cells under the *Multiple Pets in Same Unit* columns and split them into two columns. Key the following information in these cells:

   a. In the *Standard units* row, key **Two** in the first cell and **Three** in the second cell.

   b. In the *Small* and *Medium* pet rows, use the Formula command to add $10 extra per day for two pets and $15 extra per day for three pets. (In the *Daily Cost* column, add $10 to the daily cost for two pets and add $15 to the daily cost for three pets. In the *Weekly Cost* columns, multiply $10 × 5 days for two pets and $15 × 5 days for three pets and add it to the weekly cost.) Use the 0.00 number format.

   c. In the *Large* row under the *Multiple Pets in Same Unit* column, key **Not available**.

   d. In the three remaining rows under the *Multiple Pets in Same Unit* column, key **No extra charge**.

8. Add a row at the top of the table, merge all cells, and center-align in uppercase and bold the heading **PET BOARDING FEES**. Change font to 14-point Cambria.

9. Apply Medium Shading 1 – Accent 2 style; under Table Style Options, remove the check from First Column; on the Table Tools Design tab, in the Borders and Shading dialog box, change the border color to Red, Accent 2. Bold all headings.

10. Increase the height of rows 3–9 to 0.3"; left-align and center text vertically in column A; center text vertically and horizontally in all other columns except for the *Daily Cost* and *Weekly Cost* headings, which should be aligned Bottom Center.

11. Center the table vertically on the page.

12. Proofread and check; click Next to continue. (*proj2-d4*)

Unit Type and Pet Size	Daily Cost	Weekly Cost	Doggie Day Camp
Standard units			20
Luxury suite	75.50		NA
Junior suite	70.25		NA
Luxury unit	60.75		30
Small: < 35 pounds	35.50		
Medium: 35–75 pounds	42.75		
Large: > 75 pounds	46.25		

Greeting
Line

- In the Mail Merge task pane, in the far right pane, click Greeting line (or from the Write & Insert Fields group, in the Mailings tab, click the Greeting Line button). The Insert Greeting Line dialog box displays. Click the drop-list arrow to the right of the comma and select none ❼. Click OK. Tap ENTER one time and continue keying the letter until you reach the merge field code for Speech.

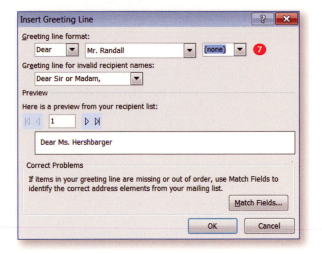

- Insert the merge field for Speech:

  a. From the right pane, click More Items (or on the Write & Insert Fields group, click the Insert Merge Field button).

  b. Select Speech, click Insert, and then click Close. (*Tip:* When necessary, tap the Space Bar to insert a blank space between fields. Insert punctuation as needed between fields or at the end of a field.)

Insert Merge
Field ▾

  c. Continue keying the letter shown below. Insert the merge fields for *Time* and *Room* at the appropriate places.

April 6, 201- (ENTER 2 times)

«AddressBlock» (ENTER 1 time)

«GreetingLine» (ENTER 1 time)

Thank you for agreeing to present your paper titled «Speech» at the International Conference on Technology to be held at the Omni Hotel in San Francisco on May 12. Your presentation is scheduled for «Time» in the «Room».

You are also invited to be our special guest at the annual awards luncheon on Friday at 11:45 a.m. in the Grand Ballroom. Your conference registration materials and a luncheon ticket will be held for you at the hotel registration desk. If you need assistance when you arrive at the hotel, please call conference headquarters at ext. 7532.

«Title» «Last_Name», we look forward to your presentation and to your outstanding contribution to our program.

Sincerely (ENTER 2 times) | Jacqueline VonKohn | Program Coordinator | xx worked meet and exceed all of the requirements for receiving academic credit for my internship. Dr. Faulk and Mr. Schmidt both agreed to evaluate my work and complete the necessary forms required for the internship. Therefore, I respectfully request that you approve this internship for academic credit.

Please let me know if you need additional information.

Document 2
Modified Block Letter

 pbpc letterhead

TIP

Save the closing lines, including your initials and the copy notation for Dr. Faulk, as a Quick Part named **Schmidt Closing Lines** to enhance your productivity.

1. Use the *pbpc letterhead* template to prepare the modified block letter for Mr. Schmidt. Mr. Schmidt uses modified block style with mixed punctuation for his letters.
2. Insert the current date at 2". Use **Sincerely,** | **Douglas C. Schmidt** for the closing lines.
3. Send Dr. Faulk a copy of the letter; use her name and title: **Erin A. Faulk, DVM**.
4. Proofread and check; click Next to continue. (*proj2-d2*)

Ms. Gabriella Anez | Palm Beach Professional Services | 2486 S. Lake Avenue | West Palm Beach, FL 33401-7828

Erin Faulk and I have reviewed all of the materials that you and her professional advisors submitted to us. We were pleased that both of our legal and financial advisors provided the same options and very similar analyses.

Each of the alternatives has unique advantages and disadvantages. However, after much discussion, we both agree that the joint venture with each party having 50 percent equity is the best option. The values of the ongoing Palm Beach Pet Care business, the ten acres of adjacent property, and the proportionate shares of construction costs are equitable.

Our accountants presented proformas that make this venture a very exciting one, and we are ready to begin work on the project immediately. We have both signed the form authorizing our professional representatives to finalize the transaction. Your copy is enclosed. We hope to have the transaction completed within the next two weeks.

Thank you for the excellent work you have done on this project.

Document 3
Block Letter

 dcs advisor

TIP

Save the closing lines including your initials and the copy notation for Mr. Schmidt as a Quick Part named **Faulk Closing Lines** to enhance your productivity.

Dr. Faulk and Mr. Schmidt agreed to send the same letter to their professional advisors; therefore, you will adapt Mr. Schmidt's letter for Dr. Faulk.

1. In the open document (*dcs advisor*), make the changes directed in the following steps.
2. Dr. Faulk uses block format with open punctuation for her letters and signs them: **Sincerely** | **Erin A. Faulk, DVM**.
3. The address information for Dr. Faulk's advisor is: **Mr. Lee Tims** | **Tims and Associates** | **423 Fern Street** | **West Palm Beach, FL 33401-5939**.
4. Modify the first sentence so that it reads: **Doug Schmidt and I . . . and his professional advisors** . . . .
5. Change the copy notation to **Douglas C. Schmidt**.
6. Proofread and check; click Next to continue. (*proj2-d3*)

Non-*Keyboarding Pro DELUXE 2* users:

Click Save to update the changes made to the main document (*78-drill1main*).

Mail Merge

Preview your letters

One of the merged letters is previewed here. To preview another letter, click one of the following:

| < | Recipient: 1 | > |

Find a recipient...

Make changes

You can also change your recipient list:

Edit recipient list...

[Exclude this recipient]

When you have finished previewing your letters, click Next. Then you can print the merged letters or edit individual letters to add personal comments.

Step 5: Preview your letters

- Remove the extra spacing between the lines of the letter address ❽.
- Click the navigation buttons to preview and proofread each of your letters. (*Tip:* Should you need to edit one of the letters, click Edit recipient list and make the necessary changes to the data source file.)
- Click Next: Complete the merge.

Ms.·Alison·Hershbarger¶

Hershbarger·&·Ward·Attorneys¶ ❽

844·Locksley·Way¶

Salt·Lake·City,·UT·84110-0844¶

Dear·Ms.·Hershbarger:¶

Step 6: Complete the merge

- Click Edit individual letters ❾. Click All; then OK. The merge letters will **not** appear on the screen. You will see the message: **Mail merge is done and document is generated.** Click OK.
- Check. The merged letters will appear on the screen as the checked document. Click Next to continue. (*78-drill1*)

Mail Merge

Complete the merge

Mail Merge is ready to produce your letters.

To personalize your letters, click "Edit Individual Letters." This will open a new document with your merged letters. To make changes to all the letters, switch back to the original document.

Merge

Print...

Edit individual letters... ❾

EDIT MAIL MERGE DOCUMENT

(Mailings/Start Mail Merge/Start Mail Merge/Step by Step Mail Merge Wizard)

Often it is necessary to edit the main document. Perhaps the user did not finish the job before closing the document, or perhaps changes are now needed in the main document.

With the main document open, follow the path above and open the Mail Merge Wizard. Click the Next or Previous buttons until you locate the desired step to be edited. Make the desired changes or continue creating the main document.

Troubleshooting Tips

1. When you open the main document, you will be prompted that data from your database will be placed in the document. Click Yes to accept the data if the desired data source is connected to the main document. If you wish to use another data source, click No and select the new data source.
2. When in the Write your letter step of the wizard, the merge field codes will display; but when in Preview your letters, actual data from the data source will display. Click Next or Previous to move to the correct step.

STANDARD OPERATING PROCEDURES (SOPs)

Dr. Faulk has talked with you about setting up and following standard operating procedures for the new business. SOPs are important in creating a consistent image and establishing the company brand. SOPs can enhance productivity and provide employees with access to information needed to work independently. You will be involved in helping to set up additional SOPs.

1. Proofread, preview, and print each document you prepare.
2. Use the Palm Beach Pet Center *letterhead* and *memo* data files for letters and memos.
3. Spell out *pbpc* as Palm Beach Pet Center each time it appears in documents.
4. Use the letter format indicated by each partner now. After the business is established, block letter format with open punctuation will be the standard style.
5. Use *Dear* + the title and last name as the salutation on all letters unless directed otherwise.
6. Add enclosure or attachment notations and copy notations when they are referenced in a letter or memo.
7. Use the document theme specified for each document. The letterhead and memo forms have been prepared using a customized theme. In Project 3, you will customize the theme and apply it to all documents you prepare.
8. Use the current date on all memos, letters, and reports unless directed otherwise.

TIP

You can enhance your productivity by creating an AutoCorrect option to replace *pbpc* with Palm Beach Pet Center each time it is keyed.

Document 1
Memo

  pbpc memo

TIP

Do not add your initials to the memo since you are preparing it for yourself.

1. Use the *pbpc memo* template to prepare a memo from you to Dr. Lynn F. Hudson.
2. Proofread and check; click Next to continue. (*proj2-d1*)

SUBJECT: Request for Internship Credit

This week I was offered and accepted an internship at the newly created Palm Beach Pet Center, which is a joint venture between Dr. Erin Faulk, owner of Palm Beach Pet Care, a veterinary clinic, and Mr. Douglas Schmidt, an entrepreneur. The new business integrates the veterinary clinic with a full-service luxury pet boarding, grooming, and boutique center.

This position offers me a great opportunity to work in an environment that I have learned about in my Small Business Management and Financial Management courses at the same time that I apply the word processing and document formatting skills that I have learned in your class. I will work with Dr. Faulk and Mr. Schmidt to develop standard operating procedures and to standardize the formats for letters, memos, reports, table styles, and for documents that are specifically related to the business. They both have indicated to me that they expect me to take full responsibility for my position and to expect very little direct supervision.

I agreed to work for a minimum of six months at least 10 hours per week, and I have the option to work as many as 25 hours a week. My plan is to average 20 hours per week. The type of position and the number of hours

78-d1

Mail Merge

1. In the open document (*78-d1main*), create the data source. Customize the address list to include the fields shown below.

2. Key the following data for each of the three records. Save the data source as *78-d1datasource*.

Field names	Record 1	Record 2	Record 3
Title	Mrs.	Mr.	Ms.
First Name	Jessica	Allen	Paje
Last Name	Quarrels	Bouchillon	Vang
Company Name	Hendrix Plastics	Magnolia Chemicals	Faulkner Florists
Address Line 1	5689 Old Vinton Road	538 Hill Street	885 N. Third Street
City	Starkville	Columbus	West Point
State	MS	MS	MS
ZIP Code	39759-5689	39701-0538	39773-0885
County	Oktibbeha	Lowndes	Clay

3. Key the main document that follows and insert the merge fields in the main document. Use open punctuation. Save the changes. (**Reminder:** The date should update automatically.)

4. Preview and proofread the document.

5. Merge the data source and the main document.

6. Check; click Next to continue. (*78-d1*)

Insert Date

«AddressBlock»

«GreetingLine»

Thank you for submitting your proposal for enacting a more culturally diverse employment program for city workers to the American Studies Association.

The American Studies Association continually strives to work with city governments in three area counties to provide work environments that value diversity. The goal, of course, is to employ persons who reflect differences in age, lifestyle, and interests. Different people solve problems differently, and that leads to better decisions.

You may be contacted, «Title» «Last_Name», to represent «County» County on the special Council for Managing Diversity that is being established in our three-county region. Again, thank you for letting us know what you are doing to ensure diversity at «Company_Name».

Sincerely | Hunter Nyiri, Director | xx

Palm Beach Pet Center I

LEARNING OUTCOMES

- Apply keying, formatting, and word processing skills.
- Create a variety of documents.
- Follow standard operating procedures.
- Work independently and with few specific instructions.

PALM BEACH PET CENTER I

Palm Beach Pet Center

1985 Parker Avenue | West Palm Beach, FL 33401-7239

Telephone: 561-555-0127 | Fax: 561-555-0159 | www.pbpc-sw.com

Welcome to the creation of Palm Beach Pet Center. This project is the first of two projects that you will complete on the center. Save all documents for future reference in Project 3, Palm Beach Pet Center II.

Palm Beach Pet Center is a new joint venture between a veterinarian, Dr. Erin A. Faulk, and an entrepreneur, Mr. Douglas C. Schmidt. Dr. Faulk owns a veterinary clinic, Palm Beach Pet Care, which offers a wide range of services to dog owners. Mr. Schmidt owns ten acres of property adjacent to the veterinary clinic. They have agreed to create a new business named Palm Beach Pet Center. The business will integrate the veterinary clinic with a full-service luxury pet boarding, grooming, and boutique center. The center is located near a very high income residential and resort area.

Legal and financial consultants are working on the formal documents for the new business. Since neither Dr. Faulk nor Mr. Schmidt had office staff to handle the paperwork involved, they hired you, an intern, to work on a part-time basis for both of them.

1. Decide on a form letter that would be useful to you personally or to your class. Secure the names and addresses of the recipients of the form letter.

2. In the open document (*78-d2main*), create the data source. Save it as *78-d2datasource*.

3. Compose the main document and insert the merge fields in it.

4. Proofread and preview the document.

5. Merge the data source and the main document.

6. Check and close. (*78-d2*)

FUNKY BUSINESS/PHOTOLIBRARY

! WORKPLACE SUCCESS

Managing Information Overload

Business employees are under siege with the volume of information that is coming at them from all sides—text messages, voice mail, e-mail, the Internet, television, radio, fax, magazines, news feeds, and many others. Interestingly, much of the data that business employees review is not relevant to their jobs. Because managing information overload is a critical skill needed by today's business employees, please consider the following technology and behavior suggestions.

Technology—Use e-mail information filters to screen messages that do not demand your attention. Use delegation features to allow an assistant to respond to e-mail when possible. Delete participation in list servers not desired. Take advantage of RSS feeds to compile data from the Internet and to allow the review of one set of data. Locate reputable blogs in the area of your research to decrease search time on the Internet and provide views of many individuals.

Behavior change—Maintain responsibility in e-mail use; do not copy to another person just in case he or she may need it. Limit the control information has on your life and set the hours you will work per week. Set limits on when you check e-mails and use the cell phone, including vacation time.

82-d3

Post Cards

82-d3data

Prepare cards for the individuals who have ordered bakery goods from your organization.

1. In the open document (*82-d3cards*), use the *Access* file *82-d3data* as the data source.

2. Prepare the note card below (Avery US Letter 3259 Embossed Note Cards) as the main document. Include the fields shown. Format the card attractively. Sort by Delivery Date in ascending order.

3. Preview, proofread, and complete the merge.

4. Check the test and close. (*82-d3*)

«Customer Name»

«Delivery_Location»

«Delivery_Date»

«Order_Item_1»

«Order_Item_2»   Tap ENTER twice.

We appreciate your bakery order and wish you a happy holiday.

662-555-0109

❖ **BOOKMARK**

www.collegekeyboarding.com
Module 13 Practice Quiz

Lesson 79 | Edit the Data Source

- Edit Data Source
- Sort Data Records
- Filter Data Records

Skill Building

79b   Textbook Keying

1. Key each line once; concentrating on using good keying techniques. Tap ENTER twice after each 4-line group.
2. Repeat the drill if time permits.

i	1	sit in said did dirk city did fin its lit iris wit hit ilk simmer
e	2	gem ewe men eke ever me le hen cede key led fen eye be pen leader
i/e	3	pie lei piece feign mein feint neigh lie reign die veil vein diem
i/e	4	Either Marie or Liem tried to receive eight pieces of cookie pie.
w	5	new jaw awe win we was awe away hew saw flaw law wan pew wit wavy
o	6	to onto rot job coho sox box oboe wok roe out oil dot tote oriole
w/o	7	ow wows how won worn now woe wool mow row work cow woke flows low
w/o	8	Women won't want to work now; we are worn out after woeful worry.

| 1 | 2 | 3 | 4 | 5 | 6 | 7 | 8 | 9 | 10 | 11 | 12 | 13 |

Communication

79c

KEYBOARDING PRO DELUXE 2

References/Communication Skills

1. Complete the Quotations and Italics pretest, rules, and posttest in *Keyboarding Pro DELUXE 2* before completing this exercise.
2. Key your name on the first line and right-align it.
3. Key each sentence, correcting the errors in quotation marks and italics. Use the Numbering command to number each sentence.
4. Proofread again to ensure that you did not make any other keying errors. Correct any errors you find.
5. Proofread and check; click Next to continue. (*79c*)

QUOTATIONS AND ITALICS

1. Dr. Waites recommended, When you are a guest in a new country, experience the culinary differences by dining at authentic restaurants.

2. Excellent reads for an overseas trip are the book International Travel Made Easy; and the magazine International Travel.

3. The lyrics for the song International Fiesta were written by a music student.

4. What Is Your Cultural IQ, an article published in the International Journal, won best article for 2011.

5. The word diversity is clearly explained in the opening scene of the movie Today's World.

6. Do you know who coined the phrase bottom line that is used often by American business executives?

82-d1

continued

Directions to Hathorn Hall, the residence hall designated for summer workshop participants, are enclosed. You may check in at Hathorn from 8 a.m. to 10 p.m. Housing payment can be made at the residence hall.

«First_Name», should you have any questions about the workshop, please call me at 555-0123. I look forward to your being a part of our workshop series.

Sincerely, | Jane D. Gunter | Workshop Coordinator

82-d2

Sort and Filter

82-d2datasource

Prepare form letters for your dental patients who are 90 days delinquent on their dental payments.

1. In the open document (*82-d2main*), prepare the form letter below as the main document. Use block letter style and open punctuation. Send a copy of this letter to Justin Langberg.

2. Choose the *Excel* worksheet *82-d2datasource* as the data source; select Sheet 1.

3. Sort the data source by ZIP Code in ascending order. Filter to select those patients whose Days Past Due are greater than or equal to 90 days.

4. Preview, proofread, and complete the merge.

5. Continue to the next document. (*82-d2*)

March 1, 201-

«AddressBlock»

«GreetingLine»

Your unpaid balance of $ «Unpaid_Balance» is now past due. We have requested payment from you on «No_Contacts_Made» occasions; however, we have received neither payment nor an explanation as to why payment has not been made.

Although we have no desire to cancel your credit privileges, we are forced to disallow any increase to your balance until payment of the past-due amount is paid. Future dental services for you and your family can be provided on a cash basis only.

Please call me at 305-555-0135 and make arrangements for paying your overdue amount. If we do not hear from you regarding a revised payment schedule, please pay $ «Minimum_Payment», a minimum payment. This payment must be received by March 20.

Sincerely | Paul Vanzandt | Office Manager | xx

USE MERGE COMMANDS ON MAILINGS TAB

An alternate method for creating and editing a mail merge document is to access the merge commands on the Mailings tab.

Use the Address Block **1**, Greeting Line **2**, and Insert Merge Field **3** buttons to create the placeholders for the merge fields in the main document. The Edit Recipient List **4** button is used to edit the data source, while the Finish & Merge button **5** is used to complete the merge.

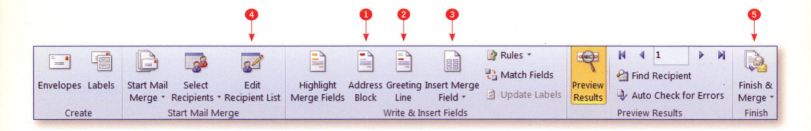

EDIT DATA SOURCE

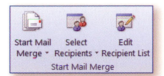

Sometimes you will need to edit the data source (list of variables) by changing individual records or revising the fields for all records.

To edit records:

Mailings/Start Mail Merge/Edit Recipient List

1. Follow the path above to display the Mail Merge Recipients dialog box.
2. In the Data Source box, click the data source, e.g., *78-drill1datasource* **1**. Click Edit. The Edit Data Source dialog box displays.
3. Click the desired entry **2** or click Find **3** to locate a record quickly.
4. Make the desired changes.
5. Click New Entry to add a new record, or click Delete Entry to delete a record. Click OK.

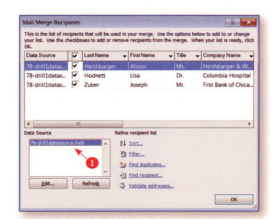

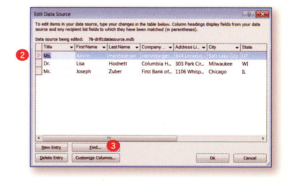

Prepare the main document and data source for a form letter to participants of a summer workshop. You will need to edit your data source after you create it.

1. In the open document (*82-d1main*), create the data source as shown below and save as *82-d1datasource*.

Field names	Record 1	Record 2	Record 3
Title	Mr.	Ms.	Ms.
First Name	Phillip	Anele	Anna
Last Name	Lancaster	Nyiri	Skelton
Company Name	Fulton High School	Curtis Middle School	Curtis Middle School
Address Line 1	35 Wallace Circle	16060 Aspen Road	1355 Palomino Drive
City	Norfolk	Richmond	Richmond
State	VA	VA	VA
ZIP Code	23501-3849	27173-5721	27173-0616
Date	June 15–16	June 23–24	June 23–24
Room	204	205	205

2. Move Ms. Skelton to the June 15-16 workshop. Change Mr. Lancaster's address to **89 Castle Road**.

3. Key the main document (block style with mixed punctuation style) and insert the merge fields. Add notations as needed. Key the date as **May 1, 201-**. Save the changes.

4. Sort by ZIP Code in ascending order.

5. Preview, proofread, and complete the merge.

6. Continue to the next document. (*82-d1*)

Date

«AddressBlock»

Dear «First_Name»:

I am delighted that you will be attending the Principles and Applications of Web Design Workshop on «Date» at Braswell Community College. Please arrive at Room «Room» of the Harper-Kock Union Building at 8 a.m. for registration and a brief orientation.

As the workshop title indicates, the objectives include learning principles of Web design and applying these principles in realistic exercises. The first day is filled with outstanding assignments highlighting important principles of Web design. During the second day, you will team with one of your colleagues to plan and design impressive Web pages for «Company_Name». Do take time before coming to the workshop to locate materials from your office that you will need to create these Web pages.

(continued)

Changes to fields are made by editing the data source. Once the change is made, all of the records are revised.

To edit fields:

Mailings/Start Mail Merge/Edit Recipient List

1. In the Edit Data Source dialog box, click the Customize Columns button.
2. Edit as follows:
   a. Add new field: Click the Add button; key the field name. Use the move buttons to position correctly. (**Reminder:** Be sure to update the main document by inserting the new merge field.)
   b. Delete field: Select the field to be deleted. Click the Delete button.
   c. Rename field: Select the field to be renamed. Click the Rename button. Key new name.
3. Save your main document to update your data source.

DRILL 1   EDIT RECORDS AND FIELDS

1. In the open document (*78-drill1main*), add Fax Number as a new field after the ZIP Code field. **Note:** You will be prompted that data from your database will be placed in the document. Click Yes to accept the data unless instructed to select another data source.

2. Update the records with the following fax numbers:

   Ms. Hershbarger **217-555-0181**

   Dr. Hodnett **414-555-0194**

   Mr. Zuber **708-555-0192**

3. Change Ms. Hershbarger's address to 206 Fourth Avenue, Springfield, IL 62701-0206.

4. Check and click Next to continue. (*78-drill1main*)

UNKNOWN/RUBBERBALL/JUPITER IMAGES

! WORKPLACE SUCCESS

Multicultural Skills

What is your multicultural quotient? Companies are seeking employees who have multicultural awareness, knowledge, and skills. These valuable employees are aware that their attitudes, beliefs, assumptions, etc., do affect how they work with others who are of different cultures. These employees are very knowledgeable of the many aspects of these cultures, including history, practices, and values. They also have developed skills that are needed to interact effectively with those of different cultures. One skill might be learning the language of that culture.

Spend some time in this module increasing your own multicultural literacy. Develop an awareness, knowledge, and skills in another culture.

Lesson 82 | Assessment

Skill Building

82b **Timed Writing**

Key two 3' timed writings.

	gwam	3'	5'

Dining etiquette is necessary as good impressions are made on both important business clients and friends. Table manners tell so much about a professional. Just notice as the well orchestrated and zealous expert makes sure that the guest has the best place at the table and gives excellent advice on the best food items. Finally, the napkin is placed on his or her lap to signal the beginning of the meal.

To understand a seemingly difficult table setting more easily, think of a line down the middle of the serving plate. Then always remember liquids are positioned on the right of the line and solids are placed on the left. Notice very carefully that glassware, cup and saucer, knives and spoons are positioned on the right side of the line. Notice also that the bread and butter plate, salad plate, napkin, and forks are positioned on the left side. Returning these items to the same specific position after using each one will keep the table looking very good.

Never begin eating until the host unfolds his or her napkin. Upon this important signal, open your napkin and position it carefully on your lap. Should you need to leave the table momentarily, position your napkin on your chair. Remember, never move your plate away from you when completed. Wait until the host has placed his or her napkin on the table; then you may position yours to the right of the dinner plate.

gwam values (3'|5'):
4 | 3 | 59
9 | 5 | 62
14 | 8 | 64
18 | 11 | 67
23 | 14 | 70
27 | 16 | 72
28 | 17 | 73
32 | 19 | 76
37 | 22 | 78
41 | 25 | 81
46 | 27 | 84
50 | 30 | 86
55 | 33 | 89
59 | 35 | 92
64 | 38 | 94
66 | 39 | 96
70 | 42 | 98
75 | 45 | 101
79 | 47 | 104
83 | 50 | 106
88 | 53 | 109
92 | 55 | 112
94 | 56 | 112

3' | 1 | 2 | 3 | 4
5' | 1 | 2 | 3

Applications

82c

Assessment

 Continue

 Check

When you complete a document, proofread it, check the spelling, and preview for placement. When you are completely satisfied, click the Continue button to move to the next document. Click the Check button when you are ready to error-check the test. Review and/or print the document analysis results.

SORT DATA RECORDS

Sorting records determines the order in which the records are merged. You might sort records in ZIP Code order, Last Name order, or City order. Occasionally, a multiple sort is needed to sort first by one field and then a second field, and so forth. For example, merged name badges or registration letters might be sorted first by state, then by city, and then by last name. Records are sorted either in ascending order (A to Z or 1, 2 …) or descending order (Z to A or 100, 99, etc.).

To sort records by one field:

Mailings/Start Mail Merge/Edit Recipient List

1. Open the main document and follow the path above to display the Mail Merge Recipients dialog box.

2. Click the column heading of the field to be sorted to display the data (such as Last Name) in ascending order **1**.

   Click again to display in descending order. Click OK.

   Note: You may also click the drop-list arrow by each field **2** and select Sort Ascending or Sort Descending.

3. To merge, in the Finish group, click the Finish & Merge button. Click one of the merge options.

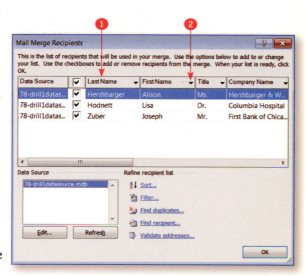

To sort records by multiple fields:

Mailings/Start Mail Merge/Edit Recipient List

1. Open the main document and follow the path above to display the Mail Merge Recipients dialog box.

2. From the Refine recipient list, click Sort.

3. From the Filter and Sort dialog box, select the Sort Records tab **1**.

4. Click the Sort by **2** drop-list arrow and select the first field to be sorted in the multiple sort.

5. Click the drop-list arrow for Then by **3** and select the second field, and so forth. Click OK.

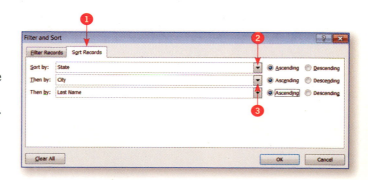

81-d3

Alternate Data Source

 81-d2datasource

1. In the open document (*81-d3envelopes*), prepare envelopes for a mailing to selected members registered for the conference referenced in *81-d2*.   Choose *81-d2datasource* as the data source.

2. Sort by last name in ascending order and then first name. Filter to merge those with luncheon fee equal to 30.

3. Preview, proofread, complete the merge, and check; click Next to continue. (*81-d3*)

81-d4

Invitation

 81-drill1datasource

▶▶ **REVIEW**

Center Page

Page Layout/Page Setup/ Layout tab/Vertical alignment

1. Prepare the invitation shown below on special paper size A5 as a mail merge document. Center the invitation vertically.

2. Format as follows:

   Title: Bold, Dark Blue, Text 2 font, 20 pt.

   Table: Apply the Colorful List - Accent 3 table style. Adjust spacing after the table.

   E-mail address: Remove the hyperlink.

3. Choose the Access database *81-drill1datasource*. Insert the five merge fields shown in the table.

4. Sort by department and then last name and first name in ascending order. Filter to merge only the Accountancy Department.

5. Preview, proofread, and complete the merge. Check and close. (*81-d4*)

ANNUAL FACULTY RETREAT

August 15, 201-

8:30 a.m. to 10: 30 a.m.

Sweeney Union Building

Assignments	
Name	«First_Name» «Last_Name»
Department	«Department»
Location	«Location»
Discussion Group	«Discussion_Group»

Discussion topics include:

A   Using Wikis to Enhance Student Learning

B   Using Wikis to Encourage Faculty Collaboration

C   Using Technology to Assess Learning Outcomes for Accreditation Response ↓1

Please RSVP by August 1 to Sheena Zhang at
szhang@college.edu
Call 662-555-0100

DRILL 2   SORT IN ASCENDING ORDER

1. In the open document (*78-drill1main*), sort by ZIP Code in ascending order.

2. Preview and proofread.

3. Complete the merge and check; click Next to continue. (*79-drill2*)

DRILL 3   SORT IN DESCENDING ORDER

1. In the open document (*78-drill1main*), sort by ZIP Code in descending order and merge to a new document.

2. Preview and proofread.

3. Complete the merge and check; click Next to continue. (*79-drill3*)

DRILL 4   MULTIPLE SORT

1. In the open document (*78-drill1main*), sort in ascending order first by State, then by City, and then by Last Name.

2. Preview and proofread.

3. Complete the merge and check; click Next to continue. (*79-drill4*)

FILTER RECORDS

Filtering records before merging the main document and the data source allows you to select a specific set of records to merge. For example, you can create a target mailing to individuals in a specific state or ZIP Code area.

To filter data records:

Mailings/Start Mail Merge/Edit Recipient List

1. Open the main document and follow the path above to display the Mail Merge Recipients dialog box.

2. From the Refine recipient list, click Filter.

3. From the Filter and Sort dialog box, select the Filter Records tab **1**.

4. Choose the appropriate data field **2** (e.g., State); click a comparison phrase **3** (e.g., *Equal to*); and key the text or data you will use for the comparison **4** (e.g., *IL*). Click OK. (**Note:** Click the drop-list arrow for comparison and note the comparison phrases.)

5. Note the records displaying in the Mail Merge Recipients dialog box to determine if you have filtered correctly. Click OK.

(**Reminder:** In the Filter and Sort dialog box, click the Clear All button to remove filters before using the main document again to ensure all records will merge.)

1. In a blank document, change the paper size to Legal 8.5" x 14". From Print Preview, note the width and length of the paper.

2. Change the paper size to Executive 7.25" x 10.5". Key your name at the top of the document. From Print Preview, note the width and length of the paper.

3. Proofread and check; click Next to continue. (*81-drill3*)

Applications

81-d1

Create Directory

81-drill1datasource

1. In the open document (*81-d1main*), choose Directory as the type of mail merge document.

2. Choose the *Access* database *81-drill1datasource* as the data source. Sort the mail merge recipients list by last name in ascending order and then first name.

3. Arrange the main document to include the fields shown below. Set a right leader tab (#2) at 6.5" to position the telephone number at the right. Be sure to tap ENTER once after the last field to ensure a blank line between entries. Bold the Last_Name field.

> **«Last_Name»**, «First_Name» ....«Telephone_Number»
> «Department»
> «Rank»

4. Insert the Alphabet footer on each page. Key **Central Watson University** at the left margin.

5. Key the main heading **Directory of University Faculty** in the header; apply the Title style. Use the Keep with Next command to ensure all data for a record remain on the same page.

6. Preview and proofread.

7. Complete the merge and check; click Next to continue. (*81-d1*)

81-d2

Edit Letter

81-d2main

81-d2datasource

1. In the open document (*81-d2main*), access the Step by Step Mail Merge Wizard. Choose the *Excel* file *81-d2data* as the data source. Select Sheet 1 in the Select Table dialog box. Click OK.

2. Insert the Address Block and Greeting Line merge fields below the date. Use open punctuation. Add the subject line **Registration Acknowledgment**.

3. Insert the following merge fields in the table cells as shown below. Press CTRL + TAB to move to the right tab in the table cell. Key the **$** signs as shown.

4. Preview, including all records, and proofread.

5. Complete the merge and check; click Next to continue. (*81-d2*)

Registration Receipt	
Registration Fee	$«Registration_Fee»
Association Dues	«Association_Dues»
Luncheon Fee	«Luncheon_Fee»
Total	$«Total»

DRILL 5   FILTER DATA RECORDS

1. In the open document (*78-drill1main*), filter as follows:

   Field: *State*

   Comparison Phrase: *Equal to*

   Compare to: *Illinois (IL)*

2. Preview and proofread.

3. Complete the merge and check; click Next to continue. (*79-drill5*)

DRILL 6   FILTER DATA RECORDS

1. In the open document (*78-drill1main*), clear filters used in Drill 5 if necessary.

2. Filter to select records of speakers who live in Illinois and are scheduled to speak at 8:30 a.m. (*Hint:* Because both conditions must be met, select *and;* then key the requirements for the second condition.)

3. Preview and proofread.

4. Compete the merge and check; click Next to continue. (*79-drill6*)

Applications

79-d1
Edit Data Source

1. In the open document (*78-d1main*), edit data source as follows:
   - Mr. Bouchillon now works for **Prestage Technology Company**.
   - Ms. Vang's new address is **983 Old Cedar Place**; ZIP Code is **39704-0983**.

2. Add two new records:

Ms. Brenda Andres	**Mr. Juan Seuffer**
Gifts and More	**Kubly and Ross Associates**
1456 W. 18th Street	**356 Airline Road**
Starkville, MS 39759-1456	**West Point, MS 39773-0356**
Oktibbeha County	**Clay County**

3. Add *Representative* as a new field.

4. Edit the records with the following data:

Record	Representative
Quarrels	**Beth Stevens**
Bouchillon	**Kelly Cancienne**
Vang	**Patrick Konscak**
Andres	**Wade Sanford**
Seuffer	**Jennifer Fleming**

5. Edit the writer's name and title in the closing lines. Delete *Hunter Nyiri, Director* and insert the merge field *Representative*. Add the word **Representative** as the writer's title.

6. Sort by Last Name in ascending order; preview and proofread.

7. Complete the merge and check; click Next to continue. (*79-d1*)

79-d2
Filter Data Source

1. In the open document (*78-d1main*), filter the data source to select records in Oktibbeha County. Check that the records are still sorted by last name in ascending order.

2. Preview and proofread.

3. Complete the merge and check; click Next to continue. (*79-d2*)

1. In the open document (*81-drill2postcards*), use *81-drill2datasource* (*Word* table) as the data source. Sort the mail merge recipients list by team in ascending order.

2. Choose Avery US Letter 3263 Postcards – Wide labels.

3. Prepare the main document below. Remove the extra space between the professor's name and title. Remove the hyperlink in the e-mail address.

4. Preview, including all records, and proofread.

5. Complete the merge and check; click Next to continue. (*81-drill2*)

February 6, 201- ↓ 2

Dear «Name»

The Team Building Unit for MGT Business Communication is designed to prepare you to function as an effective member of a team. You have been assigned membership on Team «Team».

Your first team meeting is Monday, February 25, at 5 p.m. in Room «Meeting_Room» of Greene Hall. Your team will complete the scavenger hunt described in Team Activity 1 in your *Team Building Handbook*. After your team has finished this activity, you will select your team leadership.

Good luck. You may e-mail me at cf@itc.edu if you have questions or comments. ↓ 2

Andy Peavey, Professor
Business Communication

PAPER SIZE

On some occasions it is appropriate to print documents on different-sized paper than the standard 8½" by 11". For example, invitations are often printed on special-sized paper and legal documents are often printed on 8½" by 14". However, with the use of printers and copiers today, many legal documents are accepted on standard paper.

To change paper size:

Page Layout/Page Setup/Size

1. Follow the path above.
2. Click on the desired paper size or click More Paper Sizes to display the Page Setup dialog box. If a different size is needed, key the desired width and height of the paper.

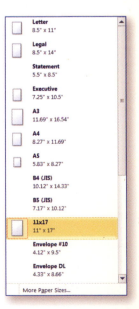

79-d3

Directory

1. In the open document (*79-d3directory*), prepare a directory of stocks. Choose Directory as the document type.

2. Create a data source (*79-d3datasource*) with these fields: Symbol, Name, Industry, and Trade. Search the Internet for current stock information for five stocks. One useful site is http://finance.yahoo.com. Key the following as the first stock entry:

   Symbol: **WMT**; Name: **Wal-Mart Stores, Inc.**; Industry: **Discount, Variety Store**; and Trade: **55.06**

3. Arrange the directory as follows. Set left tabs at 0.5" and 2" and right tab at 5.5".

   Name

       Symbol   Industry   Trade

4. In the header key **Directory of Stocks** and apply the Title style. Sort by name in ascending order and merge.

5. Preview and proofread.

6. Complete the merge, check and close. (*79-d3*)

QUICK ✓

Check your document design against the illustration below. Your solution will include five stocks sorted by name in ascending order.

Directory of Stocks

Wal-Mart Stores, Inc.
    WMT   Discount, Variety Store   55.06

Lesson 81 | Merge with Alternate Sources

New Commands
- Merge with Alternate Sources

New Commands

81b

MERGE A DOCUMENT USING ALTERNATE SOURCES

Word can perform a mail merge using a data source created in other programs such as *Access*, *Excel*, and *Outlook*. *Word* tables can also be used as a data source when they contain a header record in the first row. The header record contains the field names that will be used in the mail merge. Each row in the table (below the header) contains data for one record. Each column in the table contains data for one field. If a record doesn't have information for a certain field, the cell for that field can be left blank.

To perform a mail merge using an alternate data source:
Mailings/Start Mail Merge/Start Mail Merge

1. In the main document, follow the path above and click Step by Step Mail Merge Wizard.
2. Select the document type (e.g., Letters, Envelopes, Labels, Directory). Click Next: Select recipients.
3. Under Select recipients, choose Use an existing list.
4. Click Browse, select the data source filename, and click Open.
5. Prepare the main document by inserting merge codes and keying any constant text.
6. Preview and proofread.
7. Complete the merge.

DRILL 1 | ACCESS ALTERNATE SOURCE | 81-drill1datasource

1. In the open document (*81-drill1labels*), *select 81-drill1datasource* (*Access* database) as the data source. Sort the mail merge recipients list in ascending order by department, then last name, and then first name.

2. From the label option, choose Avery US Letter 5066 File Folder labels. Include these fields in the label.

«Last_Name», «First_Name»
«Department»

3. Change the font of the merge fields to Cambria. Preview, including all records, and proofread.

4. Complete the merge and check; click Next to continue. (*81-drill1*)

Lesson 80 | Merge with Envelopes and Labels

New Commands
- Merge Envelopes
- Merge Labels

New Commands

80b

MERGE ENVELOPES

Envelopes can be merged from the data source. When printing envelopes, you will need to know the type of envelope feeder your printer uses. In this lesson, you will create #10 landscape envelopes (standard business envelope).

To create envelopes:

Mailings/Start Mail Merge/Start Mail Merge

1. The main document automatically opens and is saved when the drill or application is selected.
2. Follow the path above and click Step by Step Merge Wizard to display the Mail Merge pane at the right of the screen.
3. Under Select document type, select Envelopes. Click Next: Starting document.
4. Under Select starting document, check that Change document layout is selected.
5. Under Change document layout, click Envelope options. The Envelope Options dialog box displays. The Size 10 envelope is default. Click OK; then Next: Select recipients.
6. Under Select recipients, click Use an existing list. Under Use an existing list, click Browse. From the appropriate disk drive, select *78-drill1datasource*, the data source created in Lesson 78. The Mail Merge Recipients dialog box displays the records. Click OK. Click Next.
7. Under Arrange your envelope, position the insertion point in the letter address area. Click Address Block to insert as a merge field. Click Next.
8. Under Preview your envelopes, click the navigation buttons to preview and proofread the envelopes. Click Edit recipient list if changes are needed in the data source. Click Next.
9. Click Edit individual letters. Click All; then OK. The merge envelopes will **not** appear on the screen. You will see the message: **Mail merge is done and document is generated.** Click OK.
10. Check. The merged envelopes will appear on the screen as the checked document.

TIP

Non-Keyboarding Pro DELUXE 2 users:

Open a new document and save it as the main document with an appropriate name, e.g., *80-drill1envelope*. Remember to resave when the main document is complete.

DRILL 1 — PREPARE ENVELOPES

1. In the open document (*80-drill1envelope*), follow the steps provided above to prepare envelopes for the data source *78-drill1datasource*.
2. Preview and proofread.
3. Complete the merge and check; click Next to continue. (*80-drill1*)

80-d1

continued

The Holland Eye Center invites you to attend a special seminar sponsored for our patients who are potential candidates for laser vision correction. This seminar held at our clinic on «Date» at 7 p.m. will feature a panel of doctors and patients and a live laser vision correction procedure. A question/answer period will also provide an opportunity to have all your questions answered by these laser vision correction experts. You'll also have an opportunity to enter your name in a drawing for a complimentary laser vision correction procedure to be presented at the close of the seminar.

Would you like to join the millions of people who have chosen laser vision correction and be free of the daily hassles of glasses and contact lenses? Get started today by completing the enclosed reservation card indicating you will attend the seminar on «Date» and learn for yourself the details of laser vision correction.

Sincerely | Edward S. Vickery, M.D. | xx | Enclosure

3. Sort by Last Name in ascending order and then First Name in ascending order. Preview and proofread.

4. Complete the merge and check; click Next to continue. (80-d1)

80-d2

Edit Data Source

1. In the open document (80-d2main), edit the data source as follows:
   - Invite Dr. Jantz to the February 25 seminar.
   - Ms. Wiseman's new address is **235 N. Fifth Street, Omak, WA 98841-3592**.

2. Add two new records for the February 25 seminar.

   Mrs. Darlene Chism   Mr. James Lee
   830 Yorkville Street   332 Matilda Road
   Tonasket, WA 98855-1251   Omak, WA 98841-2028

3. Filter to select records of patients invited to the February 25 seminar. Preview and proofread.

4. Complete the merge and check; click Next to continue. (80-d2)

80-d3

Envelopes

Prepare envelopes for all the patients invited to the February 25 laser vision correction seminar.

1. In the open document (80-d3envelopes), prepare envelopes for the records stored in the data source 80-d1datasource.

2. Filter appropriately and sort by Last Name and then First Name.

3. Preview, proofread, complete the merge, and check; click Next to continue. (80-d3)

80-d4

Name Badges

All the patients you invited to the February 25 laser vision correction seminar have agreed to attend the seminar. Prepare name badges for their use at the seminar.

1. In the open document (80-drill4labels), prepare name badges (Avery 5095) for the records stored in the data source 80-d1datasource. Include the First Name and Last Name fields on the name badge. Sort by Last Name and First Name in ascending order. Format attractively (e.g., font, size, alignment, etc.).

2. Preview, proofread, complete the merge, check, and close; click Next to continue. (80-d4)

1. In the open document (*80-drill2envelope*), prepare envelopes for the records stored in data source *78-d1datasource*. From the More items list, select the following merge fields and arrange as shown here:

   Title First Name Last Name

   Company Name

   Address Line 1

   City, State ZIP Code

2. Sort by ZIP Code in ascending order. Preview and proofread.

3. Complete the merge and check; click Next to continue. (*80-drill2*)

MERGE LABELS

Labels designed for printers are available in all sizes and for many purposes, including file folder labels, mailing labels, name badges, and business cards. The data source is often used for merging letters, registration forms, envelopes, and numerous types of labels. Merging labels is very similar to merging envelopes.

To create labels:

Mailings/Start Mail Merge/Start Mail Merge

1. Follow the directions on page 412 for merging envelopes.

2. Under Select document type, select Labels. Click Next: Starting document.

3. Under Select starting document, be sure Change document layout is selected.

4. Under Change document layout, click Label options. Choose Avery US Letter from the label vendor list and 5160 from the product number list. Click OK. Click Next: Select recipients.

5. Under Select recipients, click Use an existing list. Under Use an existing list, click Browse. From the appropriate disk drive, select *78-drill1datasource*. The Mail Merge Recipients dialog box displays the records. Click OK and Next: Arrange your labels.

6. Under Arrange your labels, click Address Block and click OK. Click Remove Space Before Paragraph to remove the extra spacing between the address lines. (Click More Items to select the merge fields individually for the address block.)

7. Under Replicate labels, click Update all labels to replicate the address block merge field on each label on the page. Save the main document again. Click Next.

8. Under Preview your labels, click the navigation buttons to preview and proofread the labels. Click Edit recipient list if changes are needed in data source. Click Next.

9. Click Edit individual letters. Click All; then OK. The merge labels will **not** appear on the screen. You will see the message: **Mail merge is done and document is generated.** Click OK.

10. Check. The merged labels will appear on the screen as the checked document.

1. In the open document (*80-drill3labels*), prepare address labels for the data source file *78-drill1datasource*. *Hint:* Click Remove Space Before Paragraph after inserting the Address block. Be sure to update all labels.

2. Preview and proofread.

3. Complete the merge and check; click Next to continue. (*80-drill3*)

1. In the open document (*80-drill4labels*), prepare file folder labels (5066-Filing Labels) for the records stored in data source *78-d1datasource*.

2. Sort by Last Name in ascending order.

3. From the More Items list, select the following merge fields. Select both lines and remove extra space between the lines.

   Last Name First Name Title

   Company Name

4. Preview and proofread. Complete the merge and check; click Next to continue. (*80-drill4*)

Applications

80-d1

Mail Merge

The Holland Eye Center is hosting two seminars to inform its patients about laser vision correction. Prepare the form letters for the records shown below.

1. In the open document (*80-d1main*), create the datasource and save as *80-d1datasource*.

Field names	Record 1	Record 2	Record 3
Title	Mr.	Dr.	Ms.
First Name	Angelo	Karen	Mary
Last Name	Seay	Jantz	Wiseman
Address Line 1	P.O. Box 88	137 Sonoma Drive	539 Swoope Avenue
City	Tonasket	Omak	Tonasket
State	WA	WA	WA
ZIP Code	98855-3918	98841-0174	98855-8296
Date	January 31	January 31	February 25

2. Key the main document and insert the merge fields in it. Use open punctuation. Save the changes. (**Note:** The date should update automatically.)

«AddressBlock»

«GreetingLine»

Do you ever imagine being able to see the alarm clock when you wake up? Do you ever imagine no more hassles of daily contact lens maintenance? Perhaps you may have imagined playing your favorite sport with complete peripheral vision—no fogging or slipping glasses. Millions of people across the world have chosen laser vision correction as an alternative to glasses and contact lenses. They now are enjoying these freedoms that you have only imagined.

(continued)

Reference Guide

Capitalize

1. First word of a sentence and of a direct quotation.
   We were tolerating instead of managing diversity.
   The speaker said, "We must value diversity, not merely recognize it."

2. Names of proper nouns—specific persons, places, or things.
   Common nouns: continent, river, car, street
   Proper nouns: Asia, Mississippi, Buick, State St.

3. Derivatives of proper nouns and geographical names.
   American history   English accent
   German food   Ohio Valley
   Tampa, Florida   Mount Rushmore

4. A personal or professional title when it precedes the name or a title of high distinction without a name.
   Lieutenant Kahn   Mayor Walsh
   Doctor Welby   Mr. Ty Brooks
   Dr. Frank Collins   Miss Tate
   the President of the United States

5. Days of the week, months of the year, holidays, periods of history, and historic events.
   Monday, June 8   Labor Day   Renaissance

6. Specific parts of the country but not compass points that show direction.
   Midwest   the South   northwest of town

7. Family relationships when used with a person's name.
   Aunt Helen   my dad   Uncle John

8. Noun preceding a figure except for common nouns such as line, page, and sentence.
   Unit 1   Section 2   page 2   verse 7   line 2

9. First and main words of side headings, titles of books, and works of art. Do not capitalize words of four or fewer letters that are conjunctions, prepositions, or articles.
   Computers in the News   *Raiders of the Lost Ark*

10. Names of organizations and specific departments within the writer's organization.
    Girl Scouts   our Sales Department

Number Expression

General guidelines

1. Use **words** for numbers *one* through *ten* unless the numbers are in a category with related larger numbers that are expressed as figures.
   He bought three acres of land. She took two acres.
   She wrote 12 stories and 2 plays in the last 13 years.

2. Use **words** for approximate numbers or large round numbers that can be expressed as one or two words. Use **numbers** for round numbers in millions or higher with their word modifier.
   We sent out about three hundred invitations.
   She contributed $3 million dollars.

3. Use **words** for numbers that begin a sentence.
   Six players were cut from the ten-member team.

4. Use **figures** for the larger of two adjacent numbers.
   We shipped six 24-ton engines.

Times and dates

5. Use **words** for numbers that precede o'clock (stated or implied).
   We shall meet from two until five o'clock.

6. Use **figures** for times with a.m. or p.m. and days when they follow the month.
   Her appointment is for 2:15 p.m. on July 26, 2011.

7. Use **ordinals** for the day when it precedes the month.
   The 10th of October is my anniversary.

Money, percentages, and fractions

8. Use **figures** for money amounts and percentages. Spell out cents and percent except in statistical copy.
   The 16% discount saved me $145; Bill, 95 cents.

9. Use **words** for fractions unless the fractions appear in combination with whole numbers.
   one-half of her lesson   5 1/2   18 3/4

Addresses

10. Use **words** for street names First through Tenth and **figures** or ordinals for streets above Tenth. Use **figures** for house numbers other than **one**. (If street name is a number, separate it from house number with a dash.)
    One Lytle Place   Second Ave.   142--53rd St.

Punctuation

Use an apostrophe

1. To make most singular nouns and indefinite pronouns possessive (add **apostrophe** and **s**).

   computer + 's = computer's   Jess + 's = Jess's
   anyone's   one's   somebody's

2. To make a plural noun that does not end in s possessive (add **apostrophe** and **s**).

   women + 's = women's   men + 's = men's
   deer + 's = deer's   children + 's = children's

3. To make a plural noun that ends in s possessive. Add only the **apostrophe**.

   boys + ' = boys'   managers + ' = managers'

4. To make a compound noun possessive or to show joint possession. Add **apostrophe** and **s** to the last part of the hyphenated noun.

   son-in-law's   Rob and Gen's game

5. To form the plural of numbers and letters, add **apostrophe** and **s**. To show omission of letters or figures, add an **apostrophe** in place of the missing items.

   7's   A's   It's   add'l

Use a colon

1. To introduce a listing.

   The candidate's strengths were obvious: experience, community involvement, and forthrightness.

2. To introduce an explanatory statement.

   Then I knew we were in trouble: The item had not been scheduled.

Use a comma

1. After an introductory phrase or dependent clause.

   After much deliberation, the jury reached its decision. If you have good skills, you will find a job.

2. After words or phrases in a series.

   Mike is taking Greek, Latin III, and Chemistry II.

3. To set off nonessential or interrupting elements.

   Troy, the new man in MIS, will install the hard drive. He cannot get to the job, however, until next Friday.

4. To set off the date from the year and the city from the state.

   John, will you please reserve the center in Billings, Montana, for January 10, 2011.

5. To separate two or more parallel adjectives (adjectives could be separated by and instead of a comma).

   The loud, whining guitar could be heard above the rest.

6. Before the conjunction in a compound sentence. The comma may be omitted in a very short sentence.

   You must leave immediately, or you will miss your flight. We tested the software and they loved it.

7. Set off appositives and words of direct address.

   Karen, our team leader, represented us at the conference.
   Paul, have you ordered the DVD-ROM drive?

Use a hyphen

1. To show end-of-line word division.

2. In many compound words—check a dictionary if unsure.

   - Two-word adjectives before a noun:
     two-car family
   - Compound numbers between twenty-one and ninety-nine.
   - Fractions and some proper nouns with prefixes/suffixes.
     two-thirds   ex-Governor   all-American

Use italic or underline

1. With titles of complete literary works.

   College Keyboarding   *Hunt for Red October*

2. To emphasize special words or phrases.

   What does *professional* mean?

Use a semicolon

1. To separate independent clauses in a compound sentence when the conjunction is omitted.

   Please review the information; give me a report by Tuesday.

2. To separate independent clauses when they are joined by conjunctive adverbs (*however, nevertheless, consequently,* etc.).

   The traffic was heavy; consequently, I was late.

3. To separate a series of elements that contain commas.

   The new officers are: Fran Pena, president; Harry Wong, treasurer; and Muriel Williams, secretary.

Use a dash

1. To show an abrupt change of thought.

   Invoice 76A—which is 10 days overdue—is for $670.

2. After a series to indicate a summarizing statement.

   Noisy fuel pump, worn rods, and failing brakes—for all these reasons I'm trading the car.

Use an exclamation point

After emphatic interjections or exclamatory sentences.

Terrific! Hold it! You bet! What a great surprise!

Proofreading Procedures

Proofread documents so that they are free of errors. Error-free documents send the message that you are detail-oriented and a person capable of doing business. Apply these procedures after you key a document.

1. Use Spelling & Grammar to check the document.
2. Proofread the document on screen to be sure that it makes sense. Check for these types of errors:
   - Words, headings, and/or amounts omitted.
   - Extra words or lines not deleted during the editing stage.
   - Incorrect sequence of numbers in a list.
3. Preview the document on screen using the Print Preview feature. Check the vertical placement, presence of headers or footers, page numbers, and overall appearance.
4. Save the document again and print.
5. Check the printed document by comparing it to the source copy (textbook). Check all figures, names, and addresses against the source copy. Check that the document style has been applied consistently throughout.
6. If errors exist on the printed copy, revise the document, save, and print.
7. Verify the corrections and placement of the second printed copy.

Proofreaders' Marks

Mark	Meaning	Mark	Meaning
#	Add horizontal space	/ or lc	Lowercase
‖	Align	☐	Move left
∼	Bold	☐	Move right
Cap or ≡	Capitalize	☐	Move up
⌒	Close up	☐	Move down
ℓ	Delete	#	Paragraph
∨	Insert	𝒮𝓅	Spell out
⌄⌄ " "	Insert quotation marks	∼ or tr	Transpose
... or stet	Let it stand; ignore correction	—	Underline or italic

Addressing Procedures

The Envelope feature inserts the delivery address automatically if a letter is displayed. Title case, used in the letter address, is acceptable in the envelope address. An alternative style for envelopes is uppercase with no punctuation.

Business letters are usually mailed in envelopes that have the return address preprinted; return addresses are printed only for personal letters or when letterhead is not available. The default size of Word is a size 10 envelope (4⅛" by 9½"); other sizes are available using the Options feature.

An address must contain at least three lines; addresses of more than six lines should be avoided. The last line of an address must contain three items of information: (1) the city, (2) the state, and (3) the ZIP Code, preferably a 9-digit code.

Place mailing notations that affect postage (e.g., REGISTERED, CERTIFIED) below the stamp position (about line 1.3"); place other special notations (e.g., CONFIDENTIAL, PERSONAL) below the return address about line 1".

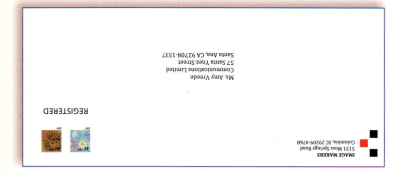

IMAGE MAKERS
5131 Moss Springs Road
Columbia, SC 29209-4768

REGISTERED

Ms. Amy Vreede
Communications Limited
57 Santa Ynez Street
Santa Ana, CA 92708-1537

Folding and Inserting Procedures

Large envelopes (No. 10, 9, 7¾)

Step 1   Step 2   Step 3

Step 1: With document face up, fold slightly less than 1/3 of sheet up toward top.

Step 2: Fold down top of sheet to within 1/2" of bottom fold.

Step 3: Insert document into envelope with last crease toward bottom of envelope.

Formatting Decisions

Decisions regarding document formats require consideration of four elements: (1) attractiveness of the format, (2) readability of the format, (3) effective use of space on the page, and (4) efficiency in producing the format. Please note several formatting decisions made in this text regarding defaults in *Word 2010*.

Styles

Word 2010 offers a quick gallery of styles on the Home tab, and a gallery of cover pages. Using these styles results in efficient production of an attractive title page.

Default 1.15 Line Spacing

The default line spacing of 1.15 in *Word 2010* provides readers with a more open and more readable copy.

Space after the Paragraph

The default space after a paragraph in *Word 2010* is 10 point after the paragraph. This automatic spacing saves time and creates an attractive document.

Remove Space after the Paragraph

While enjoying the benefits of efficiency, it is also necessary to the space that is being consumed. For example, extra spacing between the lines of the letter address requires too much space and is not an attractive layout. Note the formats in this book when the extra space is removed by simply clicking on options of the Line Spacing command.

Margins

The default margins for *Word 2010* are 1" top, bottom, left side, and right side. With the side margin default of 1", additional space is needed for the binding of leftbound reports.

Fonts and Document Themes

Microsoft provides true type fonts in *Office 2010* and a number of new document themes that incorporate color and a variety of fonts depending on the theme selected. Color printing has become increasingly popular and more cost effective. Many documents presented in the text are based on the default document theme, *Office*, and use the default heading font, Cambria, and the default body text font, Calibri, 11 point, black text. See the illustration below of the default headings and fonts.

Title (26 pt., Cambria, Color Text 2)

Subtitle (12 pt., Cambria, Italic, Color Accent 1)

Heading 1 (14 pt., Cambria, Bold, Color Accent 1, Darker 25%)

Heading 2 (13 pt., Cambria, Bold, Color Accent 1)

Heading 3 (11 pt., Cambria, Bold, Color Accent 1)

Heading 4 (11 pt., Cambria, Bold, Italic, Color Accent 1)

The default body text is Calibri, 11 pt. Color Automatic (Black).

Default Document Theme: Office:  Office

Letter Parts

Letterhead. Company name and address. May include other data.

Date. Date letter is mailed. Usually in month, day, year order. Military style is an option (day/month/year).

Letter address. Address of the person who will receive the letter. Include personal title (*Mr., Ms., Dr.*), name, professional title, company, and address. Remove the extra spacing in the letter address.

Salutation. Greeting. Corresponds to the first line of the letter address. Usually includes name and courtesy title; use *Ladies and Gentlemen* if letter is addressed to a company name.

Body. Message. Key in default 1.15 line spacing; tap ENTER once between paragraphs.

Complimentary close. Farewell, such as *Sincerely*.

Writer. Name and professional title. If the name and title are keyed on two lines, remove the extra spacing between the lines.

Initials. Identifies person who keyed the document (for example, *tr*). May include identification of writer (*ARB:tri*).

Enclosure. Copy is enclosed with the document. May specify contents. If more than one line is used, align at 1" and remove the extra spacing between the lines.

Copy notation. Indicates that a copy of the letter is being sent to person name. If more than one line is used, align at 0.5" and remove the extra spacing between the lines.

Note: To remove extra spacing between lines, click the down arrow on the Line Spacing command and select Remove Space After Paragraph.

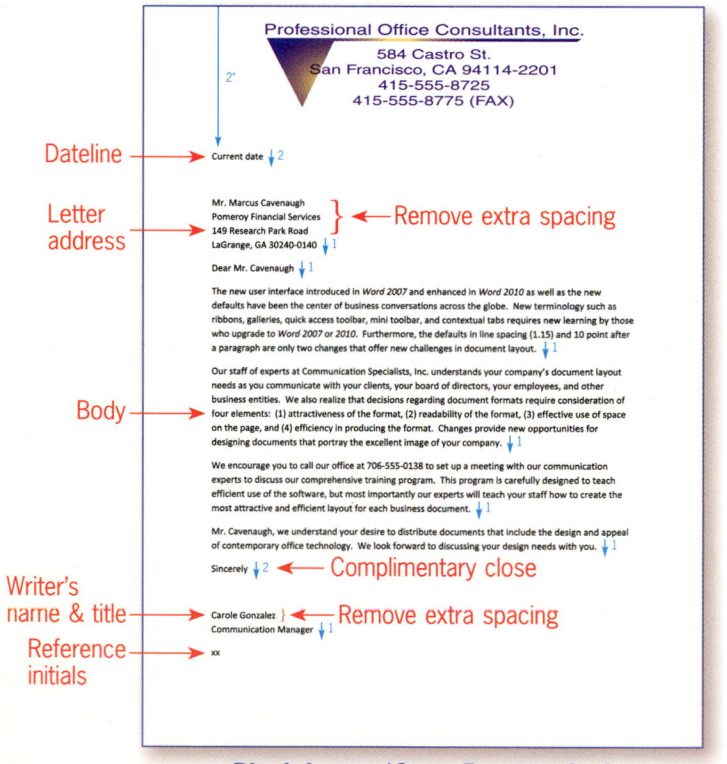

Block Letter (Open Punctuation)

Modified Block Letter (Mixed Punctuation)

Envelope

Letters and memos longer than one page require a header on the second and subsequent pages. Appropriate placement of the following special letter parts are illustrated below: mailing notation, postscript, attention line, subject line, blind copy notation, and reference line.

**Attention Line, Subject Line, and
Blind Copy Notation**

Reference Line

Memo with Table

TO:	Parents
FROM:	Lynn Marshall
DATE:	May 15, 201-
SUBJECT:	Tuition

The Board of Directors has reviewed our financial statements, the proposed budget for next year, and our current tuition plan. Although we have tried to maintain tuition at the current rate, it is not possible to do so. Our costs for utilities, food, supplies, and gasoline for the buses have increased substantially. Therefore, we have applied a 2.5% increase in tuition for next year. The following table summarizes our new weekly rates.

Age Group	Single-Child Rate	Multi-Child Rate	Half-Day Rate
Infant/Toddler	$268	$245	$150
Preschool 2	$253	$233	$140
Preschool 3	$240	$230	$125
Preschool 4	$237	$228	$122
Preschool 5	$235	$225	$122

The new rates take effect on July 1 and will be guaranteed not to change for one full year. The Children's Center will continue to accept credit cards and personal checks as it has always done. Tuition may be paid weekly, monthly, and annually.

If you wish to pay the annual tuition at one time prior to July 1, you may pay the current rates rather than these new rates with the 2.5% increase shown in the table. If you have any questions about tuition or other financial issues, please check with our business manager at the Children's Center.

We look forward to seeing all of you at the annual picnic next week.

xx

Memo with Table

Newsletter with Graphics

PBPC News and Views

Palm Beach Pet Center now provides full-service, luxury pet care. Our services are now offered to owners of both dogs and cats. Our survey to all of our current clients strongly endorsed broadening our services to include cats.

Grand Opening—Huge Success
Thanks to all of you who turned out for the Grand Opening ceremony. The attendance far exceeded our expectations and was a fun event for both owners and pets. Many clients enjoyed the tour of the new cat facility and meeting the new veterinarians who specialize in medical services for cats. Sadie was the first to use these new facilities.

Picture-Taking Sessions
We encourage all clients to have pictures taken of their pets. The schedule is posted in the main office and on our website. Your written permission is required to feature the pets in our publications and on the website. The form is provided at the picture taking sessions. Lizzie was the first to have her picture taken.

Suites
Andy laid first claim to reservations in one of the luxury suites and tried out the new leather couch that arrived this week. Three levels of luxury suites are available in addition to the standard units. Luxury suites feature all of the comforts of home—couches, comfortable beds, rugs, TV/VCR, toys, windows, climate control, premium food, a play yard, and a homey atmosphere.

Multiple Pets Per Unit
Standard units can accommodate two or three small or medium-size dogs or cats. All three levels of luxury suites are large enough to accommodate any size pets. Henry and Choo were happy that they can stay together in one of the luxury suites with comfortable furniture and a climbing tree.

1985 Parker Avenue | West Palm Beach, FL 33401-7239 | Page 1

Newsletter with Graphics

Personal Business Letter

Po-Ling Huang

1001 Hogan Street, Apartment 216A • Mobile, AL 36617-1001 • 334-555-0103 • plhuang@cu.edu

Current date

The return address may be keyed immediately above the date, or you may create a personal letterhead as shown here.

Mr. Coleman Stanberry
Managing Editor
Forde Financial News
840 Montclair Road
Birmingham, AL 35213-1943

Dear Mr. Stanberry

My bachelor's degree with double majors in graphic design and information technology and my graphic design work qualify me for the position of a junior graphic designer for *Forde Financial News* that you advertised.

As a result of my comprehensive four-year program, I am skilled in the latest Office suite as well as the current versions of desktop publishing and graphics programs. In addition, my excellent research and writing skills played a very important role in the Cother University Design Award I received last month. Being able to locate the right resources and synthesize those data into useful information for your readers is a priority I understand well and have practiced in my positions at the Cother University Alumni Office and the Cother University Library.

My technical and communication skills were applied as well as I worked as the assistant director and producer of the *Cother University Alumni News*. I understand well the importance of meeting deadlines and also producing a quality product within budget that will increase newspaper sales.

After you have reviewed the enclosed resume as well as my graphic design samples located on my Web page at www.netdoor.com/~plhuang, I look forward to discussing my qualifications and career opportunities with you at *Forde Financial News*.

Sincerely

Po-Ling Huang

Enclosure

Personal Business Letter

Resume

Po-Ling Huang

Permanent Address: 583 Post Oak Road | Savannah, GA 31418-0583 | Telephone: 912-555-0171

Temporary Address: (May 30, 201-): 1001 Hogan Street, Apt. 216A | Mobile, AL 36617-1001 | Telephone: 334-555-0103 | plhuang@cu.edu

CAREER OBJECTIVE	To obtain a graphic design position with an opportunity to advance to a management position.
SUMMARY OF ACHIEVEMENTS	Bachelor's degree with double major in graphic design and information technology; certified in major software applications and programming language. Relevant work experience in two organizations; earned design award.
EDUCATION	B.S. Graphic Design and Information Technology (double major), Cother University, Mobile, Alabama. May 2010. GPA: 3.8/4.0 (Magna Cum Laude).
SPECIAL SKILLS	Microsoft Certified Application Professional. C++ Certification. Know Java and Visual Basic Script programming languages. Keyboarding skills: 70 wpm.
EXPERIENCE	Cother University Alumni Office. Mobile, Alabama. Assistant editor and producer of the Cother University Alumni News, 2008 to present.

- Designed layout/production of six editions; met every publishing deadline; received the Cother University Design Award.
- Assisted editor in design of Alumni Office webpage (www.cu.edu/alumni).

Cother University Library, 2006-2008.

- Created Multimedia Catalog using computerized database.
- Prepared monthly and annual reports using database.
- Designed brochure to promote library services (www.cu.edu.plhuang/samples/brochure).

HONORS AND ACTIVITIES	Dean's Scholar (3.5 GPA or higher), President, Cother University Graphic Design Association, Recipient of Cother University Design Award.
REFERENCES	Letters from references and a transcript are available from Cother University Placement Office, Cother University, P.O. Drawer 3418, Mobile, AL 36617-3418	Telephone: 334-555-0134.

Resume

Margins: Tap ENTER three times to begin first page of report and reference page at 2"; default 1" top margin for succeeding pages; default 1" for bottom margin.

Unbound report: Side margins 1"

Leftbound report: Side margins 1.5"

Titles: Title style. Main words capitalized.

Spacing: Default 1.15 line spacing; paragraphs blocked. Tap ENTER once between paragraphs.

Page numbers: Second and subsequent pages are numbered at top right of the page. One blank line follows the page number.

Side headings: Heading 1 style. Main words capitalized.

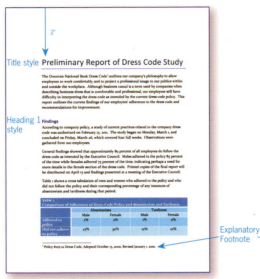

Page 1, Leftbound Report with Explanatory Footnote

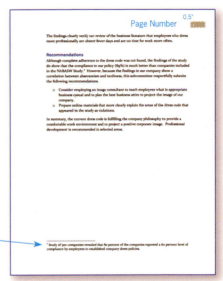

Page 2, Leftbound Report (Page Number Style)

Reports with Preliminary and Appendix Pages

Take advantage of the reference features of *Word 2010* when producing reports. The table of contents, bibliography page, and index are generated automatically. The references are entered in the report using the Citations command.

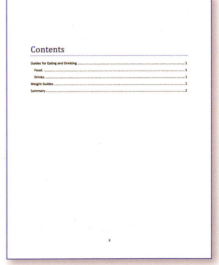

Title Page Using Cover Page Feature

Table of Contents

Unbound Report with Citations, Page 1

Nutrition Guides for Good Health

Good health is a high priority for most people. Yet many individuals know relatively little about nutrition and make dietary choices that are detrimental to their health. Studies show that at least one-third of all cancer and heart attack deaths are directly related to diet. This report presents valuable guides to eating and drinking as well as weight guides.

Guides for Eating and Drinking

Diet consists of both the foods and beverages consumed daily. The foods and beverages consumed should be selected carefully to ensure good nutrition as well as healthy guides for preparing and making wise food choices.

Food. A wide variety of foods should be eaten each day since no one food contains all of the nutrients needed. Foods that are rich in vitamins and high in dietary fiber should be eaten daily. Fruits, vegetables, and whole-grain breads are particularly good sources of vitamins and fiber.

A good diet also avoids harmful foods. Sodium, saturated fat, high-fat dairy products, salt, and sugar should be eaten in moderation.

Selecting the proper food and beverages is only one part of a healthy diet. The quantity consumed and the manner in which foods are prepared are equally important. A person's diet should be planned carefully to maintain a desirable weight for the body size. Obesity increases the risk of many diseases. Being underweight can also create problems.

Foods should also be prepared in a manner that does not add fat to the food. Baking, steaming, poaching, roasting, and cooking in a microwave are the best ways to prepare foods.

Wise food choices are important for a healthy diet. Many health-conscious individuals have learned to make the following substitutions for foods that are high in fat and calories (Wright).

(Bulleted list)

- Diet soda for regular soda
- Skim, 1%, or 2% milk for whole milk (begin with 2% and work down to skim milk)
- Egg whites for whole egg
- Low-fat cheese for full-fat cheese

Drinks. The body needs a significant amount of fluids. The daily minimum of water is eight glasses per day. Rosa Sanchez (59), a well-known nutritionist, states, "Increase the minimum requirement

---

Page 2 of Report with Alphabet Header and Footer

of water when exercising briskly, when weather temperatures are hot, and when dieting to burn fat."

Consider creative ways to consume the daily requirement of water, such as drinking water at all meals, keeping a measured container of water in your work area, and substituting water for a snack.

If alcoholic beverages are consumed, they should be consumed in moderation. Alcoholic beverages are high in calories and low in food value. In addition, excessive drinking can lead to major health problems.

Weight Guides

A person's body frame helps to determine the desirable weight for that person. Desirable weight for a person with a small frame is less than for a person with an average or large frame. For example, the desirable weight for a 6'0" male with a large frame is 195-205 pounds, while the weight for a 6'0" male with a medium frame is 180-190. On the other hand, the desirable weight for a 5'4" female with a medium frame is 118-130 and a female with a small frame is 110-120 (Kwon). Desirable weights based on body frame size are helpful to guide individuals in healthy body weight.

Summary

Health-conscious individuals make wise choices daily related to foods and drinks realizing that health issues can become problematic. Maintaining the desirable weight level for the size frame is equally important.

Bibliography Page

Kwon, Chinn. "What Should I Weigh?" May 2011. Nutrition Notes. 23 July 2011 <www.doctorsandnurseshi-energy.com/whatishouldiweigh.html>.

Sanchez, Rosa. "Did You Get Your Water Today?" Nutrition Journal 10.1 (2011): 58-60.

Wright, Dona. Nurse Practitioner Dean Young. 4 November 2011.

Index

Command Summary

AutoCorrect	File/Options/ Proofing/AutoCorrect Options	
Align Text	Home/Paragraph/Click desired alignment (Align Text Left, Center, Align Text Right, or Justify)	
Arrange All	View/Window/Arrange All	
Bibliography	References/Citations & Bibliography/ Bibliography	
Blank Page	Insert/Pages/Blank Page	
Bookmark	Insert/Links/Bookmark	
Breaks	Page Layout/Page Setup/Breaks	
Building Blocks Organizer	Insert/Text/Quick Parts/Building Blocks Organizer	
Bullets and Numbering	Home/Paragraph/Bullets or Numbering	
Center Page	Page Layout/Page Setup/Dialog Box Launcher/ Layout tab/Vertical alignment/Center	
Character Spacing	Home/Font/Dialog Box Launcher/Advanced tab	
Citations—Insert Citation—Add Source	References/Citations & Bibliography/Insert Citation Click Insert Citation and then select Add New Source from drop-down list.	
Citation—Edit	Click citation; Select Edit Citation from drop-down list.	
Citation—Delete	Click citation; Select Convert to static text and tap DELETE.	
Citations—Manage Sources	References/Citations & Bibliography/Manage Sources	

Feature	Location	Button
Clip Art—Format	Picture Tools/Format	Picture Tools Format
Clip Art—Insert	Insert/Illustrations/Clip Art	Clip Art
Close Document	File/Close or Close button at top right of screen	Close ☒
Columns—Create	Page Layout/Page Setup/Columns	Columns
Columns—Unequal Width	Page Layout/Page Setup/Columns/More Columns	More Columns...
Comments	Review/Comments/New Comment, Delete, Previous, or Next	New Comment, Delete, Previous, Next (Comments)
Cover Page	Insert/Pages/Cover Page	Cover Page
Custom Themes	Page Layout/Themes/Colors/Create New Theme Colors Page Layout/Themes/Fonts/Create New Theme Fonts Page Layout/Themes/Save Current Theme. Add desired effects and then save the current theme.	Create New Theme Colors... Create New Theme Fonts... Save Current Theme...
Cut, Copy, and Paste	Home/Clipboard/Cut, Copy, or Paste	Cut, Copy, Paste
Date and Time—Insert	Insert/Text/Date & Time	Date & Time
Default Theme—Set as Default	Home/Styles/Change Styles/Set as Default	Set as Default
Document Themes	Page Layout/Themes/Themes	Themes (Colors, Fonts, Effects)
Document Properties	File/Info/Properties display on right side	Info
Drawing Canvas	Insert/Illustrations/Shapes/New Drawing Canvas	New Drawing Canvas

Drop Cap	Insert/Text/Drop Cap	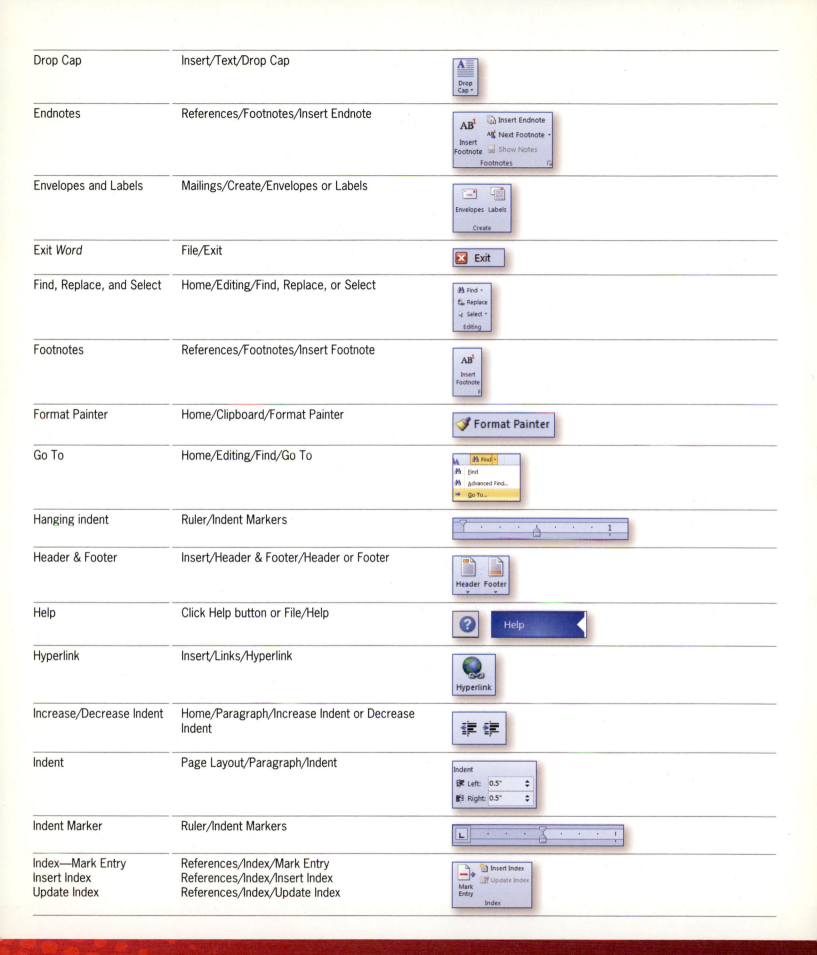
Endnotes	References/Footnotes/Insert Endnote	
Envelopes and Labels	Mailings/Create/Envelopes or Labels	
Exit *Word*	File/Exit	
Find, Replace, and Select	Home/Editing/Find, Replace, or Select	
Footnotes	References/Footnotes/Insert Footnote	
Format Painter	Home/Clipboard/Format Painter	
Go To	Home/Editing/Find/Go To	
Hanging indent	Ruler/Indent Markers	
Header & Footer	Insert/Header & Footer/Header or Footer	
Help	Click Help button or File/Help	
Hyperlink	Insert/Links/Hyperlink	
Increase/Decrease Indent	Home/Paragraph/Increase Indent or Decrease Indent	
Indent	Page Layout/Paragraph/Indent	
Indent Marker	Ruler/Indent Markers	
Index—Mark Entry Insert Index Update Index	References/Index/Mark Entry References/Index/Insert Index References/Index/Update Index	

Insert File	Insert/Text/Object/Text from File	
Line and Page Breaks	Home/Paragraph/Paragraph Dialog Box Launcher/Line and Page Breaks tab	
Line Spacing	Home/Paragraph/Paragraph Dialog Box/Line and Paragraph Spacing	
Mail Merge Select Recipients Edit Recipient List Insert Merge Fields Address Block Greeting Line	Mailings/Start Mail Merge/Start Mail Merge/Step by Step Mail Merge Wizard/Select Recipients, or Edit Recipient List Mailings/Write & Insert Fields/Insert Merge Field, Address Block, or Greeting Line	
Margins	Page Layout/Page Setup/Margins	
Mini toolbar	Appears when text is selected	
Multilevel List	Home/Paragraph/Multilevel List	
Open New/Existing Document	File/New or Open; then locate the file	
Orientation	Page Layout/Page Setup/Orientation	
Page Borders	Page Layout/Page Background/Page Borders	
Page Break	Insert/Pages/Page Break	
Page Color	Page Layout/Page Background/Page Color	

Page Numbers—Insert	Insert/Header & Footer/Page Number	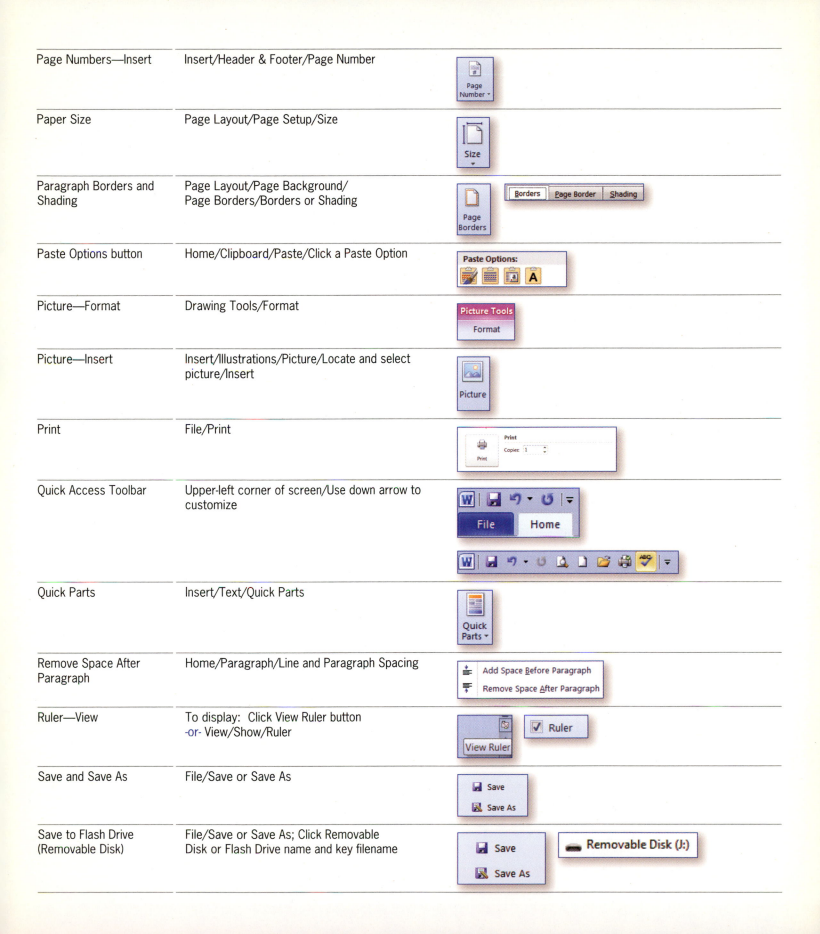
Paper Size	Page Layout/Page Setup/Size	
Paragraph Borders and Shading	Page Layout/Page Background/ Page Borders/Borders or Shading	
Paste Options button	Home/Clipboard/Paste/Click a Paste Option	
Picture—Format	Drawing Tools/Format	
Picture—Insert	Insert/Illustrations/Picture/Locate and select picture/Insert	
Print	File/Print	
Quick Access Toolbar	Upper-left corner of screen/Use down arrow to customize	
Quick Parts	Insert/Text/Quick Parts	
Remove Space After Paragraph	Home/Paragraph/Line and Paragraph Spacing	
Ruler—View	To display: Click View Ruler button -or- View/Show/Ruler	
Save and Save As	File/Save or Save As	
Save to Flash Drive (Removable Disk)	File/Save or Save As; Click Removable Disk or Flash Drive name and key filename	

Save in New Folder	File/Save or Save As; Click New Folder and key name	
Save As Template	File/Save As; Word defaults to Templates folder; Key name and in Save as type box, select Word Template	
Section Breaks	Page Layout/Page Setup/Breaks; Select the desired section break from the list.	
Shapes—Add Text to Shapes	Click in the shape and key the text	
Shapes—Format	Drawing Tools/Format	
Shapes—Insert	Insert/Illustrations/Shapes	
Show/Hide	Home/Paragraph/Show/Hide	
Show/Hide White Space	Print Layout View/Position insertion point at top or bottom of page/Click to show or hide white space	
Slider: Zoom in or out	Click Slider/Move left or right to zoom in or out	
SmartArt—Design or Format	SmartArt Tools/Design or Format	
SmartArt—Insert	Insert/Illustrations/SmartArt	
Sort	Home/Paragraph/Sort	
Space After Paragraph	Page Layout/Paragraph/Spacing	
Special Characters	Insert/Symbols/Symbol/More Symbols/Special Characters tab	
Spelling and Grammar	Review/Proofing/Spelling & Grammar	

Split Panes	View/Window/Split	
Status line		
Styles—Change	Home/Styles/Change Styles	
Styles—Insert	Home/Styles/Quick Styles	
Symbol	Insert/Symbols/Symbol	
Table of Contents	References/Table of Contents/Table of Contents	
Table of Figures	References/Captions/Insert Table of Figures	
Table Tools/Design or Layout	Table Tools/Design or Layout	
Tables—Adjust Column Width using the Ruler	Ruler/Column Marker/Drag to appropriate position	
Tables—Decimal Tab in Table	Select Column/Click Tab Selector button/Select decimal tab/Click appropriate position on Ruler	
Tables—Insert using the Insert Table command	Insert/Tables/Table/Insert Table	
Tables—Insert Using the Table Grid	Insert/Tables/Table/Drag to select number of rows and columns	
Tabs—Leaders	Home/Paragraph/Paragraph Dialog Box Launcher/ Tabs/Select desired leader tab	
Tabs—Bar, Left, Center, Right, and Decimal	View Ruler/Tab Alignment Button/Click on Horizontal Ruler	
Tabs—Modify Tabs using Horizontal Ruler	Select desired tab; Click and drag the tab to the desired location on the ruler	

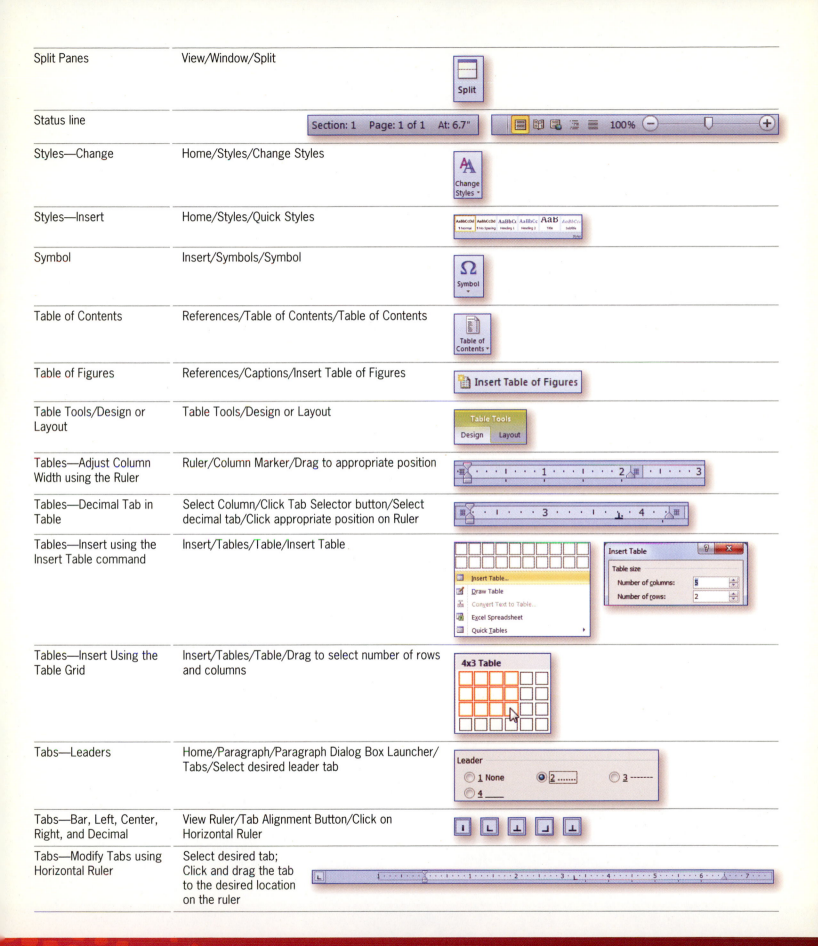

Track Changes—Change Tracking Options	Review/Tracking/Track Changes/Change Tracking Options
Track Changes—Show Markup	Review/Tracking/Display Markup Options, Show Markup, or Reviewing Pane
Track Changes—Review Changes	Review/Changes/Accept, Reject, Previous, or Next
Track Changes	Review/Tracking/Track Changes
Thesaurus	Review/Proofing/Thesaurus
Text Formats —	Home/Font/Click desired text format command (Font, Font Size, Grow Font, Shrink Font, Change Case, Clear Formatting, Bold, Italic, Underline, Strikethrough, Subscript, Superscript, Text Effects, Text Highlight Color, Font Color)
Text Box	Insert/Text/Text Box
Templates	File/New/Available Templates
Tabs—Set Underline Tab	Home/Paragraph/Paragraph Dialog Box Launcher/Tabs; Use Leader 4 to set Underline tab.
Tabs—Modify Tabs using the Tabs dialog box	Home/Paragraph/Paragraph Dialog Box Launcher/Tabs

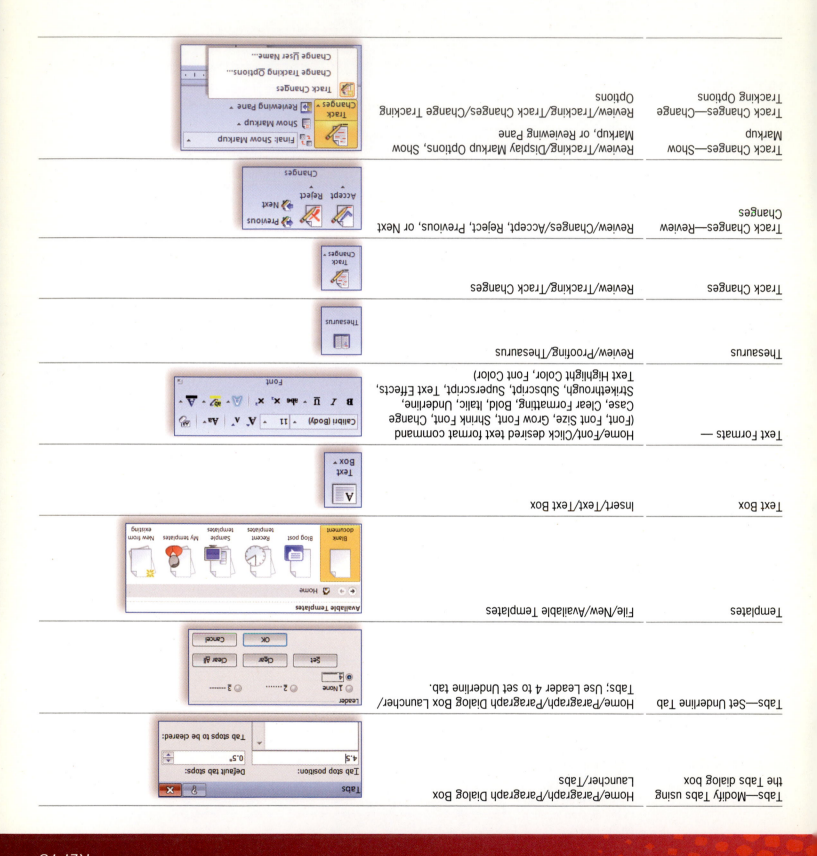

Translate	Review/Language/Translate/Choose Translation Language/Select word to translate and Bilingual Dictionary displays	
Vertical Page Position	To turn on: Right-click status bar/Click Vertical Page Position	Section: 1 Page: 1 of 1 At: 6.7"
Views—Document	View/Document Views/Select view	Print Layout Full Screen Reading Web Layout Outline Draft Document Views
Views—View Buttons	Select view buttons on status bar	
View Side by Side	View/Window/View Side by Side	View Side by Side
Watermark	Page Layout/Page Background/ Watermark	Watermark
Word Options	File/Options	Options
Word-Art—Format	Drawing Tools/Format	Drawing Tools Format
WordArt—Insert	Insert/Text/WordArt	WordArt
Wrap Text	Select graphic/Format/Arrange/Wrap Text	Wrap Text

Section 1 | *Microsoft Windows 7*

OVERVIEW

Windows 7 is the newest operating system software released by Microsoft. The operating system software controls the operations of the computer and works with the application software. *Windows* 7 works with *Word* in opening, printing, deleting, and saving files. It also allows you to work with photos and pictures, play music, and access the Internet.

When you turn on your computer, *Windows* displays a login screen followed by a password screen. See your instructor for login and password information. The *Windows* 7 desktop displays after you have logged in.

MICROSOFT WINDOWS 7 DESKTOP

★ TIP

The Windows desktop and its components are described on the next page.

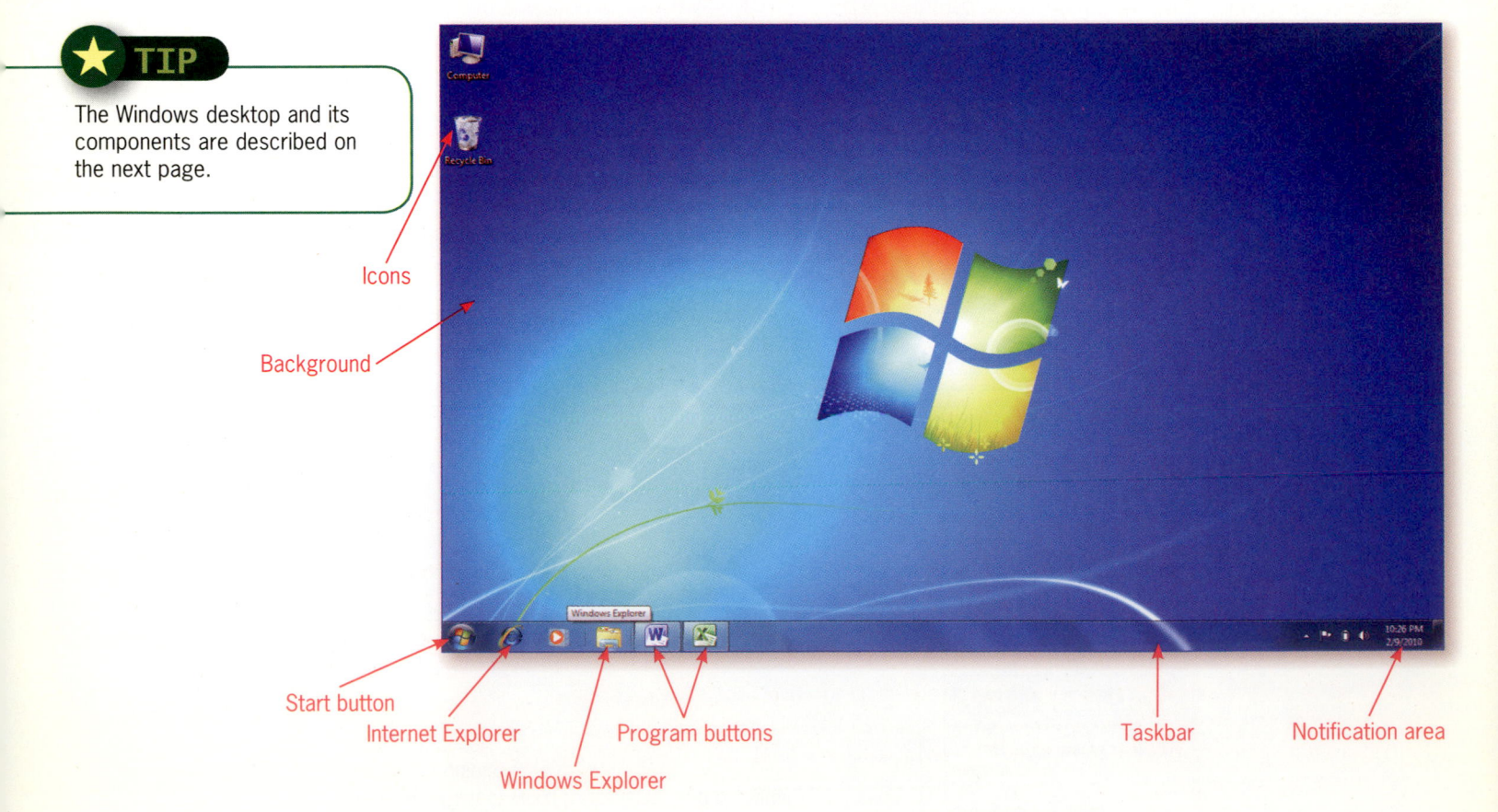

Icons

Background

Start button

Internet Explorer

Windows Explorer

Program buttons

Taskbar

Notification area

WINDOWS DESKTOP COMPONENTS

The illustration on the previous page shows the default *Windows* 7 Aero desktop. The Aero theme has a semitransparent glass design that gives a three-dimensional appearance. In order to see the graphical enhancements of the Aero theme, your computer hardware and version of *Windows* 7 must support it. Your screen may have the *Windows* 7 Basic theme.

Read the description of each component and hover the mouse over each object to display the ScreenTip that identifies each element.

- *Taskbar.* The taskbar displays across the bottom of the screen and contains the elements listed below.

  - *Start button.* Click the Start button to display the Start menu. The Start menu provides access to programs and files on your computer.

  - *Program and file buttons.* Buttons display for the programs that are open or pinned to the taskbar and allow you to switch between them easily. The illustration shows that *Internet Explorer, Windows Explorer, Word,* and *Excel* either are open or have been pinned to the taskbar so that they remain on the desktop.

  - *Notification area.* The notification area provides helpful information, such as the date and time and the status of the computer. When you plug in a USB drive, *Windows* displays an icon in the notification area letting you know that the hardware is connected.

- *Icons and Shortcuts.* Icons, small pictures representing certain items, may be displayed on the desktop. The Recycle Bin, which represents a wastepaper basket, displays when *Windows* is installed. Other icons and shortcuts may be added.

- *Background.* The default background is the *Windows* logo on a blue background. The background can be changed or customized to include a personal picture or a company logo.

START MENU

The Start menu enables you to access all programs, documents, and other computer resources. The programs listed in the left pane of the Start menu vary depending on which programs you have used recently. However, all programs can be located by clicking All Programs. The right pane contains links to files and resources on your computer. One of the key links that will be useful is Help and Support. Note that the Shut down button is also located on the Start menu.

To display the Start menu, click the Start button. The Start menu is illustrated on the next page. Review the callouts on the illustration on the next page.

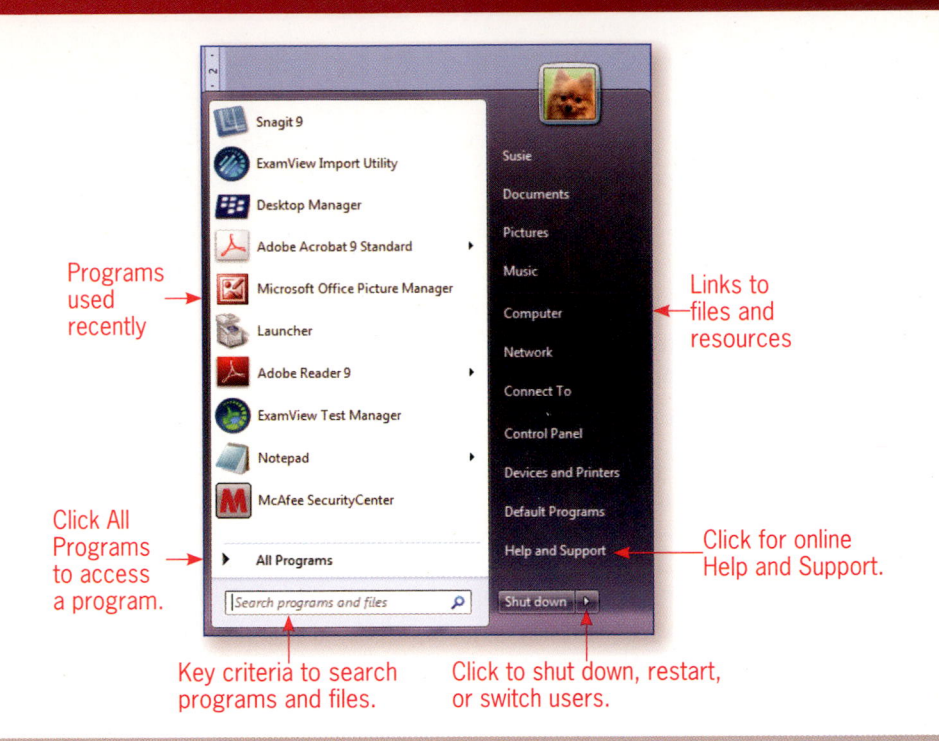

Programs used recently

Click All Programs to access a program.

Links to files and resources

Click for online Help and Support.

Key criteria to search programs and files.

Click to shut down, restart, or switch users.

 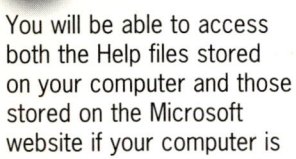

You will be able to access both the Help files stored on your computer and those stored on the Microsoft website if your computer is connected to the Internet.

WINDOWS 7 HELP AND SUPPORT

The fastest way to get help is to key a word or phrase in the Search Help box and tap ENTER; all the Help pages that contain the word or phrase will display. You can also click the Browse Help topics link and then click an item in the contents listing of subject headings that appear. Some subject headings contain Help topics within a subheading. Click the Help topic to open it, and click the subheading to narrow your search.

COMPUTER DRIVES

You will be working with auxiliary drives, including CD/DVD and universal serial bus (USB) flash drives. USB flash drives vary in size and shape and can hold gigabytes of information. They are also called thumb drives, memory keys, pen drives, and key drives. The USB drive needs to be plugged into a USB port in order for the computer to read the drive. Your computer may have several USB ports.

To access drives on your computer:

1. Click the Start button to display the Start menu.
2. Click Computer in the right pane to view the drives and storage devices connected to your computer.

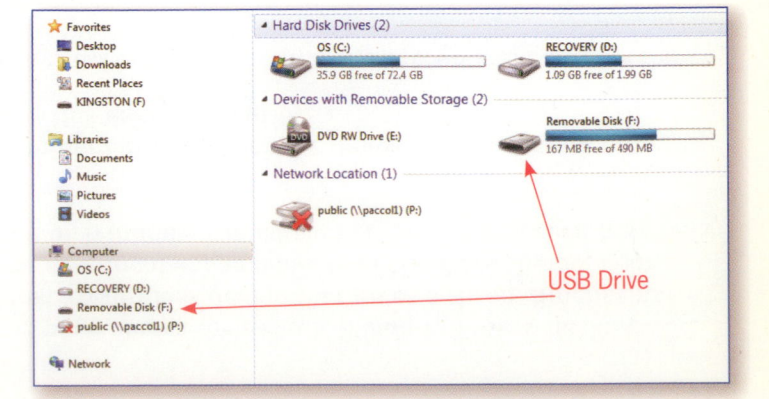

USB Drive

Section 2 | *File Management*

WINDOWS EXPLORER

Windows Explorer is a file management program provided with *Windows 7* Accessories. In the previous section, *Windows Explorer* was shown pinned to the taskbar. If your computer does not have it pinned to the taskbar, you can access *Windows Explorer* by right-clicking the Start button and selecting Open Windows Explorer.

LIBRARIES

When *Windows Explorer* opens it displays four libraries—Documents, Music, Pictures, and Videos as shown in the illustration below.

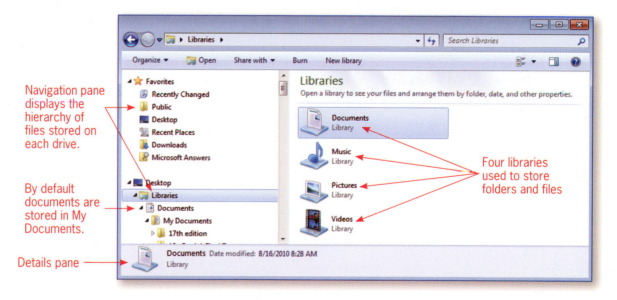

Navigation pane displays the hierarchy of files stored on each drive.

By default documents are stored in My Documents.

Details pane

Four libraries used to store folders and files

DOCUMENT MANAGEMENT

A logical system for storing documents enables you to locate and retrieve the documents when you need them. *Keyboarding Pro DELUXE 2* stores your files in a logical system for you. However, if you were not using *Keyboarding Pro DELUXE 2*, think how you could structure files for your *CK Advanced Word Processing* class so that you could locate them quickly and easily. Your class has ten modules and two projects. Each module and project may have data files, solutions, and materials from your instructor. Having a folder for each module and subfolders for data files, solutions, and materials from your instructor would make it easy to locate and retrieve files.

FOLDER STRUCTURE

Note the file structure in *Windows Explorer* if you set up a folder on the hard drive for each module of the CK Advanced Word Processing Class and subfolders in each module for data files, materials from instructor, and solutions. Files relating to each of these areas would be stored in the appropriate folder.

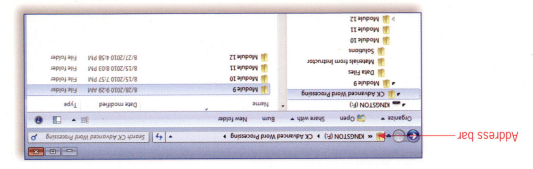

Address Bar

Note the first level folder—the CK Advanced Word Processing class is under My Documents.

These modules are folders under CK Advanced Word Processing and have subfolders for data files, materials from instructor, and solutions.

FOLDER ADDRESSES

A folder is a location for storing files or other folders. The Address Bar shows the location of the folders. Compare the address bar in the illustration above in which the folders are saved in My Documents on the hard drive OS (C:) and the illustration below in which the folders are saved on a USB (flash) drive.

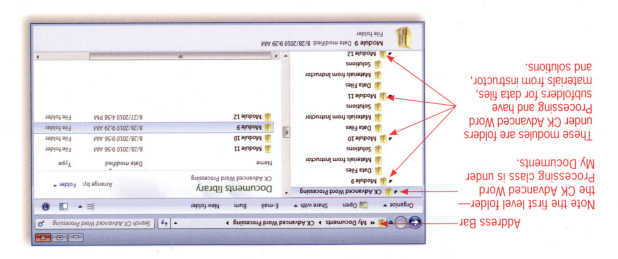

Address bar

In the Address bar, each level of the hierarchy is separated with a ► symbol; the highest level folder displays at the left side of the Address bar. The ► symbol indicates the next lower level.

NAMING CONVENTIONS

The names given to both folders and files should be logical and should reflect the content of the folder or file. The names of folders are usually keyed with initial capital letters. The names of files are typically keyed using lowercase.

Filenames can be up to 255 characters long (but in practice you won't use filenames that long). In addition, the following symbols cannot be used in a filename: \ / : * ? " , . The descriptive name is followed by a period (.), which is used to separate the descriptive name from the file extension. The file extension is three or four letters that follow the period. When renaming a file, do not delete or change file extensions as this may cause problems opening the file.

WORKING WITH FOLDERS AND FILES

Effective file management involves a number of tasks including creating folders, renaming folders and files, and copying, moving, and deleting folders and files. These tasks can be accomplished using *Windows Explorer* or using the Save As dialog box in applications such as *Word*, *Excel*, and *PowerPoint*. *Windows Explorer* is used for the following instructions.

To create a folder or subfolder:

1. In the Navigation pane, click the drive that is to contain the new folder. If a subfolder is desired, highlight the folder that will contain the new folder.

2. Click the New folder button to display a new folder.
3. Key the name of the new folder and tap ENTER.

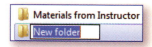

To copy a file or folder:

1. Highlight the file or folder that is to be copied. Click Organize and then click Copy.

2. Navigate to the desired location, such as a flash drive, and click the icon.
3. Click Organize and then click Paste.

To rename a file or folder:

1. Right-click the file or folder icon.
2. Left-click Rename from the Shortcut menu.
3. Key the new name and tap ENTER.

To move a file or folder:

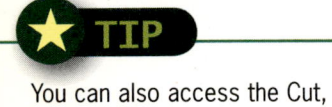

TIP

You can also access the Cut, Copy, and Delete commands by selecting the filename; then right-click and choose the desired command from the menu.

1. Highlight the file or folder that is to be moved and click Organize.
2. Click Cut.

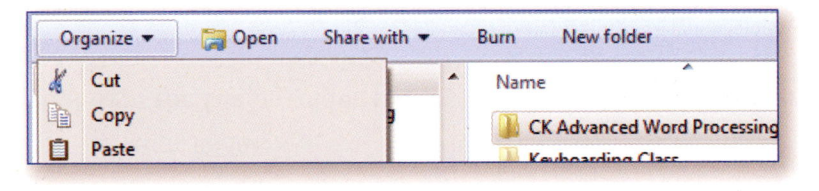

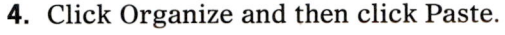

3. Navigate to the desired location, such as a flash drive, and click the icon.
4. Click Organize and then click Paste.

To delete a file or folder:

1. Highlight the file or folder that is to be deleted.
2. Click Organize and then click Delete.
3. The Delete Folder dialog box displays to confirm the Delete request. Click Yes.

Note: Deleting a file removes it from its current location and sends it to the Recycle Bin; the file remains there until the Bin has been emptied.

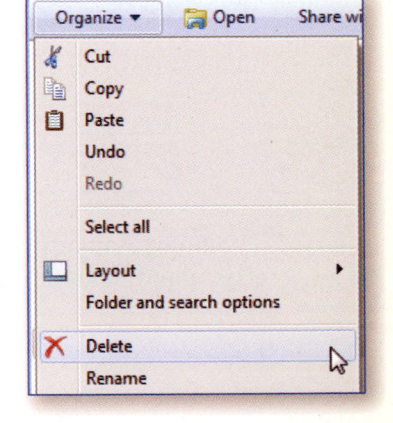

RECYCLE BIN

The Recycle Bin provides temporary storage for deleted files. If you accidentally delete a file, you can select the file and click Restore this item. To permanently remove all files, click Empty the Recycle Bin.

Web-Based Computing: Internet, Cloud, and Web 2.0

Web-Based Computing 1 | Internet

OVERVIEW OF WEB-BASED COMPUTING

Three key components of web-based computing—Internet, Cloud, and Web 2.0—are covered in this section. These topics are overlapping and have many common advantages and disadvantages, but looking at them separately makes it easier to understand the concepts and to apply them in a useful manner.

INTERNET

Most students have had significant experience surfing the Web. If you haven't, a quick terminology review might be helpful.

Internet	A global collection of interconnected networks used to share information. To access the Internet, you must have an Internet connection and a browser.
Browser	A software program, such as Internet Explorer, Chrome, or Firefox, that enables you to view web pages.
URL	A **U**niform **R**esource **L**ocater is a unique web address for each web page. Clicking the URL http://www.collegekeyboarding.com will take you to the College Keyboarding website. The protocol is **http://**, the location is **www** (World Wide Web), and the domain is **com** (commercial). Each segment of the address is separated by a period.
Search Engine	A software program, such as Bing, Google, or Yahoo, that enables you to locate specific information efficiently on the Web by using keywords that describe the topic.
Bookmark	A bookmark is a saved URL that you can access quickly by adding it to a **Favorites List**. To visit the website again, click Favorites and select it.

ADVANCED SEARCH

Google, *Bing*, and *Yahoo* are the most frequently used search engines. *Google* and *Yahoo* offer an advanced search option. To search efficiently, click Advanced Search and complete the text boxes to specify language, region, dates of inclusion, and specific words or phrases. With *Bing*, placing quotes (" ") around the keywords will limit the results to articles containing the keywords in the search.

CLOUD COMPUTING

Cloud computing is an evolving concept and, as such, is very difficult to define. Cloud computing can be simplified by examining the following concepts involved in cloud computing:

- A cloud computing system consists of many high-powered computer resources, such as servers, networks, storage applications, software applications, and information technology (IT) services that can be easily accessed with a basic computer and an Internet connection.

- The resources can be accessed anytime, from any location, and without any involvement of the organization providing the services. An example would be Hotmail or Gmail from Google. They are Web-based, available on demand, and accomplished without interaction with the provider.

- The IT services provided to businesses are fee-based services. Some services may be provided free, such as Google Docs and Microsoft Web Apps. Both of these Web applications are also often referred to as Web 2.0 applications. Cloud computing serves as a bridge between the Internet and Web 2.0.

WEB-BASED E-MAIL

Information on creating an e-mail account is presented on page xiv in your textbook. If you have not read that information, you should read the information carefully and set up a free Hotmail account before moving to the next section. If you have already set up the account and sent or received e-mail using it, you have used cloud computing. Your next venture into cloud computing will be to learn more about Web Apps.

WEB APPS

Microsoft Web Apps provide both Word 2010 and storage space on the SkyDrive (Internet). Documents stored on the SkyDrive can be viewed and edited. Documents stored on the Web can be accessed on the Internet with a browser at any time and from any location. New documents can also be created. Word 2010 software is not necessary on the computer used to create or access the documents. Your Hotmail e-mail address and your password serve as your Windows Live™ ID.

To access the SkyDrive and add a document:

www.windowslive.com

1. Sign in using your Hotmail address and Password.
2. Hover the mouse over Windows Live.
3. Click SkyDrive.

To access the SkyDrive and create a document:

1. To create a document, click New and select Word document. The *Word* ribbon and screen displays. Key the document name in the Name box and click Save. Then key and format the desired document.

2. Click File and select Save when you have finished; close and exit SkyDrive.

To access the SkyDrive and add a document:

1. Use the three steps on the previous page to access the SkyDrive.

2. To add a file, click Add files and then select documents from your computer.

3. Select the desired file and it uploads. Double-click the filename to open it.

4. Click the View tab to view it in Editing View or Reading View. The first illustration below is in Editing View. The second illustration is in Reading View.

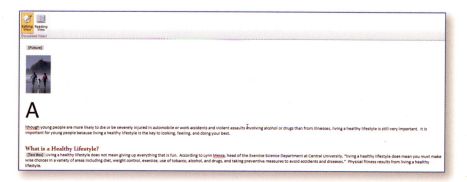

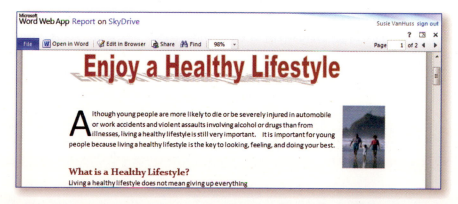

Web-Based Computing 3 | Web 2.0

WEB 2.0

Most people think of the first generation of the Internet as a vast online collection of information that can be accessed easily and at little or no cost. The role of the Internet user is simply to access information in a passive way for whatever purpose the user needs the information. Most people think of the second generation of the Internet (Web 2.0) as an interactive tool that enables the user to contribute and collaborate with others. The role of the Web 2.0 user is that of an active participant. Web 2.0 applications are often thought of as social networking.

SOCIAL MEDIA TOOLS

Many options exist that enable Web 2.0 users to participate actively. The group of social media tools listed below is just a few of the different options available to users who want to participate actively in the second generation of the Internet.

Social networks are generally thought of as tools for sharing information with an online community of people with common interests. Facebook, LinkedIn, and MySpace are examples of frequently used social networks.

Micro-blogging sites enable users to send brief messages (often 140 or fewer characters) to a group of people which in turn can be sent to other groups. Twitter and Tumblr are examples of micro-blogging sites.

Video sharing sites provide a platform for people to post videos to share with others. YouTube, Metacafe, Break, and Google Video are examples of video-sharing sites.

Photo sharing sites provide a platform for people to post photographs to share with others. Examples include Flickr, Photobucket, Webshots, and Fotki.

Blogs are sites that provide publishing tools for people to post articles and various types of information to share with others and accept comments from readers. Examples of blog hosting sites include Blogger from Google, WordPress, and Live Journal.

Bookmarking sites allow users to bookmark or tag sites that they recommend. Examples are Delicious, Furl, Reddit, and StumbleUpon.

WEB 2.0 FOR BUSINESSES

Even though Web 2.0 was popularized by teenagers, today many businesses and non-profit organizations have a presence on social media sites. The most common usage by businesses is for marketing and promotion. The primary advantage is that the costs are very inexpensive and consist primarily of staff time. The primary disadvantage is that businesses have little or no control over what others can post about them. The demographics of social networks are changing significantly, which makes them more appealing to businesses.

Index